ZERO

MARTIN CAIDIN was the author of over fifty books and more than a thousand magazine articles and was recognized as one of the outstanding aeronautics and aviation authorities in the world. The National War College, the Air Force's Air University and several other institutions use his books as doctrine and strategy guides, historical references and textbooks. He twice won the Aviation/Space Writers Association award as the outstanding author in the field of aviation. Caidin died in March 1997.

AVAILABLE NOW

Helmet for My Pillow
The General
The March to Glory
By Robert Leckie

Samurai!
By Saburo Sakai with Martin Caidin
and Fred Saito

Thunderbolt!
By Robert S. Johnson and Martin Caidin

Fork-Tailed Devil: The P-38
The B-17: The Flying Forts
By Martin Caidin

When Hell Froze Over
By E.M. Halliday

The World War II Reader
By the Editors of *World War II* magazine

Vietnam: A Reader
By the Editors of *Vietnam* magazine

The Civil War Reader: 1862
By the Editors of
Civil War Times Illustrated and
America's Civil War

The Battle for Jerusalem
By Lt. General Mordechai Gur

The Lost History of Gettysburg
By Colonel James K. P. Scott

Operation Vulture
By John Prados

ZERO

By MASATAKE OKUMIYA
and JIRO HORIKOSHI
with MARTIN CAIDIN

ibooks
new york
www.ibooks.net

DISTRIBUTED BY SIMON & SCHUSTER, INC.

This book is dedicated to . . .
all the airmen who fought with
and who fought against the Zero fighter.

Acknowledgements

The authors wish to express their appreciation to all the persons and institutions without whose assistance this book would not have been possible. Particular thanks are due to ex-Vice-Admiral Misao Wada, whose suggestions and encouragement brought the Japanese authors to assemble the material for *ZERO!*; I wish particularly to thank Otto v. St. Whitelock, whose editorial assistance has always been invaluable; Sally Botsford, whose long hours of hard work and typing helped so much; and the former editors of *Impact*, who produced probably the most dramatic record of the Pacific War.

Contents

CONTENTS

CONTENTS

CONTENTS

CONTENTS

Introduction

Some years ago when Lee Iacocca was C.E.O.'ing at Chrysler someone suggested that he use the following line in a commercial:

> On your way to buy a Toyota,
> It still isn't too late
> To remember Pappy Boyington
> And our boys from Torpedo 8

Being an astute businessman, Iacocca researched and tested this advertisement only to find out that the vast majority of his potential customers, particularly the younger ones, didn't know anything about either Boyington or Torpedo 8.

This lack of familiarity with World War II was and continues to be unfortunate particularly in view of the violence that has been loosened in our world today.

Zero by Martin Caidin was told to him by two of Japan's major military players, Masatake Okumiye and Jiro Horikoshi. It is an in-depth account of Japanese air power in the years between 1937 and 1945. A very vital part of this narrative is the development of Japan's Zero fighter which during the opening years of the war was superior to any fighter plane that showed our star on its wings.

It was as late as June 4, 1942, that a fantastic stroke of luck left a Zero fighter on an island in the Aleutians. Its pilot had attempted an emergency landing which resulted in a slightly damaged aircraft. The Japanese aviator was not so lucky. His head struck the instrument panel, killing him instantly. Retrieved by American forces, the Zero was rushed to research facilities in the States and its powerful capabilities were carefully noted as the Grumman Company put together the F6F. Finally we had a plane that was the equal to or even superior to the Zero. Its days of ascendancy were over, but this did not prevent it from fighting actively right up to the very end of the war.

As the air war drew to an end and American bombers ranged over the Japanese islands, a new form of warfare was developed by the Japanese. Two very different cultures were at war. For a Japanese soldier or marine, death was preferable to the shame of capture. With this orientation it was not a large step to design a Kamikaze program where the pilots in explosive-laden planes suicidally crashed them into American warships and our B-29 bombers. In those final months of the war the Japanese even designed glider bombs and manned torpedoes to be directed by a living pilot on a one-way trip to targets of opportunity.

We speak of being at war today, and I guess we are. However there are differences. In one night, B-29s burned nearly seventeen square miles of Tokyo with resulting casualties that no one has ever been able to count.

I don't think we can ever see the present clearly if we neglect windows into the past. *Zero* is a revealing account of an American victory over an extremely violent culture that was very different from our own.

It was also a culture that didn't give up easily. With almost every city of any size burnt to the ground the Japanese government was willing to desperately fight on until the last of its citizens was killed. Only the use of the ultimate violence of atomic weapons elicited the Emperor's surrender. Many are critical of this violence.

My question and particularly for the younger critics is,

INTRODUCTION

"Which of the home islands of Japan were you planning to invade on or about the end of 1945?"

David Ballantine
Bearsville, NY

unusual nor unique. Since that time, I have found that many other historians, writers, game designers, defense analysts, and military enthusiasts shared the same adventure with me. *Zero* was just that kind of book for all of us.

Today, I still look back in awe and respect at *Zero*, both for its effect on me personally, along with how well it has stood the test of time. Written in Japan five decades ago, *Zero* was among the first of a handful of books written by Japanese veterans of the Great Pacific War. The Japanese authors of *Zero*, Masatake Okumiya and Jiro Horikoshi, though generally unknown outside of Japan were men at the center of Japanese naval aviation during that period. Okumiya was an air operations officer aboard carriers and at land bases throughout the war, giving him a unique perspective on the conduct of Japanese naval aviation in combat. Horikoshi on the other hand, was the chief designer of the Type 0 *Reisen* (Zero fighter) for Mitsubishi. His exceptional engineering skills made him a contemporary of such legendary American designers as Kelly Johnson (whose creations included the P-38 Lightning and P/F-80 Shooting Star) and Ed Heinniman (lead engineer on the SBD Dauntless, A-20 Havoc, and A-1 Skyraider). Horikoshi's understanding of Japanese design and production practices help give *Zero* an unparalleled clarity on just why Japan failed to field more and better aircraft in the second half of the Great Pacific War. *Zero* also provides readers with something else: an understanding of just what Imperial Japan's Navy was doing and thinking prior to the attack on Pearl Harbor on December 7th, 1941. Japanese records of that period are sparse at best, most being destroyed as the result of systematic destruction by Japan's leadership, American firebombing, and Allied postwar editing and discarding by occupation forces. The personal memories and diaries of Okumiya and Horikoshi represent an important contribution to insights into Japanese political, cultural, and military society before the war, something lacking from so many other volumes on the Great Pacific War. As such, *Zero* may well have been the first book in both Japan and the United States to explore such topics in the post-World War II period.

The ten years from the mid-1930s to 1945 is a historical black hole to most Japanese citizens, and today the general population shuns almost any open signs of respect or interest in the period. This lack of historical perspective remains one of the major social shortcomings within Japan, something the Japanese continue to struggle with even at the dawn of a new Century. Amazingly the handful of books about World War II written by military veteran authors like Masatake Okumiya, Jiro Horikoshi, Saburo Saki (along with "Fred" Saito and Martin Caiden, the author of *Samurai*), and Tameichi Hara (writer of the classic *Japanese Destroyer Captain*) may well become the primary way Japanese youngsters will learn about the darkest days and intentions of their country in the years ahead. In writing *Zero*, Okumiya and Horikoshi did a great service, as much to the future of their homeland as to the documenting of aviation history. After the war, Japan made a conscious effort to put their sense of manifest destiny and desires for conquest behind, as the country tried to recover from one of the worst beatings ever inflicted upon a defeated nation. Nevertheless, Okumiya and Horikoshi wrote their story with pride and passion, along with a sense of remorse and frustration, feelings that come through clearly in *Zero*.

Another bit of respect needs to be paid to the efforts of the late Martin Caiden, who brought *Zero* to American readers in the mid-1950s. *Zero* was one of three books Caiden found in Japan, the other two being *The Zero*

Fighter and Saburo Saki's superb *Samurai!* These three classics of historical aviation literature have helped several generations of military professionals gain some insight into the mysteries of why Japan acted as it did in World War II, and how they could possibly evolve their operations to include the seeming insanity to Western minds of planned *kamikaze* (suicide) operations. Today, military officers at service schools around the world still study *Zero* for insights into just how Japan managed to conquer almost a quarter of the world's surface in just six months, the greatest overwater military conquest in the history of the world. Caiden was a man with an eye for good and unusual books, something that made him a legend in publishing and a favorite among readers like myself.

Zero is more than just a book about an airplane, even though that aircraft was the key to Japanese plans and successes in the first year of the war in the Pacific. It is the story of Japanese naval aviation, the force that allowed Japan to spread out faster and farther than any other nation in history. At the core of this community was the Type 0 *Reisen* fighter and its highly skilled pilots, which enabled Japan to achieve air supremacy wherever it flew early in World War II. The Zero fighter flew with the Imperial Japanese Navy everywhere that it went, from 1940 in China until the end of the war with America in 1945. Between those dates, the *Reisen* was both Japan's combat edge, and later its downfall as it fought against increasingly longer and tougher odds. Ironically, the very qualities that made the Zero a world-beater in 1940 would make it vulnerable to superior models of Allied aircraft and improved tactics just two years later. In this way, the *Reisen* was a metaphor for the entire philosophy of the Imperial Japanese Navy in World War II, and *Zero* is the book that tells that story.

Today, *Zero* still remains the best general narrative of Japanese naval aviation in World War II. Here readers will find the Imperial Japanese Navy's many early successes and long decline that ended in 1945. Within the pages of *Zero* you will find what military professionals call "ground truth," a raw and honest personal view of events through the eyes of two men who were there to see for themselves. Such accounts are always rare in wartime, made even more so by the terrible casualty rates of both Japanese naval personnel and later civilians as American firebombing of urban centers became standard tactics. That either man survived World War II is a minor miracle. That they cared enough to write *Zero* at all for posterity is their legacy. None of us enjoys admitting our failures to ourselves, much less sharing them with others. In *Zero*, Okumiya and Horikoshi have done so for the whole world to see, something almost inconceivable given the cultural nature of Japanese society. In this way, their honesty and bravery in postwar Japan is certainly the equal of their actions during World War II.

Zero is hardly a perfect book, though today it stands up well even when compared to newer accounts of the Pacific War. It suffers in a few areas, most of them more due to when it was written than any error or personal bias of the authors. As a point of reference, Samuel Elliot Morrison's fifteen volume masterpiece, *History of United States Naval Operations in World War II*, was not even finished until 1962, fully five years after the first American edition of *Zero* had been released. In fact, the Great Pacific War had been over only five years when Okumiya and Horikoshi began writing the book that became *Zero*. That they got so much right so early is a tribute to their own experience, along with an obvious personal honor and integrity to the subject of their labors. Both had lost many close acquaintances in the war, and they clearly intended *Zero* as a respectful homage to all those who lost their lives fighting for Japan.

Nevertheless, even the imperfections in *Zero* provide us insights into the shortcomings of Japanese military culture, one of the most important being the matter of codebreaking. The first public insights into U.S. efforts to penetrate Japanese code and cipher systems was revealed during the Congressional investigations of the Pearl Harbor attack in 1946. This should have raised the equivalent of a warning klaxon to Okumiya, whose obvious knowledge of classified documents and plans clearly shows in *Zero*. Nevertheless, the lack of emphasis on intelligence matters in *Zero* is itself a clear indication of a major lapse in the prosecution of the Japanese war effort. A similar fault is reflected in Okumiya's lack of insight on radar and other supporting electronic and mechanical aids to aerial warfare. In fact, Okumiya seems almost wondrously mystified and befuddled at times by the growing power of the American war machine as the book progresses, a feeling shared by many Japanese military leaders of the time. This was hardly his fault though. Having spent his entire life being raised in a society which preached the racial and moral supremacy of Japanese warriors over their enemies, it was a difficult misconception to overcome when looking at the United States as a military opponent. Add to this the Imperial Navy doctrine of emphasizing the *offensive* fighting qualities of individual planes and ships over building a larger and more balanced force as America did, and it is easy to see how by 1943 the Japanese began to be overwhelmed.

Several other misconceptions in *Zero* are based in Horikoshi's lack of understanding at just what his designs were facing out on the battlefields of the Pacific and East

Asia. During the design and development phase of building the *Reisen*, Horikoshi was operating under the misconception that his new fighter was big (compared with earlier Japanese carrier fighter designs), powered by a huge radial engine, and even fueled by state of the art (for Japan) 93 octane aviation gasoline. In fact, by Western standards of the day, the Zero was light and small, with a tiny radial engine and powered by fuel with much less stored energy than the 100+ octane blended fuels being produced in the United States. So fixed and limited were the tools and technologies he had to work from, that he did not even realize the handicaps he and his fellow Japanese designers had operated under until after the surrender in Tokyo Bay. That the Zero was so dominate early in the Great Pacific War is perhaps his greatest tribute.

In the case of the Type 0 *Reisen*, these shortcomings showed in details like the lack of self-sealing fuel tanks and armor plating for pilots in planes like the Zero. While comparatively contemporary American aircraft became virtual flying fortresses for their aircrews, Japanese planes frequently became funeral pyres. The lack of protective crew armor meant that aircrew that might have bailed out and lived to fight another day went down with their planes, lost forever to an ever shrinking pool of Japanese naval aviators. This downward spiral would reach a point that by the end of 1944, the Imperial Japanese Navy could not gather enough planes and crews to put air groups onto carriers to oppose the American landings at Leyte in the Philippines. By the end of that great battle general use of *kamikaze* suicide tactics was in effect and would remain that way until the end of World War II. It is a tragic story, one that you will find documented in amazing detail here in *Zero*.

Preface

On the first day of World War II, the United States lost two thirds of its aircraft in the Pacific theater. The Japanese onslaught against Pearl Harbor effectively eliminated Hawaii as a source of immediate reinforcements for the Philippines. And on those beleaguered islands, enemy attacks rapidly whittled down our remaining air strength until it could no more than annoy a victory-flushed foe.

Japan controlled as much of the vast China mainland as she desired at the time. She captured Guam and Wake. She dispossessed us in the Netherlands East Indies. Singapore fell in humiliating defeat, and brilliantly executed Japanese tactics almost entirely eliminated the British as combatants. Within a few months fearful anxiety gripped Australia; its cities were brought under air attack. Japanese planes swarmed almost uncontested against northern New Guinea, New Ireland, the Admiralties, New Britain, and the Solomons. Enemy occupation of Kavieng, Rabaul, and Bougainville not only threatened the precarious supply lines from the United States, but became potential spring-boards for the invasion of Australia itself.

No one can deny that during those long and dreary months after Pearl Harbor the Japanese humiliated us in the Pacific. We were astonished—fatally so—at the unexpected quality of Japanese equipment. Because we committed the unforgivable error of underestimating a potential enemy, our antiquated planes fell like flies before Japan's agile Zero fighter.

At no time during these dark months were we able to more than momentarily check the Japanese sweep. The bright sparks of the defenders' heroism in a sea of defeat were not enough. There could be no doubt that the Japanese had effected a brilliant coup as they opened the war.

It is astonishing to realize, then, that even during this course of events Japan failed to enjoy a real opportunity for ultimate victory. Despite their military successes, within one year of the opening day of war the Japanese no longer held the offensive. The overwhelming numerical superiority which they enjoyed, largely by destruction of our own forces with relative impunity, began to disappear. By the spring of 1943 the balance clearly had shifted. Not only were we regaining the advantage of quantity; we also enjoyed a qualitative superiority in weapons. The Japanese were on the defensive.

The majority of the Japanese military hierarchy could not agree to this concept. They viewed the setbacks in the Pacific as no more than temporary losses. They basked in their successes of the first six months and reveled in a spirit of invincibility. Enhanced by centuries of victorious tradition, cultured by myths and fairy tales, and bolstered by years of one-track education, Japanese confidence of victory was even greater than our own.

There are many reasons why the Japanese failed in their

bid to dominate half the world. One reason, it has been said, is that while Japan fought for economic gain, we fought a strategic war of vengeance, a war which promised a terrifying vendetta for the people of Japan.

We can be much more specific than this. The Japanese failed, primarily, because they never understood the meaning of total war. Modern war is the greatest co-operative effort known to man; the Japanese never were able to fuse even their limited resources into this effort. They limped along with a mere fraction of our engineering skill. Throughout the war they were constantly astonished at the feats of our construction crews which hacked airfields out of solid coral and seemingly impenetrable jungle, at the rapidity with which we hurled vast quantities of supplies ashore at invasion beachheads. Air logistics in the form of a continued flow of airborne supplies was unknown to them.

The Japanese lacked the scientific "know how" necessary to meet us on qualitative terms. This was by no means the case early in the war when the Zero fighter airplane effectively swept aside all opposition. In the Zero the Japanese enjoyed the ideal advantage of both qualitative and quantitative superiority. The Japanese fighter was faster than any opposing plane. It outmaneuvered anything in the air. It outclimbed and could fight at greater heights than any plane in all Asia and the Pacific. It had twice the combat range of our standard fighter, the P-40, and it featured the heavy punch of cannon. Zero pilots had cut their combat teeth in China and so enjoyed a great advantage over our own men. Many of the Allied pilots who contested in their own inferior planes the nimble product of Jiro Horikoshi literally flew suicide missions.

This superiority, however, vanished quickly with our introduction of new fighter planes in combat. As the Zeros fell in flames, Japan's skilled pilots went with them. Japan failed to provide her air forces with replacements sufficiently trained in air tactics to meet successfully our now-veteran airmen who made the most of the high performance of their new Lightnings, Corsairs, and Hellcats.

At war's end half of all the Japanese fighter planes were essentially the same Zero with which the Japanese fought in China five years before.

In the critical field involving the development of new weapons Japan was practically at a standstill while we were racing ahead. Her few guided missiles were never used in combat. She had in preparation *one* jet airplane, and that flew but once. Japanese radar was crude. They had nothing which even approximated a B-17 or a B-24—let alone a B-29. And Japan constantly was perplexed and bewildered by a profusion of Allied weapons—air-to-ground rockets, napalm, computing sights, radar-directed guns, proximity fuses, guided missiles, aerial mines, bazookas, flame throwers, and brilliantly executed mass bombing. It was the Japanese inability to counter these weapons, let alone produce them, which had them on the ropes during the last two years of war.

The Japanese failed because their high command made the mistake of believing its own propaganda, to the effect that there was internal dissension in the United States, that we were decadent, that it would require years for us to swing from luxury production to a great war industrial effort. This in itself was a fatal error for, despite the drain of the fight against Germany, even by sheer weight of arms alone we eventually would have overwhelmed an enemy whose production was never ten per cent of our own at its peak.

Japanese strategists and tacticians fought their war entirely out of the rule books. These were never revised until ugly experience taught the Japanese that the books were obsolete, that we were fighting a war all our own—on *our* terms. The enemy became dumbfounded; they were incapable of effective countermeasures.

The Japanese high command was inordinately fond of the words "impregnable, unsinkable, and invulnerable." That such conditions are myths was unknown to them.

Their conception of war was built around the word *attack.* They could not foresee a situation in which they did not have the advantage. Once on the defensive, they threw away their strength in heroic *banzai* charges where massed firepower slaughtered their ranks. Sometimes when the trend was against them, they lost their capacity for straight thinking and blundered, often with disastrous results.

The Japanese failed because their men and officers were inferior, not in courage, *but in the intelligent use of courage.* Japanese education, Japanese ancestor worship, and the Japanese caste system were reflected time after time in uninspired leadership and transfixed initiative. In a predicted situation which could be handled in an orthodox manner, the Japanese were always competent and often resourceful. Under the shadow of frustration, however, the obsession of personal honor extinguished ingenuity.

The execution of Japanese plans was totally unequal to the grandiose demands of their strategy. Never was this so true as in the Japanese failure to understand the true meaning of air power. Because they themselves lacked a formula for strategic air power, they overlooked the possibility that it would be used against them and so were unprepared to counter it. Japanese bombers never were capable of sustaining a heavy offensive. To the Japanese, the B-17s and B-24s were formidable opponents; the B-29 was a threat beyond their capacity to counter.

The collapse of Japan brilliantly vindicated the whole strategic concept of the offensive phase of the Pacific War.

While ground and sea forces played an indispensable role which can in no sense be underestimated, that strategy, in its broadest terms, was to advance air power to the point where the full fury of crushing air attack could be loosed on Japan itself, with the possibility that such attack would bring about the defeat of Japan without invasion.

There was no invasion.

Japan was vulnerable. Her far-flung supply lines were comparable to delicate arteries nurtured by a bad heart. The value of her captured land masses and the armed forces which defended them was in direct proportion to the ability of her shipping to keep them supplied, to keep the forces mobile, and to bring back to Japan the materials to keep her factories running. Destroy the shipping, and Japan for all practical purposes would be four islands without an empire ... four islands on which were cities made-to-order for destruction by fire.

Destroy the shipping and burn the cities. We did.

To the submarines goes the chief credit for reducing the Japanese merchant fleet to a point where it was destroyed or useless. Air power also played a great part in this role by sinking ships at sea (the A.A.F. destroyed more than one million tons in 1944) and sealing off Japanese ports with aerial mines.

We burned the cities. The B-29s reaped an incredible harvest of destruction in Japan. Her ability to continue the war collapsed amid the ashes of her scarred and fire-trampled urban centers. The two atomic bombs contributed less than three per cent of the destruction visited upon the industrial centers of Japan. But they gave the Japanese, so preoccupied with saving face, an excuse and a means of ending a futile war with honor intact.

The full story of the vast Pacific war, however, never has been told. It is one thing to study that war from your own viewpoint, but quite another to examine it from that of the enemy.

Therein lies the reason for this book. In its entirety, *ZERO!* is a Japanese story, told by the Japanese. The liberties I have taken in writing this book for the American public do not infringe upon the story of the two Japanese authors. There are instances where I do not agree with Masatake Okumiya and Jiro Horikoshi, but it is their story, not mine, which you will read.

Where readability is aided I have replaced the complicated Japanese aircraft descriptions and designations with terms more familiar to the American reader. For example, the *Claude* is the Type 96 Carrier Fighter, the *Jack* is the Raiden fighter plane, the *Val* is the Aichi Type 99 Carrier-Based Bomber, and so forth. All code names are those employed by U.S. forces in World War II.

Questionable passages and data have been carefully checked against official American histories, and the apparent inconsistencies put before the Japanese for clarification. However, the writer must emphasize again that the sentiments and feelings, the data and reports, are those of the Japanese authors. Every word in this book has been carefully studied by them to produce, from the Japanese point of view, an accurate history and appraisal of the Pacific War. Okumiya and Horikoshi, aided by many of their wartime colleagues, have provided us with a fascinating new perspective of that great conflict.

These Japanese are what I would call "complimentary to their enemies." In *ZERO!* they are completely forthright, honest, and prepared to call a spade a spade. While you will read of the humiliating victories of the Japanese over our own forces, you will find equally honest accounts of Japanese defeats and routs—as told by our former enemies. There are no attempts at evasion; there is frank admission of Japanese inadequacies in planning and in fighting.

Both Masatake Okumiya and Jiro Horikoshi are ideally suited to present the Japanese side of the World War II story. Okumiya is a former flying officer of the Japanese Navy with active service and combat flying experience over a period of fifteen years. A graduate of Japan's Naval Academy, Okumiya as a Commander engaged in most of the major sea-air battles in the Pacific from 1942 to 1944, as a staff officer of carrier task forces. The Midway-Aleutian Sea Battle, the Guadalcanal Campaign, the Santa Cruz Battle in 1942 and the Marianas Campaign in 1944, are only a few. Okumiya was actively engaged in the crippling air campaigns fought in the Solomon Islands and the New Guinea area. For the last year of the war he was placed in command of Japan's homeland air defense as a staff officer of General Headquarters in Tokyo.

He is considered one of Japan's leading air-sea strategists, and today holds a high position in the new Japanese Air Force. The combat material in this book is his contribution.

Jiro Horikoshi is considered by his associates as one of the world's greatest aeronautical engineers and, indeed, is held in the highest esteem in international circles. A graduate of Tokyo Imperial University, he joined the Nagoya Aircraft Works of Mitsubishi Heavy Industries, Ltd., in 1927, and with that firm served in many engineering and director capacities. From his drafting board emerged several of Japan's greatest fighter planes, the Claude, the famous Zero, the Raiden, and the spectacular but ill-fated Reppu.

Horikoshi's contributions to Japan's aeronautical industry played a great part in enabling that nation to achieve originality of design, to gain her first independence of foreign aeronautical science and products. His engineering background and the vital role played by his design products in China and during World War II, make Jiro Horikoshi's story a unique and revealing look into a hitherto untold chapter of Japan's history.

Prior to the Pearl Harbor attack, not all the members of the Japanese high command wished a war with the United States. Especially among the Naval staff were three men with the ability to foresee the dire consequences of such a conflict. More than any other Japanese military officer, Admiral Isoroku Yamamoto, Commander-in-Chief of the Combined Fleet, protested vigorously against the war. He accurately forecast that, if the war continued beyond 1943, Japan was doomed to defeat. But Yamamoto's warnings, as well as those of other officers and government statesmen, fell on deaf ears. Hideki Tojo committed his ill-equipped nation to a bitter defeat. Isoroku Yamamoto died in air combat in 1943, but his predicted conduct of the war proved astonishingly correct.

It is refreshing not to find in *ZERO!* the bungled attempts at evasion of responsibility for the war which are so prevalent in the biographies prepared by former members of the German High Command. It is astonishing indeed, to learn that so many German generals and statesmen had absolutely nothing to do with their nation's preparations for war. With weary familiarity the ex-leaders of Germany "prove" their innocence of participation in the schemes which produced history's greatest blood bath. You will not find such insultingly naïve passages in this book.

By mid-1943 the Empire of Japan was beaten. There was no longer any question as to the outcome of the war. The peculiarities of the Japanese, however, would not permit any such official admission, even to themselves. And so the war continued, with mounting Japanese casualties, with frenzied suicide attacks, with the incredible savagery of fire bombing which the Japanese brought upon themselves by their own unwillingness to end a useless struggle.

The defeat of Japan is a story which becomes a monumental tragedy. The question now is not how the Japanese ever accomplished as much as they did in the Pacific, but rather why it took us so long to end that war.

(With thanks to *Impact*)

Martin Caidin
New York, 1955

We feel that we can justify the thesis taught to the Japanese masses whereby they were, subsequent to the Sino-Japanese and Russo-Japanese wars, led to believe that Japan would not and could not lose a war. Be that as it may, the military and political leaders in whose hands lies the future of a nation should concentrate their efforts on devising means not merely of winning a war but of preventing defeat, should armed conflict prove inevitable. Should these national leaders be misled by the outward appearance of the armed might at their disposal and throw their nation into the cataclysm of war without an exhaustive study of the implications of their actions, they cannot themselves escape the consequences of their acts. Their actions are nothing short of outrageous or, in modern parlance, subversive, regardless of theoretical justifications.

It has been the tragedy of modern Japan that those great and humane statesmen who attempted to follow the principles of "fair play" in international conduct often met death, and that several cabinets composed of such men fell by the wayside before the pressure of the military cliques.

We, the Japanese, must never forget that it was criminal to permit this situation to exist; that because of this intolerable political blindness we pushed millions of our good neighbors into misery and suffering beyond the comprehension of most Japanese civilians; and, finally, that our own foolish actions hurled Japan into the present economic abyss from which she finds it so difficult to emerge. We must provide some form of compensation for those countries on which we have visited destruction; we must maintain the utmost vigilance to prevent the repetition of past mistakes.

Despite this attitude, so necessary to peaceful international conduct, there arise occasions when armed might is indispensable to a nation's welfare. Those persons who have been invested with their nation's military responsibility must, without regard to politics, do their utmost to execute the duties entrusted to them.

To meet its military requirements, a nation will strive for the most effective weapons and manpower. Several decades ago Japan recognized adequate airpower as the weapon most suited to solve its national defense problems and accordingly stressed the growth of that arm, notably in the naval field.

On July 7, 1937, the Sino-Japanese Incident flared on the Asian mainland, almost a quarter of a century after we had undertaken to develop our naval air power. At this time the Navy was prepared to counter any eventuality with this striking force:

CARRIER STRIKING FORCE

FIRST CARRIER DIVISION

Under command of Rear Admiral Shiro Takasu, in Ryujo:
    Ryujo, Captain Katsuo Abe
      12 Type 95 carrier-based fighters
      15 Type 94 carrier-based dive bombers
    Hosho, Captain Ryunosuke Kusaka
       9 Type 95 carrier-based fighters
       6 Type 92 carrier-based attack bombers

SECOND CARRIER DIVISION

Under command of Rear Admiral Rokuro Horie, in Kaga:
    Kaga, Captain Ayao Inagaki
      12 Type 90 carrier-based fighters
      12 Type 94 carrier-based dive bombers
      12 Type 89 carrier-based attack bombers
      12 Type 96 carrier-based attack bombers

LAND-BASED AIR FORCE

FIRST COMBINED AIR FLOTILLA

Under command of Captain Mitchitaro Tozuka, at Taipei (later Shanghai):

Kisarazu Air Corps, Captain Ryuzo Takenaka
  6 Type 95 land-based attack bombers
 24 Type 96 land-based attack bombers

Kanoya Air Corps, Captain Sizue Ishii
  9 Type 95 carrier-based fighters
 18 Type 96 land-based attack bombers

SECOND COMBINED AIR FLOTILLA

Under command of Rear Admiral Teizo Mitsunami, at Ohmura (later Shanghai):

12th Air Corps, Captain Osamu Imamura
 12 Type 95 carrier-based fighters
 12 Type 94 carrier-based dive bombers
 12 Type 92 carrier-based attack bombers

13th Air Corps, Captain Sadatoshi Senda
 12 Type 96 carrier-based fighters
 12 Type 96 carrier-based dive bombers
 12 Type 96 carrier-based attack bombers

Total strength: 66 carrier-based fighters
             51 carrier-based dive bombers
             54 carrier-based attack bombers
             <u>48</u> land-based attack bombers
           219 combat-ready warplanes

There were also available the thirty scout and observation seaplanes of the costal defense ship *Izumo*, the flagship of the Third Fleet (stationed at Shanghai); the seaplane tender *Kamoi*; and various cruisers.

When the fighting spread to Shanghai on August 13, 1937, our intelligence reported that the Japanese garrison in that city was completely encircled by a strong Chinese force, supported by three hundred planes based in the Nanking area. Additional reports revealed that a concerted Chinese attack could in a few days wipe out to the last man the Japanese marines who were isolated in Shanghai. The marine garrison faced overwhelming numbers of Chinese troops; since no airfield within Shanghai was usable, our men were denied local air coverage.

On August 14, following a series of sharp land battles, the Chinese planes opened bombing attacks against our forces in and around Shanghai. Even as the raids began, a single Type 90 scout-observation seaplane of the *Izumo* attacked the enemy formations, downing one fighter. This first aerial battle forecast greater commitments of planes by both sides.

On the evening of August 14, the Type 96 land-based attack bombers (Nells) of the Kanoya Air Corps based at Taipei (Formosa) attacked Chinese positions. On the following day Nells of the Kisarazu Air Corps from Ohmura Base on Kyushu Island began their bombing raids, and, commencing on the sixteenth, the carrier planes joined the rising tide of raids against the enemy's forces. These attacks of the Nells constituted the first "transoceanic" bombing raids.

For many years the Japanese Army and Navy had hidden their armament and weapons; the public saw only the obsolete models of heavy guns, warships and planes. In contrast to this policy, other countries obviously attempted to frighten their enemies into submission through constant exhibition of their military forces. Knowledge of the true performance of foreign weapons was denied the public; the propaganda mills ground out exaggerated reports of the actual strength of each nation.

By importing many foreign aircraft and weapons, we in Japan were able to gauge approximately what these weapons could and could not do. By keeping our planes and other armament within our borders and free from prying eyes, we led the world seriously to underestimate the combat strength of our naval aviation.

The so-called transoceanic bombing missions of the Sino-Japanese Incident revealed for the first time the actual capabilities of Japanese warplanes. The long-distance raids by the Nell bombers, averaging two thousand kilometers (1250 miles) for each raid, exceeded by a considerable margin the previous maximum-range attacks of any country's planes. Further appreciation of this startling advance in aerial warfare was possible when it was revealed that these airplanes were carrying out their attacks in extremely poor weather, flying from Formosa and Kyushu against targets in and around Shanghai, Nanking, Hanchou, and other cities.

The elation which swept the Japanese populace with the announcements of the bombing was understandable. We had a powerful, long-range, fair-and-foul-weather, day-and-night bombing force. Our planes constantly set new records; the only air battles fought across an appreciable expanse of water up to this time had been those undertaken in World War I across the Straits of Dover and its vicinity.

Despite the obvious quality of our planes and the caliber of our pilots, the Navy's Air Force suffered heavy losses in the early days of the incident. There was much to be learned in the art of long-distance attack which could be acquired in peacetime, but the price which the Chinese exacted for those lessons was severe.

We learned—almost at once, and with devastating thoroughness—that bombers are no match for enemy fighter planes. We lost many men as this lesson was administered, including Lieutenant Commander Nitta, Air Group Commander, Lieutenant (JG) Umebayashi and Ensign Yamanouchi of the land-based attack-bomber groups, and other pilots well known in Japan.

The planes of the aircraft carrier *Kaga* suffered disastrously. The twelve Type 89 carrier-based attack bombers, led by Group Commander Lieutenant Commander Iwai, left the *Kaga* on August 17 for a raid against Hangchou. Bad weather prevented a rendezvous with an expected fighter escort and near their target the bombers were attacked by a group of Chinese fighter planes. Eleven bombers, including the commander's, were shot down. Lieutenant (JG) Tanaka managed to bring his bullet-riddled and crippled bomber safely back to the carrier; otherwise, the fate of the attacking group would never have been known, and another bomber formation might have suffered a similar fate. Tanaka's report astonished the officers of the fleet, and immediate warnings were issued to all bomber groups to take special precautions against the defending Chinese fighters.

We discovered that when our fighter planes provided escort to, over, and from the target such incidents did not occur. Comparing the shattered unescorted bomber groups with the relatively unharmed formations which were protected by fighters, the Navy reacted quickly. The *Kaga* was ordered to return immediately to Sasebo and to receive a full complement of the new Type 96 carrier-based fighters (Claudes).

Although the fighters had never flown in service operations from an aircraft carrier, the gravity of the situation warranted the risk of accidents. In early September the Second Combined Air Flotilla, equipped with the powerful Claudes, returned to Shanghai.

In the Second Combined Air Flotilla were Lieutenant Commander Okamura, Lieutenant Commander Genda, and Lieutenant Nomura, three of Japan's outstanding veteran fighter pilots; later they were joined by another combat veteran, Lieutenant Nango. The flotilla's first raid against Nanking on September 18 was followed by wave after wave of attacks, made chiefly with dive bombers and the powerful Claude fighters.

The Chinese air force put up a desperate air defense, hurling fighters of international repute against the Mitsubishi fighter planes. Chinese pilots attacked the Claudes with such planes as the English Gloster Gladiator, the American Curtiss 75, and the Russian N-15 and N-16 fighters. There was no doubt about the outcome of the protracted aerial engagements; from the outset the Claudes proved their superiority in a series of air victories. Within two months of the initial attacks against the Chinese targets, the enemy's fighter planes disappeared from the arena; the last combat on December 2, when Lieutenant Nango's Claudes blasted ten N-16's from the sky over Nanking, was a glorious victory. All through October and November the Japanese people rejoiced at the brilliant combat successes of the Claudes, which battled numerically superior forces.

The Chinese moved their air-base facilities to rear areas beyond the flight range of the marauding Mitsubishi fighter planes, establishing new headquarters at Nanching in central China, about 335 miles southwest of Shanghai. Attacking their planes from Shanghai with Claude fighters required new tactics. Lieutenant Commander Genda, air staff officer of the 2nd Combined Air Flotilla, proposed that the Navy set up special refueling bases close to the Chinese lines to be used by the fighters on their way to the enemy.

Employing Type 95 land-based attack bombers as emergency transport planes, the Navy flew fuel and mechanics for the fighters into Kuangte Air Field. Although occupied by the Japanese Army, the airfield was partially isolated, since the enemy still controlled the supply lines. Our fighter planes landed at Kuangte for refueling, then resumed their flights for the Nancheing area. Those planes with sufficient fuel to return directly to Shanghai flew nonstop from the target area; the remainder with short fuel reserves made another stop at Kuangte.

The novelty of the new tactics proved completely successful, as repeatedly our fighters made disastrous surprise raids against the unsuspecting Chinese. Japan gained a hero in this series of attacks; Flight Petty Officer Kashimura had just downed his second enemy plane in a single engagement when the falling fighter rammed the Claude, shearing off more than one third of its left wing. Through superb piloting Kashimura managed to return his crippled fighter to Shanghai.

The demands of battle forced the naval planes into unexpected situations for which they had not been trained. Carrier-based dive bombers, attack bombers, and Type 95 carrier-based fighters repeatedly reconnoitered, bombed, and machine-gunned enemy forces in direct cooperation with our army units, which were advancing steadily westward from the Shanghai area to Nanking. Although lacking in training and experience, the naval pilots performed these missions so successfully that they received the greatest praise of the ground units, who benefited materially from their supporting attacks.

These special operations were discontinued after three months of fighting, marked by the fall of Nanking. Many lessons were gained in the way of new tactics and operations from the campaign, especially (1) that air groups and combat planes trained at sea for sea duty can serve successfully without special training in any air campaign over land, and (2) that the key to success in any land or sea operation depends upon command of the air.

The outstanding combat successes of the Claude fighter planes ended a long-standing controversy in Japan, destroying once and for all the validity of the arguments of those who insisted upon retaining biplane-type fighters. Even with due consideration for its exceptional maneuverability, the short range and slow speed of the Type 95 carrier-based fighter doomed it to extinction. It required the final test of combat to determine which of these two fighter types would be the most effective in war.

The China air battles vindicated completely the Navy's insistence upon the strictest training for all pilots and air crews. Although the naval pilots were trained specifically for operations against enemy surface fleets, their quality enabled them to perform with an efficiency superior to that exhibited by our Army pilots. Conversely, it was also determined that pilots trained specifically for maneuvers over land experienced great difficulty in overwater operations, even in merely flying long distances over the ocean.

We discovered that the extended range of our Navy bombers opened new vistas of aerial warfare and that with these far-flying aircraft we could attack enemy positions far behind the front lines or while several hundred miles at sea. Most important of all, perhaps, we learned that certain types of air campaigns could not be strictly defined as either strictly "land" or "sea" battles, but required of the pilots the ability to fight under any conditions.

Despite these more obvious results of aerial warfare in China, the farsighted younger officers of the Navy Air Force encountered a solid wall of conservatism among the military hierarchy. The situation within the Army proved similar; there was little change in the basic concept of air power as an auxiliary to sea and land forces. Aware that they must first overcome the obstacles of outmoded thinking before they could hope to modernize our aerial weapons, our naval air officers again bent every effort to obtain greater authority and increased funds for their Air Force.

In the succeeding years, these efforts proved their worth; modern equipment, better training, and increased numbers of planes gave the Navy the strength of modern air power. Despite radical changes within its own organization, the Army failed to keep pace with the constant and rapid advances in air power achieved by the Navy, and was especially deficient in general reliability and ground maintenance. Except for a few plane types such as the Type 100 headquarters plane, far superior to any comparable Navy aircraft, the performance of the Army's planes fell below those of its sister service.

Despite vigorous attempts to modernize the Army's air training policies, it remained particularly deficient in overwater and night-flying capabilities. The Army Air Force never quite emerged from its position as the "crippled air force" whose dominion was confined entirely to the land.

Even as Japan drifted toward the Pacific War, men of foresight recognized the need for a land-based air power capable of operating under any conditions. These men, outside the military organization, failed in their efforts to convince the Army's leaders of their views.

We have often wondered about this misfortune of Japan, whose particular military, political, and social system did not permit the views of people outside the military hierarchy to affect the nation's armament. Certainly, we could have done much to improve the effectiveness of our air strength had we at least listened.

CHAPTER 2

Peace Attempts Fail—The Fighting Continues

T HE WAR IN CHINA WAS now three years old. We discontinued temporarily military operations in middle China, commencing with the occupation of Nanking in December of 1937. By the year's end the Japanese government was making every possible effort to settle politically the regrettable conflict between Japan and China. The attempts at negotiation failed completely, due primarily to the interruption of the Japanese Army hierarchy, as well as to the desire of influential Chinese parties to see the war continued. Indeed, in January, 1938, Army officers compelled Prime Minister Konoye against his will to announce: "We will not negotiate with the Nationalist Government of Chiang Kai-shek."

The inevitable happened; the war continued and no end appeared in sight. The Japanese people, concerned with the rapid spread of open fighting in China since July 7 of the previous year, still believed optimistically that despite the Prime Minister's obvious surrender to the Army, the war would soon end. Several leaders of our country publicly warned the government of the foreseeable grave consequences of extended fighting with China. A number of patriots in and outside of Government service openly opposed the influential Army groups which, acting through the timorous prime minister, had so effectively diverted national policy and had committed the nation to war. These protests proved of little avail, as history relates.

Thus the fighting spread rapidly, soon enveloping most of China. In January of 1938 Japanese troops triumphantly concluded the Hankow Operation; thirteen months later they controlled Hainan Island and also temporarily and successfully halted the Shansi Campaign. In the interim our naval air units flew constant sorties, mainly in southern and central China. Once the Chinese air groups retreated beyond the range of the Type 96 carrier fighters to rebuild their shattered strength, the air war became a protracted struggle confined almost entirely to the bombing attacks of the Type 96 land-based attack bombers. Despite the best intentions of our commanders, the war situation demanded the presence of the naval air units at the Chinese front, a situation in which their maximum potentialities could not possibly be developed.

CHAPTER 3

Zero Fighters in China

FOLLOWING THEIR ADVANCE in late 1938 to the Hankow Air Base, the Navy Air Force flew close-support missions for Army troops and Navy surface forces with Type 97 carrier attack bombers (Kates) and with Type 99 carrier dive bombers (Vals). The Type 96 land-based attack bombers (Nells) bombed Chungking and other interior bases. The Type 96 carrier fighters (Claudes) defended our air bases and engaged enemy fighters whenever the Chinese pilots ventured within the range of the Claudes.

Between May and September of 1939, the Nells attacked Chungking from Hankow bases with twenty-two separate raids, aggregating an overtarget total of two hundred bombers. On November 4, 1939, Nells flew from the Hankow bases to attack Chengtu, and from late November to late December the Nells flew from Yucheng bases in Shansi to raid Lanchow (in Kansu).

The continuous aerial assaults noticeably weakened the Chinese Air Force's offensive power. Despite the effectiveness of the attacks, however, within six months we noticed definite signs of recovery. From mid-May to early September of 1940 Nells repeatedly battered the Chungking area. There were in the Hankow area in mid-1940 130 Type 96 bombers assigned to the four China-based air corps—Kanoya, Takao, the 13th, and the 15th. Every flyable airplane flew in each mission against Chungking for a total of 168 daytime attacks and 14 night raids, aggregating 3,717 bombers over target.

These were the heaviest raids of the China air war. On eight raids, Army Type 97's joined the Nells, aggregating seventy-two planes over target. The limited range of the Claude fighters prevented them from escorting the bombers to their objectives, where waiting Chinese fighters pounced upon the raiders. We suffered heavy losses; nine planes were destroyed or missing, and a total of 297 bombers were damaged. During some raids the percentage of lost or damaged bombers rose beyond the "prohibitive" figure of 10 per cent. The Chinese fighters inflicted at least half the damage sustained by our bombers, while antiaircraft fire was responsible for the remainder. We could alleviate this unsatisfactory situation only by securing command of the air over the targets.

The Zeros were the answer. With their two machine guns and two 20-mm. cannon they outgunned every airplane which opposed them. Their 300-mile per hour speed enabled them to pursue—and to catch—all enemy aircraft within their range. Combining the advantages of speed, rapid climb, excellent maneuverability and heavy firepower, our pilots had in their new Zero fighter an airplane which shattered enemy opposition.

Besides the two skilled squadron commanders, Lieutenants Tamotsu Yokoyama and Saburo Shindo, and other well-known fighter pilots including Lieutenant (JG) Ayao

Shirane, Flight Warrant Officers Koshiro Yamashita and Ichiro Higashiyama flew with the new planes.

On August 19, 1940 Lieutenant Yokoyama led a squadron of twelve Zero fighters on an escort mission of fifty Nell bombers over Chungking, but failed to encounter any Chinese fighters. The following day Lieutenant Shindo made another sweep over Chungking escorting fifty bombers, but again failed to find an opportunity to engage in combat. Our intelligence officers believed that the Chinese had already learned of the arrival of the Zeros in China and, accordingly, had carefully dispersed their planes. Despite the lack of action which our pilots coveted, the initial two combat flights proved valuable in that they enabled our pilots to become familiar with the combat area. The missions also established new world records for the combat flights of fighter planes; the Zeros flew a round trip of more than one thousand nautical miles.

By early September the Navy concluded its major offensive and expeditionary operations and recalled from the continent all units except the 12th Air Corps with Zero fighters, and the 13th Air Corps with several squadrons of Nell bombers station in the Hankow area.

On September 12 Lieutenant Yokoyama led twelve Zeros on an escort mission for twenty-seven Nells in an attack against Chungking. Unopposed in the air, the Zero pilots sighted five enemy planes on the ground at Shihma-chow Air Field, and dove earthward in a strafing attack. The enemy planes were decoys, and the Zeros then strafed airfield structures and other military establishments. Despite the lack of active aerial opposition against the Zeros, photographs taken the same day by a Type 98 reconnaissance plane confirmed the presence of thirty-two Chinese planes on the bases about the city.

On September 13 thirteen Zeros under the command of

Lieutenant Shindo and Lieutenant (JG) Shirane escorted Nell bombers from Hankow on the thirty-fifth raid of the 13th Air Corps against Chungking. After the bombing runs the pilots put into effect a long-planned ruse to lure the Chinese fighters out of hiding. The Nells turned and started for Hankow, accompanied by the fighter planes. Approximately at two o'clock in the afternoon, with our bombing force already out of sight of the city, our reconnaissance plane radioed Lieutenant Shindo that Chinese fighters had appeared over Chungking.

The Zeros wheeled, climbing for altitude as they returned to the city and the unsuspecting Chinese fighters. Diving out of the sun, the Zeros swarmed over the startled Chinese pilots, spreading havoc with their machine guns and cannon. Within thirty minutes our pilots cleared the sky of all the Chinese fighters, later identified as twenty-seven Russian-made N-15 and N-16 airplanes.

Japan gained a new hero in Flight Warrant Officer Koshiro Yamashita, who in this single combat became an ace by destroying five enemy fighters. Flight Petty Officer (2nd Class) Oki, despite damage to his fuel tanks, pursued and destroyed an N-15 fighter. Two desperately evading enemy planes smashed into and exploded against a mountainside. Utterly confused by the flashing, swirling Zeros, three Chinese pilots hastily bailed out of their undamaged fighters. With the last enemy plane cleared from the sky, Warrant Officer Yamashita and Petty Officers Kitahata and Yoneda flew to Paishihyi Air Field, strafing and burning several Chinese planes which were just returning from other missions. Our pilots were overjoyed. Only four Zeros suffered light damage, and every one of our pilots escaped injury.

Vice-Admiral Shigetaro Shimada, the Commander in Chief of the China Area Fleet, immediately dispatched a special commendation to the Zero Fighter Squadron, which stated:

SPECIAL COMMENDATION

TO: THE 12TH AIR CORPS FIGHTER SQUADRON COM-
   MANDED BY LIEUTENANT SABURO SHINDO:

ON 13 SEPTEMBER 1940 THIS SQUADRON MADE A SUC-
CESSFUL LONG-RANGE FLIGHT OVER THE MOUNTAIN-
OUS SSUCHUAN-SHENG (SZECHWAN PROVINCE) AREA,
ESCORTING THE CHUNGKING BOMBING EXPEDITION OF
THE LAND-BASED ATTACK BOMBER GROUP. AFTER
COMPLETING THEIR ESCORT MISSION AND APPEARING
TO LEAVE THE TARGET AREA FOR THE PURPOSE OF
LURING ENEMY FIGHTERS FROM HIDING, THE
SQUADRON RETURNED TO CHUNGKING TO ATTACK A
NUMERICALLY SUPERIOR ENEMY FIGHTER FORCE, SUC-
CEEDING IN DESTROYING ALL ENEMY FIGHTER PLANES
THROUGH GALLANT AND COURAGEOUS COMBAT. THIS
OUTSTANDING SUCCESS DESERVES THE *DISTIN-
GUISHED MILITARY MERIT.*

I HEREBY AWARD THIS DIPLOMA OF MERIT.
OCTOBER 30, 1940.

> SHIGETARO SHIMADA
> COMMANDER IN CHIEF
> CHINA AREA FLEET

Obviously the inability of the Chinese pilots to present a determined front to the attacking Zero fighters, accentuated by two crashing enemy planes and the three pilots who needlessly bailed out, contributed heavily to the one-sided victory of September 13. Much of the credit, however, rested directly with the Zero fighter which, by virtue of its superior flight range, staying power, high speed, heavy firepower, and unexcelled maneuverability, imparted to our pilots a tremendous advantage in dogfighting. This was enhanced, of course, by the superior flying ability of our pilots.

Informed of the brilliant first combat success of the Zero fighters, Vice-Admiral Teijiro Toyota, Chief of the Naval Bureau of Aeronautics, forwarded a letter of appreciation (reproduced below) to each of the three companies—Mitsubishi, Nakajima, and Dai Nihon Heiki (the Japan Weapons Company)—which had manufactured the airframes, engines, and 20-mm. cannon. The Navy expressed its great satisfaction with its new fighter by granting the Nakajima company a large production order for Zero fighter airframes.

LETTER OF APPRECIATION

TO: MR. KOSHIRO SHIBA, CHAIRMAN
    BOARD OF DIRECTORS
    MITSUBISHI HEAVY INDUSTRY COMPANY, LTD.

THE RECENT OUTSTANDING SUCCESS OF THE 12TH AIR CORPS ZERO FIGHTER SQUADRON IN ATTACKING AND DESTROYING TWENTY-SEVEN CHINESE FIGHTERS OVER CHUNGKING ON SEPTEMBER 13, 1940, WITHOUT LOSS TO OUR AIRPLANES, IS DUE IN GREAT PART TO THE EXCELLENT PERFORMANCE OF THE ZERO FIGHTER AIRPLANE.

I HEREBY EXPRESS MY SINCERE GRATITUDE, AND THE GRATITUDE OF THE NAVY, FOR THE OUTSTANDING

AND MERITORIOUS WORK OF YOUR COMPANY IN COM-
PLETING WITHIN A SHORT DEVELOPMENT TIME THIS
EXCELLENT FIGHTER.

> SEPTEMBER 14, 1940
> TEIJIRO TOYOTA
> *VICE-ADMIRAL*
> *CHIEF, NAVY BUREAU OF AERONAUTICS*

Encouraged by the success of the Zero fighters against
the enemy planes over Chungking, later in the afternoon of
September 13, the 12th Air Corps launched the first attack
against the city with Val bombers, flying from Ichang Air
Base. Two days later, Kate bombers also flew from Ichang
to attack Chungking. With its newly won command of the
air over the Chinese objectives the Zeros made it possible
for the Navy to apply all of its available bomber force
against the enemy. On September 16 six Zero fighters
attacked and destroyed a single large Chinese plane over
Chungking; this was their last combat engagement for the
month. Our pilots and mechanics devoted the final two
weeks of the month solely to maintenance, preparing for
the forthcoming flights deep within enemy territory to
where the Chinese planes had fled.

On October 4 Lieutenants Yokoyama and Shirane led
eight Zeros on an escort mission for twenty-seven Nells of
the 13th Air Corps in their first raid against Chengtu in
Szechwan Province. The two formations broke through
thick clouds over the city at 2:30 P.M., and the bombers
inflicted heavy damage on their targets. Unopposed in the
air, the Zeros attacked nearby Taipingssu Air Field, shooting down five N-16 fighter planes and one SB bomber. Our
pilots then strafed airplanes and airfield installations.

With ground facilities burning and Chinese personnel

scattered from the field, Flight Warrant Officer Higashiyama and Flight Petty Officers Hagiri, Nakase, and Oishi landed on the field while the remaining Zeros flew top cover. Leaving their planes with engines running, the four pilots attempted to set afire the remaining undamaged Chinese airplanes. The fierce gunfire of returning Chinese troops forced them to abandon their plan and to take off immediately.

The Zeros again had struck had, shooting down five fighters and one bomber, burning nineteen additional planes on the ground, and damaging four others, for a total confirmed kill of twenty-five enemy planes destroyed. Only two Zeros received light damage. Again Admiral Shimada forwarded a special commendation to the Corps.

The following day, October 5, Lieutenant Fusata Iida led seven Zeros in strafing attacks against Fenghuangshan Air Field near Chengtu. Our pilots set afire six large and four small planes and damaged two additional large aircraft. Fourteen decoys were burned.

As a consequence of these attacks, the backbone of Chinese air strength in the Chungking and Chengtu areas was broken. For weeks afterward the skies over these two cities were conspicuously free of enemy planes.

Immediately prior to the initial combat successes scored by the Zero fighters, elements of our Army and Navy were enabled to advance into French Indochina as a result of diplomatic negotiations with the French Vichy Government. (Although our entry into French Indochina resulted from diplomatic-political negotiations with France, this action eventually created strong friction between Japan and the United States, Great Britain, and other nations in the Allied fold. It could accurately be described as the first noticeable move in a series of events which finally resulted in the Pacific War.)

Our naval air units stationed in southern China few immediately to their new bases in northern French Indochina. The proximity of these new stations to Chinese targets enabled us to launch single-engine bombers to attack Kunming, an area of great strategic importance in southwestern China which, previously, could be reached only by the long-range Nells. As soon as the French air bases could receive them, squadrons of the 14th Air Corps' Claude fighters, Kate attack bombers, and Val dive bombers were transferred to their new facilities. The 12th Air Corps in Hankow detached one squadron of Zero fighters, transferring them to French Indochina for long-range escort work.

On October 7 seven Zero and nine Claude fighters escorted a group of Val dive bombers to Kunming. Nearly twenty enemy fighter planes opposed the Zeros and Claudes, which definitely destroyed thirteen enemy planes and probably destroyed another. The Vals wrecked four enemy planes on the ground.

On December 12 seven Zero fighters escorted ten dive bombers and two bomb-carrying reconnaissance planes in an attack against Siangyun. Our fighters strafed and destroyed twenty-two enemy planes on the ground. From October 8 to the end of December Zeros flew an additional twenty-two sorties, in which they definitely shot down two enemy planes.

While the Indochina-based planes attacked southern Chinese targets, on October 10, the Double Ten Festival Day of China, the 12th Air Corps Zeros in the Hankow area raided Chungking without encountering enemy opposition. On October 26 eight Zeros caught a large group of Chinese planes over Chengtu, destroying five enemy fighters, one transport plane, and four other types. On December 30 eight Zeros returned to Chengtu for their fourth attack, sweeping in a strafing attack over the Fenghuangshan, Taipingssu, Shuanglin, and Wenchiang airfields. They burned eighteen enemy planes, and wrecked fifteen others by cannon fire. The Zeros also set afire one large fuel storehouse and shot up other ground installations. Only two of our fighters suffered damage from antiaircraft fire.

Thus ended the year 1940 and the Zero fighter's baptism in combat. It drew first blood in an almost miraculous fashion, for in the period from August 19 to the end of the year the Zeros ran up this record:

Number of attacks made	22
Total number of planes used	153
Chinese planes shot down (one probable)	59
Chinese planes destroyed (air and ground)	101
Number of Zeros damaged by enemy fire	13
Number of Zeros lost	0

However brilliant these combat successes, and however outstanding the record of our Navy Air Force in China, from the first transoceanic bombing of 1937 to the close of 1940, our pride can be justified only from the military standpoint.

No Japanese citizen can recall the events of these years and find justification for the *national* conduct of our country. No one can deny the record, for history will relate only that Japan forced her friendly neighboring nations into an unreasonable and unnecessary war, transformed their fields and cities into battlegrounds, and visited misery and deprivation on millions of innocent people.

CHAPTER 4

Eve of the Pacific War

AS JAPANESE, WE FIND it difficult and more than a little embarrassing to discuss in retrospect our military successes in China immediately prior to the Pacific War. We would prefer to relegate our nation's inexcusable conduct in the Sino-Japanese Incident to oblivion; however, in order to present accurately certain phases of that incident not previously included in this book I (Okumiya) must review a certain aspect of these events.

In late October of 1940 the Navy recalled from China all its Type 96 land-based attack bombers (Nells) for reorganization into new combat units. During the six months from October to April of 1941, the Zero fighter planes remaining on the continent were the only aerial forces capable of attacking on all fronts the Chinese units which had retreated beyond the effective range of our single-engine bombers and our Claude fighters. The task assigned to the remaining groups was enormous, for they were equipped with only thirty-odd fighter planes. Nevertheless, the Zeros maintained their one-sided superiority over enemy aircraft and, on March 14, 1941, scored another tremendous victory when our fighters slashed into large Chinese formations over Chengtu. Our pilots destroyed twenty-four planes and probably destroyed three others.

In May of 1941 several units of Type 96 and Type 1 twin-engined bombers returned to China to resume heavy bombing operations, which augmented the marauding raids of the Zero fighters. On May 20, unable to ferret out Chinese fighters over Chengtu, the Zeros strafed and set afire fuel storage installations and destroyed two planes on the Taipingssu and Shuanglin airfields.

This strafing raid, however, marked the end of the incredible good fortune of the Zeros against enemy opposition. Antiaircraft fire riddled Chief Flight Petty Officer Kimura's airplane, which subsequently crashed; this was the first Zero lost in combat. Three other fighters sustained damage from enemy ground fire that day.

On May 22 nineteen Zeros attacked Chengtu, shooting down two enemy planes and burning ten on the ground in strafing attacks. Five Zeros were damaged. Nancheng was visited next; on May 26, nine Zeros destroyed five out of twenty Chinese fighters in aerial combat, and then burned eighteen additional planes in strafing runs. Twenty Zeros raided Lanchow on the twenty-seventh, but failed to arouse the enemy pilots; they burned two planes on the ground. On June 7 four Zeros caught two Chinese fighters over Chungking, blasting one from the air. Twenty-two Zeros made the biggest attack in months on the eighteenth against Lanchow, but failed to encounter enemy planes. They strafed and burned two planes, and suffered damage to two Zeros. On the twenty-second, nine of our fighters raided Chengtu, burning one plane and damaging another in a low-level sweep.

On the same day, six Zeros swept over Kanyuan, catching at least an equal number of Chinese fighters in the air, and destroying three of these. Later that afternoon the day's third long-range patrol raided Tienshui; seven Zeros shot down one enemy plane. On the twenty-third six Zeros strafed Ipin, burning two and damaging five additional planes.

We lost our second Zero later in the day on the twenty-third. Three fighters escorting two Type 98 reconnaissance planes on a low-altitude flight between Lanchow and Yuncheng were caught suddenly by a heavy antiaircraft barrage, causing pilot Kobayashi's Zero to crash. Subsequently, for more than two weeks, our fighters searched in vain for enemy planes. The Chinese refused to give battle.

On August 11, however, sixteen Zeros escorting seven Type 1 bombers over Chengtu swarmed over a large group of Chinese fighters which for the first time in weeks opposed our bombers. Three enemy planes flamed before the Zeros' cannon, and the bombers destroyed two others. The attack proved successful; the bomber raid against enemy airfields destroyed seven planes on the ground, and damaged an additional nine.

On August 31 the Zeros embarked on their most difficult and also their final mission of the war in China. Their target was Sungfan, China's northwesternmost stronghold, which lay some five hundred nautical miles west of our Yuncheng base. Towering mountain ranges of twenty-three thousand feet jutted into the ever-present clouds along the route which our planes must follow. Since the beginning of the Sino-Japanese Incident, Sungfan had been attacked but once, when on June 23 Mihoro Air Corps bombers raided the stronghold.

Two Type 98 land-based reconnaissance planes led five Zero fighters, each flown by one of our best pilots in

China, against the distant target. The planes met the expected heavy cloud cover and managed to maintain formation by flying at different heights where clearer air beckoned. Finally the cloud masses almost completely filled the visible sky, forcing the seven airplanes to turn back. The Zero's role in China was completed.

From early 1941 to September of the same year, Zeros flew 354 sorties, during which they shot down forty-five enemy planes and damaged sixty-two. During this same period we lost two fighters to anti-aircraft guns, while twenty-six suffered damage both from enemy planes and from ground fire.

The battle score for the Zeros in all engagements on the Chinese mainland totaled seventy attacks against enemy targets, during which an aggregate of 529 fighters participated. They shot down ninety-nine planes, and probably shot down four others, while damaging an additional 163 planes. Thirty-nine Zeros sustained damage, and enemy ground fire destroyed two.

The largest single attack was a raid by thirty fighters on May 20, 1941, against Chengtu. Zero fighter groups received five Letters of Commendation from the Commander in Chief of the China Area Fleet, awarded for meritorious accomplishments in the missions against Chungking on September 13, 1940; against Chengtu on October 4 and December 30, 1940; against Chengtu on March 14, 1941; and against Nancheng on May 26, 1941.

By March of 1941 the land-based attack bomber groups which had returned to Japan for reorganization were ready for new assignments. In early April the Genzan and Mihoro Air Corps of the newly organized 22nd Air Flotilla returned to central and north China. They were joined in late July by the Kanoya and the 1st Air Corps of the 21st Air Flotilla, and by the Takao Air Corps of the 23rd Air Flotilla.

Escorted by Zero fighters, these bombers repeatedly attacked the cities of Chengtu, Chungking, and Lanchow. The Navy ordered the 3rd Air Corps of the 23rd Air Flotilla to northern French Indochina, from which the bombers raided Kunming.

In late August and early September of 1941, their missions accomplished, the China-based bombers reported to new stations in both Japan and Formosa. During their second combat tour of four months, we placed twenty-six hundred bombers over enemy targets. Of this number, we lost only one bomber, and that airplane fell to enemy anti-aircraft fire. In the dozens of raids which the bombers carried out, they encountered only ten Chinese fighter planes which managed to slip past the escorting Zero fighters. Even so, the enemy fighter planes failed to destroy any of our planes.

These facts clearly demonstrate the Zero's effectiveness in the China campaign. Where once we had reached the point of prohibitive bomber losses to enemy fighters and anti-aircraft, the arrival of the Zeros entirely destroyed the enemy planes' effectiveness as intercepters. In summation, the Zero gave us undisputed command of the air over both our own territory and that of the enemy.

By now, of course, we recognized the imminent possibility of a major war in the Pacific. The Navy completely reorganized its combat forces and alerted all units for possible immediate war. We intensified our training program, concentrating on those tactics most likely to be needed in a war of major scope. The long combat missions in China proved of immense value in reforming our front-line groups, for in Asia we had flown both day and night missions with large formations; coordinated closely operations between our escort fighters, attack bombers, and reconnaissance planes; improved our planes as dictated by the lessons of battle; effected fighter sweeps; and increased greatly the efficiency of our bombers and fighters. We felt that even with the vast expanse of the Pacific Ocean as the next area of battle, the lessons we had learned from combat in China would prove their value.

By late November of 1941, with the special three months' period of intensive training completed, all the Navy's air units were fully prepared for battle, confident in their men, their planes, and their ground-support groups.

War however, is seldom a one-sided affair. Despite our brilliant successes in China, we felt uneasy about a mass conflict with the United States and England. The vast strength of those two powers destroyed any basis for optimism. We knew that in a war against those two nations we would face an array of weapons terrifying both in quality and in quantity.

It must be admitted that this appraisal of a potential conflict with America and England was made only by few people within the Navy. The vast majority of our airmen, experienced only in combat against the Chinese, or basing their conclusions on reports of the China Incident, could only visualize victory against any possible opponent.

CHAPTER 5

Opening of Hostilities Followed by Anxiety

A T MIDNIGHT TODAY, the eighth of December, our Army and Navy have opened hostilities with American and British forces."

This totally unexpected broadcast on the early morning of December 8, 1941, struck the Japanese people like a thunderbolt. Bewilderment and open disbelief greeted the words of the announcer. It was true, of course, that the populace realized that diplomatic relations between their country and the United States were strained. The political maneuverings of the two countries since the summer of 1940 had been clouded by uncertainty and oppressiveness, partly due to the American government's freezing of Japanese assets in the United States and to the sudden suspension of the commercial treaty between the two nations.

The public had little understanding of the actual deterioration of international relationships, and found it difficult to accept an announcement of total war. However, the subsequent broadcast of the Imperial Rescript of the declaration of war left little doubt. The Japanese people soon concerned themselves with domestic adjustment as their nation plunged into war with two of the world's greatest powers.

Our people faced an enigmatic situation. They had been led into war with little preparation for an impending major conflict. Despite national pride, no one could deny the awesome combined strength of the United States and Great Britain. The great majority of our people tried, anxiously and unsuccessfully, to evaluate their situation. Their desire to criticize bitterly the autocratic government which without warning had swept the nation into war was countered by the tendency to place full support behind that government in the hope that the war had been undertaken with some plan for avoiding any physical destruction to the homeland. Only time would provide the answer.

On December 8 I (Okumiya) was air staff officer of the 11th Combined Air Flotilla with headquarters at Kasumigaura, in charge of training the pilots and other air crew members for the Navy. The sudden announcement of war complicated enormously my training program which, I realized, would soon require considerable expansion.

The experience of the Sino-Japanese Incident, and the recently completed three-month period of intensive flight training, meant that the Navy was well prepared to engage in "limited operations" with the enemy. However, our experience in large-scale conflict was insufficient for us to hold any confidence in our ability to maneuver against our opponents. The British, meanwhile, already had experienced nearly two years of war in Europe. America's military forces, while not yet actually engaged in open conflict, studied closely the lessons of the European battle and modified their own military organizations accordingly. This experience would improve the position of our enemies, giving them an advantage in addition to their numerical superiority in military aircraft and in matériel. At best, our expeditions in China were of limited usefulness; we lacked battle experience against strong enemy air forces.

We enjoyed one distinct strategic advantage. The air war in China had taught us clearly that the key to any successful military operation lay in command of the air. Without effective air control, our sea and land forces would at best be placed in disadvantageous positions and, indeed, might even forfeit victories which they could otherwise attain with adequate air power. It was also obvious, from past experience, that the primary means of attaining the coveted command of the air was through the possession of a superior fighter plane. Neither did we entertain any doubts that, in any large-scale protracted war in which planes and warships played the dominant roles, the outcome would depend largely on the basic national economy and our industrial potential.

The secret document, *Japanese Navy Wartime Organization Table*, of which I was assigned a copy, listed the front- and second-line naval air strength at the war's outset. As given in the document, this was:

(Abbreviations are explained immediately below.)

ABBREVIATIONS

VF . . . . .fighter plane
VB . . . . .dive bomber
VCB . . . . .carrier-based attack bomber
VLB .land-based attack bomber
VR . . . . .land-based reconnaissance plane
V2S . . . . .two-seat scout-observation seaplane
V3S . . . . .three-seat scout seaplane

VT . . . . .trainer plane
VST . . . . .trainer seaplane
VPB . . . . .patrol bomber (flying boat)
BB . . . . .battleship
CA . . . . .heavy cruiser
CL . . . . .light cruiser
CV . . . . .aircraft carrier
CVL . . . . .light aircraft carrier
Bat Div . . . . .battleship division
Cru Div . . . . .cruiser division

I. FIRST LINE STRIKING FORCE

A. COMBINED FLEET

FIRST FLEET

1st Bat Div (BB) *Nagato, Mutsu*   each 2 V2S
2nd Bat Div (BB) *Ise, Hyuga, Fuso, Yamashiro* each 2 V2S
3rd Bat Div (BB) *Kongo, Haruna, Kirishima, Hiei* each 3 V2S
6th Cru Div (CA) *Aoba, Kinugasa, Kako, Furutaka* each 2V3S
1st Destroyer Squadron (CL) *Abukuma* (flagship) 1 night-
scout seaplane
3rd Destroyer Squadron (CL) *Sendai* (flagship) 1 night-
scout seaplane
3rd Carrier Division (CVL) *Hosho* 11 Type 96 VF,
8 Type 96VCB
Zuiho   16 Type 96VF,
12 Type 97VCB

SECOND FLEET

4th Cru Div (CA) *Atago, Takao, Maya, Chokai*
5th Cru Div (CA) *Myoko, Nachi, Haguro*   each 2 V2S

7th Cru Div (CA) *Kumano, Suzuya, Mogami, Mikuma*1 V3S
8th Cru Div (CA) *Tone, Chikuma*   2 V2S (or) 2 V3S
2nd Destroyer Squadron (CL) *Jintsu* (flagship) 1 night-
                                              scout seaplane
4th Destroyer Squadron (CL) *Naka* (flagship) 1 night-scout
                                              seaplane

THIRD FLEET

16th Cru Div (CA) *Ashigara*   2 V2S, 1V3S
          (CL) *Nagara, Kuma*   each 1 V3S
5th Destroyer Squadron (CL) *Natori*   1 V3S
6th Submarine Squadron (Tender) *Chogei*   1 V3S
2nd Naval Base Force (Seaplane Tender) *Sanuki-Maru* 8 V2S
12th Carrier Division (Seaplane Tender)
                    Kamikawa-Maru   8 V2S, 4 V3S
                    Sanyo-Maru   6 V2S, 2 V3S

FOURTH FLEET

          (CL) *Kashima*   1 V3S
19th Squadron (Mine Layer) *Okinoshima*   1 V3S
24th Air Flotilla, *Chitose*Air Corps   36 Type 96 VLB
          Yokohama Air Corps   24 Type 97 VPB
3rd Naval Base Force, 16th Air Corps   6 V3S
4th Naval Base Force, 17th Air Corps   6 V3S
5th Naval Base Force, 18th Air Corps   6 V2S, 6 V3S
6th Naval Base Force, 19th Air Corps   8 V2S, 10 V3S
Attachment (Seaplane Tender) *Kiyokawa-Maru*   8 V2S,
                                              4 V3S

FIFTH FLEET

7th Naval Base Force, *Chichijima* Air Corps	6 V3S
21st Squadron (Seaplane Tender) *Kimikawa-Maru*	8 V3S

SOUTHERN AREA FLEET

CL *Kashii*	1 V3S
9th Naval Base Force (Seaplane Tender) *Sagara-Maru*	8 V2S

FIRST AIR FLEET

1st Carrier Division (CV) *Akagi*

Kaga	each 18 Type Zero	VF
	18 Type 99	VB
	27 Type 97	VCB

2nd Carrier Division (CV) *Soryu*

Hiryu	each 18 Type Zero	VF
	18 Type 99	VB
	18 Type 99	VCB

4th Carrier Division (CVL) *Ryujo*

	22 Type 96	VF
	18 Type 97	VCB
Shoho		*none*
Kasuga-Maru		*none*

5th Carrier Division (CV) *Zuikaku*

Shokaku	each 18 Type Zero	VF
	27 Type 99	VB
	27 Type 97	VCB

ELEVENTH AIR FLEET

21st Air Flotilla Kanoya Air Corps	72 Type	1 VLB
1st Air Corps	48 Type	1 VLB
Toko Air Corps	24 Type 97	VPB

22nd Air Flotilla Mihoro Air Corps	48 Type 96	VLB
Genzan Air Corps	48 Type 96	VLB
Attachment	6 Type 98	VR
	36 Type Zero	VF
23rd Air Flotilla Takao Air Corps	72 Type 96	VLB
Tainan Air Corps		
3rd Air Corps	each 92 Type Zero	VF
	72 Type 96	VLB
	12 Type 98	VR

ATTACHMENT OF COMBINED FLEET

11th Carrier Division (Seaplane Tender) *Mizuho*

Chitose each 16 V2S

4 V3S

B. CHINA AREA FLEET

| Attachment | 8 V3S, 12 VCB |

II. SECOND LINE STRIKING FORCE

YOKOSUKA NAVAL STATION FORCE

Yokosuka Air Corps	24	VF
	12	VB
	36	VCB
	12	VLB
	12	V2S
	6	V3S
	3	VPB
Tateyama Air Corps	12	VCB
	6	V2S
Kisarazu Air Corps	60	VLB

11th Combined Air Flotilla

Kasumigaura Air Corps	164	VT
Tsukuba Air Corps	108	VT
Yatabe Air Corps	108	VT
Hyakurigahara Air Corps	108	VT
Kashima Air Corps	132	VST
Tsuchiura Air Corps	48	VST
Suzuka Air Corps	36	VCB
144 Navigation and Aircrew Trainers		

KURE NAVAL STATION FORCE

Kure Air Corps	24	V2S
Saeki Air Corps	16	VB
Iwakuni Air Corps	72	VT

12th Air Flotilla

Oita Air Corps	52	VF
	24 Trainer	VF
	45	VCB
Usa Air Corps	36	VB
	63	VCB
Hakata Air Corps	48	V2B
	54	V3S
Omura Air Corps	36	VF
	42	VCB

MAIZURU NAVAL STATION FORCE

Maizuru Air Corps	6	V3S

SASEBO NAVAL STATION FORCE

Sasebo Air Corps	16	VF
	6	V3S
	15	VPB

OMINATO NAVAL STATION FORCE

Ominato Air Corps	16	VF
	8	VCB
	8	V3S

OSAKA NAVAL STATION FORCE

Komatsujima Air Corps	8	V2S
	8	V3S

CHINKAI NAVAL STATION FORCE
(Chinhaeman, Korea)

Chinkai Air Corps	6	V3S

BAKO NAVAL STATION FORCE
(Makung, Formosa)

Attachment	4	VB

From the preceding lists, I drew up a table of total aircraft types which would assist me in determining pilot and aircrew training program requirements, which stated:

TYPE OF PLANE	2nd Line Striking Force	1st Line Striking Force	Total
Trainer	560	—	560
Seaplane Trainer	180	—	180
Navigation and Aircrew Trainer	168	—	168
Fighter Trainer	24	—	24
Carrier-Based Fighter (Type 96)	144	49	193
(Zero)		322	515
Carrier-Based Dive Bomber	68	126	194
Carrier-Based Attack Bomber	242	194	436
Land-Based Attack Bomber			
(Type 96)	52		204
(Type 1)		120	376
Land-Based Reconnaissance Plane	—	30	30
Two-Seat Seaplane	98	144	243
Night Scout Plane	—	44	
Submarine-Based Plane	—	66	
Three-Seat Seaplane	94	111	205
Flying Boat	18	48	66
Transport	—	23	23
TOTAL	1648	1381	3029

In the first-line striking force, all carrier-based dive bombers were Type 99's; carrier-based attack bombers were Type 97's; two-seat observation seaplanes were Type 95's and Type Zeros; three-seat scout seaplanes were Type Zeros and some Type 94's; and all flying boats were Type 97's.

Since we required two pilots to man each land-based attack bomber, flying boat, and transport plane listed in the above category, we needed a minimum of thirty-five hundred pilots merely to operate the Navy's regular aircraft strength. This figure increased with the pilots required for the Navy's auxiliary aircraft, which numbered one third the total of first- and second-line forces. At the very least, then, we required a total of nearly five thousand pilots, and an equal number of observers, navigators, gunners, bombardiers, radiomen, and other aircrew personnel to maintain operational status with existing planes.

We realized that the war with the United States and England would drain Japan's limited resources, and that such attrition would create tremendous problems in the steady replacement of planes and matériel. I was fully aware, however, that our greatest weakness lay not in physical supplies, or in bulk manpower, but in the steady replacement of qualified flight crews. The difference between the veteran flier and the new pilot is far greater than is generally realized; one might compare the two to a man and a child.

When I assumed my position in January of 1940 as an instructor at the Kasumigaura Training Air Corps, I learned that, despite the seeming low number of less than thirty-five hundred naval pilots, we actually maintained in active service a greater number of pilots than did the American Navy. At that time I was approached by Lieutenant Takekatsu Tanaka, my division officer, who felt concern for what he believed would surely be a future shortage of competent pilots. Farsighted and capable, and deeply concerned with the wellbeing of the Navy, Tanaka prepared and submitted to me for study his proposed "Plan for Training Fifteen Thousand Pilots." Tanaka's work and able consideration of training problems so impressed me that I forwarded the report with favorable recommendations to my immediate superior.

In comparison to the then-existing Navy pilot training program, however, the number of pilots Tanaka proposed to train each year was so great that my superiors dismissed the recommendation merely as the wild dream of a young air force officer. It is regrettable that the "dream" was not afforded the attention it deserved. In August of 1941, when I was appointed as an air staff officer at Kasumigaura, the Navy circulated a new mass-training program which called for the special training of fifteen thousand pilots. World events, and the demands placed upon our naval air units, had changed so rapidly that accurate predictions became impossible. The Navy's new training program came too late; it was impossible to train effectively the flight crews demanded by the Navy in the short space of time allowed.

On that fateful morning of December 8, 1941, I felt that it was more than likely that, either quickly or through attrition, our shortage of pilots would result in victory for the United States and England. The mathematics were simple. Numerically, the Navy's trained flight crews, i.e., those who had received operational "on-the-job" service following a year's preliminary training, could not possibly man all the regular service aircraft listed in the *Japanese Navy Wartime Organization Table,* which I studied. Obviously the greater majority of those pilots who were assigned to the spare planes were those who lacked even a full year's training within the combat air corps. The over-all figures hid further deficits in our manpower; many of our veteran pilots, then assigned to front-line combat units, could not possibly withstand the rigors of actual combat. A combination of age and ill health would effectively further reduce our ranks even before hostilities commenced.

I realized intuitively that the percentage of pilots who lacked sufficient training, already a problem at the very outset of the war, would rapidly increase. We would not feel the effect of the proposed mass-training program for at least another two to four years.

At the end of the first week in December of 1941 the Navy's required training periods for student noncommissioned officer pilots were as follows:

Noncommissioned Officer Pilot

Preliminary Ground Training Pilot Training

Class	Age	School (Minimum)	Training Period	Training Period
A	15–17	Completed 3rd year Middle School	14 months	12 months or less
B	15–17	Completed 4th grade	28 months	12 months or less
C	Below 24	From regular conscripts	3 months	12 months or less

The Navy selected its air force officers from its lieutenants (J.G.) and ensigns, training these men for at least twelve months. These students were regarded as adequate pilots following a year of preliminary flight training in the combat air corps, but they required at least one additional year of training to qualify as carrier-based pilots and forward combat area pilots.

We maintained the strictest requirements for these young men, for, despite their age, they were responsible for the operation of elaborate and expensive machines and apparatus of which Japan was continually in short supply. Once in the air, they were literally "on their own;" they must be fully competent to fulfill the responsibilities with which they had been entrusted. Time and again this policy proved its worth, notably so in the excellent performance of our pilots during the Sino-Japanese Incident.

CHAPTER 6

Prewar Anticipation

THE LARGE-SCALE AIR battles of the Sino-Japanese Incident, and of the first two years of World War II in Europe, were fought chiefly over the land areas of the Asian and European continents. Because there did not exist any proof of the effectiveness of bombing planes against large warships at sea, at the time of the Hawaiian Operation on December 8, 1941, our Navy backed its confidence in the superiority of the warship against any other type of armament. The proponents of maximum surface fleet strength pointed out the indecisiveness of mass aerial attacks against enemy objectives even on land, and further stressed the fact that the battles we could expect in the vast regions of the Southwest Pacific would be determined primarily by the performance of our sea and land forces. They stipulated that air units would obviously be relegated to support roles. They further strengthened their arguments by employing as the classic example the case of the German dreadnaught Bismarck which, despite the superiority of British naval air power, was destroyed mainly by the shells and torpedoes of numerous British warships.

Despite the overwhelming argument of current history which favored surface power, there were in our Navy a sufficient number of farsighted officers who realized the potentialities of the bombing plane. Accordingly, the Navy exerted every possible effort to insure the maximum efficiency of all available bombing units. This effort received further impetus when in mid-1941 the American government froze the assets of all Japanese residing in the United States. This move clarified the general drift toward a war between the two great powers, and our Army and Navy officers discussed privately the conflict which must inevitably flare between Japan and the United States and Great Britain.

The vast expanse of the Pacific Ocean showed clearly that a war with these two foreign powers would be most likely decided upon the open sea. In the fall of 1941 our Army lacked aircraft capable of bombing from any base under our control the vital British installations at Singapore and similar American installations at Manila. Nor did the Army have available any fighter planes which, operating from our southernmost base in Formosa, could raid the American airfields on Luzon. Occupation of the Singapore and Manila installations was vital to any extension of Japanese control in the Pacific. Consequently, as in the case of our operations in central and south China in the early months of the Sino-Japanese Incident, the Navy was assigned the responsibility for supplying air support for our ground forces.

By their very nature the United States and Great Britain were formidable adversaries in the air. We realized fully that, unlike the chaotic misuse of air power by China, America and England, long our seniors in aviation and the two greatest international sea powers, would employ their fighters and bombers with maximum efficiency. We expected only light resistance from enemy aviation at the outset, for we knew that only limited numbers of fighters and bombers were in the Orient in late 1941. This fact, however conducive to immediate Japanese successes, could not be regarded as an accurate appraisal of enemy air potential. We knew only too well that the two countries would quickly multiply by many times their Oriental complements of planes and men.

Despite our enemies' awesome industrial might, the Navy had confidence in the ability of our Zero fighter planes to wrest air control from the enemy over any battle area. Our intelligence and our technical groups stated flatly that the excellent performance and technical superiority of the Zero fighter meant that, in battle, one Zero would be the equal of from two to five enemy fighter planes, depending upon the type. Because of this unshakeable faith in the Zero, the Navy felt extremely confident of victory in initial campaigns.

We expected, however, severe losses to our Type 1 land-based attack bombers, which constituted our major aerial striking forces. Where the Zero clearly could best any known enemy fighter, we realized that each bomber would be grounded for extensive repairs after two or three missions. The fuel tanks of the Type 1 bombers were not of the selfsealing, or bulletproof, types, and their repair was extremely difficult.

I agreed that we might achieve outstanding initial combat success against America and England. The prospects of victory dimmed rapidly, however, in the face of a prolonged war in which the United States could bring to bear upon our forces its great industrial force. Attrition would cripple our strength just as effectively as enemy guns.

During the summer of 1941, Army and Navy staff officers frequently discussed with government officials the possible ramifications of a war against the United States and England. Admiral Isoroku Yamamoto, Commander in Chief of the Combined Fleet, fully realized the difficulties we would face in an extended struggle. Cognizant of the almost insurmountable problem of maintaining and increasing qualified flight crews and supplying minimum numbers of combat planes to the front, Admiral Yamamoto frankly informed Premier Konoye:

"If you tell me that it is necessary that we fight, then in the first six months to a year of war against the United States and England I will run wild, and I will show you an uninterrupted succession of victories; I must also tell you that, should the war be prolonged for two or three years, I have no confidence in our ultimate victory."

Soon afterward, at the Imperial Council immediately prior to the decision to enter war, Admiral Mitsumasa Yonai stated to the assembly that "... at all cost we must avoid the war with the United States and Great Britain which means a sudden deterioration in our national situation; we can afford the risk of gradual loss of our national political and economic situation...."

Ex-premier Yonai's advice, supported by many high-ranking naval officers and civil officials, provided an excellent summation of the actual prewar situation. Admiral Yamamoto, however, not only properly evaluated the excellent chances for initial Japanese military success, but also foresaw with foreboding clarity the inevitable defeat which lay ahead.

High naval staff officers realized fully the pitfalls in the way of maintaining effective strength against the enemy and emphasized that the war would of necessity be fought mainly at sea. Despite the apprehensions of these officers,

who commanded the air combat units which would spear-
head the proposed mass attack against American and English forces, the Imperial Council decided in favor of war.

The Navy's past experience in testing foreign planes
enabled us to evaluate accurately the performance of these
aircraft we would be most likely to encounter in the opening phases of the war. Equally important, however, was the
foreign evaluation of *our* military aircraft, and in this
respect we enjoyed an undisputed advantage. Our potential
enemy was sadly misinformed as to the true performance
capabilities of our warplanes, and American aviation magazines especially went to great lengths to deride our air
forces. Clearly they dismissed as inconceivable the possibility that Japanese planes could effectively carry the war
to the Americans and the British.

In September of 1941 the "authoritative" American
magazine *Aviation*, in an article titled "Japanese Air
Force," stated that our military and civilian pilots suffered
from the world's highest accident rate and that our Army
and Navy trained fewer than one thousand pilots each
year. We could not help but wonder at the source of the
magazine's information when we read that our pilots definitely were inferior in the Sino-Japanese Incident to Chinese pilots, and that in the campaign at Nomonhan,
Manchuria, the Soviet Air Force defeated our combat units.

The magazine continued in this pompous fashion to
state that while our Air Force was aggressive, it lacked
experience in such large-scale operations as were being
conducted in Europe. We could not hope, claimed the
anonymous authority, ever to develop effective air power.
The story ended on the note that our industry could not
possibly meet the requirements of a war; that our aviation
engineering depended entirely upon the "handouts" of the
United States, Great Britain, Germany, Italy, and the

Soviet Union; and, finally, that "America's aviation experts can say without hesitation that the chief military airplanes of Japan are either outdated already, or are becoming outdated. . . ."

The magazine's observations reflected not merely this single publication's views, but rather the international evaluation of Japanese military air power. It is true that to foreign observers our training methods may have appeared unduly reckless with regard to student casualties in a program which suffered from an insufficient number of training planes.

Unknowingly, however, the magazine paid our military services an excellent compliment, for we had long bent every effort to conceal from foreign observation our actual military strength. In this respect we were obviously most successful! Our Navy's chief training grounds were not in the homeland, but far at sea where even our own people remained unaware of the true extent of air-sea maneuvers. Further, we concealed in every possible fashion the particulars of our military weapons and especially the performance of our aircraft. Foreign observers saw only what we allowed them to see.

So effective was our armaments censorship that prior to the Pearl Harbor attack not a single American publication realized the existence of the Zero fighter, and not until several months following the opening of hostilities did the American public receive even a reasonably accurate impression of this airplane. Again we determined the trend of American thought by observing in another magazine, published several months before December of 1941, that: "The Japanese Navy's air force consists of four aircraft carriers with two hundred planes."

In his memoirs Winston Churchill testified to the effectiveness of our military censorship and to the erroneous impressions of our air power held both by England and America. Referring to the battle of Malaya fought on December 10, 1941, during which our planes sent to the bottom the *Prince of Wales* and the *Repulse*, Churchill defended the actions of Vice-Admiral Sir Tom Phillips, who dispatched the ships under his command to the sea off Kuantan without fighter plane cover. On the basis of all data available to Admiral Phillips, Saigon, the Japanese base nearest to Kuantan, lay more than four hundred nautical miles to the north, and the admiral had every reason to believe that no torpedo bomber then in existence could carry out a mission over this distance.

Admiral Phillips was, of course, in error, as we demonstrated so clearly by destroying the two mighty battleships. As Churchill himself stated, both England and America greatly underestimated the battle capabilities of our warplanes; this contributed greatly to the success of our operations.

The unforgivable error of "underestimating the enemy" made by the Americans and the British was perhaps best illustrated in the reliance placed upon the antiquated Brewster F2A Buffalo fighter plane, which American aviation experts boasted was "the most powerful fighter plane in the Orient," and a "fighter plane far superior to anything in the Japanese Air Force." Against the Zero fighters, the Buffalo pilots literally flew suicide missions.

On the first day of the war we jammed the message rooms, anxiously awaiting the initial combat reports which would inform us of initial victory, or of setbacks. Our exuberance rose steadily as an unending stream of radio messages described the courageous and amazing victories won by our naval air units. My apprehension faded with the increasing number of reported victories; incredibly, the first hours of war were totally in our favor.

The evening of December 8, Commander Ikegami, the Senior Staff Officer of our air flotilla, returned from Navy General Headquarters in Tokyo with detailed combat reports. From these we learned that Vice-Admiral Chuichi Nagumo commanded the First Air Fleet's task force of 376 planes (108 Zeros, 126 Type 99 dive bombers, and 142 Type 97 carrier-based attack bombers) which attacked the Hawaiian Islands; and that the Navy land-based Air Force of 566 planes (224 Zeros, 288 Type 1 and Type 96 land-based attack bombers, 30 Type 99 land-based reconnaissance planes, and 24 Type 97 flying boats) of the Eleventh Air Fleet under Vice-Admiral Nishizo Tsukahara was in the Malayan and Philippines theaters of operations, flying from bases in Formosa, southern French Indochina, and Palau. Coordinating their attacks with Admiral Tsukahara's forces, and the 4th Carrier Division under Rear-Admiral Kakuji Kakuda operating in the Davao area, the planes of Rear-Admiral Eiji Goto's 24th Air Flotilla flew from their Marianas and Marshall Islands bases to lash out at Wake and Guam.

Without exception, every combat report recorded only smashing victories. Our successes exceeded by far even the most optimistic preattack estimates.

In all military history I do not know of any country which simultaneously launched so many battles of such magnitude and, in addition, so completely defeated its opponents as we did on that fateful morning of December 8, 1941. We coordinated our combat operations across a distance of six thousand nautical miles, spanning the ocean between Hawaii and Singapore.

What I would like history most to record, however, is that this abrupt reversal of the Asiatic-Pacific balance of power was accomplished with the total of only approximately one thousand planes of the Japanese Naval Air

Force and that this same force suffered only the barest minimum of losses. An excellent evaluation of our available naval air power may best be had by referring to the air strength hurled by the Allies against Europe in the Normandy division—more than eleven thousand aircraft!

The initial anxiety of the Japanese people changed to wild joy when they learned of our astonishing military gains. Our own air force personnel jubilantly cheered each new message of conquest. To be perfectly honest, I personally was astounded at the enemy's inexplicably weak resistance. We expected our forces to fight hard and to achieve a certain minimum of successes, but prior to the attack no one would have dared to anticipate the actual results of our initial assaults. Despite our brilliant gains, however, I and several other senior officers with a more intimate knowledge of the long-range consequences of the new war could not help but harbor anxiety as to the future of our nation.

I remember clearly the special reactions of our young officers, who clamored for combat duty. The war was hardly more than a month old when rumors spread among the personnel of the air flotilla that before long the war would end in a smashing victory for Japan. Frontline duty appealed much more to these young pilots than did the prosaic training duties of the home air flotillas, and they thought of nothing but their own participation in air battles. We could not disabuse these overenthusiastic youngsters of their belief that the war would end too quickly for them to try their mettle against the enemy; we stressed the tremendous industrial potential of our adversaries, but with no effect. Our junior pilots were fully convinced that the war would end too soon to enable them to participate.

CHAPTER 7

The Pearl Harbor Attack: Overwhelming Victory as the War Begins

THE ATTACK ON PEARL HARBOR was a military feat so daring and so successful as to deserve a special place in history. In a single masterful stroke, Japan not only launched the opening phase of the Pacific War, but wrought mass devastation through the powerful American fleet which was caught unaware in the Hawaiian Islands.

The success of this attack stemmed directly from the brilliant planning and the decisive measures taken by Admiral Isoroku Yamamoto, Commander in Chief of the Combined Fleet, who for the eighteen years prior to the Pacific War had, with a fervor amounting almost to religion, devoted all his efforts to the end of creating a powerful Japanese naval air force.

When our intelligence tabulated the final results of the Hawaiian Operation (this was its official designation), we discovered that the surprise attack had inflicted far greater damage to the American warships in Hawaii than our most optimistic advance estimates had anticipated. The crippling of a large and powerful segment of the American fleet placed Japan's naval units in a position of strength sufficient to permit our rapid movement elsewhere throughout the Pacific and Indian oceans.

The great majority of Americans will undoubtedly be surprised to learn that the Pearl Harbor assault was not intended to be a sneak blow, although it has come to be accepted in the public mind as such. The conditions and timing of the attack, as related to diplomatic activities conducted simultaneously in Washington, D.C., unhappily created a situation in which it appeared our Navy deliberately struck without any prior notice of hostilities.

This unfortunate eventuality occurred despite the fact that the Japanese government had forwarded an ultimatum to the United States through the Japanese Embassy in Washington. Although the ultimatum was dispatched to the Embassy in sufficient time to permit translation and delivery to the State Department prior to the actual attack, the Japanese Embassy's inexcusable delay in making the translation resulted in delivery of the message after our planes had commenced their attack.

Actually, this statement does not embody any unusual revelation, since the truth has already been revealed during the international war criminal trials at Tokyo. The writer wishes, however, to "set the record straight" in these pages.

The Hawaiian Operation was carried out under the direct command of Vice-Admiral Chuichi Nagumo, who was given command of a special carrier task force for the Pearl Harbor operation. The attacking fleet was composed of twenty-three vessels, including six aircraft carriers. These were the *Akagi* and the *Kaga* of the 1st Carrier Division; the *Soryu* and the *Hiryu* of the 2nd Carrier Division; and the *Zuikaku* and the *Shokaku* of the 5th Carrier Division. Augmenting the carrier force were the battleships

Hiei and *Kirishima*, the two heavy cruisers *Tone* and *Chikuma*, one light cruiser, nine destroyers, and other vessels.

On November 22, 1941, while United States-Japanese diplomatic talks were under way, the Nagumo Force gathered at Hitokappu Bay on Etorofu Island, in the southern part of the Kuril Arch. All commanding officers assembled for special meetings with Admiral Nagumo, who took special pains to outline his plans for the attack, which would be launched should negotiations fail.

At this time, no definite date for the assault was set. The final disposition and schedule for battle, should there be any, would be determined by the outcome of the diplomatic maneuvers going on in the American capital.

On November 26, according to plan, the warships and supporting vessels of the Nagumo Force weighed anchor and slipped out of Hitokappu Bay. Under strict secrecy, the task force set sail for its position north of Hawaii whence, should it prove necessary, the attack would be launched against Pearl Harbor. Admiral Yamamoto personally directed the sailing order to Admiral Nagumo.

Even as the fleet made its way across the northern Pacific waters, the diplomatic negotiations in Washington foundered. The Japanese government felt that the worst possible international situation had resulted.

On December 2, 1941, Admiral Yamamoto dispatched new orders to Admiral Nagumo: "The date for the declaration of war is fixed for December 8."

Upon receipt of his combat orders, Admiral Nagumo ordered the carrier task force to increase speed and to prepare for battle. Early on the morning of December 8 the attacking force reached its destination, approximately two hundred nautical miles north of Oahu Island.

At 1:30 A.M., Tokyo time, the first bombers roared off their carrier decks, bound for Pearl Harbor.

At exactly 3:23 A.M. (Tokyo time) on December 8, Commander Mitsuo Fuchida of the *Akagi*, supreme air commander of the Pearl Harbor Attack Air Groups, issued the following order to all his pilots in the air over or approaching Pearl Harbor: *"All aircraft immediately attack enemy positions."* Commander Fuchida then sent a wireless report to Admiral Nagumo: *"We have succeeded in the surprise attack."*

These two wireless messages were the signals for raising the curtain of war all across the Pacific and the Indian Oceans. Immediately thereafter Japanese air fleets launched their attacks against enemy installations over a front of thousands of miles.

The fundamental rule of any air battle is to gain immediate control of the local air by eliminating the defensive activities of enemy fighter planes. This precept was rigidly adhered to in the Pearl Harbor attack.

Under Commander Fuchida's control, Lieutenant Akira Sakamoto led twenty-five Type 99 (Val) dive bombers of the first attacking wave in a screaming assault on Hoiler Air Base. Before the attack, Japanese intelligence had reported that Hoiler was the main center of American fighter-plane operations in Hawaii; Lieutenant Sakamoto's mission was designed to eliminate fighter opposition before the American planes could leave the ground.

Immediately behind Sakamoto's group came twenty-six dive bombers under the command of Lieutenant Commander Kakuichi Takahashi. Takahashi's planes swarmed over Hickam Air Field, which was reported to be the major heavy-bomber base for the enemy army air force; simultaneously, a portion of the Takahashi attacking force was diverted for an attack against Ford Island. The latter was reported as a base for navy carrier fighter, and Takahashi's attacking wave effectively shattered the enemy's fighter strength.

While a few enemy planes managed to get off the ground, our attacking aerial forces were relatively free from enemy fighter opposition, and our fleet was now protected from an American aerial counterattack.

As the dive bombers plunged from the sky, Commander Fuchida's level and torpedo bombers assaulted the enemy battleships anchored in the harbor. Under Commander Fuchida's direct control were forty-nine Type 97 carrier-based attack bombers; coordinated with this bombing effort was the torpedo bombing assault of forty Type 97 carrier-based attack bombers under the leadership of Lieutenant Commander Shigeharu Murata.

As the dive bombers, level bombers, and torpedo bombers carried out their attacks, Lieutenant Commander Shigeru Itaya led forty-three Zero fighters in a low-level strafing sweep, shooting up enemy antiaircraft positions, ground installations, planes, and ships in the harbor. The Zeros intercepted and destroyed four enemy fighters which had managed to leave the ground during the attack and which were attempting to disrupt the bombing operations.

One hour and fifteen minutes after the first attacking force ripped into the American naval bastion, the second wave of 170 aircraft under the command of Lieutenant Commander Shigekazu Shimazaki of the *Zuikaku* reached attack position above Oahu. Commander Shimazaki's fifty-four level bombers pounded the enemy fighter and bomber air bases; immediately afterward Lieutenant Commander Takashige Egusa's eighty dive bombers plunged earthward and sent their missiles into the anchored battleships and other enemy warships. Thirty-six Zero fighters led by Lieutenant Saburo Shindo in a combination strafing and air-strike mission swept the air clear of opposing enemy fighters and carried out strafing attacks against their air bases.

By approximately 8:30 A.M. all our planes had completed their attacks and had returned to their respective aircraft carriers.

Chief Flight Petty Officer Juzo Mori of the *Soryu* flew the second torpedo bomber in the attack led by Lieutenant Tsuyoshi Nagai; this is Juzo Mori's story:

"The assigned objectives of the *Soryu* torpedo bombers were the American battleships which we expected to find anchored along the wharf of the Oahu Naval Arsenal. We dropped in for our attack at high speed and low altitude and, when I was almost in position to release my own torpedo, I realized that the enemy warship toward which I was headed was not a battleship at all, but a cruiser. My flight position was directly behind Lieutenant Nagai, and we flew directly over Oahu Island before descending for our attack.

"Lieutenant Nagai continued his torpedo run against the cruiser, despite our original plan to attack the enemy battleships. However, I did not expect to survive this attack, since I and all the other pilots anticipated heavy enemy resistance. If I were going to die, I thought, I wanted to know that I had torpedoed at least an American battleship.

"The attack of the *Soryu*'s planes was met with intense antiaircraft fire from the enemy fleet, since the bombing waves from the *Akagi* and the *Kaga* had already passed over. My bomber shook and vibrated from the impact of enemy machine-gun bullets and shrapnel. Despite my intention of swinging away from the cruiser, now dead ahead of my plane, and attacking the group of battleships anchored near Ford Island, I was forced to fly directly forward into a murderous rain of antiaircraft fire.

"Because of this and the surrounding topography, I flew directly over the enemy battleships along Ford Island, and then banked into a wide left turn. The antiaircraft fire did not seem to affect the plane's performance, and I chose as my new objective a battleship anchored some distance from the main group of vessels which were at the moment undergoing torpedo attack from the *Soryu*'s planes. The warship separated from the main enemy group appeared to be the only battleship yet undamaged.

"I swung low and put my plane into satisfactory torpedoing position. It was imperative that my bombing approach be absolutely correct, as I had been warned that the harbor depth was no more than thirty-four feet. The slightest deviation in speed or height would send the released torpedo plunging into the sea bottom, or jumping above the water, and all our effort would go for naught.

"By this time I was hardly conscious of what I was doing. I was reacting from habit instilled by long training, moving like an automaton.

"Three thousand feet! Twenty-five hundred feet! Two thousand feet!

"Suddenly the battleship appeared to have leaped forward directly in front of my speeding plane; it towered ahead of the bomber like a great mountain peak.

"Prepare for release.... Stand by!

"*Release torpedo!*

"All this time I was oblivious of the enemy's antiaircraft fire and the distracting thunder of my plane's motor. I concentrated on nothing but the approach and the torpedo release. At the right moment I pulled back on the release with all my strength. The plane lurched and faltered as antiaircraft struck the wings and fuselage; my head snapped back and I felt as though a heavy beam had struck against my head.

"But . . . I've got it! A perfect release!

"And the plane is still flying! The torpedo will surely hit its target; the release was exact. At that instant I seemed to come to my senses and became aware of my position and of the flashing tracers and shells of the enemy's defensive batteries.

"After launching the torpedo, I flew directly over the enemy battleship and again swung into a wide, circling turn. I crossed over the southern tip of Ford Island.

"To conceal the position of our carrier, as we had been instructed to do, I turned again and took a course due south, directly opposite the *Soryu*'s true position, and pushed the plane to its maximum speed.

"Now that the attack was over, I was acutely conscious that the enemy antiaircraft fire was bracketing and smashing into my bomber. The enemy shells appeared to be coming from all directions, and I was so frightened that before I left the target area my clothes were soaking with perspiration.

"In another few moments the air was clear. The enemy shells had stopped. Thinking that now I had safely escaped, and could return to the carrier, I began to turn to head back to the *Soryu*. Suddenly there was an enemy plane directly in front of me!

"As my plane, the Type 97 carrier-based attack bomber, was armed only with a single rearward-firing 7.7-mm. machine gun, it was almost helpless in aerial combat. I thought that surely *this* time my end had come.

"As long as I was going to die, I reasoned, I would take the enemy plane with me to my death. I swung the bomber over hard and headed directly for the enemy aircraft, the pilot of which appeared startled at my maneuver, and fled! Is this really, I questioned, what is called war?"

* * *

At the time of the Pearl Harbor attack the Japanese naval air force had attained what was probably the world's highest rate of accuracy in level-bombing aircraft attacks, including the use of conventional aerial bombs and of aerial torpedoes. The credit for such outstanding accuracy of bomb and torpedo hits as was dramatically illustrated at Pearl Harbor, as well as in the sea battle off Malaya two days later, belongs largely to Admiral Yamamoto.

During the period 1939–1940 the accuracy of Japanese level bombers was incredibly poor. It was so bad that it was doubtful whether one hit could be achieved when three or four groups of nine-plane formations released their bombs from a height of ten thousand feet against an evading battleship-size target on the open sea.

On the other hand, an attack by three dive bombers against the same type of objective almost always guaranteed at least one successful hit on target. High official circles were of the opinion that, for attacking warships, dive bombing and torpedoing were the preferred methods of attack. The feeling that level bombing should be eliminated entirely dominated the Navy's air-power hierarchy.

At this time Admiral Yamamoto took an active hand in the development of bombing techniques. Recently made Commander in Chief of the Combined Fleet (he was a Vice-Admiral then), Yamamoto firmly declared:

"As long as I am the Commander in Chief of the Combined Fleet, I will not do away with level bombing. True, our level bombing accuracy at sea has been poor, but the reason for the poor ratio of bomb hits lies in the free, evasive movement of the target vessel. There is no reason compelling us to select only these difficult targets. At any rate, I hope that much further study and practice will be conducted hereafter. . . ."

Admiral Yamamoto had also issued the order to pursue and destroy, either at the Singapore Naval Base or on the high seas, the British fleet which was, at the time of the Hawaiian Operation, somewhere in the Malaya area. As will be related in later pages, our naval air force in this theater, under far greater operating difficulties and hazards than were encountered at Pearl Harbor, accomplished a mission no less vital than the Pearl Harbor attack.

The fighters and bombers of the Nagumo Force which attacked Pearl Harbor fought brilliantly and heroically; within a very short space of time they destroyed the major strength of the United States Pacific Fleet. In this operation our losses consisted of nine Zero fighters; fifteen Type 99 carrier-based dive bombers; five Type 97 carrier-based attack bombers; and fifty-five officers and men. Among the casualties were Lieutenant Saburo Makino, group leader of the *Kaga*'s dive bombers, and Lieutenant Fusata Iida, squadron leader of Zero fighters from the *Soryu*.

Lieutenant Iida participated in the Pearl Harbor attack as the leader of the 3rd Covering Fighter Squadron, composed of nine Zero fighters, which struck in the second attacking wave. Near the Kaneohe Air Field his squadron, with the aid of accompanying fighter units, intercepted five or six enemy planes and quickly destroyed them all. They then strafed the air field, shooting up all enemy aircraft in sight. Lieutenant (JG) Iyozo Fujita, who participated with Lieutenant Iida in the attack as the second section leader, relates what happened to Lieutenant Iida's plane during the assault:

"When our planes machine-gunned the airfield at Kaneohe, I looked for but failed to see any antiaircraft guns on the field. Later, however, when all the fighters assembled their formations over the field I noticed a white spray of gasoline shooting out from Lieutenant Iida's plane. There appeared to be no other damage to his fighter, and I assumed he would be able to return to the carrier.

"Such was not the case, however. Lieutenant Iida circled over the Kaneohe Air Field until he was sure that all our fighters were assembled in formation. Then, and only then, he closed his cockpit canopy and began to descend toward the airfield. Suddenly the Zero whipped over into an inverted position and dove vertically for the enemy positions below.

"Thinking that he was going to make another strafing run on the field, I immediately began a wingover to follow his plane down. I realized abruptly, however, that Lieutenant Iida was flying in a most unusual manner, quite different from his usual tactics. I watched his plane as it dove in its vertical, inverted position until it exploded on the ground between the Kaneohe airfield hangars."

Thus died one of Japan's leading fighter pilots on the first day of the war. Lieutenant Iida had flown as a Zero fighter pilot since September of 1939, and had fought successfully against Chinese fighters over the Asiatic mainland. He was twenty-seven years old when he died, and was the highest ranking officer among the Nagumo Force's fighter pilots to die this day.

[After the war I [Okumiya] had the opportunity carefully to review the American photographs of the Pearl Harbor attack. In one picture I saw the funeral ceremony at Pearl Harbor of an air force lieutenant of the Japanese Navy. It was not possible to discern from the photographs any difference in the burial services afforded the American dead and those given the Japanese lieutenant. I point this out especially, since those Americans were killed because of a Japanese air attack in which this Japanese lieutenant participated. We—all former Japanese airmen—should take heed of this fact, and long remember the attitude of the American officers and men who did not make any discrimination between their own and the enemy's officers, even after such an event as the Pearl Harbor attack.)

Following the final assault against the enemy installations at Hawaii, Commander Fuchida, the supreme air commander of the operation, returned safely to his aircraft carrier with the second attack force. Lieutenant Masaharu Suganami, group leader of the *Soryu*'s Zero fighters, left his carrier at 1:30 A.M. when the Japanese fleet was still two hundred nautical miles north of Oahu; after convoying the bombers of the first attacking wave and strafing the enemy's airfield, he remained alone over Oahu Island and joined the second attack group in its assault. He returned to his carrier at approximately 8:30 A.M.

From such incidents we can well appreciate the high quality and air-combat superiority of the officers and men of the Nagumo Force. This was their first introduction to airsea combat on a large scale, and the men and planes accomplished their tasks magnificently.

Thus ended successfully the greatest aerial operation ever seen up to this time. In a single smashing blow a total of 353 planes from six aircraft carriers completely wrecked the powerful battleship fleet of the United States. This feat astounded the entire world.

Who would have thought, up to this time, that the Japanese Navy, without firing a single shot from its guns, would be able to destroy almost completely and within so short a time the powerful dreadnaughts of the United States Pacific Fleet? The battleship had long been regarded as the king of the sea. Ever since the birth of the modern navy, the battleship had reigned supreme in America's fleet. And this same fleet which, with only eight battleships, had been holding the Japanese Navy at a distance of more than three thousand nautical miles, now lay crushed and useless as the result of a single telling air blow!

What is most amazing about the Hawaiian Operation is that, of the 353 planes launched by the Nagumo Force to attack Pearl Harbor, *only 154 planes were assigned to attack the American warships*. The remaining 199 aircraft were dispatched to strafe and bomb the enemy airfields, to destroy on the ground and in the air any enemy aircraft, the attacking Japanese force might have undisputed local air superiority.

If the American air force had detected in advance the approach of the Japanese fighters and bombers and had thrown up an air defense of fighter planes, our accomplishments would surely have been lessened and our losses increased. It is conceivable that, had Pearl Harbor been protected by air defenses, the assault against Hawaii could have lost much of its effectiveness, and the nature of the Pacific War proportionally altered.

CHAPTER 8

Zero Fighters Assure Victories: Operations in the Philippines and the Dutch East Indies

THE NATURE OF THE Hawaiian Operation prevented the Zero fighters from demonstrating fully their exceptional combat performance. Our planes so quickly eliminated all enemy aerial opposition that the Zeros confined their sweeps mainly to strafing attacks. In the Philippine Islands and the Dutch East Indies campaigns, however, our success rested directly on the ability of the Zero fighters to establish control of the air. Neither campaign could possibly have achieved its success with a fighter plane of lesser performance than the new Zero which so completely surprised the enemy.

Our main land-base air strength lay in Formosa, to which our planes flew immediately prior to the war. Separating these bombers and fighters from crucial Clark and Iba fields on Luzon was the impressive distance of more than four hundred and fifty nautical miles. We considered these two bases, as well as the city of Manila, which lay some five hundred nautical miles from Formosa, as targets of the highest priority. Our intelligence reported that at Clark and Iba fields rested the bulk of American air power in the Philippines; it was necessary to destroy this if our operations were to proceed with any degree of safety.

This distance between our Formosa bases and the Philippine Islands created a tremendous obstacle. Our planes in China often flew long missions, especially between Hankow and Chungking, but the proposed Formosa-to-Philippines-and-return raids exceeded even the most strenuous flights of the Sino-Japanese Incident. Further complications arose from the fact that the greater portion of the Formosa-Philippines flight would have to be made over water, which increased the possibilities of navigational error. Even were these obstacles to be overcome, we still faced the hazards of excessive bomber losses, since the distances involved appeared far beyond the maximum capabilities of our fighter planes. The Chinese with inferior fighters had effectively defended their cities against our unescorted bomber formations, and we realized only too well that the superior caliber of American pilots and planes promised severe bomber losses.

It was possible that in the Zero we possessed the world's first fighter airplane capable of flying the nine hundred nautical miles for the round trip between Formosa and Luzon. Actually we would have to provide for the equivalent of at least thirteen hundred nautical miles of flight, since the Zeros would inevitably be called on to engage in fuel-consuming dogfights.

We had also to consider additional factors. The effective flight range of an airplane is determined by more than merely still-air flight. The size of the formations would in great part determine the eventual fuel consumption of our planes, and much would depend upon our pilots' flying skill. Experience had taught us that a pilot well versed in the art of flying "by the seat of his pants" could extend by a considerable margin the maximum range of his airplane, as compared to the individual who flew mechanically. In China we always realized maximum efficiency from our formations, and were assured that our men possessed the highest flying skill. Circumstances then permitted us to select for Zero fighter operations only our crack pilots, and our formation flights never exceeded in size the thirty-Zero mission against Chengtu.

Once we placed the Zero in mass production and assigned large numbers to operational fleet units, we forfeited the luxury of critical pilot selection. Our commitment to a decisive war with America and England demanded the use of every available Zero fighter against the enemy, although we might lack what we considered a desirable number of "crack pilots." Consequently, in the summer of 1941 we assigned to our aircraft carriers half of those pilots who had fought in China under Lieutenant Saburo Shindo's command. The remaining veterans, under Lieutenant Tamotsu Yokoyama's leadership, were transferred to the land-based air forces.

Thus the difficulties of the Formosa-Philippines operation mounted steadily. To raid Luzon with Zero fighter planes, we were required to use the relatively few seasoned pilots as a nucleus around which we built a force of nearly two hundred and fifty Zero fighters, including spare planes which we assigned to the Tainan and the 3rd Air Corps.

The magnitude of the forthcoming Luzon assault demanded that we employ larger fighter-plane formations than we have ever sent into combat. The difficulties of maintaining formation with large groups of airplanes complicate enormously the pilots' efforts to maintain minimum fuel consumption. The mass formations inevitably resulted in a reduction in the Zero's operating radius of action.

Perhaps our greatest worry lay in the fact that the American and Philippine forces would expect our attack and consequently would be able fiercely to resist our planes with a maximum number of interceptors. Since we were to open the war with the Hawaiian Operation, the Philippines would have ample time in which to bolster their defenses. The unfavorable timing demanded that we attack Luzon with every available airplane. Everything depended upon the ability of the Zero fighters to wrest control of the local air from the defenders. Cognizant of our difficulties, the General Staff in Tokyo and the Combined Fleet General Staff ordered every possible action taken to increase the flight endurance of the Zero fighters in Formosa. Again we were faced with a problem other than that of range. We had to calculate the effect upon our pilots of the long hours spent in the air within the small Zero cockpits; our pilots must engage American fighters after spending what we considered was a prohibitive number of flying hours before entering combat.

In early October of 1940 three small aircraft carriers, the *Ryujo, Zuiho*, and *Kasuga-Maru*, arrived in southern Formosa. We commenced special deck take-off and landing training, for our plan was to move the carriers as close as possible to Luzon before launching our attack in the Philippines. By so doing we would reduce effectively the time spent in the air by our fighter pilots; further, our planes would not have to take off in early-morning darkness to coordinate their attack with that of the Nagumo Force (there is a difference of five hours and twenty minutes in the time of sunrise between Pearl Harbor and Luzon). The carrier operation would allow our planes to attack Luzon, engage in air combat, and return directly to Formosa.

Subsequent events forced us to review critically our proposed carrier attack. Our larger carriers were all committed to specific operations for the morning of December 8, 1941, and the three carriers assigned to the Philippines campaign were maddeningly slow, had small carrier decks, and could accommodate no more than seventy-five planes in all. For long months our pilots would be limited to practicing carrier operations, and would never receive the special simulated combat training which they required. The performance of each plane would suffer from the added weight of aircraft-carrier-operation equipment.

In early 1941 there were in Formosa many of Japan's outstanding fighter-plane strategists and pilots, including Commander Motoharu Okamura, Commander Yasuna Kozono, Commander Takeo Shibata, Lieutenant Hideki Shingo, and the China veteran, Lieutenant Tamotsu Yokoyama. For months the renowned flier Captain Masahisa Saito of the Tainan Air Corps and Captain Yoshio Kamei of the 3rd Air Corps drove their pilots near to exhaustion, steadily improving the range of their Zero fighters, increasing the efficiency of formation flights, and extending the flight-endurance time of the fighters. Captain Saito and Captain Kamei were hard taskmasters; day after day they sent their pilots into the air under conditions which exceeded our worst experiences in China.

The severe training discipline reaped a golden harvest. Saito's pilots steadily increased the endurance time of their Zeros, ranging further and further in nonstop flights from their home bases. Ten-hour flights became routine; then this figure jumped to eleven, and finally our fighter pilots flew simulated combat missions of twelve continuous hours in the air. In flights up to and exceeding ten hours, our pilots reduced their fuel consumption to twenty-one gallons per hour. Flight Petty Officer Saburo Sakai achieved the amazing fuel consumption of only eighteen gallons per hour.

The reduction in fuel consumption with its accompanying greater range and flight endurance brightened the prospects of the Luzon attack. With a guaranteed minimum of ten hours of flight time, the Zeros would be able to fly from Formosa to Luzon, combat the American fighters, and return to their home bases with fuel to spare. Our biggest problem was solved. Vice-Admiral Nishizo Tsukahara, Commander in Chief of the Eleventh Air Fleet and the commander of land-based air forces in the Formosa theater, informed Navy General Headquarters that the three aircraft carriers were no longer required for the Philippines attack.

Here was concrete proof that our ceaseless efforts to achieve in the Zero hitherto "impossible" performance had paid handsome dividends. The fighter's unparalleled range enabled the Navy to relieve the three carriers of their intended mission; the *Ryujo* steamed to Palau Island to join in the campaign against Davao (Mindanao Island), and the *Zuiho* and *Kasuga-Maru* returned to Japan for other assignments. On the very eve of the impending war we thus gained the equivalent of three vitally important aircraft carriers for our initial thrusts against the enemy.

The intended naval air force distribution for the opening of the Philippines campaign on December 8, 1941, was:

	Japanese Name	*Chinese Name*
Takao Air Corps		
3rd Air Corps	Takao Base	*Kaohsung*
Tainan Air Corps		
1st Air Corps	Tainan Base	*Tainan*
Kanoya Air Corps	Taichu Base	*Taichung*
1001st Air Corps	Kagi Base	*Chiai*
Toko Air Corps	Toko Base	*Tungkan*

We assembled at these bases a total of 184 Zero fighters; 192 land-based attack bombers (120 Type 1 and 72 Type 96); and twenty-four Type 97 flying boats. Only 108 Zeros and 144 attack bombers were capable of joining the difficult long-range operations; later this number diminished even further when we transferred to southern French Indochina approximately half the strength of the Kanoya Air Corps, leaving us with 117 operational attack bombers.

Our intelligence selected as priority targets the well-equipped Clark and Iba fields on Luzon Island; we dismissed as unimportant the secondary Nichols Field in the Manila suburbs.

Early in the morning of December 8, 1941, thick fog rolled in from the sea completely to shroud our air bases. On the very first day of the war, when a coordinated effort was of the utmost importance, our planes could not leave their fields. We cursed and fumed, for even as we paced helplessly in the swirling gloom the Nagumo task force planes turned Pearl Harbor into a shambles. If the enemy in the Philippines had the opportunity to counterattack quickly, he could disrupt completely our carefully laid plans. Finally the initial reports of the Pearl Harbor raid reached us through Tokyo; still the fog did not lift.

After long hours of chaining us to the ground, the fog dispersed before the morning sun. We wasted no time and, as quickly as their engines could be warmed, the fighters and bombers thundered from the field and headed southward. As the gods of war would have it, the crippling fog proved to be a tremendous asset in our attack against the American air bases. Our planes reached Luzon Island at 1:30 P.M., Tokyo Time, several hours later than we had originally scheduled. By this quirk of circumstances, we caught the American fighters completely off guard. Receiving the reports of the Pearl Harbor attack, the fighters took to the air in anticipation of a forthcoming raid. After waiting in vain for several hours for our planes, which were then sitting helplessly on the ground, the enemy planes, their fuel exhausted, returned to their fields. Almost immediately afterward our fighters and bombers swept in to attack.

Admiral Tsukahara's battle report of the day's events follows:

"On the morning of December 8, fifty-four Type 1 land-based attack bombers, the majority of the 1st Air Corps, bombed and destroyed forty to fifty of the sixty enemy planes on Clark Field. Thirty-four Zero fighters of the Tainan Air Corps led by Lieutenant Shingo flew escort; immediately following completion of the bombing runs, the Zeros descended to treetop level and in sweeping attacks strafed and destroyed almost all the remaining enemy planes. Fifty-four Type 96 land-based attack bombers of the Takao Air Corps, escorted by fifty Zero fighters of the 3rd Air Corps under command of Lieutenant Yokoyama, bombed and destroyed all of approximately twenty-five planes at Iba Field.

"Two of our Zero Fighter Units encountered an estimated fifteen enemy planes in the air and in the ensuing battle shot down the entire enemy fighter force. The effectiveness of our attacks has exceeded our fondest expectations."

The sweeping raids reduced in a single stroke the major American offensive power in the Philippines. Our intelligence estimated an enemy strength of some three hundred airplanes throughout the Philippine Islands on the first day of the war; our initial attack destroyed at least one third of this number. The sudden destruction of so large a segment of the air power of the United States, an enemy whom we expected to offer bitter resistance, infected our air crews with the desire to destroy the remaining enemy air force completely. (After the war we learned that the United States Army Air

Forces had on Luzon Island on December 8, 1941, 160 planes, including thirty-five B-17 heavy bombers. Our initial attack destroyed or rendered useless at least sixty of these.)

On the war's second day, severe storms reduced the effectiveness of our attacking planes. High winds and rain forced several fighters into the sea. On December 10, however, a savage aerial attack effectively neutralized the Cavite Naval Base area in south Manila. Forty-eight hours later not a single enemy plane remained on Luzon Island to contest our rampaging Zero fighters. Within these three days the aerial operations against Luzon Island ceased; by the fourth day, December 13, we dismissed the possibility of any form of enemy aerial counterattack. In three days our Zero fighters had given us absolute aerial supremacy in this theater of war.

At first glance these successes closely resemble the operations of the German Air Force in its overwhelming victories against Poland and France in the early days of World War II. A closer appraisal of the two air campaigns, notably of the numbers of aircraft employed both by our naval air forces and those of the *Luftwaffe*, reveals the slim numerical margin with which our forces operated. Ours was a battle resting entirely upon qualitative superiority and tactics, while the *Luftwaffe*, as can be seen in the accompanying charts, enjoyed both qualitative and overwhelming quantitative advantages.

GERMAN OPERATION AGAINST POLAND

Type of Plane	Poland	Germany
Bomber	180	2,000
Fighter	400	500
Other	200 (multipurpose)	500 (mainly Stuka dive bombers)

GERMAN OPERATION AGAINST FRANCE

Type of Plane	France	Germany
Bomber	1,500	3,000
Fighter	1,500 (including RAF)	1,500
Light Bomber	200	500 (mainly Stuka dive bombers)

JAPANESE NAVY OPERATION IN PHILIPPINES

Type of Plane	U.S.A.	Japan
Fighter	110	123
Attack	440 (est.)	146
Other	66 (36 flying boats)	39 (24 flying boats)

After the beginning of the war, we learned that, although the Zero fighter had appeared in battle in China more than a year prior to December of 1941, the Allies professed astonishment at the sight of our new fighter and were caught completely unaware by the Zero's performance. Months after the Philippines campaign, the Allies still did not realize the true flight capabilities of the Zero. When Zeros raided Port Darwin, Australia, early in 1942, the enemy accepted without question the fact that the Zeros must have flown from our carriers, when in reality they flew from our newly captured land bases on Timor Island.

In every operation in December of 1941 we quickly attained numerical as well as qualitative superiority. We fully appreciated the fact that the geographical isolation of the Pacific and Asiatic battle areas would prevent the enemy from rapidly reinforcing his air forces, and that by quick, decisive onslaughts we would not only achieve local air supremacy but would retain this advantage.

Within ten days of the opening bombing attack, the enemy planes disappeared entirely from the Philippines. Our forces wasted no time in pressing their newly won gains. On December 25, our task force swarmed ashore on Jolo Island in the southern part of the Sulu Sea and occupied its airfield. To obtain local air coverage we dispatched twenty-four Zero fighters of the Tainan Air Corps in a mass nonstop formation flight of twelve hundred nautical miles. The flight of the single-seat fighter planes was unprecedented in aviation history.

Our fighters experienced little difficulty in ridding the skies of the remaining enemy planes; by early March of 1942, our naval land-based air forces had landed in the string of south Pacific Islands. Quickly the entire Dutch East Indies came under the control of our air force. The Tainan Air Corps advanced to Bali Island in the Dutch East Indies through Jolo Island, Tarakan, Balikpapan, and Bandjermasin; the 3rd Air Corps flew to Davao, Menado, and Kendari (Celebes), then divided into two groups, the first of which advanced through Makassar to Bali Island. The second group moved into Dilly on Timor Island by way of Amboina.

Under Admiral Tsukahara's command, the naval land-based air forces in the southern Pacific area definitely shot down in air combat and destroyed on the ground a total of 565 enemy planes from December 8, 1941, until the close of the Java Operation. Of this number, our Zero fighters accounted for 471 planes, or 83 per cent of the total.

We can judge the effectiveness of our Zero fighters by observing that in all our operations in the first months of the war, the Zero fighters of our land- and carrier-based air forces destroyed 65 per cent of all the enemy planes lost.

This accomplishment contributed directly to the success of our operations in many respects other than the destruction of the enemy aircraft; without control of the air, our bombers and torpedo planes could not possibly have eliminated enemy resistance so thoroughly.

We have stressed, perhaps repetitiously, the role of this one airplane in the initial phases of the Pacific War. We feel, however, that at Pearl Harbor, as well as in the Philippines and Dutch East Indies, we could not possibly have achieved our sea, land, and air victories with a fighter plane of lesser performance than the Zero. Our entire strategy depended upon the success of this aircraft.

CHAPTER 9

The Sea Battle Off the Coast of Malaya

ON DECEMBER 10, 1941, the third day of the Pacific War, Japan received news of a tremendous victory which was greatly to affect our future military operations in Pacific and Asiatic waters. Two of England's most powerful warships, the dreadnaught *Prince of Wales* and the battle cruiser *Repulse* of the British Asiatic Fleet, had been sent to the bottom off the Malayan coast.

The victory was accomplished without the participation of Japanese surface vessels. Seventy-five twin-engine, land-based attack bombers of the Navy's 22nd Air Flotilla, under the command of Rear Admiral Sadaichi Matsunaga, had carried out the devastating attack and, in a single blow, rendered Britain's Asiatic sea power impotent.

Even more dramatically than the Pearl Harbor attack, this action typified the sudden changes in a balance of military power which could be wrought by bombing aircraft. Japan's air power accomplished England's reduction from her position as a major naval power in the Indian Ocean to

77

a state of helplessness at the unbelievably low cost of only three bombing airplanes, all of which succeeded in crashing into a British warship as they went down.

During the summer of 1941, the 22nd Air Flotilla had been undergoing intensified combat flight training at the Naval Air Force Base in southern Formosa. In late October the flotilla was ordered to move its headquarters to Saigon, the capital of French Indochina. Two air corps of the flotilla were simultaneously transferred to new bases. The Genzan Air Corps, consisting of forty-eight Type 96 land-based attack bombers, moved to Saigon via Hainan Island; and the Mihoro Air Corps, similarly equipped with forty-eight Type 96 bombers, transferred to Thudaumot, north of Saigon.

The flotilla's fighter-plane unit, consisting of thirty-six Mitsubishi Zero fighters, and the reconnaissance plane unit with six Type 98 land-based reconnaissance planes, were moved under direct command of Rear Admiral Matsunaga to the advanced base at Soctrang, south of Saigon.

These air units were specifically charged with (1) destruction of enemy fleet forces and the protection of our troop transports carrying the Army Malaya Landing Force; (2) destruction of the enemy's air forces stationed around Singapore; (3) maintaining a sea patrol.

The strategy adopted just prior to the opening of hostilities in the Pacific War called for the Army Air Force to assume air responsibility for this area. At this time, however, the Army Air Force lacked striking power and was almost useless for air combat operations. The Navy had little faith in the ability of Army units to attack with any success the enemy's surface vessels; indeed, the Army was sadly deficient in the means and the experience with which to carry out overwater military activities.

Had the war broken out at this time (October) rather

than during the planned date of the first week in December, the Army would not have possessed a single aircraft capable of bombing Singapore, the largest and most powerful British base in the area, from our main base in French Indochina.

This deporable situation prevailed despite the fact that the British fleet and the bombers based at Singapore were considered the greatest menace to the Army transports which had been scheduled to carry the Army Landing Force from French Indochina for the invasion of Malaya. Considering the vital objectives at hand, Admiral Isoroku Yamamoto, Commander in Chief of the Combined Fleet, personally interceded and ordered the 22nd Air Flotilla to move immediately to its new bases in French Indochina.

In late November of 1941, we received intelligence reports stating that two British battleships had been sighted moving in an easterly direction through the Indian Ocean. Additional reports from the area indicated later that the two warships had arrived at Singapore on December 2 or 3. It was also determined that the commander of the newly strengthened fleet was Vice-Admiral Sir Tom Phillips, and that the two large warships were the new *King George V* and the fast battle cruiser *Repulse*.

Subsequent to the action of December 10, the battleship was identified as the *Prince of Wales*, of the same class as the *King George V*, which six months previously had played an important role in the sinking of the German dreadnaught *Bismarck*.

The Japanese plans for the Malayan invasion were seriously threatened by the unexpected appearance of the two powerful British warships in the area. Conservative estimates by our intelligence indicated that the two British warships were even more powerful than our fast battleships *Kongo* and *Haruna*, then under the command of

Vice-Admiral Nobutake Kondo, the leading Japanese Navy commander in the theater, and Commander in Chief of the Second Fleet.

Admiral Kondo had under his direct command not only the two battleships, but also two heavy cruisers, one light cruiser, and ten destroyers. In addition to this force, five heavy cruisers, one light cruiser, and fourteen destroyers were under Vice-Admiral Jisaburo Ozawa, Commander in Chief of the Malaya Force.

To support this surface strength Admiral Yamamoto, when informed of the appearance of the *Prince of Wales* and the *Repulse* at Singapore, ordered twenty-seven Type 1 land-based attack bombers of the Kanoya Air Corps, which had been stationed in South Formosa, to move immediately to a new base in French Indochina. They were placed under the command of Rear Admiral Matsunaga.

This was the final disposition of our forces in the area as the scheduled date for initiating the war approached.

By the middle of the first week in December our air, sea, and ground forces were poised to strike against the enemy. Our operations involved the taut period of waiting and patrolling. We paid particularly close attention to the movements of the British Asiatic Fleet. Starting early in December, partly for the purpose of tracking the *Prince of Wales* and the *Repulse*, we patrolled the ocean waters surrounding French Indochina, Malaya, and Borneo daily with land-based attack bombers.

Tension among the air units was at a high pitch. To date all our movements had been carried out successfully, but at any moment the enemy might discover our plans and cause confusion among the closely coordinated activities of our air, sea, and land elements.

Lieutenant Sadao Takai, a squadron leader of the Genzan Air Corps, who participated in the preattack sea patrol and later in the Malaya sea battle, kept detailed notes of activities at the time:

"Two days before the scheduled date of opening hostilities, we patrolled the ocean as far as one hundred nautical miles south of Singapore. Patrol duty was an unpleasant experience; we were a single lonely plane flying through the cloudless skies over the southern sea. My crew uttered hardly a word during these long flights, almost constantly holding their breath, their eyes turned toward Singapore. The great British military base had been set as our target on the first night of the war, in the event that the British fleet should fail to leave the protection of the shore guns. Perhaps my men were carrying out their duties too intently; they seemed to be attempting to gain useful experience from every moment spent in the air during the tedious patrol missions. Everyone in the aircraft was in a confused state of mind, which was caused by the need for constant caution, by anticipation as to what would occur when the fighting began, and by a strong desire to be as proficient as possible in his duties.

"Not a single vessel or airplane was seen. The sea stretching endlessly before our bomber was so calm that not a wave was visible. It was hardly believable that only two days from now the war would start."

Full-scale patrol of the ocean area in which the first attacks would take place had commenced several days before the scheduled opening of hostilities but, as is evident from Lieutenant Takai's detailed report, many of the searching bombers failed to sight any movement on the part of the British fleet or air forces. Some British planes were observed by the Japanese bombers, but without hostile action taken by either side.

Lieutenant Takai's report continues:

"The Navy had ordered that all personnel engaged in

search missions were to concentrate on the movement of the two British battleships. We flew our patrols every day, seeing nothing, growing more and more tense as the attack date approached. The nerve-racking stillness over the ocean might well be described as the 'calm before the storm.'

"December 6, 1941. The troop transports carrying the Army landing force scheduled to invade the east shores of Malaya were proceeding westward off the south Indochina coast. Troop convoys are always infuriatingly slow in their movement; this phase of the attack operation was the bottleneck in our scheduled invasion of the enemy-held territory. Under constant fighter-plane cover, however, the fleet was advancing slowly toward Kota Bharu in Malaya. Fortunately, the sea was calm and the transports went unobserved, but this Japanese feudal-lord procession-like fleet could not remain completely safe forever!

"On this same day our worst fears were realized. British flying-boat patrol bombers discovered the convoy of troopships! Our entire invasion plan was completely exposed to the enemy long before we were able to launch the invasion of Malaya. It was perfectly clear to the British what a fleet composed of thirty vessels in formation represented, to what area it was headed, and when it would arrive at its destination. We were compelled to immediately change our tactics from secret operation to open movement. The possibility of an enemy aerial attack on our air bases in French Indochina was a cause for grave concern. Immediately we began to disperse our bombing squadrons to bases covering a wider area than they embraced.

"The day before the opening of the war dawned quietly. We hoped and prayed that the enemy would not take any action. Every radio dispatch was carefully studied for a hint of possible attack. We were worried that the British might attack the troopship convoy. Whenever a long interval went by without receipt of a radio dispatch, we feared we might have missed the news of possible fighting. On the other hand, whenever a radio message was received, we were afraid it would bring bad news. The scope of the area and the size of the forces involved were so great that almost anything could happen. We all wondered if our meticulously laid plans would really succeed. The constant waiting and wondering made sleep almost impossible.

"My most important duty was to have all my bombers prepared to launch an attack at a moment's notice. The armament we were to carry would, of course, depend upon the object of any attack. If land objectives were to be bombed, then special bomb racks would have to be mounted, because we would carry a large number of small-size bombs.

"If enemy ships were to be attacked, we would carry either heavy bombs or torpedoes. Unless my airplanes were in constant readiness to be loaded with any of these three types of weapons, they would be useless for the forthcoming air battles, in which even the slightest delay in joining the action could prove disastrous. The ground crews which maintained our planes in combat-ready condition were little known to the public in contrast to the attention bestowed upon the flight crews. It often happens, however, that the armament and ground crews hold the key to victory or defeat.

"No sign was received to indicate that the British fleet would leave Singapore to attack our surface vessels. The order was given; we would bomb Singapore on the first night of the war as originally scheduled.

"The flight crew of every airplane had been trained to perfection. This was our final moment. We had studied the bombing and attack plans so many times we had memorized every detail. Special preparations were unnecessary. Beyond the normal need for mechanical maintenance and the loading of our aircraft with bombs or torpedoes, we were ready to attack. Our only worry was the strength of possible enemy aerial counterattacks.

"However, as the war was to be opened in this theater by bombs dropped by our own aircraft, everyone was in high spirits. We were determined to frighten the enemy out of their wits. This was to be our first large-scale naval action, and our concern was not for our safety, but rather how much damage our aerial bombs and torpedoes would inflict on the enemy battleships.

"December 7, 1941. The day just before the opening of the war passed quietly and without incident. The British failed to attack. Three squadrons (twenty-seven planes) of the Mihoro Air Corps and three squadrons of the Genzan Air Corps roared from their bases in south Indochina into the black of night for Singapore, as scheduled.

"The southern sky was filled with cumulo-nimbus clouds which were peculiar to this area. My fears of very bad weather were realized when the twenty-seven bombers of the Genzan Air Corps, to which I belonged, suddenly were enveloped in thick clouds as we were climbing. As squadron leader of the 2nd Squadron, I placed my plane at the head of a nine-bomber flight.

"Visibility was so poor that it was almost impossible to recognize the formation lights of the two aircraft immediately behind me. The air was extremely rough; the plane rocked and shook. Sheets of rain drummed on the wings and fuselage and smashed against the cockpit windshield. Without changing course I began a descent to a lower altitude.

"Behind me, some high, others low, could be seen the glowing red, green, and yellow lights of the bombers in my squadron as they struggled to maintain formation in the rough air. Every now and then great flashes of lightning were reflected from the whirling propeller blades of the bombers. The pilots were trying desperately to hold the group together, so that they would not be left behind or separated from the formation, to become lost over the sea.

"I was still losing altitude when directly below the aircraft there appeared the dull white crests of waves streaking the black ocean surface. I pulled up from the steady descent, and searched for the other bombers; only two of the original squadron of nine were in sight. It seemed almost impossible to reorganize the formation. I was still looking vainly for an area of clear sky amidst the boiling clouds and rain when a "Return to base" order was received by wireless from Lieutenant Commander Niichi Nakanishi, our wing commander. All bombers returned to their takeoff points.

"Later that night we received a radio message telling of the successful first bombing attack on Singapore. The Mihoro Air Corps bombers were unobstructed by weather and had carried out their raids as scheduled. Our bomber crews were annoyed and disgusted that, in the first attack of the war, the Genzan Air Corps had not even reached its bombing objective and, because of weather conditions, had been scattered all over the sky.

"December 8, 1941. This morning dawned quietly. By some miracle the enemy had still not attacked our air bases in French Indochina, much to the relief of all pilots and crew members. Our Army planes were already active and were carrying out their bombing missions against the enemy forces. It was inconceivable that the enemy would not launch a heavy attack against our airfields, and my squadron moved at once to a nearby French army air base.

"A French army officer approached my bomber this

morning, smiling broadly and speaking rapidly in his native tongue. It had been a long time since I studied French at the Naval Academy, and I was unable to understand a word he was saying. We later discovered that the French officer had been congratulating us for our Navy's successful attack on Pearl Harbor.

"Until that moment, when we discovered what the excited French officer was trying to tell us, we were unaware of the great assault on the American air and naval bastion.

"Neither our constant bomber patrols over the ocean, or the reconnaissance flights over Singapore, had yet discovered any activity by the British battleships. We could not understand what caused the enemy to delay throwing these powerful vessels into action.

"Today was the most critical phase of our operations; the Army troops were scheduled to invade Malaya. Should the British warships or their bombers attack our transports during the assault operation, we might be in serious trouble. The absence of the enemy fleet made us feel that something was amiss, that the British might spring a sudden attack upon us. I know that, had I been the commander of those two mighty warships, I would have taken them out to sea off Kota Bharu, the Army's invasion point on Malaya, and attacked.

"While we were standing by, waiting for orders to take off in the event of enemy action, we received word that our transports were moving into Kota Bharu.

"All the men of the Genzan Air Corps were sorely disappointed that the first great bombing of the war was made by the aircraft carriers attacking Pearl Harbor. On the other hand, our questions as to the effectiveness of our aerial bombs and torpedoes were fully answered by the smashing success of the carrier planes which had raided the Hawaiian Islands.

"December 9, 1941. This morning one of our Type 98 reconnaissance planes flew over the Singapore Naval Base. All squadrons anxiously awaited the crew's report which might reveal the location of the British battleships.

"The news was good; the two battleships were still anchored at Singapore. Everybody relaxed; our troopships were free of the threat of the big British guns. Although we had nothing to fear from the warships as long as they remained in Singapore, at any moment the British might move the ships out to sea where they would be in a position to attack.

"Rear Admiral Matsunaga called a staff conference in his headquarters to determine the feasibility of having our bombers make a mass torpedo attack against the warships while they remained within the base.

"All pilots and aircrew members were in high spirits. We had found the battleships, and the opportunity to gain even more glorious fame than the men who had successfully attacked Pearl Harbor beckoned to us. Everybody was busy investigating the water depths at the Singapore Naval Base, the best directions from which to attack, and the most advantageous flight formations to utilize.

"At 5:00 P.M. we received a radio message from our submarine *I-56*, which had been patrolling east of Singapore. The submarine commander stated: '*3:50 P.M.* Two battleships proceeding northward.'

"We could not understand the discrepancy between the report of the reconnaissance plane, which stated that the warships were still within the British base, and the submarine report that the *Prince of Wales* and the *Repulse* had taken to the high seas. Whatever the outcome, the Genzan

Air Corps was ordered to assemble immediately for torpedo attack.

"Had the two powerful warships actually left the Singapore Naval Base? Or were there other enemy battleships in the area? Perhaps heavy cruisers had been mistaken for the battleships. Whatever the character of the British ships, their speed would bring them off the coast of Kota Bharu the following day. They must be located and destroyed before their powerful guns had the opportunity to destroy the invasion fleet.

"The order for torpedo attack was shortly received.

"The Type 98 reconnaissance plane returning to its base from the Singapore flight was ordered to change its destination and land immediately at the Saigon airfield. The photograph negatives were hurriedly developed. Now we knew the truth. What had appeared to the naked eye from a great altitude to be warships were actually two large cargo vessels.

"The absence of the *Prince of Wales* and the *Repulse* from Singapore Naval Base was confirmed. Delay was not permissible. The enemy's intentions were very clear; they were moving against the Kota Bharu invasion force. Our submarines, however, had lost contact with the enemy fleet and the exact whereabouts of the British vessels remained a mystery.

"7:00 P.M. All preparations for the torpedo attack were completed. With hopes of locating and attacking the British warships that evening or even during the night, we took off from our base in high spirits.

"We could not understand how the Army discovered that we were leaving in search of the enemy ships, but large numbers of our Army men had assembled at the base to see us off. The torpedoes were a great source of wonder to them. They waved and cheered loudly as our bombers left the ground.

"I do not understand why, but the occurrences of this day remain clearly in my mind. I was anxious to press the attack against the enemy. I can remember every small detail involving tonight's mission.

"Cumulo-nimbus clouds filled the sky as we flew south along the French Indochina coast, indicating that the weather might prove unfavorable. However, I did not fear for the safety of my men in the event we should run into storms. Every one of my planes that were scattered by the storm of two days ago had returned safely to the base, attesting to the ability of their pilots. Tonight we were determined to carry the attack to the enemy even if storms should break up the formations, and if no more than two planes could fly together. We were determined not to be balked by the weather.

"All planes descended below cloud level in search of the enemy.

"A radio order received from Vice-Admiral Nobutake Kondo, Commander in Chief of the South Area Force, indicated that all available surface and air units would be mobilized for night attack. Our submarine had sighted the enemy battleships; now, it was our air force's turn to destroy them. We did not intend to let our surface fleet take this big game away from us! Our fighting spirit was high!

"The sun had dropped below the horizon. Visibility was very poor, and we were flying in three-plane formation.

"Unfortunately, there was still a serious problem to be solved. We had not decided, when the operation began, on any definite measures for differentiating between the enemy vessels and our own warships during close-range sea battles, when such identification can be extremely difficult. We did not know the definite location of the enemy warships; furthermore, we had no information as to the location of our own ships this night. How were we to distinguish one from another?

"Even during daylight, identification of warships is generally difficult; at night, it becomes almost impossible. There is actually great danger of attacking our own warships and airplanes during combined operations of our sea and air forces except under special conditions, such as when the vessels of either the enemy or friendly forces remain stationery.

"Not having received any training on this matter, and not having had time to discuss warship identification before we took off, our air and sea forces were rushing into the battle blindly. It seemed as if we might be caught in our own traps!

"The clouds seemed to stretch endlessly over the ocean. We could not emerge from them, and the task of observing the ocean surface was becoming increasingly difficult. We could not fly much higher than one thousand feet. Under such conditions our chances for discovering the enemy fleet were doubtful unless we happened to fly directly over the British ships, or crossed their wakes.

"However, the situation was not hopeless. We had many airplanes searching the ocean and any one of them might sight the enemy forces. There was also the chance that we might discover the enemy inadvertently in the event that he sighted our planes and fired upon them. When one flies in almost total darkness one feels that the enemy might appear suddenly and without warning before one's eyes.

"Farther and farther we flew southward in search of the enemy fleet.

"A radio report from one of our searching bombers

brought jubilation to our hearts. The anxiously sought enemy vessels had been sighted!

"The radio report continued: *'We have dropped a flare bomb.'*

"One of the Mihoro Air Corps bombers had succeeded in sighting the enemy. With high spirits we drove our planes to maximum speed and hastened toward the location of the enemy ships. Already the attack might be under way! We extracted the last ounce of power from our motors trying to make the airplanes go faster and faster. Soon another radio message was received.

" *'The vessel under our flare is the* Chokai.'

"Good heavens! Instead of being disappointed, I was appalled! We were in great danger of bombing our own fleet in place of the enemy's. Instead of attacking the British warships, we must now be extremely careful to avoid bombing and torpedoing the Japanese vessels in the area. Had we missed this last message, we would have pressed the attack against the *Chokai*, a heavy cruiser and the flagship of Vice-Admiral Ozawa!

"We were sorely dejected. It appeared that we did not have very good opportunity this night to discover the whereabouts of the enemy and to launch an attack. Soon after the *Chokai* was sighted an order was received from Rear Admiral Matsunaga:

" *'Discontinue operation. All planes return to base.'*

"The order to call off the search for the enemy enabled us to relax our tense muscles. Yet, we remained undecided as to what to do. It was possible that the British warships had broken through our air-sea screen and might even now be hurling their shells against our transports lying off Kota Bharu. That was my greatest fear. We stifled the urge to continue searching for the enemy for a little while longer, and turned back toward the base. Orders must be followed without hesitation.

"It seemed as if our problems this night would never end. To attempt a landing with a torpedo after the safety pin had been pulled is an extremely hazardous undertaking; we were anxious to dump the deadly weapons into the sea before landing. But no, we could not do this because the supply of torpedoes at the French Indochina bases was sorely limited.

"There was only one torpedo for each airplane. We could not afford to lose a single one.

"To insure against possible landing accidents on the blacked-out field, each plane was kept in the air until the moon had risen. It was not until midnight that the landing strip became visible in the moonlight, and the planes could land.

"Despite the exhaustion brought on by the harrowing flight through stormy weather, the long hours spent in the air, and the nerve-racking landings with armed torpedoes, we were not given a chance to rest. Calling on our reserve stamina and courage, we worked through almost the entire night preparing for the next day's mission.

"Our primary duty involved reconnaissance. Since the movement of the enemy warships was completely unknown after our submarine lost the British vessels, it was the task of the bombers to search out their whereabouts. While every effort would be made to locate the enemy ships if they were still at sea, we had to consider the possibility that the warships might have returned to Singapore.

"Should they already be within the port, the enemy's resistance would be much greater and our attacks less effective. We would have to contend not only with the antiaircraft weapons of the ships, but also with those of the naval base. Our airplanes would be limited in their attack formations. The worst problem of all was that, should we be forced to attack with torpedoes in Singapore itself, our bombers would not have sufficient fuel to return to their bases.

"We must by all means seek out and destroy the enemy vessels this morning. It was thereupon decided to send out nine attack bombers and two Type 98 reconnaissance aircraft to search for the British warships early in the morning of December 10. At the same time we would dispatch a strong attack force to Singapore, regardless of the movement of the enemy vessels.

"Today's search mission was so difficult that, according to the pilots' calculations, only about half of the area in which the British ships might be found could possibly be covered. Although the desire of the commanding officers to use as many planes as possible out of the total available force of a hundred aircraft was understandable, I did not think these tactics intelligent. The men were almost worn out.

"December 10. The sky was clear—good visibility today! No unexpected troubles developed, and all battle preparations were completed on time for takeoff.

"At 6:25 A.M. all reconnaissance planes left their bases simultaneously. Between 7:35 and 9:30 A.M. torpedo and bombing units took off. The airplanes mobilized for action this day included nine Type 96 attack bombers, and two Type 98 reconnaissance aircraft for search duty; twenty-six Type 96 attack bombers and twenty-six Type 1 attack bombers to carry torpedoes; and thirty-four Type 96 attack bombers carrying bombs.

"The leader of the reconnaissance group took a position in the center part of the search area, where the chance of sighting the enemy ships would be the greatest. The airplane carried many cameras with which to photograph the enemy ships and the scene of battle. The reconnaissance aircraft flying parallel to the leader succeeded in sighting the enemy first; unfortunately, this latter plane did not carry cameras.

"I participated in this operation as 2nd Squadron Leader of torpedo bombers of the Genzan Air Corps.

"In torpedo practice with my bomber on the ground, the aircraft released its torpedo without trouble. We knew when the torpedo had left the airplane by the strong vibrations transmitted to the airframe at the moment of release.

"As my particular bomber was a most dependable aircraft assigned for my exclusive use, I was completely at ease with both the plane and its engines. Everyone in the corps had full confidence in his craft.

"All the crew members are veterans of the battles in China. But this was their first sea battle, and torpedoing enemy vessels is a hazardous operation. All my men felt pleasure as well as anxiety as we anticipated the coming battle.

" 'Sir, what angle of fire shall I follow?' I was asked by a faithful young pilot in my squadron. Many factors enter into the final decision for the angle of fire to release the torpedo, but most of these must be determined by visual observation. The general principle of torpedo attack is easily understood. However, under combat conditions where the position of the target relative to the aircraft changes from moment to moment, only a considerable amount of past practice can accurately determine the precise angle of fire to release torpedoes.

"After giving the young pilot general instructions, I told him, 'If you become too confused to determine the proper angle of fire, fly very low and aim your torpedo directly at the bow.'

"Our commander, Admiral Matsunaga, painstakingly

and kindheartedly gave all the men their orders. When he had finished, Captain Kosei Maeda, our commanding officer, lectured the men severely. He told them to calm down and to put their strength in their abdomen. Commander Kamero Sonokawa, the corps flight officer, issued detailed instructions on the possible movement of the enemy, and outlined the plan of assault. Lieutenant Commander Niichi Nakanishi, the wing commander for the day, elaborated further on the attack plans.

"It was then my turn, as the 2nd Squadron Leader, to speak, but there was nothing left for me to say.

"By the time my men had heard the instructions from the section leader, and the chief of each plane who followed me, they had forgotten the previous lengthy instructions. The young crew members were thinking perhaps not of the long orders but about the lunch in the planes.

"Young crew members are usually innocent of battle. A tasty lunch boosts their morale more than medals of valor or certificates of merit. Of all the food carried in the bombers, bean-paste-coated rice cake, called *ohagi*, is the best liked. If, in addition, coffee syrup is carried in the vacuum bottles, they are in very high spirits, and exhibit their great pleasure by the expressions on their faces even before the airplane takes off.

"It is an indisputable fact that there usually appears a trace of anxiety or uncertainty on the face of every man while on a bombing mission. When, however, a man exhibits calmness and efficiency in his duties, we feel proudly that he is really a crack crew member. Just how well the men will actually perform their duties in combat rests upon the skill and ability of the wing commanders and the squadron leaders.

"It is now 7:55 A.M., and the reconnaissance planes which left before dawn should be beyond the French

Indochina coast and over the open sea. All the torpedo bombers took to the air and set a course straight for Singapore. Our foremost concern was our fuel supply.

"Ever since September the Genzan Air Corps had made continuous studies on how to save fuel and increase the flight endurance of our bombers. We learned how to take advantage of wind conditions, and what were the best power settings. Through careful use of the mixture-control lever we had succeeded in increasing our range by 20 per cent without adding to our fuel load, as compared to our missions in China.

"As our planes carried torpedoes today, we had in our tanks about 30 per cent less fuel than normal. We flew in a very large formation, and for reasons of safety our radius of operation was fixed at a maximum of four hundred nautical miles. However, should we find the enemy ships more than four hundred nautical miles from Saigon, we would naturally press home the attack. All pilots were trying to use as little fuel as possible.

"As the miles slipped beneath our wings and we flew farther south, the weather constantly improved. Finally the sky was completely clear. We maintained a flight altitude of between 8,300 and 10,000 feet.

"Nearly 10:00 A.M. What is the matter with our reconnaissance planes? Still no sign of the enemy. In spite of the good weather and clear visibility, is it possible the reconnaissance planes still cannot find the British warships? By now our planes should be more than five hundred nautical miles from Saigon. Wing Commander Nakanishi, flying just ahead of my bomber, must also be growing very impatient.

"We have passed the danger line of four hundred nautical miles from Saigon. Still no report on the enemy ships. It is as though we were enveloped in complete darkness.

The pilots are becoming more and more anxious about their remaining fuel. We measured the rate of fuel consumption as carefully as possible and reduced it to the lowest possible level. It was not the best way to treat the engines, but we had little choice. Perhaps because of our severe mixture control, one of my bombers developed engine trouble and was forced to leave the formation and return to base. I could not send even one plane as escort. Including my own, the number of planes in my squadron was reduced to seven.

"At 11:45 A.M. we sighted a small vessel off to our left. The sea was absolutely calm. The ship appeared to be a cargo vessel of about five hundred or six hundred tons. Singapore was near. Since it was possible that other enemy vessels might be in the vicinity, I ordered my men to stay alert. No other object could be seen; this was unusual.

"Keeping a sharp lookout above and behind us for enemy planes, we tightened all formations and maintained our flight due south.

"Without warning the entire 3rd Squadron dropped out of the mass formation and flew toward the small cargo vessel. Soon they circled over the ship. I could not understand what the squadron leader could possibly be doing.

"The enemy vessel suddenly changed its course, and no sooner had it begun its twisting evasive action than a salvo of bombs fell more than seven hundred feet away from the ship without inflicting any damage! What was wrong with the 3rd Squadron leader? Nine 1,100-pound bombs were lost, dissipated without results, after all the trouble of carrying them for such a long time!

"The level-bomber squadron had already wheeled out of formation and was returning to its home base. We continued to fly southward. Far ahead and to our right we could make out the southern tip of the Malayan peninsula.

"If the enemy fleet was on the high seas, we certainly should have been able to sight it. Our commander appeared determined to seek out the enemy vessels right in Singapore if he failed to find them on the ocean.

"We were dangerously close to passing the 'point of no return,' when we would lack the fuel to return to our base. Our only hope, in the event that we passed this point, was to make a forced landing at Kota Bharu, which our troops had already invaded.

"All this time we were without word as to what had happened to the Mihoro and Kanoya Air Corps wings. There was no information as to their whereabouts. Perhaps, however, they purposely silenced their radios for fear of alerting the enemy.

"At 12:20 P.M. my wireless operator informed me that he had just received a message. I instantly left the pilot's seat and used the code book to decipher the message, which revealed that the enemy fleet had been found! On the face of everyone aboard the plane there appeared excitement and a joy at having finally discovered the enemy. Soon there would be battle! The message read:

" *'Sighted two enemy battleships. Seventy nautical miles southeast of Kuantan. Course south-southeast. 1145.'*

"The enemy was right *behind* us. I watched closely for the signal to turn and reverse our course. Strangely, the 1st Squadron continued to fly southward. We waited and waited but no signal was received from the 1st Squadron to turn about and head for the enemy.

"Ten minutes went by, and I was becoming very anxious. Finally I relayed the message concerning the sighting of the battleships to the other planes and, at the same time, began gradually to reverse our course in order to take over the lead of the formation. Seeing my maneuver, the planes of the 1st Squadron also reversed their course and fell in behind my squadron.

"Our new heading was north-northwest. Anticipating the coming battle, all planes moved in and took up a close formation. We were flying just above eighty-three hundred feet. Clouds had begun to fill the sky, but they did not restrict our view of the ocean below us. In spite of repeated warnings to the crew members not to relax for a moment their vigilance to the rear and above our airplanes, everybody was straining to look ahead of our bomber to sight the enemy fleet. Everybody wanted the honor of being first to see the British warships.

"It was just past one o'clock. Low clouds were filling the sky ahead of us. Fully five hours had passed since we left Saigon that morning. The enemy fleet should become visible any moment. I became nervous and shaky and could not dismiss the sensation. I had the strangest urge to urinate. It was exactly like the sensation one feels before entering a contest in an athletic meet.

"At exactly 1:03 P.M. a black spot directly beneath the cloud ahead of us was sighted. It appeared to be the enemy vessels, about twenty-five miles away. Yes—it was the enemy! Soon we could distinguish the ships. The fleet was composed of two battleships, escorted by three destroyers, and one small merchant vessel. The battleships were the long-awaited *Prince of Wales* and the *Repulse!*

"The 1st Squadron picked up speed and moved ahead of my squadron. Lieutenant Commander Nakanishi ordered, *'Form assault formation!'* A little later, *'Go in!'*

"The enemy fleet was now about eight miles away. We were still flying at eighty-three hundred feet and were in the ideal position to attack. As we had planned, Nakanishi's bomber increased its speed and began to drop toward the enemy fleet. He was headed to the right and a little ahead of the warships. Trying to maintain the same distance and not be left behind, the bombers of my squadron also increased their speed as I started a gradual dive. I headed toward the left flank of the enemy formation. It was a standard practice among us for the 1st Squadron to attack the largest vessel, and the 2nd Squadron the next largest.

"All crew members searched the sky vigilantly for the enemy fighters which we expected would be diving in to attack us at any moment. Much to our surprise not a single enemy plane was in sight. This was all the more amazing since the scene of battle was well within the fighting range of the British fighters; less than one hundred nautical miles from both Singapore and Kuantan.

"Except for the planes which at this moment were screaming in to attack, no other aircraft could be seen. We learned later that the third reconnaissance plane, piloted by Ensign Hoashi, had first sighted the enemy battleships and alerted all the bombers. As soon as he had reported the presence of the enemy fleet and was informed that our bombers were rushing to the scene, Hoashi left the area to bomb the Kuantan air base, to prevent the enemy fighters from taking off.

"Without interference from enemy fighters we could make our attacks freely. Coordinating my movements with those of the 1st Squadron, I led my squadron to the attack so that the enemy ships would be torpedoed from both flanks. The 1st Squadron was circling about four miles to the left and forward of the enemy ships and was about ready to begin its torpedo run. Antiaircraft shells were exploding all around the circling bombers. The planes could be seen between the flashing patches of white smoke as the shells exploded.

"Not a single antiaircraft shell exploded near my squadron. Perhaps the clouds hid us from the enemy gunners.

"Through my binoculars I studied the enemy's position. The large battleships were moving on a straight course, flanked by the three destroyers. The destroyers were just ahead of the battleships and making better than twenty-six knots. I could see clearly the long, white wakes of the ships as they cut through the water.

"A long, narrow plume of white smoke drifted upward from the second battleship. Later I discovered this was due to a direct hit scored by the level bombers of the Mihoro Air Corps which had made the first attack at 12:45 P.M.

"There was no doubt that it was a battleship. However, when I studied carefully the details of the vessel, it resembled—it even appeared to be—our battleship *Kongo!* We were completely unaware of the whereabouts of our own surface forces in this area; it was not impossible that it was actually the *Kongo* below us. The narrow escape of the *Chokai* from our bombers last night was still fresh in my memory, and my blood ran cold at the thought that we might be attacking our own vessels.

"However, the 1st Squadron bombers were plunging into the attack, one after the other, and the enemy gunners (if it really was the enemy!) were filling the sky with bursting antiaircraft shells.

"I was still undecided about attacking. I called our observer and inquired as to the identity of the ship below us, stating that it greatly resembled the *Kongo*. I was shocked to hear the observer reply, 'It looks like our *Kongo* to me, too.'

"It was a terrible situation to be in. I could not decide whether or not the vessel was a British battleship or actually the *Kongo*. I had been on the *Kongo* three years ago, and I was trying to remember details of the battleship. To confess, I had not studied to any extent the details of British warships, but had concentrated instead on American vessels. My knowledge of the British vessels was very meager.

"What further confused the situation was the repeated flag signal from the third plane of my squadron, *'Is not the fleet ours?'* Both the second and third bombers were watching my plane as if asking for my decision.

"Even if the fleet now under attack was friendly, it would have no alternative but to open fire fiercely when some airplanes started action preparatory to an assault. And our level bombers had already attacked a short while ago. I could not assume the fleet to be hostile merely because it was defending itself and firing upon our planes.

"My squadron was requesting information again from me. I did not know what to do.

"Meanwhile our bombers had passed the ideal point to commence the torpedo attack. We were now flying at 1,700 feet.

"The clouds were increasing steadily, and visibility was already reduced. It would be to our disadvantage to attack from the sterns of the enemy ships. Boldly the formation circled out from the protection of the clouds, and checked once again the position of our targets. We were able to get a very good look at the battleship.

"I was greatly relieved. I was sure of it—the vessel below was not the *Kongo.*

"I was nervous and upset, and starting to shake from the excitement of the moment. We turned and flew into the clouds again. We changed course while in the clouds to confuse the enemy and came out from beneath the clouds in attack position. This was possible because of a stratum of scattered clouds between 1,000 and 1,700 feet.

"We began the attack at an altitude of 1,000 feet and about a mile and a half from the enemy. No sooner had we emerged from the protection of the clouds than the enemy gunners sighted our planes. The fleet opened up with a tremendous barrage of shells, trying to disrupt our attack before we could release our torpedoes. The sky was filled with bursting shells which made my plane reel and shake.

"The second battleship had already started evasive action and was making a hard turn to the right. The target angle was becoming smaller and smaller as the bow of the vessel swung gradually in my direction, making it difficult for me to release a torpedo against the ship. It was expected that the lead torpedo bomber would be compelled to attack from the most unfavorable position. This was anticipated, and it enabled the other planes following me to torpedo the target under the best of conditions.

"The air was filled with white smoke, bursting shells, and the tracers of antiaircraft guns and machine guns. As if pushed down by the fierce barrage thrown up by the enemy, I descended to just above the water's surface. The airspeed indicator registered more than two hundred knots. I do not remember at all how I was flying the airplane, how I was aiming, and what distance we were from the ship when I dropped the torpedo. In the excitement of the attack I pulled back on the torpedo release. I acted almost subconsciously, my long months of daily training taking over my actions.

"A giant battleship suddenly loomed before the plane. Passing very close to the towering stern I swung into a hard turn and sped away from the warship. I began a wide circling turn in a clockwise direction, hastily easing the complaining bomber out of its steep climbing turn.

"Not many shells appeared to be bursting about us. The engines were still roaring loudly and only moderate damage had been inflicted upon my airplane. I pulled up again in a steep climb and leveled off, once we were within the clouds. I took a deep breath, and forced my taut muscles to relax.

"Suddenly my observer came stumbling forward through the narrow passageway, crying 'Sir! Sir! A terrible thing has happened!' When I looked at him in surprise, he shouted, 'The torpedo failed to release!'

"I felt as though cold water had been dashed over my head and entire body. We were still carrying the torpedo! I forced myself to be calm and reversed our course at once. I passed on my new orders to the men. 'We will go in again at once.'

"I began to lower our altitude as we flew through the clouds. The second torpedo run on the battleship would be very dangerous; the enemy gunners were fully alert and would be waiting for us. I did not like the idea of flying once again through a storm of antiaircraft fire which would be even worse than before.

"We dropped below cloud level. We were on the side of the enemy battleship, which was just swinging into a wide turn. Our luck was good—no better chance would come!

"I pushed the throttles forward to reach maximum speed and flew just above the water. This time I yanked hard on the torpedo release. Over the thudding impact of bullets and shrapnel smashing into the airplane, I felt the strong shock through the bomber as the torpedo dropped free and plummeted into the water. It was inexcusable that we did not notice the absence of this shock during the first torpedo run.

"The 1st Squadron commander was sending out the attack reports by radio. '*Many torpedoes made direct hits,*' and '*The lead battleship is listing heavily but is returning to normal position,*' etc.

"As the outcome of my squadron's attack was impossible for me to determine, I merely radioed, 'The 2nd Squadron has finished its torpedo runs.'

"I waited for the bombers of my squadron to assemble.

"All through the attack we had concentrated only on scoring direct hits on the enemy vessels. We had ignored everything but the release of our torpedoes into the British battleships. We had even forgotten to worry about our own safety. Once we had released the torpedoes, however, we were able to study the situation about us. Tracer bullets and antiaircraft shells filled the sky all about the airplanes, and we could feel the thud and shock vibrating all through the fuselage and wings as bullets and shrapnel ripped through the plane metal. It seemed to each of us that all the guns were aimed at our own plane. We became afraid of losing our own lives.

"Might this not be considered a normal reaction of human nature, this anxiety for one's own life? Pilots fare better in this respect than the crew members because they are so preoccupied with the many things necessary to fly their airplanes. It seems that the other crew members are unable to sit idly by as the bomber thunders in toward the enemy, flying right into the spitting orange and red flashes of his gun muzzles. They must have something to do, to occupy themselves, or their fear may become overpowering.

"The machine gunners later told me they could not help but open fire against the enemy battleships, to sweep the decks with their bullets. In past days when our missions over the China continent were to bomb Chungking and Chengtu, it was the time spent between reaching the target and releasing the bombs that was most uncomfortable for the pilot. When our bombers were bracketed by enemy antiaircraft and a shell would explode ahead and above the airplane, the acrid smell of the powder would fill the cockpit. It penetrated our nostrils and brought fear to our hearts; the shells were so close that we might be hit next. Only after we released our bombs and sped away from the city could we relax. In this respect torpedo bombing and level bombing are the exact opposite of each other.

"I banked my airplane and studied the battle scene below us. White smoke poured from the second large battleship. This was due to a direct torpedo strike scored about twenty minutes before we attacked; the hit had been made by Lieutenant Yoshimi Shirai's bomber squadron of the Mihoro Air Corps. The level bombers had made their attack from a height of 11,700 feet, and in the first bombing run a 550-pound bomb scored a direct hit. In the second attack two 550-pound bombs scored near misses.

"Commanded by Lieutenant Hachiro Shoji, the wing of the Mihoro Air Corps had actually left the French Indochina bases after we had taken off. Lieutenant Shirai's squadron of the Mihoro Air Corps wing, which had first bombed the enemy battleships, took off about thirty minutes after we left. Its course, however, was in a direct line with the enemy fleet and it arrived on the scene first, immediately attacking the enemy.

"Sixteen bombers of the Genzan Air Corps torpedo squadrons had torpedoed the British fleet for about nine minutes. One of the 1st Squadron planes was hit immediately after releasing its torpedo; somehow the pilot managed to keep control of the bomber and finally made a suicide crash with his crippled plane into the enemy.

"About four minutes later eight bombers of the Mihoro Air Corps torpedo squadron sent their torpedoes toward the second large battleship. Lieutenant Katsusaku Takahashi of the 2nd Squadron could not release his torpedo in the first attack. Once beyond the range of the enemy guns he turned and hurtled once again into the deadly barrage thrown up by the enemy ships. Again the torpedo failed to release. Somehow Lieutenant Takahashi's bomber managed to survive the gantlet of antiaircraft fire. It was discovered later that the torpedo release mechanism had been hit by shrapnel and had jammed.

"Immediately behind the Mihoro Air Corps torpedo squadron twenty-six Type 1 bombers of the Kanoya wing attacked the two battleships. They were led by Lieutenant Commander Shichizo Miyauchi. The Kanoya wing carried out their attacks over a period of twenty minutes. Two of the bombers made suicide dives into the enemy ships after releasing their torpedoes.

"During a period of slightly less than one hour, fifty land-based attack bombers assaulted the two battleships, roaring in one after the other to release their torpedoes. The cumulative effect of the torpedo strikes was evident in the gradual loss of speed and control of the two battleships.

"When the Kanoya torpedo squadrons had completed their torpedo runs, two level-bomber squadrons of the Mihoro Air Corps arrived at a position directly above the enemy fleet, which was trying desperately to evade the constant torpedo attacks. The Mihoro Air Corps bombers were flying at 8,400 feet when they moved in to make their bombing runs.

"By now the *Repulse* was a shattered hulk. It was still moving, but slowly, and was gradually losing speed. It had completely lost all fighting power and was no longer considered a worth-while target. It was only a matter of minutes before the battle cruiser went down.

"To all appearances, the *Prince of Wales* was intact, and defending herself furiously with an intense antiaircraft barrage. She was selected as the next bombing target. Fourteen 1,110-pound bombs were dropped; several scored direct hits on the enemy warship. The bombs struck directly in the center of the battleship.

"All the bombs of one squadron were wasted. While attempting to obtain an accurate bombing fix on the *Prince of Wales*, the squadron leader accidentally tripped his bomb release. He was still far from the enemy battleship when his bombs dropped; the other planes in the squadron, when they saw the bombs falling from the lead aircraft, immediately released their own bombs, which fell harmlessly into the sea.

"Ensign Hoashi's plane caught the dramatic last moments of the two battleships. Minute by minute, as he circled above the stricken warships, he radioed back a vivid report of what was happening far below him. Twenty minutes after being hit by torpedoes, the *Repulse* began to sink beneath the waves. By 2:20 P.M. the great ship was gone.

"A few minutes later a tremendous explosion ripped through the *Prince of Wales*. Twenty minutes after the *Repulse* had sunk, the *Prince of Wales* started her last plunge and disappeared quickly.

"All pilots and crew members in the bombers returning to their bases were jubilant and flushed with victory. We happily listened to each of Ensign Hoashi's radio reports as he told how the burning and exploding enemy ships were sinking.

"Back at the airfields in French Indochina, a second wave of bombers was being readied for another assault on the enemy battleships. The base had not been able to obtain accurate information on the progress of the battle, and was prepared to launch another mass attack. However, as soon as it received the reports from Ensign Hoashi's plane as he circled the area, the attack was called off.

"While he observed the sinking *Prince of Wales*, Hoashi sighted eight enemy fighters racing to the scene. Their belated appearance was of no avail, for the *Repulse* and the

Prince of Wales had already disappeared beneath the waves.

"Hoashi immediately fled to the protection of nearby clouds. As the enemy fighters searched vainly for his reconnaissance plane, he skillfully eluded his pursuers and returned safely to base.

"This was indeed fortunate for us. Had Hoashi's plane failed to confirm the results of the battle, our future operations would necessarily have been based on the assumption that the two mighty warships had not been destroyed. Our freedom of action would have been severely curtailed, for we dared not send surface units in an area in which the big guns of the British warships might destroy them.

"The great ability of our pilots to wrest every possible mile of range out of their bombers was soon made apparent in dramatic fashion. We feared that many of our planes would be compelled to make forced landings at Kota Bharu, since we had flown beyond our calculated 'point of no return,' and then engaged in fuel-consuming battle maneuvers. Actually, not a single plane was forced to make an emergency landing at Kota Bharu, and all bombers were able to return to their respective bases in Indo-China.

"Furthermore, only the three planes which fell in flames during the sinking of the enemy warships failed to return! And all three planes had managed to crash into the battleships. It was a great and glorious victory."

Subsequent interrogation of pilots indicated that thirty-five torpedo bombers and eight level bombers had attacked the swift battle cruiser *Repulse*. The Genzan Air Corps released seven torpedoes against the *Repulse*, of which four struck the ship. Of the more than twenty torpedoes released against the *Repulse* by the Kanoya Air Corps, at least ten were seen to explode against the warship. Four of seven torpedoes released by the Mihoro Air Corps bombers went true to their target.

Sixteen 550-pound bombs were dropped against the *Repulse* by Mihoro Air Corps bombers; one scored a direct hit and two fell as near misses.

The *Prince of Wales* was attacked by fifteen torpedo bombers. The Genzan Air Corps released nine torpedoes, of which four struck the battleship. Each of six Kanoya Air Corps bombers dropped a torpedo, scoring four hits on the *Prince of Wales* and one hit on an escorting destroyer.

Eight level bombers of the Mihoro Air Corps dropped fourteen 1,100-pound bombs on the battleship; of these, two were direct hits. Nine other bombers of the same air corps dropped eighteen 1,100-pound bombs but failed to score any hits.

A total of forty-nine torpedoes were released in the attack. More than twenty-six of these struck the two battle-ships and one of the escorting destroyers. Of the sixteen 550-pound bombs dropped, only one scored a direct hit. Forty-one 1,100-pound bombs were released (eighteen were prematurely dropped) and two direct hits were obtained.

The *Repulse* was attacked initially by the Mihoro Air Corps under the command of Lieutenant Hachiro Shoji, who first dropped bombs on the *Repulse* at 12:45 P.M. The first torpedoes struck the *Repulse* at 1:22 P.M. The battle cruiser went down at 2:20 P.M.

At 1:14 P.M. the first four torpedoes crashed into the *Prince of Wales*. The battleship sank at exactly 2:30 P.M.

Our search aircraft, which had remained over the battle area to confirm the destruction of the two British warships, discovered eight approaching enemy fighters at 3:00 P.M., and immediately left the scene.

The Battle of Malaya was fruitful in more ways than only in the destruction of Britain's two most powerful warships in this area. The lesson to be learned from the battle was different from that at Pearl Harbor, where an anchored and unsuspecting enemy fleet was surprised.

The British commanders were fully aware that a Japanese carrier task force had only recently assaulted Pearl Harbor with devastating results, and that surface ships did not actually participate in the destruction visited upon the American installations. It was a mistake leading to the most serious consequences that the British failed to heed this lesson and provide air protection for their prized battleships. This was the more surprising since it was most obvious from the moment our reconnaissance planes discovered the whereabouts of the British fleet, which seriously threatened Japanese surface operations, that we would launch an intensive aerial assault against the *Prince of Wales* and the *Repulse*.

It was completely incredible that the two warships should be left naked to attack from the skies. Interception of our level and torpedo bombers by British fighter aircraft might have seriously disrupted our attack and perhaps permitted the two warships to escape destruction.

The battle of Malaya illustrated in the most forcible manner that a surface fleet without fighter protection was helpless under enemy air attack. The battleship, long the ruler of the seas, had been toppled from its dominant position and was now just another warship to be destroyed by aerial assault.

CHAPTER 10

The Wake Island Operation

ON THE DAY FOLLOWING the sinking of the *Prince of Wales* and the *Repulse* one hundred miles from Singapore, our Navy was subjected to its only defeat in the opening months of the war. The dramatic victory of air power over sea power as demonstrated in the Malaya sea battle was still being jubilantly received in Japan when the invasion force which had attacked tiny Wake Island was soundly thrashed by small defending American forces and forced to flee for safety.

Considering the power accumulated for th invasion of Wake Island, and the meager forces of the defenders, it was one of the most humiliating defeats our Navy had ever suffered.

At the time of this operation, our Navy was hard-pressed for the services of every available aircraft carrier, and none could be spared for the invasion of Wake Island on December 11. The Navy did not have fighter aircraft capable of reaching the island from the nearest Japanese base on Kwajalein, six hundred nautical miles distant in the Marshall Islands.

The offensive action against the American garrison on Wake Island consisted of repeated bombing with some thirty attack bombers during the three days of December 8 to 10.

On December 11 the invasion forces moved in to take the island. Rear Admiral Sadamichi Kajioka, Commander of the 6th Destroyer Squadron, led the invading forces. At his disposal was the Wake Invasion Force composed of the light cruiser *Yubari* with six destroyers and accompanying vessels, and the light cruisers *Tenryu* and *Tatsuta*, commanded by Rear Admiral Kuninori Marumo.

The enemy guns on Wake Island resisted this attempted invasion so violently that the cruiser *Yubari* was damaged and the destroyer *Hayate* sunk, compelling the attack force to withdraw beyond range of the enemy defenses.

Also opposing the invasion force were about four Grumman F4F Wildcat fighters of the United States Marine Corps. Our fleet was at the mercy of these few fighter airplanes, which made consistent machine-gun and bombing attacks upon our ships. Their persistent strafing and bombing caused considerable damage to the light cruisers *Tenryu* and *Tatsuta*, and sank our destroyer *Kisaragi*. The destroyer sinking resulted indirectly from bombing by the little American fighters, a bomb from which exploded amidst depth charges stored on deck, causing a greater explosion which tore the ship apart.

The Wildcats were among the few American fighters most active in the early days of the war. Their pilots were indeed gallant men.

His confidence in the invasion shaken by the fierce resistance of the enemy shore guns and the elusive Grumman fighter planes, Rear Admiral Kajioka withdrew his fleet to Kwajalein in the Marshall Islands, where he could reorganize his forces for another assault upon the enemy. Fully cognizant of the gravity of the situation, Admiral Isoroku Yamamoto, Commander in Chief of the Combined Fleet, ordered Admiral Chuichi Nagumo to assist Admiral Kajioka in the Wake Island invasion. Admiral Nagumo was at this time returning from his devastating attack upon Pearl Harbor.

On December 15 Rear Admiral Tamon Yamaguchi's 2nd Carrier Division, with the aircraft carriers *Soryu* and *Hiryu*, escorted by four destroyers, was ordered to proceed immediately to the area north of Wake Island. Accompanying the carrier force was Rear Admiral Hiroaki Abe's 8th Cruiser Division, with the heavy cruisers *Tone* and *Chikuma*.

Approximately five days were required for the aircraft carriers, cruisers, and destroyers to assemble off Wake Island for the second invasion attempt. In the interim, our landbased attack bombers pounded the island constantly, but could do little to stop the harassing attacks of the defending Grumman fighters.

By December 21 Yamaguchi's 2nd Carrier Division was approximately two hundred nautical miles northwest of Wake Island. Yamaguchi dispatched eighteen Type 99 dive bombers (Vals), escorted by eighteen Zero fighters, to attack the island. Heavy clouds prevented the Zero fighters from engaging in combat with the enemy Wildcats.

The following day eighteen Type 97 bombers (Kates), escorted by eighteen Zeros, again bombed Wake Island. As the Zero fighters, under the command of Lieutenant Masaharu Suganami, could not see any enemy fighters in the air, they dropped down to strafe enemy ground positions. Their strafing runs were timed to hit the island simultaneously with the attack of the bombers.

As the fighters swept low over the island, Lieutenant Heijiro Abe's bomber group was suddenly attacked by a single Grumman fighter. The enemy pilot had skillfully eluded our Zeros by remaining hidden in nearby clouds, diving in to attack the bombers as the Zeros made their strafing runs.

Before the Zeros could reach the scene, two bombers had been shot down. The Grumman was quickly destroyed by the Zeros; no further flights were made by the defending enemy planes.

Once we had achieved command of the air over the island, the invasion became the responsibility of the surface force plus covering aircraft. The powerful enemy shore guns which had been so effective against the first invasion fleet could not manifest their full strength with our bombers and fighters waiting to attack the moment their positions were revealed.

With the aid of constant dive bombing by the planes of the carriers *Soryu* and *Hiryu*, our marines moved in to take the island on December 23. They were most anxious to vindicate themselves for the disgraceful failure of their first attempt, and succeeded in capturing the island on this date.

According to American military reports made available after the war, on December 21 Rear Admiral Fletcher's aircraft carrier *Saratoga* was about six hundred nautical miles northeast of Wake Island. The *Saratoga* was racing to aid the beleaguered American garrison. Had Rear Admiral Yamaguchi's 2nd Carrier Division not been hastily dispatched to Wake Island, or had the order to assist Rear Admiral Kajioka been delayed even a few days, the second landing operation might also have been shattered by the American aircraft carrier force.

Our humiliating defeat during the initial landing operation (and this was the only such defeat early in the war) and the valuable lessons obtained at such high price appeared to have been quickly forgotten. Japan was much too jubilant at the news of victory which rolled in from all corners of the Pacific to heed the bitter lesson of Wake Island.

In contrast to our failure fully to assimilate the lesson of this battle and that of the Malaya sea battle into our military organization, the United States frankly accepted the lessons of defeat in the early days of the war. Realizing that the war in the Pacific would be decided not on the ground or on the sea, but in the air, the United States mobilized all its resources and gave the highest priority to the mass production of military aircraft and the expansion of its air forces.

CHAPTER II

The Indian Ocean Operation

WITH THE EXCEPTION OF Rear Admiral Yamaguchi's 2nd Carrier Division, which joined the Wake Island Operation, all units of the victorious Nagumo Force on December 23 returned from Pearl Harbor to Hiroshima Bay, where Admiral Yamamoto awaited the fleet.

Refueled and re-equipped, the task force under Vice-Admiral Nagumo's command, with the aircraft carriers *Akagi, Kaga, Shokaku*, and *Zuikaku*, left Hiroshima Bay on January 5, 1942, for the main battle areas of the south Pacific. In late January our Army and Navy landing forces invaded Rabaul (New Britain) and Kavieng (New Ireland). Nagumo Task Force planes assisted the assault operations by raiding Rabaul, Kavieng, Lae, and Salamaua, the latter two objectives on the northeast coast of New Guinea, and quickly eliminated enemy air resistance.

In mid-February, with the invasion operations successfully concluded, Admiral Nagumo ordered Admiral Hara back to Japan with the 5th Carrier Division's *Shokaku* and *Zuikaku*. These he replaced with the *Soryu* and *Horyu* of the 2nd Carrier Division, commanded by Rear Admiral Yamaguchi, thus maintaining his original strength of four large aircraft carriers.

On February 15 the reformed Nagumo Force left Palau Island and worked its way southward through the Dutch East Indies islands, moving toward Port Darwin, the powerful enemy stronghold on Australia's northwest coast. On the nineteenth, Commander Fuchida led a mass formation of 190 planes against the enemy bastion, during which his fighters wiped out an opposing force of eight enemy fighter planes. We wrecked or set aflame an additional fifteen planes on the ground. Our bombers sank two destroyers and eight other vessels, some seven smaller ships received bomb hits or near misses, and low-level ground attacks set three aircraft hangers aflame.

The Port Darwin attack revealed to our pilots that they had little to fear in the way of enemy fighter-plane opposition. The Zero clearly outflew all of the enemy fighters encountered over Australia and, despite our advantage in numbers during this initial attack, our pilots felt no qualms about future engagements. Its mission accomplished in its first assault, the Nagumo Force swung about and anchored within Staring Bay, on the southeast coast of Celebes Island.

Simultaneously with the Port Darwin raid, our Navy land-based air forces under Vice-Admiral Tsukahara, operating from newly occupied fields in southern Borneo, repeatedly blasted enemy targets in the Java Sea area. On February 27 Tsukahara's reconnaissance planes sighted the United States seaplane tender *Langley* on the open sea south of Java Island. Immediately Tsukahara dispatched six Zero fighters and nine Type 96 Nell bombers against the American ship, which they caught approximately seventy-five nautical miles south of Java's Tjilatjap Port. The Nells turned in an outstanding performance for level bombers, hitting the enemy vessel directly with five bombs and scoring several near misses. Shattered and apparently without power, the *Langley* soon drifted helplessly. Later the crippled and abandoned hulk went under from torpedoes fired by an escorting American destroyer.

Our intelligence reported that the *Langley* had entered the Java Sea to assist the beleaguered Dutch East Indies forces, especially those on Java Island, by ferrying thirty-two Curtiss P-40 Tomahawk fighter planes and their pilots from Australia. We could only conclude that the Americans risked the *Langley* in an area known to be under constant surveillance by our planes because the Dutch need for fighters was so desperate and because the Allies lacked a fighter plane capable of flying nonstop between Australia and Java.

Again we took satisfaction from the excellent long-range characteristics of the Zero fighter. The strategic significance of the Zero's ability to fly long distances was clearly demonstrated by this incident. Because of the Zero's long range, our Navy "gained" at the war's outset three aircraft carriers which were relieved of their original Philippines attack assignment; conversely, the United States Navy lost its seaplane tender *Langley* simply because of the inferior performance of the early-1942 American fighter planes.

The following day, February 28, we capped the destruction of the American ship with another severe blow at the enemy's dwindling sea power. Our land-based attack bombers caught the British cruiser *Exeter*, damaged on the twenty-seventh in a running sea battle, and sent it to the bottom. Also destroyed in the bombing attack were the British destroyer *Encounter* and the American destroyer *Pope.*

Early in March the Nagumo Force left Staring Bay and steamed for the open sea south of Java Island. On March 5 its planes raided Tjilatjap, catching a large number of enemy vessels. Our planes swarmed over the assembled enemy ships, sinking two American destroyers and many other small vessels. This action literally cut off the escape route of the Allied forces then in Java which, pressed by our advancing troops, now stood on the edge of total collapse. Without further targets to occupy it in southern Java waters, the Nagumo Force returned to Staring Bay.

Vice-Admiral Nagumo now increased his aircraft carrier strength. He dispatched the *Kaga* to Japan for repairs and supplies, and added to his force the 5th Carrier Division under Rear Admiral Hara, bringing his strength to five carriers: the *Akagi, Soryu, Hiryu, Shokaku,* and *Zuikaku.*

On March 26 the Nagumo Force left Staring Bay and steamed at full speed for the Bay of Bengal, where our intelligence reported powerful units of the British fleet. Vice-Admiral Nagumo fully appreciated the tremendous enemy strength which would face him in his attempt to destroy British sea power, for the English had steadily reinforced their original fleet units of two aircraft carriers, two battleships, three heavy cruisers, and several light cruisers and destroyers. The Indian Ocean was fast becoming a "British lake," and Nagumo's orders were to smash this enemy strength. His intelligence reported to Nagumo that he might also face more than three hundred British warplanes, then based on Ceylon Island and on fields along the Bay of Bengal.

On the evening of April 4 a British flying-boat patrol sighted the Nagumo Force sailing under full steam for Colombo on Ceylon, hoping to catch unawares the British warships. It was only twenty-four hours before the first scheduled raid against Colombo. Zero fighters hastily launched from the carriers destroyed the enemy plane, but we feared the plane might have reported by radio its discovery of our fleet. This made it imperative that the initial Colombo attack be a maximum-strength aerial assault.

The following morning our carriers launched their planes: thirty-six Zeros, thirty-six Type 99 Val dive bombers, and fifty-three Type 97 Kate attack bombers. We discovered all too quickly that the British patrol bomber *had* managed to get out a sighting report on our fleet, for a swarm of enemy fighter planes plunged from the sky against our air formations. Again the inferior performance of the Allied fighter airplanes and the superior skill of our pilots paid handsome dividends. The ensuing air battle between the approximately sixty enemy planes and our Zero fighters resulted in the destruction of almost all the enemy aircraft, which the Zeros prevented from disrupting the bomber formations. Even as the fighter planes swirled over the ocean, bombs hurtled down toward the British port. We sank one British destroyer, one large merchant ship and ten smaller vessels, and heavily damaged land installations.

Even as the Colombo raid continued, a radio message from one of his reconnaissance planes to the southwest was handed to Admiral Nagumo. The message read: *"Two enemy destroyers sighted. Heading south-southwest. Speed twenty-five knots."* The enemy ships were placed at approximately three hundred nautical miles south-southwest of the air battles raging over Colombo. As there were no longer any worthwhile targets in the blasted British port, Nagumo immediately launched every available dive bomber on his carriers, which had been held in readiness for a possible second attack against Colombo.

Destruction of the destroyers would complement the Colombo attack.

Led by Lieutenant Commander Takashige Egusa, Air Group Commander of the *Soryu*, the eighty Type 99 Val dive bombers began their hunt for the two destroyers. Even as the planes raced toward the enemy ships, Admiral Nagumo received a corrected message. The enemy vessels were not destroyers as originally reported, but actually cruisers.

On the flagship Nagumo's staff officers waited for word from the dive-bomber force. Finally the first report from Lieutenant Commander Egusa was handed to the admiral.

"Sighted enemy vessels."

"Get ready to go in."

"Air Group, 1st Cardiv, take the first ship; Air Group, 2nd Cardiv, take the second ship."

Several minutes passed without further messages. Then:

"Ship Number One has stopped. Dead in water. Listing heavily."

"Ship Number Two is aflame."

"Ship Number One has sunk."

"Ship Number Two has sunk."

The entire attack involved only nineteen minutes, from 1:40 to 1:59 P.M. (Tokyo Time). Reconnaissance photographs of the two ships under attack identified them as the British cruisers *Cornwall* and *Dorsetshire*.

Commander Egusa's dive-bomber force established an all-time record in bombing accuracy in the destruction of the two cruisers. Perhaps the bombing conditions were perfect; whatever the reason, every bomb literally either struck the enemy ships or scored a near miss. So thick were the explosions from the rain of bombs that many plane crews could not determine whether they had actually released their missiles. Only after all our planes had assembled in formation and the pilots could visually check the racks of other planes could we tell whether or not several planes were still armed.

Following the Colombo attack and the sinking of the two cruisers, the Nagumo Force regrouped and moved eastward, planning to attack Trincomalee on Ceylon on April 9. Again, we encountered the far-searching British patrol bombers; on April 8 a flying boat sighted our fleet and reported its finding to enemy headquarters. Admiral Nagumo again anticipated heavy fighter-plane opposition, and ordered another maximum-strength assault to be flown.

Early on April 9 125 bombers and fighters thundered against Trincomalee. The enemy obviously expected our attack, for the harbor was empty of major shipping and "a large number" of fighter planes met our aerial formations head on. Our post attack tabulations indicated that the Zeros shot down fifty-six enemy fighters, including ten Hawker Hurricanes. (Postwar investigation revealed that the British lost nine out of eleven Hurricane fighters this day.) Our bombers sank one merchant vessel, damaged several other ships, and set aflame harbor installations.

For the first time since the opening day of the war, enemy bombers attacked the Nagumo Force's aircraft carriers. Even as our formations bombed Trincomalee, nine British Blenheims made a daring assault against our warships. None of the twin-engined bombers succeeded in their attack; Zeros destroyed the entire enemy force.

We were to be still further elated by the events of the day. Admiral Nagumo could not believe that Trincomalee had not harbored major British warships; these same vessels, he reasoned, upon receipt of yesterday's patrol bomber report had fled Trincomalee for the greater safety of the open sea. Simultaneously with the raid against the enemy harbor, our reconnaissance planes fanned out in a wide search for the ships which the admiral was convinced were in the area. His efforts did not go unrewarded, for the flagship deck soon received the electrifying news that a reconnaissance plane had sighted the British aircraft carrier *Hermes*, accompanied by a single destroyer (later identified as the *Vampire*), close to Trincomalee.

Again Nagumo launched his eighty Type 99 dive bombers under the command of Lieutenant Commander Egusa. Led to the long-sought British carrier, the dive bombers plummeted from the sky in devastatingly accurate attacks. Hit after hit wracked the two enemy warships, and more often than not flames and smoke rather than the slender plumes of near misses billowed upward. Our planes were literally unopposed and swarmed furiously over the warships. Egusa's men once again achieved an incredible percentage of direct bomb hits; so unusual was this accuracy, unparalleled even in future operations, that to calculate the number of hits we had to count the misses and subtract these from the total number of bombs released!

Within ten minutes of the first bomb drop, the *Hermes* was a gutted, flaming hull, its deck ripped to splinters, its sides shattered by bomb explosions. Five minutes later, only fifteen minutes after the first dive bomber dropped from the sky, the *Hermes* slipped beneath the waves. The *Vampire* was already gone, literally torn into great pieces of wreckage. With their remaining bombs, Egusa's men sighted and sank an enemy merchant ship and two smaller vessels.

Our planes were establishing new records and changing the accepted concept of sea-air warfare. At Pearl Harbor a limited number of fighters and bombers from this same fleet broke the back of American battleship power; off Malaya for the first time in history our planes sank enemy battleships without the aid of surface vessels; and, today, for the first time, aircraft without the support of surface vessels had sent a carrier to the bottom.

Lieutenant Commander Egusa was my (Okumiya's) classmate both at Etajima (the Japanese Annapolis), and in the Navy Flying School at Kasumigaura. We both were Navy senior dive-bomber pilots. Shortly after the Indian Ocean Operation, in which Egusa figured so prominently, we were able to have a reunion in Japan. At the time, as an air staff officer of the 2nd Carrier Task Force, I was preparing for the Midway and the Aleutian Operations; I asked my old friend how his planes had sunk the British warships.

Egusa looked at me and shrugged. "It was much simpler than bombing the *Settsu*. That's all."

The *Settsu!* Simpler than bombing Japan's old target battleship!

With the Indian Ocean Operation concluded with these brilliant victories, the activity of the famed Nagumo Force, which had swept aside all enemy opposition from Pearl Harbor to Ceylon, came to its end. Our gains were consolidated, and now there were new tasks for the powerful naval and air units. We who knew intimately the actions of these battles realized only too well that the greatest single factor contributing to our victory was the superior performance of the Zero fighter airplane. Except in the battle in which our torpedo and level bombers destroyed the *Prince of Wales* and the *Repulse*, our bombers were able to cause such havoc only because the Zero had won control of the air. Perhaps only a few of us were cognizant of the fact, but the Zero had become the symbol not only of our land- and sea-based air power but of the entire Japanese military force.

CHAPTER 12

The Coral Sea Battle

PRIOR TO THE OUTBREAK of hostilities between Japan and the United States, the majority of the Navy's high-ranking officers foresaw defeat for our surface vessels in a showdown struggle against America's powerful array of warships. Because our naval carrier- and land-based air forces so aggressively attacked and pursued the enemy, however, we gained a tremendous, if unexpected, margin of victory. As early as the first week of April of 1942, an incredible four short months after the explosive outbreak of war, the Navy completed its prearranged First Phase Operations. We roamed the greater part of the Pacific and the Indian oceans, securely entrenched in our conquests, and our naval air and surface forces kept the enemy at a respectable distance.

To the disappointment of many naval officers (and to the relief of others), our carrier force had failed to engage the American aircraft carriers in combat since the opening of hostilities. Once they saw the outstanding superiority of the Zero fighter sweep aside all enemy opposition, the majority of our officers looked forward to the first carrier-*vs.*-carrier engagement. By April of 1942 we had caught and destroyed only the U.S. seaplane tender *Langley* south of Tjilatjap, Java, and the British aircraft carrier *Hermes* off Trincomalee of Ceylon Island.

Following the successful Indian Ocean Operation, we planned an offensive campaign against the Solomon Islands and the southeastern part of New Guinea. Our major goal in this offensive was the capture of Port Moresby on the latter island, which was the only air base from which enemy planes continued to strike back at our still-advancing forces. By capturing this vital enemy air-field, we would eliminate the air threat to Rabaul and Kavieng. Parallel to this operation, other surface forces would support an Army invasion against Tulagi in the southern Solomons. We needed Tulagi as a base of opera-tions from which we could subsequently strike out at New Caledonia and Fiji.

Intelligence reported that it was very likely that an American surface force, centering about at least one air-craft carrier, was at that time in the Coral Sea area, and that this fleet could seriously threaten the projected Solomons and New Guinea actions. Admiral Yamamoto directed the 5th Carrier Division of the Nagumo Force, then returning to Japan after the Indian Ocean Operation, to participate in the new campaign. Under command of Rear Admiral Chuichi Hara, the 5th Carrier Division embraced the two powerful, large-type aircraft carriers *Shokaku* and *Zuikaku*.

The impending attack received the code name "MO" Operation. Vice-Admiral Shigeyoshi Inoue, then Comman-der in Chief of the Fourth Fleet in the Central Pacific, was transferred and assigned to head the MO attack. Inoue had under his command the imposing force of two large carriers, one small carrier, one seaplane tender, six heavy cruisers, four light cruisers, and other vessels, which totaled seventy ships. Supporting his carrier-based aviation were 120 land-based bombers and fighters. Inoue broke up his forces into three groups; the invasion force, the carrier task force, and his land-based air units.

By May 3 Tulagi was in our hands. With the island secured by our ground forces, the fleet moved out to its attack positions. Vice-Admiral Inoue, over-all commander of the MO Operation, remained at Rabaul aboard his flagship, the light cruiser *Kashima*. Rear Admiral Aritomo Goto assigned the four heavy cruisers *Aoba, Kako, Furutaka,* and *Kinugasa* to Shortland Anchorage in the central Solomons; these vessels remained under his direct command. He dispatched to Rabaul the light aircraft carrier *Shoho* with sixteen Zero fighters, twelve Type 97 Kate attack bombers, and other planes. Eleven transports anchored within Rabaul Harbor to take on the Port Moresby Army Invasion Force; small warships cruised nearby as escorts. And at Deboyne, Admiral Goto had the seaplane tender *Kamikawa-Maru* with four Type-Zero reconnaissance seaplanes, and eight Type-Zero observation planes.

Vice Admiral Takeo Takagi, the 5th Cruiser Division commander, became commander of the Carrier Task Force. Takagi retained under his direct orders the 5th Cruiser Division's heavy cruisers *Myoko* and *Haguro*, and assigned to Rear Admiral Chuichi Hara the command of the 5th Carrier Division's *Shokaku* and *Zuikaku*. Each of the two carriers had twenty-one Zero fighters, twenty-one Type 99 Val dive bombers, and twenty-one Type 97 Kate attack bombers. Six destroyers and other auxiliary vessels supported the carrier force.

With the Indian Ocean campaign completed by mid-

April, Hara steamed at full speed for the Solomon Islands, arriving in the eastern seas on May 5.

Under the direction of Rear Admiral Sadayoshi Yamada, commander of the 25th Air Flotilla, the supporting land-based air force, consisting of sixty Zero fighters, forty-eight Type 96 twin-engined Nell bombers, sixteen Type 97 Mavis flying boats, and ten small-type seaplanes, assembled at their various bases. The majority of the land-based planes flew into Rabaul and its supporting installation at Lae. Approximately half the flying boats and seaplanes operated from Rabaul Harbor, the remainder from Tulagi and Shortland.

Even as we prepared feverishly for the Shortland thrusts of our combined land-sea-air forces, the day following the capture of Tulagi, May 4, eighty enemy bombers and fighters attacked our fleet units in morning and afternoon waves. There was a strong possibility that the enemy realized our intentions, for his attack was unusually fierce and damaging. We lost the destroyer *Kikuzuki* and several planes to the enemy bombers.

For the first time, however, we confirmed the existence in the vicinity of American aircraft carriers. It appeared as if the time were drawing near for the first clash between American and Japanese carriers.

On the same day, the transport convoy for the Port Moresby invasion left Rabaul. Twenty-four hours later, Admiral Goto's warships slipped out of Shortland. The fleet units would rendezvous at sea and assemble their forces for the final assault against Moresby. In concert with this operation, Admiral Takagi's carrier task force skirted the southern end of the Solomon Islands, and at noon of the fifth steamed to the west of the island group. Moving at full speed, the carriers raced to cover the southern flank of Goto's invasion forces.

At 0810 hours on the morning of May 6, a Mavis flying boat of the Yokohama Air Corps sighted an enemy surface force six hundred miles south of Tulagi. The plane's crew reported at least one aircraft carrier supported by nine other vessels.

Several hours later a single enemy four-engined B-17 bomber attacked Admiral Goto's invasion fleet. We presumed that the enemy bomber flew from Port Moresby, and we feared that the troop-laden transports might soon be attacked by enemy bombers. To protect his vulnerable transports, Admiral Inoue ordered the troopships to change course and proceed due north, in the hope that this sudden shift in course would conceal the fleet from the enemy reconnaissance planes he knew would be scouring the ocean. Expecting that he would most likely engage the enemy on the following day, Takagi refueled his ships at sea on the evening of May 6.

Early on the morning of May 7 we launched an intensive search for the enemy carriers and other surface vessels. Our reconnaissance planes flew from Rabaul, Shortland, and Tulagi; other planes from the *Kamikawa-Maru* at Deboyne, the three carriers, and the heavy cruisers took to the air to participate in the search.

We did not have long to wait. At 0532 hours a Kate bomber sighted a single enemy carrier and three destroyers two hundred miles south of the *Shokaku*. Admiral Takagi ordered Admiral Hara immediately to dispatch every available airplane from his two carriers in an assault against the enemy fleet unit. At 0610 hours Lieutenant Commander Kakuichi Takahashi left the carriers with an air attack group of eighteen Zero fighters, thirty-six Type 99 Val dive bombers, and twenty-four Type 97 Kate torpedo bombers.

Thirty minutes later, at 0640, with Takahashi's bombers and fighters racing toward the enemy ships, one of the

heavy cruiser *Kinugasa*'s Type-Zero reconnaissance seaplanes of Admiral Goto's fleet sighted another enemy
group. A single large carrier and ten other vessels steamed
only two hundred miles south of the *Kinugasa*, or two
hundred and eighty miles northwest of Admiral Takagi's
position.

Unfortunately, the rich prize of a second American carrier could not be attacked. With only a minimum force of
planes to protect his own two carriers, the admiral was
forced to wait for the return of Takahashi's sixty bombers
and eighteen fighter planes. He could only hope that the
first carrier under attack would be destroyed and that, after
hasty refueling and rearming, the group could take off
again to raid the second enemy carrier.

The Fates decreed otherwise. At 0935 Commander
Takahashi reached the position of the enemy fleet unit, as
it had been reported by the Kate. The carrier and its three
escorting destroyers could not be seen. The formation
spread out and searched the ocean surface in vain. Convinced finally that no carrier was in the area, Takahashi
ordered his planes to bomb and torpedo a large tanker and
a destroyer discovered in the area. The two enemy ships
quickly went down beneath the hail of bombs and torpedoes. We later identified the tanker, originally mistaken for
the aircraft carrier, as the *Neosho*, and the destroyer escort
as the *Sims*.

Even as Takahashi's planes returned to the *Shokaku* and
the *Zuikaku*, lookouts aboard Admiral Goto's carrier *Shoho*
excitedly reported many approaching American bombers
and fighters. An estimated ninety-five enemy bombers and
fighters plunged from the sky in a devastating raid against
the hapless *Shoho*. With most of its Zeros airborne over the
transport convoy, and with only a few remaining fighters
to intercept the large enemy force, the carrier was virtually

helpless. Heavy bombs and torpedoes split the vessel, and the *Shoho* soon went down. She was the first Japanese carrier to be lost in the war.

In view of the great number of enemy carrier-based aircraft which had destroyed the *Shoho*, Admiral Takagi reasoned that he faced at least two large enemy aircraft carriers. As soon as his first attack force had returned from their "wasted" mission to the south, mechanics refueled the planes and loaded bombs and torpedoes to prepare for an immediate raid against the American force.

Takagi faced a number of difficult obstacles, for the enemy fleet was believed to lie at least three hundred and fifty miles west of his own position, beyond the normal attack radius of his carrier planes. Further, even if he launched his planes at once, the waning afternoon meant that on their return his planes would reach their carriers after dark. The single-seat Zeros, unequipped for night flying, had to be dropped from the attack group.

At 1430 hours, a second attack group of twelve dive bombers and fifteen torpedo bombers led by Lieutenant Commander Takahashi took off to attack the enemy ship. Takagi planned to send his planes in at twilight, when the shadowy light would hamper the enemy antiaircraft gunners. The bombers ran into heavy intermittent rain squalls and, even as they fought their way through between the towering cloud formations, the sun slipped below the horizon. It was impossible to locate the enemy vessels under these conditions, and reluctantly the commander gave up the search to return to his own carriers.

Surprisingly, the battle was not yet over. Takahashi's men were exhausted, having been in the air on two missions since early morning. On the flight back to their home fleet, Takahashi's pilots failed to sight an enemy aircraft carrier passing directly beneath their planes. The enemy however, had noticed the approach of our bombers and as Takahashi's force neared the enemy carrier it was attacked suddenly by Grumman F4F Wildcat fighter planes.

The Val dive bombers, unusually maneuverable for their size, turned sharply to meet the diving Wildcats. The lumbering Kate torpedo bombers were easy targets for the enemy guns, and in the brief but sharply fought battle the Grummans shot down eight of the fifteen torpedo bombers, and also destroyed one Val dive bomber. Our pilots later reported the destruction of several enemy fighters, but this could not be confirmed.

Our planes fled from the hornet's nest into which they had flown, but soon fell victim to the delusions and "mirages" brought on by exhaustion. Several times the pilots, despairing of their position over the sea, "sighted" a friendly aircraft carrier. Finally a carrier was sighted, and the remaining eighteen bombers switched on their signal and blinker lights as they swung into their approach and landing pattern.

As the lead plane, with its flaps down and speed lowered, drifted toward the carrier deck to land, the pilot discovered the great ship ahead was an American carrier! Apparently the Americans also had erred in identification, for even as the bomber dropped near the carrier deck not a single enemy gun fired. The Japanese pilot frantically opened his throttle and at full speed swung away from the vessel, followed by his astonished men.

Our crewmen were disgusted. They had flown for grueling hours over the sea, bucked thunder squalls and finally, had lost all trace of their positions relative to their own carriers. When finally they did sight the coveted American warship, cruising unsuspecting beneath eighteen bombers, they were without bombs or torpedoes—having previously jettisoned them into the sea!

On this day occurred what is clearly the greatest confusion of the entire Pacific War. Neither before this evening, nor at any time following, did such an incredible series of events take place. Not only were our pilots completely bewildered, but the combination of exhaustion and confusion caused the loss of several planes in addition to the nine shot down by the carrier-based Grummans. This loss reduced the effective striking strength of our carrier force and subsequently resulted in our sustaining crippling blows from enemy attacks.

On the same day, May 7, another large-scale air battle was fought with unusual pilot confusion. At 0820 hours a *Kamikawa-Maru* reconnaissance plane sighted an enemy fleet of two battleships, one heavy cruiser, and four destroyers, at 150 miles, bearing 200 degrees from tiny Deboyne Island. Admiral Yamada, then at Rabaul, launched thirty-three Type 96 Nell bombers, with an escort of eleven Zero fighters, to attack the enemy fleet. Twenty of the twin-engined bombers carried torpedoes, the remainder, bombs.

Approximately five hundred miles out of Rabaul, at 1230 hours our planes sighted and attacked the enemy, now reported as consisting of two battleships, two cruisers, and two destroyers. Our pilots reported sinking the *California*-type battleship, causing serious damage to one British *Warspite*-type battleship, and leaving one cruiser flaming in the water. We lost four bombers.

When I (Okumiya) investigated this battle after the war with members of the United States Strategic Bombing Survey, I learned that the enemy fleet was commanded by Rear Admiral J. G. Crace, R.N., and consisted of the Australian heavy cruisers *Australia* and *Hobert*, the American heavy cruiser *Chicago*, and two destroyers, but no battleships. Further, I learned that not a single Japanese torpedo or bomb had struck any of the ships! This was actually the first instance in which our Navy pilots reported battle damages inflicted upon enemy vessels beyond those actually achieved; in this case, the discrepancy was so great as to be ridiculous. There were several reasons for this reporting episode. The targets were highly evasive cruisers and destroyers, which often confused the crews of the attacking bombers. Further, the pilots and crews participating in this particular attack lacked combat experience, and their efficiency ranged far below that of the crews which sank the *Prince of Wales*, the *Repulse*, and the *Langley*.

The air units which attacked Admiral Crace's fleet were manned by hastily recruited replacements. On February 20, the original unit lost fifteen out of seventeen twin-engined Nell bombers, all with veteran crews, in an attack against the enemy carrier *Lexington* which at the time was raiding Rabaul. Replacements had come in slowly, the men lacked training, and crew coordination was greatly in need of improvement.

This occasion provided an ominous warning. It was the first action which proved that our reserve supply of fully trained pilots was inadequate, and that we would be faced again with this problem in the future.

Thus the sea-air battle of May 7 came to an end. It was a poor day for our fleet; American bombers had destroyed the *Shoho* in our first aircraft-carrier loss of the war, and we had failed to inflict retaliation upon the enemy carriers. To the naval personnel involved, the destruction of the *Shoho* and the subsequent inability of our planes to attack the American carriers involved great loss of pride. Aboard the *Shokaku* and the *Zuikaku*, Admiral Hara's men grimly attended to their bombers and fighters, preparing them for combat on the following day. To "save face," they must by any means destroy the American carriers.

Before the sun broke over the horizon on the early morning of May 8, reconnaissance planes thundered off the decks of both the *Shokaku* and the *Zuikaku*. The men still smarted from the events of the previous day; this new and uncomfortable feeling could be erased only by victory against the Americans. At 0715 hours Lieutenant Commander Takahashi led into the air eighteen fighters, thirty-three dive bombers, and eighteen torpedo bombers, which fanned out in a wide search pattern to seek the American fleet.

Less than ten minutes after Takahashi's departure, the carrier bridge received the news that one of its reconnaissance planes dispatched earlier that morning had sighted the enemy fleet at a position about two hundred miles due south of the *Shokaku*. As anticipated, there were at least two aircraft carriers supported by ten other ships. The message was relayed to Takahashi, and the sixty-nine planes veered onto their new course.

A Type 97 Kate torpedo bomber first discovered the enemy carriers, and Flight Warrant Officer Kenzo Kanno, using to advantage nearby cloud formations, shadowed the American fleet, reporting by radio to the *Shokaku* the details of the warships. Finally, his fuel rapidly dwindling, Kanno turned for his own carrier. He had full confidence in the accuracy of his reporting, as well as his up-to-the-minute details of the exact positions of the enemy fleet.

Barely out of sight of the unsuspecting enemy vessels behind him, Kanno suddenly noticed the Takahashi air group racing toward its target. Kanno realized intuitively that despite the accuracy of his position readings Takahashi's group could easily fail to sight the carriers on the vast ocean expanse. Without further consideration for his own safety, for to alter course now was to place himself beyond the "point of no return," Kanno swung his bomber into a sharp turn and eased the airplane alongside that of Takahashi's.

Every pilot in that sweeping formation knew precisely what Kanno and his two crew members were doing; he now lacked sufficient fuel to return to his own carrier, more than three hundred miles to the north. The pilots could see Kanno's big three-seat torpedo bomber, swinging about and nosing up to Takahashi's plane. But there was little to be said.

Shortly afterward the air group sighted the long-sought American fleet. The planes swung immediately into the attack. As reported subsequently by Takahashi's subordinate: "Starting at 0920 hours, we made determined torpedo and bomb attacks against one *Saratoga*-type and one *Yorktown*-type aircraft carrier. At least nine torpedoes and more than ten 550-pound bombs struck the former ship, while the latter was hit with three torpedoes and eight to ten 550-pound bombs. We damaged two other vessels."

Again our pilots had erred strongly in their evaluation of torpedo and bomb strikes, for post-war investigation revealed that in this battle the U.S.S. *Lexington* was hit with two torpedoes and two bombs, and that our planes scored several near misses. The other carrier, the U.S.S. *Yorktown*, received one bomb hit and two near misses.

We sustained heavy losses in the attack, for Lieutenant Commander Takahashi, Warrant Officer Kanno, and many other officers and crewmen died. We lost more than twenty-six bombers, or more than half of the entire bombing force.

Prior to this attack, while Takahashi's force flew toward the enemy carrier force, lookouts aboard the *Shokaku* and the *Zuikaku* sighted an approaching enemy carrier plane force. Soon they made out more than eighty planes. The *Zuikaku* was fortunate; her captain placed the big ship beneath a nearby rain squall, preventing the American planes from pressing their attack. The *Shokaku* received hits by three medium bombs. Although her deck was shattered, preventing the launching or landing of any planes, the *Shokaku* was still able to maneuver with little difficulty. The extensive repairs needed forced the big ship to retire from the scene of action.

Thus ended the first naval battle which was fought entirely by the air elements of the two opponents. In this initial carrier-vs.-carrier contest, our carrier forces and those of the enemy were approximately equal in strength.

In the two days of fighting our carriers lost thirty-two planes either shot down or missing, and twelve additional aircraft which made forced landings. Our losses mounted when the *Zuikaku*'s captain ordered several planes jettisoned overboard to clear the decks for emergency landings of the *Shokaku*'s aircraft, when that carrier's own decks became tangled wreckage. Immediately after the battle there remained on the *Zuikaku* as operational aircraft only twenty-four Zero fighters, nine Type 99 Val dive bombers, and six Type 97 Kate attack torpedo bombers. This number represented barely one fourth the original total of bombers aboard both carriers prior to the air battles.

These losses indicated clearly the high cost of all-out carrier warfare and for the first time enabled us to predict the outcome of future fleet engagements in which surface vessels, despite their number or power, would play merely auxiliary roles. Over separation distances of two hundred to three hundred miles between fleets, the cruisers and battleships could contribute to the battle only by employing their antiaircraft weapons to help defend their carriers against attacking enemy planes. In the two full days of the Coral Sea Battle, the approximate total of ninety-five vessels of both contestants, twenty-five American and seventy Japanese, did not exchange a single shot.

The Coral Sea episode also taught us to study closely the use of fighter planes in air-sea engagements. We discovered that, in a long-range conflict between aircraft carriers, qualitative superiority in fighter planes was not enough to stop a determined attack by enemy bombers and fighters. Quantity also was a requisite for successful defense and, even under the best possible conditions, an attack fiercely pressed home by the enemy would result in severe air losses to both sides.

Two weeks after the Coral Sea Battle, I (Okumiya) conferred with Lieutenant Commander Shigekazu Shimazaki, who as a *Zuikaku* group commander had participated in the entire battle. Shimazaki told me:

"Never in all my years in combat have I even imagined a battle like that! When we attacked the enemy carriers we ran into a virtual wall of antiaircraft fire; the carriers and their supporting ships blackened the sky with exploding shells and tracers. It seemed impossible that we could survive our bombing and torpedo runs through such incredible defenses. Our Zeros and enemy Wildcats spun, dove, and climbed in the midst of our formations. Burning and shattered planes of both sides plunged from the skies. Amidst this fantastic 'rainfall' of antiaircraft and spinning planes, I dove almost to the water's surface and sent my torpedo into the *Saratoga*-type carrier. I had to fly directly above the waves to escape the enemy shells and tracers. In fact, when I turned away from the carrier, I was so low that I almost struck the bow of the ship, for I was flying below the level of the flight deck. I could see the crewmen on the ship staring at my plane as it rushed by. I don't know that I could ever go through such horrible moments again."

This was the frank confession of a veteran air group commander who had engaged in combat with our naval air forces since the beginning of the Sino-Japanese Incident in 1937. Shimazaki was a brilliant and courageous group commander; in the Pearl Harbor attack he commanded the second wave of 170 planes, and subsequently played a major part in our carrier operations.

Following an evaluation of his pilots' combat reports and those of his reconnaissance planes, Rear Admiral Hara confirmed the sinking of the *Saratoga*-type carrier (the *Lexington*) during the night of May 8. In his official combat report (about the second carrier) he stated: "The *Yorktown*-type aircraft carrier received hits by more than eight bombs and more than three torpedoes, and was left burning. Listing heavily to port, she is believed to have sunk, although we have not as yet confirmed the destruction of the vessel."

(As related previously, the admiral's report greatly exaggerated damage to the *Yorktown*, which suffered only from one bomb strike and two near misses.)

Tactically, therefore, we considered the Coral Sea Battle as victorious for our forces. Future events proved this evaluation to be faulty for, as strategic moves would clearly reveal, the Coral Sea Battle proved a serious Japanese setback. Cognizant of the battle's implications, Vice-Admiral Inoue postponed indefinitely the Port Moresby invasion, and recalled his troopships. These, however, were localized events.

In Japan, Admiral Yamamoto expressed deep regret at the failure of his commanders to exercise the aggressiveness necessary to exploit the damage our planes had inflicted upon the American carriers. Our ships retired from the scene of battle, although they held in their hands the opportunity to insure the destruction of the enemy carrier forces in the Coral Sea.

One of the direct reasons for this failure, of course, was the fact that few planes remained aboard the surviving *Zuikaku*. At best this could be regarded only as a poor excuse, for reduction in numbers is hardly a deterrent to the true battle commander. The truth of the matter was that our senior naval commanders in the Coral Sea area lacked the fighting spirit necessary to engage the enemy. This failure to pursue a temporary advantage later proved to be of tremendous advantage to the Americans. A postbattle study of the Coral Sea engagement brought out the fact that neither Vice-Admiral Inoue nor Vice-Admiral Takagi had on their immediate staffs a single air officer with combat experience in carrier-based or land-based air operations. It was incredible to realize also that both admirals likewise lacked any experience in this type of combat!

For years the Japanese Navy had operated against enemy forces on the principle that, while it might be numerically inferior to its opponents, our Navy could overcome any combat obstacles through superior tactics and aggressive fighting spirit. In a single stroke the Coral Sea Battle destroyed the validity of this concept, making it abundantly clear that the greatest weakness of our carefully created naval air strength lay in the lack of senior commanders who could command our crack units. Leadership, indispensable for any combat success, existed in the Coral Sea Battle only in those commanders who actually attacked the enemy forces.

None of our surviving officers of the Coral Sea Battle could have foreseen the terrible strategic implications of their colossal blunder. The crippled *Yorktown* was permitted to escape when perhaps a single torpedo or only a few bombs could have insured that vessel's destruction. A month later, that same ship which we then permitted to survive became one of the strongest factors contributing to our Navy's shattering defeat in the Battle of Midway.

Every last officer and crewman lost in the attacks on the evening of May 7 was a skilled, irreplaceable veteran. Had these men and their planes not been lost in the debacle of May 7, they could have participated in the attack against the enemy carriers on May 8 and, quite possibly, could have crippled the *Yorktown* as our remaining planes had disabled the *Lexington*.

In retrospect, it is no exaggeration to state that those few Grumman Wildcats which were in the air on May 7 and which intercepted our planes on their return to their own carriers saved not only the *Yorktown* but also eventually many other American ships then in the Coral Sea.

CHAPTER 13

The Midway and Aleutians Operations:
The Turning Point of the War

THE RESULTS OF THE Coral Sea Battle forced Vice Admiral Inoue to postpone indefinitely the planned invasion of Port Moresby. This delay in operations in the southern Pacific, however, did not seriously affect the execution of the Midway and Aleutian Operations, which our General Staff had long before decided upon. Despite its less obvious overtones, Tokyo still regarded the Coral Sea Battle only as a minor setback, and merely the first such incident after four successive months of brilliant victories. The Navy's faith in its air arm, on which it had relied so heavily and successfully, was undiminished.

The record to date justified this confidence, since from the war's outset all the major blows inflicted upon an enemy staggering from repeated defeats were struck by this same naval air force. Indeed, not only had we swept clean the vast ocean areas in which our ships and planes operated, but we had achieved our goals at an unbelievably low cost in ships, planes, and men. There existed no reason to expect that these same forces which now ruled the Pacific and Indian oceans would do otherwise than continue their victorious engagements against the enemy.

At staff conferences held in early May aboard the *Yamato*, we studied the gains and losses of both our fleet and that of the enemy, from the opening of the war until the close of the Coral Sea Battle. On December 8, 1941, at Pearl Harbor, our carrier-based planes sank or disabled the United States battleships *Nevada, California, Arizona, West Virginia, Maryland,* and *Oklahoma,* and heavily damaged the battleships *Pennsylvania* and *Tennessee.* We sent to the bottom the old target ship *Utah,* the cruiser *Helena,* and two destroyers. Several other vessels were heavily damaged, and the enemy suffered heavy damage to shore installations and the loss of many planes.

On December 10, 1941, off Kuantan, our land-based bombers sank the British dreadnaughts *Repulse* and *Prince of Wales.*

On February 4, 1942, in the sea north of Java, our land-based bombers heavily damaged the American heavy cruiser *Houston* and the light cruiser *Marblehead.*

On the twenty-seventh of the same month, off Tjilatjap, Java, the seaplane tender *Langley* went to the bottom after an attack by land-based bombers. The following day our land-based bombers struck again, sinking the British heavy cruiser *Exeter.*

Off Colombo on April 5, carrier-based bombers sank the British heavy cruisers *Cornwall* and *Dorsetshire.* Four days later, off Trincomalee, carrier-based bombers destroyed the first enemy aircraft carrier, the British *Hermes.*

On May 8, in the Coral Sea Battle, carrier-based bombers sank the 33,000-ton American aircraft carrier *Lexington,* and heavily damaged the *Yorktown,* another American carrier.

In the first six months of the war, therefore, our naval aviation alone had sunk two aircraft carriers and seriously damaged a third, sent to the bottom one seaplane tender, either sunk or heavily damaged ten battleships, destroyed four and heavily damaged two cruisers, and sunk ten destroyers.

Conversely, our damages and losses from enemy air activities in warships the size of or larger than destroyers amounted only to three vessels sunk and one heavily damaged. On December 11, 1941, Grumman Wildcat fighter planes off Wake Island sank the destroyer *Kisaragi*. At Tulagi, on May 4, 1942, we lost the destroyer *Kikuzuki*. And on May 7, in the Coral Sea Battle, we lost the aircraft carrier *Shoho*. The following day the carrier *Shokaku* received heavy damage from American carrier planes.

With the exception of the single submarine attack on January 11, 1942, in which the 33,000-ton aircraft carrier *Saratoga* was hit by torpedoes, approximately two hundred and fifty nautical miles northeast of Johnston, the only damage inflicted to enemy vessels by our warships occurred in the period between late February and early March of 1942. All engagements took place in the Java Sea, where our warships sank the Netherlands' light cruisers *De Ruyter* and *Java*, the Australian light cruiser *Perth*, the American heavy cruiser *Houston*, and five destroyers of various countries.

On the other hand, not a single Japanese warship lost during this period to enemy action other than air attack went down before the guns of enemy ships, as this listing shows:

December 12, 1941:
Destroyer *Hayate* sunk off Wake Island by enemy shore guns.

December 18, 1941:

Destroyer *Shinonome* sunk by mine explosion off Miri, Borneo.

December 24, 1941:

Destroyer *Sagiri* sunk off Kuching, Borneo, by torpedo attack of Netherlands submarine.

February 8, 1942:

Destroyer *Natsushio* sunk off Makassar, Celebes, by torpedo attack of United States submarine.

May 3, 1942:

Seaplane tender *Mizuho* sunk off southern coast of Japan proper by torpedo attack of United States submarine.

May 11, 1942:

Mine layer *Okinoshima* sunk off Rabaul by torpedo attack of United States submarine.

Compared to the losses sustained by the Allied powers in the Pacific, therefore, we suffered very lightly, indeed. The tally of enemy and Japanese ships lost in the first six months of the war was a literal realization of the Navy's concept of "ideal combat conditions," to "wage a decisive sea battle only under air control." For the ten years prior to the Pacific War we had trained our airmen implicitly to believe that sea battles fought under our command of the air could result only in our victories. The initial phases of the Pacific War dramatically upheld this belief.

War, however, is a vast drama in which it is often impossible to predict the morrow through "logic" alone. The chain of events established by previous combat engagements may be altered completely in a few short hours. Despite exhaustive planning and preparation prior to any battle, only the gods know what course that battle will take. It appears that in any conflict in which great numbers of men and machines are pitted against one another, some force beyond that exercised by man is responsible for the final decision. While the course of the Pacific War for its first six months became a parade of brilliant Japanese victories, no sensible man could honestly believe that an abrupt change was not in store for our country.

In the immense arena of the Pacific War, Japan could realize a final victory only through rapid and powerful blows against the forces of the United States and Great Britain. To accomplish our aims with our limited industrial resources, we had to strike quickly, to throw off balance an enemy of great industrial might before that enemy could bring to bear upon us the full weight of its military strength. No Japanese military student possessing any basic knowledge of military logistics could fail to foresee ultimate defeat for our nation in a prolonged war.

We who were informed of the true status of the economic-industrial strength of America and England as compared to that of Japan knew that our nation could emerge victorious from this war not merely through military gains but more probably as the result of military-political-diplomatic actions. It was imperative that we attain and consolidate initial gains, for eventually we would meet in the far reaches of the Pacific an avalanche of Allied military power.

Those people cognizant of this situation expected the government, as it had done in the Sino-Japanese and the Russo-Japanese wars, soon to resort to diplomatic negotiations at a time most advantageous to Japan. To prolong the war was only to allow America's factories the time necessary to overwhelm completely our own military strength. International diplomacy as conducted from a perspective wider than merely that of the geographical boundaries of Pacific-Asiatic combat was the only means through which we could benefit from the Pacific War. Japan did not possess the military-industrial-economic strength necessary to conclude successfully a purely military struggle against the United States and Great Britain.

Unfortunately, the vital requirements for international diplomatic negotiations never were achieved. The military heirarchy disastrously decided to continue the war strictly on a military basis.

Once committed to total conflict, positive aggressive action is the only means by which to hasten the conclusion of a war. On the theory that only by continued strikes against the enemy could Japan either expand or securely maintain her victories gained in the war's initial six months, Admiral Isoroku Yamamoto, Commander in Chief of the Combined Fleet, planned to attack American forces at Midway Island and in the Aleutians chain in a single, concerted mass sweep. The "Midway and Aleutian Operations," as we designated the assault, would be undertaken early in June of 1942 as the first step of the Second Stage Operations.

The series of major actions which emerged from this widespread campaign brought disastrous results to our Navy; especially in the Battle of Midway, where our fleet suffered a devastating defeat. So severe were the consequences of this great fleet engagement that in a single stroke Japan's favorable position in Pacific Ocean air-sea combat was altered. The Battle of Midway was the pivotal point of the Pacific War. In a single day we lost four aircraft carriers, as well as their aircraft complement, and the irreplaceable combat-veteran crews. Our defeat stemmed directly from our Navy Air Force's loss in air superiority, both on a qualitative and a quantitative basis.

We had two specific objectives in mind for the Midway and Aleutian Operations. By invading and occupying Midway Island, we would extend greatly to the east our warship and bomber patrol lines, while the occupation of Kiska and Attu islands in the western end of the Aleutians island chain would prevent United States task forces in the far north from attacking the Japanese mainland.

These island occupations constituted the campaign's initial phase. The second was to draw out the remainder of the United States Pacific fleet, and to hasten the end of the war by destroying that fleet. The Americans could not allow our eastward and northward thrusts to go unopposed; their fleet would feel compelled to oppose our attacking forces with every last plane and ship. Admiral Yamamoto, by forcing this showdown, would determine to a large extent the final outcome of the Pacific War. With Midway Island in our hands, we would have a powerful forward base from which to extend further the aggressive actions of our ships and planes.

Admiral Yamamoto assembled a tremendous striking force for his attack. His total naval strength for the combined operation included 350 vessels of all types, which exceeded a total of a million five hundred thousand tons. For an all-out aerial assault against the Americans he gathered more than one thousand warplanes; more than one hundred thousand officers and men manned his ships and planes.

Our attacking fleet dwarfed in numbers and offensive strength any previous assembly of ships, planes, and men. Not only did we enjoy great numerical strength, but we had a further advantage in that the handling and combat quality of the men and the planes aboard the aircraft carriers *Kaga, Akagi, Hiryu*, and *Soryu* were superior to those of any comparable enemy group. These battle-tested veterans, outstanding in their flying skill, went into the attack under the brilliant command of Vice-Admiral Chuichi Nagumo, who had devastated Pearl Harbor and wrought a path of destruction across the Pacific. The crews and pilots of the four carriers actually looked down upon the other two carriers under Nagumo, the *Shokaku* and the *Zuikaku*, which had participated (rather ineffectively, in the opinion of Nagumo's other veterans) in the Coral Sea Battle.

For some reason, through a series of incredible blunders on the part of our fleet, we threw away this priceless advantage. Our Navy committed so many inexcusable errors in the battle commencing on June 5 that we have often wondered if the gods of war had determined beforehand the outcome of the conflict! Through the courageous, yet costly, attacks by the American land- and carrier-based warplanes, and also the enemy submarines, the Nagumo Force was completely defeated, compelling Admiral Yamamoto to withdraw his battered fleet without attaining even a part of his original objectives at Midway.

The attack commenced at 1:45 A.M. on June 5, 1942. Under the command of Lieutenant Joichi Tomonaga of the *Hiryu*, thirty-six Zero fighters, thirty-six Type 99 Val dive bombers, and thirty-six Type 97 Kate attack bombers took off from four carriers. These planes directed their attacks against important ground facilities on Midway Island. We expected heavy resistance and posed great confidence in the ability of the Zeros to protect their bombers, no easy task when thirty-six fighter planes must escort twice their number in bombers. Approximately thirty nautical miles from Midway Island more than thirty enemy fighter planes jumped our formations, starting a running air fight which continued to directly over the island.

Under the leadership of Lieutenant Masaharu Suganami, the Zeros managed to prevent the enemy fighter planes from seriously interfering with the bombing attacks. The Nagumo Force's official combat report of this particular raid reveals that we lost two Kates, one Val, and two Zero fighters, and that it was believed that these planes were destroyed by the fierce enemy antiaircraft fire.

In his postattack intelligence briefing, Lieutenant Tomonaga reported that his fighters and bombers shot down forty enemy fighters, one light bomber, and one seaplane in their attack against Midway Island. Intelligence reduced this number appreciably, for it was obvious that "double counting" by our pilots was responsible for the unusually high number of enemy losses reported. (Postwar investigation of this particular battle with officers of the U.S. Navy Section of the Strategic Bombing Survey revealed that twenty Brewster F2A Buffaloes and seven Grumman F4F Wildcats attacked Tomonaga's force. Of these, seventeen were shot down, including the fighter commander, Major Parks. Seven other enemy fighters sustained heavy damage, and most of the surviving pilots were injured.)

The Zero fighters defending our carriers set up against the first wave of Midway-based enemy torpedo bombers an almost impenetrable wall of fire. More than sixty torpedo bombers raced in at low altitude to attack Nagumo's carriers. The American pilots pressed home their attacks with great courage, but their lumbering aircraft fell easy prey to the Zeros and the fleet's defending gunfire. The initial enemy attack became a massacre, as almost all of the American planes fell flaming into the ocean. Not a single torpedo struck our ships.

Our fleet waited apprehensively for the second attack (which came this time from large carrier-based enemy formations). They did not have long to wait, and the Zeros slashed into the enemy planes, disrupting formations and scattering the bombers. Even as the second enemy wave battled fiercely to break through the defending cordon of Zero fighters, keeping our planes occupied near the water's surface, large numbers of American dive bombers suddenly appeared on the scene. It was the beginning of the end, for our fleet was caught completely unaware by this sudden assault.

Almost unopposed, the enemy bombers plunged in vertical dives from above the clouds. Our carriers were helpless. Bomb after bomb smashed into our ships' vitals, flooding compartments, destroying gun-control systems, knocking out fire-fighting apparatus, setting aflame gasoline and oil tanks. Within an hour of the attack, the *Akagi*, *Kaga*, and *Soryu* were crippled hulks in sinking condition. Several hours later the three great ships went down. Nagumo had suffered a grievous blow, for in this single dive-bombing attack the Americans had reduced by more than half his available fighter and bomber strength.

With the first battle phase completed, and with our fleet reeling from its severe losses, we launched an attack against the American carriers. Eighteen Type 99 Val dive bombers and six Zero fighters left Rear Admiral Tamon Yamagushi's flagship *Hiryu*, the only carrier to escape the enemy's bombs. Led by Lieutenant Michio Kobayashi, the eighteen bombers dove through a hail of antiaircraft fire and defending enemy fighter planes to score more than three direct hits on the *Yorktown*.

Soon after Kobayashi left the *Hiryu*, Lieutenant Tomonaga led ten Type 97 Kate torpedo bombers and six Zero fighters in search of a second American carrier. Again our planes encountered fierce resistance, but our returning pilots reported that they had sent two torpedoes directly into the big warship. Rear Admiral Yamaguchi felt relieved, for now his planes had heavily damaged two enemy carriers. (We later discovered that actually we had twice attacked the *Yorktown*, not a second carrier as originally believed.)

Yamaguchi did not have long to enjoy the news of the attack for, shortly afterward, enemy carrier-based bombers found the *Hiryu*. The rain of bombs crippled the flagship in short order and, like her sister ships, soon the *Hiryu* became a helpless hulk, wracked with flaming explosions and abandoned by her crew.

This may appear paradoxical, but in my estimate I feel that the *Hiryu*'s air group had been superior in combat to its American carrier-based counterparts. Many factors which are not apparent to the uninformed observer influence a battle's final outcome; in the vast Midway conflict the Americans had a definite advantage in that their carriers were equipped with radar, enabling them to receive out-of-sight advance warning of air attacks, while our own vessels lacked this priceless equipment. Every Japanese aircraft committed to the attack against enemy surface ships and the installations at Midway Island performed admirably. Despite the staggering loss of our carriers, there still remained no doubt that the Zero fighter exceeded in performance any of the American planes which it contested. Our Val dive bombers and Kate torpedo bombers were at the time two of the world's best aircraft for their respective missions.

There was little to criticize in the performance and courage of our air-crew members under fire. Every man did his utmost to press home the attacks against the American warships, particularly Lieutenant Joichi Tomonaga, who on his final mission took off from his carrier with the knowledge that he could not possibly return. With three of our carriers already lost, it was imperative that we either cripple or sink the enemy aircraft carriers. Tomonaga took off in his final attack with only his right wing tank containing fuel; enemy bullets had holed the left tank over Midway. This outstanding officer would not let his aircraft remain idle while his fellow pilots flew into combat. This action, similiar to that of Flight Warrant Officer Kanno in the Coral Sea Battle, did much to uphold the morale of our men in the face of terrible losses.

Despite the determination and courage of our men, and the high performance of our airplanes, the American aircraft overwhelmed our best defenses. No one could have foreseen the effectiveness of their courageous attacks; their tenacity brought the Battle of Midway to a tragic end. The loss of the four aircraft carriers, the *Akagi, Kaga, Hiryu*, and *Soryu*, shocked the Japanese people. We could not underestimate the gravity of our defeat, for these four carriers had played the major role in the Navy's smashing victories across the breadth of the entire Pacific. An even greater blow, however, was the loss of the irreplaceable veteran air crews and the skilled maintenance crews which went down with their ships.

Even as we reeled from the debacle of Midway, another event occurred far to the north which, although lacking the drama of open conflict, was no less serious. In the Aleutians, one of our Zero fighters made a forced landing and was captured almost intact by the Americans. The subsequent detailed study of the airplane revealed fully to the Americans the Zero's advantages and faults. With the airplane's every characteristic an open book to the enemy engineers, they could quickly assure their own qualitative superiority.

Early in the morning of June 4, 1942, the aircraft carriers *Ryujo* and *Junyo* of Rear Admiral Kakuji Kakuda's 2nd Carrier Task Force approached Dutch Harbor. The task force's stealthy and unobserved move to the Aleutians actually was the opening blow of the Midway and Aleutian Operations. Lashed by cold winds and driving rain, the *Junyo* launched six Zero fighters and twelve Type 99 Val dive bombers in the first attack against the American positions. During their flight, our formations encountered several enemy flying boats, which they engaged and destroyed. This delay in flight, in addition to the violent storms encountered en route, forced the Zeros and Vals to abandon their mission.

However, six Zeros and eleven Type 97 Kate attack bombers from the *Ryujo* failed to encounter enemy aircraft on their approach to Dutch Harbor. Led by Lieutenant Masayuki Yamagami, the formation battled heavy rain and thick fog, arriving over the enemy base above a solid layer of clouds. Fortunately the sky cleared directly over the harbor and our planes dove to the attack. The Kates bombed the radio stations and pier installations, while the Zeros, free from enemy fighters, strafed a number of flying boats tied to harbor buoys.

After the attack the bombers and fighters reassembled over the eastern end of Unalaska Island, where Flight Petty Officer Tadayoshi Koga noticed that his Zero trailed a thin spray of gasoline. Informing Kobayashi that he did not have enough fuel to return to the *Ryujo*, Koga dropped low over a small island eastward of Dutch Harbor, which had been designated as an emergency landing site for crippled planes. Once down on the island, the pilots would be picked up by a submarine.

On his return to the carrier, Kobayashi reported to his superior:

"The emergency landing site appeared from the air to be flat and clear. Koga made his approach perfectly, but immediately after the wheels struck the ground the airplane tipped over, remaining upright. The Zero appeared to be heavily damaged and either the pilot died or he must have been seriously injured. Since the island surface seems to be tundra, it would be difficult to remove the wreckage. We could not discern any sign of human habitation in the vicinity."

We did not learn until many months afterward that an enemy reconnaissance plane discovered the Zero. Ground parties rushed to the site found an airplane only slightly damaged, still upright. Koga had been killed by the shock of landing; his head struck the instrument panel with great force.

Koga apparently realized that to land in the water off the island would have been certain death, for the temperature was so low that only several minutes of exposure to the cold would have killed him. Notified of the emergency crash landing, our submarine scoured the area, but did not sight the wreckage on the island.

The Americans removed the airplane to the United States, where it was repaired and subjected to exhaustive test flights. They were surprised at the Zero's unusually light weight and by the fact that the airplane's high performance was achieved with an engine of but 1,000 horsepower. It was quickly established that the Zero's greatest weaknesses lay in its poor diving ability and in its lack of armor-plate protection. The flight tests revealed also that at high speeds the Zero responded sluggishly to aileron control, and that it was limited in altitude performance. Aware of the Zero's minutest details, the Americans rushed to completion a fighter airplane intended specifically to wrest from Japan the advantages afforded by the Zero. This was the United States Navy's Grumman F6F Hellcat, one of the most versatile enemy planes to be encountered in the Pacific.

The F6F was the first plane designed by the Grumman company following their thorough study of the captured Zero fighter. Grumman engineers painstakingly reduced the thickness of the fuselage, and bent every effort to reduce structural weight. With a 2,000-horsepower engine, the new Hellcat had a higher maximum speed than the Zero, could outclimb and outdive and outgun it, and retained the desired benefits of high structural strength, armor plating, and self-sealing fuel tanks. In fact, with the exception of turning radius and radius of action, the Hellcat completely outperformed the Zero. The advantages of superior engines stood the enemy in good stead, for the Hellcat was twice as powerful as the Zero. This sudden performance increase combined with the rising tidal wave of American production forecast the overwhelming strength the enemy would soon bring to bear against the homeland itself.

In the Aleutian campaign I (Okumiya) was Admiral Kakuda's air staff officer. I could not realize at the time how far-reaching an effect this seemingly trivial incident of losing to the enemy a single intact Zero could have. We felt strongly that the unnoticed capture of the airplane, assisting the enemy so greatly in producing a fighter plane intended specifically to overcome the Zero's advantages, did much to hasten our final defeat.

Meanwhile, in Japan, our government harped on the victories of the Aleutians attacks and the island occupations. The continual emphasis on our successes in the far north was, of course, merely a diversionary effort to conceal from the people the terrible losses at Midway.

CHAPTER 14

Reorganization of the Combined Fleet

THE RESULTS OF THE Battle of Midway rudely awakened our Naval General Staffs. Only six months after Pearl Harbor, following a succession of unprecedented victories and stronger than it ever had been before in its entire existence, the Navy retreated sorely wounded from Midway. The sudden insight which this defeat afforded our commanding officers forced them to realize that Midway had voided the concept of the battleship as the prime naval power, and that victory or defeat at sea fundamentally rested on the effectiveness of the aircraft carrier. With the understanding that air power, not the usually impotent sixteen-inch guns, decided naval battles, our planning staffs came also to appreciate the thin-skinned vulnerability of the aircraft carrier, which would always experience the fury of enemy attack.

At one sweep Tokyo discarded its policy of offensive operations and substituted for it a new, curving defense line which was to be held at virtually all costs before an enemy who was now expected to commence his own assault operations. The outermost reaches of the new defense line extended west of the Aleutian Islands in the north, to the Marshall Islands in the east, from Rabaul to the northeast coast of New Guinea in the south, to the Dutch East Indies, Malaya, and Burma in the west. To most efficiently defend these lines, we reorganized the Combined Fleet. The new effort concentrated upon maximum development of our land-based air forces, and we accelerated our program of rebuilding the surface fleet around a center of aircraft carriers. On July 14, 1942, the Navy echelons received their reorganization orders, with the following tables of the new first-line Air Corps.

SECOND FLEET

Division Flotilla, etc.	Warship Air Corps, etc.	Plane Types and number	
11th Carrier Division	*Chitose* (seaplane tender)	Pete (and) Type	95
		Reconnaissance	
		Seaplane	16
		Jake	7
	Kamikawa-Maru (seaplane tender)	Pete (and) Type	95
		Reconaissance	
		Seaplane	8
		Jake	4

THIRD FLEET

Division Flotilla, etc.	Warship Air Corps, etc.	Plane Types and number	
1st Carrier Division	*Shokaku*	Zero	27
		Val	27
		Kate	18
	Zuikaku	Zero	27
		Val	27
		Kate	18
	Zuiho	Zero	21
		Kate	16
2nd Carrier Division	*Junyo*	Zero	21
		Val	18
		Kate	9
Division Flotilla, etc.	*Warship Air Corps, etc.*	*Plane Types and number*	
	Hiyo	Zero	21
		Val	18
		Kate	9
Division Flotilla, etc.	*Warship Air Corps, etc.*	*Plane Types and number*	
	Ryujo	Zero	24
		Kate	9

FOURTH FLEET

Division Flotilla, etc.	Warship Air Corps, etc.	Plane Types and number	
4th Naval Base Force	21st Air Corps	Jake	11
5th Naval Base Force	(Attachment)	Jake	6
6th Naval Base Force	19th Air Corps	Type 95 Reconnaissance Seaplane	8
		Jake	10
(Attachment)	*Kunikawa-Maru* (seaplane tender)	Type 95	

Division Flotilla, etc.	Warship Air Corps, etc.	Plane Types and number	
		Reconnaissance Seaplane	6
(Attachment)		Transport Plane	3

FIFTH FLEET

(Attachment)	Chichijima Air Corps	Jake	6
(Attachment)	Kamikawa-Maru (seaplane tender)	Jake	8
(Attachment)	5th Air Corps	Rufe	12

EIGHTH FLEET

(Attachment)	Kiyokawa-Maru (seaplane tender)	Pete (and) Type 95 Reconnaissance Seaplane	8
		Jake	4
(Attachment)	2nd Air Corps	Zero	16
		Kate	16

ELEVENTH AIR FLEET

22nd Air Flotilla	Mihoro Air Corps	Nell	36
	Genzan Air Corps	Nell	36
		Zero	36
24th Air Flotilla	Chitose Air Corps	Betty	36
		Zero	36
	1st Air Corps	Betty	36
		Zero	36
	14th Air Corps	Mavis (and) Emily	16
25th Air Flotilla	Yokohama Air Corps	Mavis	16
		Rufe	12

Division Flotilla, etc.	Warship Air Corps, etc.	Plane Types and number	
	Tainan Air Corps	Zero	60
		Type 98 Reconnaissance Plane	8
		Transport Plane	4
	4th Air Corps	Nell (and) Betty	48
26th Air Flotilla	Misawa Air Corps	Nell (and) Betty	36
	Kisarazu Air Corps	Nell (and) Betty	36
	6th Air Corps	Zero	60
		Type 98 Reconnaissance Plane	8
(Attachment)		Transport Plane	12

MALAYA AREA FLEET

12th Naval Base Force	(Attachment)	Jake	4
(Attachment)	40th Air Corps	Kate	12
(Attachment)	Sagara-Maru (seaplane tender)	Type 95 Reconnaissance Seaplane	8
(Attachment)		Transport Plane	1

DUTCH EAST INDIES AREA FLEET

21st Naval Base Force	33rd Air Corps	Kate	8
24th Naval Base Force	36th Air Corps	Jake	8
(Attachment)	35th Air Corps	Val	12

Division Flotilla, etc.	Warship Air Corps, etc.	Plane Types and number
(Attachment)	*Sanyo-Maru* (seaplane tender)	Type 95 Reconnaissance Seaplane 6
		Jake 2
(Attachment)		Transport Plane 2
Division Flotilla, etc.	Warship Air Corps, etc.	Plane Types and Number

PHILIPPINES AREA FLEET

(Attachment)	31st Air Corps	Val 16
(Attachment)	*Sanuki-Maru* (seaplane tender)	Type 95 Reconnaissance Seaplane 8
(Attachment)		Transport Plane 1

SOUTHWEST AREA FLEET

21st Air Flotilla	Kanoya Air Corps	Betty 48
		Zero 36
	Toko Air Corps	Mavis 16
	(Attachment)	Transport Plane 3
23rd Air Flotilla	Takao Air Corps	Betty 60
	3rd Air Corps	Zero 60
		Type 98 Reconnaissance Plane 8
(Attachment)		Transport Plane 4

Division Flotilla, etc. (Attachment)	Warship Air Corps, etc.	Plane Types and number
		Transport Plane 3

ATTACHED TO COMBINED FLEET

	Kasuga-Maru	
(converted carrier)	Zero	11
	Type 96 D.B.	14
	Yawata-Maru	
(converted carrier)	Kate	14

NORTHERN CHINA FLEET

(Attachment)	Jake	4

SOUTHERN CHINA FLEET

(Attachment)	Jake	3

HAINAN NAVAL STATION

(Attachment)	Kate	4

CHINA AREA FLEET

(Attachment)	Kate	8

In addition, there were aboard the fleet's various battleships, cruisers, submarines, and other vessels the following aircraft:

Pete (and) Type 95 Reconnaissance Seaplane	39
Jake (and) Type 94 Reconnaissance Seaplane	44

Type 96 Small Seaplane   14
Type 98 Night Scout Seaplane   3

Thus reorganized, the Combined Fleet's first-line naval forces had available for combat:

Carrier-based fighters	(all Zeros)	492
Carrier-based dive bombers	(mostly Vals)	132
Carrier-based attack bombers	(all Kates)	141
Land-based reconnaissance planes	(all Type 98)	24
Land-based attack bombers	(Nells and Bettys)	360
Transport Planes	(Type 96 and Type Zero)	32
Two-seat reconnaissance seaplanes	(mostly Type 95)	107
Three-seat reconnaissance seaplanes	(Type Zero and Jake)	121
Fighter seaplanes	(all Type 2, Rufe)	24
Small-type reconnaissance seaplanes	(all Type 96)	14
Night scout planes	(all Type 98)	3
Flying boats	(mostly Type 97 Mavis and some Type 2, Emily)	<u>48</u>
	TOTAL	1,498

These figures indicated only too clearly the intrinsic defects in Japan's military strength, for, compared to the number of first-line naval planes at the war's outset, we had increased our strength by only 117 aircraft. Further, we now had an increase of only seventy-four planes over the total available immediately prior to the Battle of Midway. Our naval air strength in numbers remained basically static, while the enemy feverishly prepared his industry for the production of more and more warplanes. The future looked dark indeed.

There was another weak link in our airpower chain which, although lacking the effect of total numbers of aircraft, presaged more and even severer defeats than we suffered at Midway. Since the war's outset, the Navy had adopted, or was about to adopt, only three new-type planes. These were the 13-*Shi* carrier-based dive bomber (the *Suisei*, or Type 2 carrier-based reconnaissance plane Judy); the 13-*Shi* large-type flying boat (the Type 2 flying boat Emily); and the 13-*Shi* twin-engined land-based fighter (the *Gekko*, or Type 2 land-based reconnaissance plane Irving). Our domestic aeronautical engineering and production outlook was bleak; despite the pressing demands of combat, we could not hope to accelerate any further the development and production of new-type aircraft. Geared to a specific, low pace, our industry could not, even in time of need, discard its own shackles. The over-all situation seemed even worse when one realized that, even with these difficulties, the Navy was infinitely better off than the Army.

During the first six to seven months of the war, the Zero remained the Navy's only front-line fighter airplane and bore the entire burden of all fighter operations. Even in mass production the airplane still featured outstanding performance, ease of maintenance, and dependability. We experienced but two operational difficulties, which were occasional failure of the landing-gear shaft under heavy shock loads, and poor release of the jettisonable auxiliary fuel tank. Even by mid-July of 1942 the Navy did not contemplate replacing the Zero with another fighter.

As we worked to rebuild and to reorganize the Combined Fleet's various air corps, our worst fears were realized. The enemy no longer fell back helplessly. The counterattack in Guadalcanal had begun.

CHAPTER 15

Change in Warship-Building Policy

A LTHOUGH THE NAVY ACTED immediately after the Battle of Midway drastically to change its warship-building policy, placing the aircraft carrier ahead of the battleship as the backbone of surface power, the damage had already been done. We realized too late that a preponderance of battleship strength could not strategically affect the outcome of important campaigns. Every type of surface vessel was at the mercy of carrier-borne aircraft, and American strength in carrier aviation increased by fantastic leaps and bounds. Although constantly exhorted to backbreaking efforts, our industry could do little to contest the monumental production of America's shipyards.

Up until immediately after World War I, Japan, as one of the three great naval powers, maintained a surface Navy centered about powerful battleship strength. By so doing, we established a balance of naval power with that of the United States and Great Britain. With the international conflict over, in 1919 Japan turned to its new so-called *Hachi-Hachi* Fleet Plan, which was to give our nation the strongest fleet afloat. The to-be-reorganized Navy would center around eight battleships (*Hachi*), including the *Mutsu* and *Nagato*, and eight new battle cruisers including the *Akagi* and *Amagi*, which were then under construction. At the time our largest planned battleship exceeded by a considerable margin any foreign ship, for we were to construct a giant dreadnaught of 48,000-tons' weight. However, because naval air power in 1919 was restricted to auxiliary activities, the *Hachi-Hachi* Fleet Plan called for only two small aircraft carriers of 12,500 tons each.

In 1918, one year before the Navy drafted the *Hachi-Hachi* Fleet Plan, we laid the keel for the *Hosho*, Japan's first aircraft carrier. On March 16, 1923, Lieutenant Shunichi Kira, later to become a Vice-Admiral, became the first Japanese pilot to land on a carrier deck when he brought a plane down on the *Hosho*.

Because the Washington Naval Conference restricted the maximum tonnage of our battleships, we modified our broad naval program and planned to convert the battle cruisers *Akagi* and *Amagi* into large aircraft carriers, the latter as the *Kaga*. In 1927 we decided to expand our carrier strength with the new *Ryujo*, bringing our total to four fleet aircraft carriers. Again international events interfered, for the London Naval Conference of 1930 imposed further restrictions on our warship expansion.

In 1934, after the adoption of the London Naval Treaty, we instituted the Second Supplemental Plan, which called for the powerful carriers *Soryu* and *Hiryu*. Although it seemed as if the Navy would finally receive the large and fast warships it coveted, the limitations of the two naval treaties by which we were bound halted further construction for two years.

Late in 1936 the disarmament treaties were abrogated, and the Navy instituted a new construction plan which called for maximum shipyard efforts. Under the Third Replenishment Plan (popularly known as the *Marusan* Plan), we began the actual build-up of the fleet into one of the world's greatest sea powers. Included in the new program were the famous superdreadnaughts *Yamato* and *Musashi* and the aircraft carriers *Shokaku* and *Zuikaku*, both of which exceeded by a considerable margin the performance and efficiency of the *Akagi* and the *Kaga*.

In 1938 we planned the construction of two additional *Yamato*-class (74,000 tons) battleships and an outsized aircraft carrier, the *Taiho*, with unusually heavy armament. By 1939 our shipyards began the conversion of large merchant vessels into aircraft carriers. The first of these ships to be so altered, the modern passenger ship *Kasuga-Maru*, was followed by Japan's two largest passenger ships, the 27,000-ton vessels *Izumo-Maru* and *Kashihara-Maru*. Four additional commercial vessels, each exceeding 10,000 tons, were brought into the carrier-conversion program.

Because of the changing international situation of 1942, the Navy called for a speed-up of the Wartime Construction Plan of 1941, under which we added to our shipbuilding program one more aircraft carrier, the *Hiryu*-class *Unryu*. Early in 1942, however, the Navy still regarded as its priority weapon the heavy, fast battleships, and ordered construction to begin on another 74,000-ton battleship, two new-type battleships, two 30,000-ton aircraft carriers, and one 17,000-ton aircraft carrier. The devastating defeat at Midway forced a halt in the new construction program even as the shipyards worked on the keels of the mighty new warships. The Navy abandoned further work on the fourth *Yamato*-type battleship, then in its initial stages, and ordered a halt to all battleship construction. The third 74,000-ton battleship, the *Shinano*, was converted to the greatest aircraft carrier ever built (the ship failed to see combat, for on her maiden voyage on November 28, 1944, she was crippled by the American submarine *Archerfish*, and sank the following day). To provide carrier aviation across the Pacific expanse, the Navy also ordered fifteen new *Hiryu*-type carriers and five *Taiho*-type carriers.

Our efforts came much too late. Due to a combination of circumstances, including the stoppage of raw materials to the homeland and the increasing bombardment of our shipyards by enemy planes, only four of the fifteen planned *Hiryu*-type carriers came off the ways. None of the planned *Taiho*-class carriers was completed. The following table lists the entire carrier strength of the Japanese Navy up to the close of the Pacific War; this material was compiled from official documents on August 15, 1945:

Carrier	Displacemen (Ton)[1]	Length (Meter)	H.P.	Speed (Knot)	Planes Carried[2]	(Date of Construction) or (Date of Conversion)
Hosho	9,500	165.00	30,000	25	26	Dec. 27, 1922
Akagi	34,000	249.00	131,200	31	63	March 25, 1927
Kaga	33,000	230.00	91,0002	7.5	72	March 31, 1928
Ryujo	11,700	175.39	65,000	29	48	May 9, 1933
Soryu	18,800	222.00	152,000	34.5	71	Dec. 29, 1937
Hiryu	20,250	222.00	152,000	34.3	73	July 5, 1939
Ryuho	15,300	210.00	52,000	26.5	31	March 31, 1934 (Nov. 28, 1942)
Shoho	13,950	201.43	52,000	28	30	Jan. 15, 1939 (Jan. 26, 1942)
Zuiho	13,950	201.43	52,000	28	30	Dec. 27, 1940
Chitose	13,600	185.93	56,800	29	24	July 25, 1938 (Jan. 1, 1944)
Chiyoda	13,600	185.93	56,800	29	24	Dec. 15, 1938 (Oct. 31, 1943)
Shokaku	29,800	250.00	160,000	34.2	75	August 8, 1941
Zuikaku	29,800	250.00	160,000	34.2	75	Sept. 25, 1941
Hiyo	27,500	215.30	56,250	25.5	54	July 31, 1942
Junyo	27,500	215.30	56,250	25.5	54	May 3, 1942
Taiyo	20,000	173.70	25,200	27	24	Sept. 5, 1941
Unyo	20,000	173.70	25,200	27	24	July 31, 1940 (May 31, 1942)
Chuyo	20,000	173.70	25,200	27	24	March 23, 1940 (Nov. 25, 1942)
Shinyo	20,900	189.36	26,000	33	24	(Dec. 15, 1943)
Kaiyo	16,700	159.59	52,000	23	24	May 31, 1939 (Nov. 23, 1943)
Shinano	68,060	256.00	150,000	27	120	Nov. 19, 1944
Taiho	34,200	253.00	160,000	33.3	75	March 7, 1944
Ibuki	14,800	198.35	72,000	29	27	–
Unryu	20,400	223.00	152,000	34	63	August 6, 1944
Amagi	20,400	223.00	152,000	34	63	August 10, 1944
Katsuragi	20,200	223.00	104,000	32	63	Oct. 15, 1944
Kasagi	20,400	223.00	152,000	34	63	–
Aso	20,200	223.00	104,000	32	63	–
Ikoma	20,450	223.00	152,000	34	63	–

[1]Displacement is official displacement except for Hosho, for which regular displacement is shown.
[2]Planes carried are approximate.

Carrier	Shipbuilding Yard Launching (After Launching)	Remark	History
Hosho	Asano Shipyard (Yokosuka Naval Dockyard)		[3]†
Akagi	Kure Naval Dockyard	Remodeled from battle cruiser	x
Kaga	Kawasaki Heavy Industry (Yokosuka Naval Dockyard)	Remodeled from battleship	x
Ryujo	Yokohama Dockyard (Yokosuka Naval Dockyard)		x
Soryu	Kure Naval Dockyard		x
Hiryu	Yokosuka Naval Dockyard		x
Ryuho	Yokosuka Naval Dockyard	Remodeled from *Taigei*, a submarine tender	o
Shoho	Yokosuka Naval Dockyard	Remodeled from *Kenzaki*, a submarine tender	x
Zuiho	Yokosuka Naval Dockyard	Remodeled from *Takasaki*, a submarine tender	x
Chitose	Kure Naval Dockyard (Sasebo Naval Dockyard)	Remodeled from seaplane tender	x
Chiyoda	Kure Naval Dockyard (Yokosuka Naval Dockyard)		x
Shokaku	Yokosuka Naval Dockyard		x
Zuikaku	Kawasaki Heavy Industry		x
Hiyo	Kawasaki Heavy Industry	Remodeled from *Izumo Maru*[4]	x
Junyo	Mitsubishi Nagasaki Shipyard	Remodeled from *Kashihara Maru*[4]	x
Taiyo	Mitsubishi Nagasaki Shipyard (Sasebo Naval Dockyard)	Remodeled from *Kasuga Maru*[4]	x
Unyo	Mitsubishi Nagasaki Shipyard (Kure Naval Dockyard)	Remodeled from *Yawata Maru*[4]	x
Chuyo	Mitsubishi Nagasaki Shipyard (Kure Naval Dockyard)	Remodeled from *Nitta Maru*[4]	x
Shinyo	Bremen, Germany (Kure Naval Dockyard)	Remodeled from *Shornhorst*[4]	x
Kaiyo	Mitsubishi Nagasaki Shipyard	Remodeled from *Argentina Maru*[4]	o
Shinano	Yokosuka Naval Dockyard	Remodeled from No. 3 *Yamato*-type battleship	x
Taiho	Kawasaki Heavy Industry		x
Ibuki	Kure Naval Dockyard (Sasebo Naval Dockyard)	Remodeled from cruiser not completed	xx
Unryu	Yokosuka Naval Dockyard		x
Amagi	Mitsubishi Nagasaki Shipyard		oo
Katsuragi	Kure Naval Dockyard	Not completed	‡‡
Kasagi	Mitsubishi Nagasaki Shipyard (Sasebo Naval Dockyard)	Not completed	xx
Aso	Kure Naval Dockyard	Launched but not completed; used as target; damaged near the end of the war	xx
Ikoma	Kawasaki Heavy Industry	Launched but not completed; damaged near the end of the war.	

[3]†—intact at the time of war's end
‡‡-slightly damaged but was safe at the time of war's end
o—medium damaged but was safe at the time of war's end
oo—seriously damaged but was safe at the time of war's end
x—sunk
xx—not completed
[4]Indicated commercial vessel

CHAPTER 16

Desperate Air Operations Over Long-Range Conditions: The Saga of Saburo Sakai

ESPECIALLY SIGNIFICANT IN THE first half of 1942 were the great battles of Midway and the Coral Sea. These two vital engagements were decided solely by the weight of air power, despite the commitment of numerous opposing land and sea forces.

Despite this obvious superiority of combat aerial forces to other armaments, however, the United States and Japan failed equally to evaluate properly the significant role of air power in these two engagements.

Of the land-based air forces in combat at this time, the only major command which maintained heavy and continuous air action against the enemy was the 25th Air Flotilla, consisting of the Tainan Air Corps, the 4th Air Corps, and the Yokohama Air Corps. The headquarters of these forces was at Rabaul and was under the command of Rear Admiral Sadayoshi Yamada.

The flotilla engaged in constant air attack, concentrating the full force of its strength against the enemy at Port

Moresby, New Guinea. Of lesser consequence were the intermittent attacks which it mounted against Port Darwin, Australia, with medium attack bombers of the 23rd Air Flotilla, based on Timor Island.

The air attacks against Port Moresby were always made (as was characteristic of this phase of the war) with comparatively heavy formations composed of twenty-seven or more land-based medium attack bombers and an approximately equal number of escorting Zero fighters. For some time we had been preparing for the capture of Port Moresby; in order to facilitate this undertaking a naval landing force attacked Buna, on the northeastern coast of New Guinea, on July 21, 1942.

This invading force was subjected to a fierce and damaging air attack by approximately one hundred enemy planes on the following day. As a result of this sudden assault our beleaguered naval units were placed in a precarious position, and it became necessary to neutralize the enemy air strength attacking the forces at Buna.

The greater part of the enemy's air strength was based at Port Moresby and, to a lesser extent, at the airfields at Rabi, on the southeastern end of New Guinea. Our naval air forces prepared immediately to neutralize Rabi in an all-out attack on August 7, 1942.

Preparations were well under way for the heavy assault when, abruptly, our attention was brought to bear on a little-known island in the southern group of the Solomon Islands. The enemy had invaded Guadalcanal in what proved to be only the first of a long series of attacks.

Part of the personal element of the struggle for the air over the Guadalcanal area is vividly recounted in the following battle record of Flight Petty Officer, 1st Class, Saburo Sakai (later promoted to Lieutenant [J.G.]), who was at that time a section leader of the Tainan Air Corps.

The major combatants of World War II experienced many incredible happenings in this long-drawn-out air war. Pilots and aircrew members who were severely wounded in combat miraculously continued on flying duty to an extent far beyond that previously imagined possible. Pilots who might be presumed dead continued to fly their planes; and planes which should have disintegrated under enemy fire somehow, beyond all reason, remained in the air and brought their awed and reverent crews safely home.

Petty Officer Saki at the close of World War II was the chief surviving Japanese air ace, whose combat initiation against American flyers was marked by such incidents as his being the first Japanese pilot to shoot down a Boeing B-17 Flying Fortress (Philippines, December 11, 1941). His story, even among the epic incidents of the air war in the Pacific, is one of the most incredible episodes ever related.

"Guadalcanal. A name, merely a name. We did not even know what Guadalcanal was; an island, a military base, a secret operation code name, perhaps. When the American forces stormed ashore at Guadalcanal, we had never even heard of the island.

"It was still a few hours before the people of the world unfolded and spread out their maps of the South Pacific to search for this tiny island. Japanese and American communiques did not as yet mention the name of Guadalcanal, and the constantly broadcast news programs failed to mention this new name which would soon flare into international prominence.

"Here at Rabaul, on the eastern end of New Britain Island, the sky was clear. Not even a breeze disturbed the prevalent heat and tranquillity. Simpson Bay lay in slumber like a sheltered lake, its surface an unrippled sheet of glass reflecting the blue of the sky. It was completely encircled by low, lush hills, except for the lone entrance which opened to the east. At the northeastern shore of the bay, threads of white smoke drifted lazily upward from the temporarily stilled throat of a volcano. The smoke gleamed and shone as it caught the rays of the scorching sun.

"The sides of the volcano dipped, and their inclines disappeared suddenly into the dense jungle foliage, except at the point at which the southern slope ended. Here the jungle had been hacked, ripped apart, and banished, replaced by a long narrow strip of land running from east to west. This was Rabaul Lower Airstrip.

"At Vunakanau, where the land stretched flat as the surface of a table high above the sea, another slender clearing stood out against the natural growth of the island. This was Rabaul Upper Airstrip.

"In sharp contrast to the tranquillity of the scene and the oppressive heat of the moment, a group of heavily clothed young men stood before a nondescript shack on the northern side of the fighter airstrip. In a land where even a summer shirt brings sticky sweat cascading freely down one's body, the young men were incongruously bundled into heavy flying suits, boots, awkward lifejackets, and other weighty equipment. Revolvers were cradled within well-oiled leather holsters.

"These were fighter pilots of the Tainan Air Corps, recently transferred to the blanketing heat and mugginess of Rabaul from Bali Island in the Dutch East Indies. I was one of those fighter pilots, a section leader.

"Ever since our arrival at Rabaul, we had faced the American and Australian air forces based at Port Moresby on New Guinea. This morning, however, our usual mission of fighter patrol, attack against Moresby or air-to-air combat, was to be replaced with a special attack against the

Rabi air base at Milne Bay, on the south end of New Guinea.

"The pilots spoke with enthusiasm to each other. 'Maybe today we'll have a big fight,' one said. 'I'd sure like to get a kill,' another added. Our pilots were understandably eager to engage the enemy fighter planes in combat. The results obtained with our Zero fighter against enemy airplanes had been so amazing that often the enemy appeared openly to fear our arrival and, at times, had even refused to join combat.

"As we checked each other's equipment and made the final preparations for takeoff, to escort the bombers which would attack Rabi, a messenger ran past us into the operations room with a radio message. Whatever it contained obviously created a major stir among our officers. We could see Captain Masahisa Saito, our commanding officer; Yasuna Kozono, the air officer; and Lieutenant Commander Tadashi Nakajima, who was to command today's attack, gathered around a large map spread hastily on one of the desks.

"We listened closely to the conversation of the officers, and every now and then could catch the words Guadalcanal and Tulagi. These were strange names.

" 'Where is Guadalcanal, sir?' asked Flight Petty Officer Hatori, 2nd Class, pilot of the second fighter in my section.

" 'I don't know,' I replied. Then, to the group of petty officers and pilots, 'Does anybody know where Guadalcanal is?'

"No answer. Only a shaking of heads. Hatori spoke up again. 'Nobody knows! Then, it cannot be an important place.'

"But the officers within the operations room appeared very serious. One of the officers came out and ordered all pilots to line up immediately.

"Captain Saito came out. 'At 0525 hours this morning,' he said, 'a powerful enemy invasion force under heavy cover attacked Lunga Roads, Guadalcanal Island. This is the second island from the south end of the Solomon Island group. Tulagi on Florida Island, which is northeast of Guadalcanal, was also invaded.'

"'On Guadalcanal our engineers have been in the process of constructing an airstrip. At Tulagi, our air units are seriously threatened. The main force of the Yokohama Air Corps, belonging to the 25th Air Flotilla, is stationed on Tulagi. In addition, at the time of the invasion there were about ten flying boats and ten seaplane fighters on the island.'

"'The situation is extremely serious. Our naval forces operating in the Rabaul area have been ordered to engage the enemy immediately, in full strength, and to drive back the American invasion forces at any cost.'

"Captain Saito stopped for a moment, then continued. 'Our fighter plane units have been ordered to escort the land-based medium attack bombers which will attack enemy ships. Certain fighter groups will precede the bombers and their escorts into the battle area as challenging units, to draw off the American fighter planes.'

"'It is about 560 nautical miles from this base to Guadalcanal Island. This will be the longest mission you have ever been called upon to fly. You will be taxing your airplanes to the utmost, and I want every pilot to take maximum precautions to conserve fuel.'

"Captain Saito was finished. As we were already prepared for immediate takeoff, the only change in our plans was to receive the exact location of the battle area, and to prepare the necessary air maps for each pilot. I began to outline the course we would follow to Guadalcanal, noting the great distance our planes would be flying.

"Guadalcanal is along a string of isles. This won't be any trouble!

"Just before we climbed into the Zeros, we were given a special briefing by Lieutenant (J.G.) Junzo Sasai, the second squadron leader and my immediate superior. He was unusually serious.

" 'The American fighters over the Guadalcanal area are known to have come from aircraft carriers supporting the invasion. They are probably regular American navy fighters, not army planes brought in especially for this attack. This is the first time we will be meeting American navy fighters. Be careful, and *never lose sight of my plane.'*

"United States naval planes! Just to hear that we would meet them excited me. I had been anxious to meet American carrier pilots for a long time. Now my chance had come!

"I had been flying fighters for six years, and had more than three thousand hours in the air. I had participated in our attacks on the Chinese inland cities of Chungking, Chengtu, Lanchow, and others in the Sino-Japanese Incident. Since the outbreak of the Pacific War, I had fought in the Philippines and the Dutch East Indies.

"So far I had shot down fifty-six enemy planes; and was one of the leading aces of all Japanese naval fighter pilots. But I had never met any carrier planes. As aircraft carrier fighter pilots must receive elaborate training for landing and taking off from the narrow decks of carriers, there were many unusually skilled pilots among our carrier personnel. The same situation probably prevailed among the American carrier pilots.

" 'Well, my chance has finally come,' I thought. 'Let's see how well they can fight.'

"At 0800 hours our Zero fighters left the field, one after the other, assuming three-plane formations as we climbed away from the fighter strip. We then adopted escort positions above and behind the medium attack bombers. There were twenty-seven bombers escorted by eighteen fighters, with the former flying at about fifteen thousand feet. I was flight leader of the second section of the second fighter squadron.

"We flew southward along the line of the Solomon Islands. Shortly before noon the pilots were able to make out the waters of Lunga Roads off Guadalcanal Island.

"There were scattered clouds at about thirteen thousand feet, but above and below that level the sky was absolutely clear. We searched Lunga Roads carefully and gradually distinguished the shapes of the enemy ships in the area.

"The water seemed covered with vessels. I had never seen so large a convoy before, although I had flown on many occasions over Japanese troopship fleets during our invasion operations. I couldn't help admiring the men below me, even though they were enemies.

"Action ahead! At that moment, the fighter planes of the Challenge Units, which had preceded our flight by about ten minutes, seemed to attack enemy fighter planes. Far ahead of us we could see the bright yellow flashes peculiar to burning aircraft bursting like so many sparks. Seven or eight lines of smoke streamed down toward the ground, drawing graceful, curving arcs in the sky.

"Somebody's airplanes had been shot down, but it was impossible at this distance to tell whether they were ours or those of the enemy. The dogfight broke up quickly, and we could no longer see any aircraft—friendly or enemy—in the air.

"Seeing the sky clear of enemy fighter planes, our attack bombers suddenly began shallow dives toward the enemy ships, picking up speed as they prepared to bomb. Because of the sudden change in plan from the original schedule to attack Rabi, our bombers had not had time to replace their bombs with torpedoes; consequently, they would make high-level attacks.

"'It might go well,' I thought, even though torpedo attack was invariably more successful than level bombing against ships; the absence of enemy fighters meant an uninterrupted run for the bombers.

"Unexpectedly two enemy fighters appeared, headed for our fighter formation. I swung down to attack, and the enemy planes quickly left the area. I had to curb my desire to pursue the enemy fighters, recalling our leader's instructions given to us just before takeoff. Biting my lips in frustration, I climbed back to the formation and resumed my position.

"Ahead of us, the bombers seemed to lurch slightly as each aircraft released its deadly load; the formation was bombing en masse. The missiles hurtled down toward the enemy ships and the bomb spread successfully covered the enemy convoy, but only a few of the bombs appeared to hit any ships. We could see about eighty large ships in the enemy fleet; countless landing barges were heading for the beach, the brilliant white wakes on the water surface having the appearance of brush strokes of a giant but invisible artist.

"Although it had been only five or six hours since the enemy invasion forces had stormed in to land on Guadalcanal, what appeared to be enemy antiaircraft fire could be seen coming from guns on the island. I was amazed at the ability of the enemy to place his antiaircraft weapons on shore so rapidly. From what we had been told about mass invasions, it took about a week to complete the landing of thirty ships. That was the time required for our army to unload thirty vessels during the landings at Soerabaja in March of this year.

"Our speed of landing was far behind that being carried out by the enemy below me now. It was hard to believe. I realized intuitively that any invasion force which could push ashore so rapidly would be a very tough foe indeed.

"The bombing runs were over quickly, and the bombers had already turned and were heading back from Lunga through Tulagi. The fighter escort swung into position to protect the bombers. I had not yet fired a single bullet or cannon shell.

"Without warning a group of enemy fighters jumped our formations from above. We could see the tracers spitting through our formations. With this first burst of fire, the fighter planes of both sides, about thirty in all, instantly broke formation. Planes scattered in all directions as our Zeros tried to break free of the attacking enemy. About half the planes in the air could be seen. As I pushed the stick hard over and rolled away, I noticed several aircraft plunging earthward, trailing streaks of black smoke.

"I managed successfully to dodge the attacking fighters, but in doing so lost sight of two of my boys.

" 'Damn it,' I thought, angry at myself for losing sight of my own pilots. I twisted around and, far below, I saw three Zeros pursued by a single enemy fighter. The Zeros were trying desperately to escape from the enemy plane, but the enemy pilot hung doggedly on their tails. The Zeros looked like my boys: Hatori, Yonekawa, and another pilot. The enemy plane was a new type I had never seen before, probably a Grumman F4F Wildcat, a type we were told was in the area. The enemy pilot was very skilled in combat; he was relentless in his attacks against the three Zeros.

"My pilots needed help—and quickly. I pushed the throttle forward, drawing alongside my squadron leader; signaling Lieutenant Sasai, I pushed the stick forward and dove alone from the squadron to the battle raging below us.

"Not a second could be wasted. I opened fire on the enemy fighter plane while I was still more than three thousand feet away. It was too great a distance to cause any damage, but I accomplished my purpose. The moment the enemy pilot became aware of my airplane, he abandoned pursuit of the three Zeros at once and turned sharply to meet my attack.

"This pilot was good. As we fought, twisting and turning, I realized also that the Grumman's fighting performance far exceeded that of any other American, Dutch, or Chinese fighter planes I had encountered.

"But my long experience in air combat finally gave me the margin over this enemy, too. As I had always done in the past, I took out my Leica camera and snapped a picture of the new plane as I closed in on the enemy fighter from behind. Thus far, I had taken in this manner a total of twenty rolls of film, or about seven hundred photographs of airfields and enemy planes both in the air and on the ground.

"After snapping a shot for proof of the new enemy aircraft, I resumed attack. When I closed in from the best firing angle, approaching from the rear left of the Grumman, the pilot appeared to realize that he could no longer win. He fled at full speed toward Lunga.

"I had full confidence in my ability to destroy the Grumman, and decided to finish off the enemy fighter with only my 7.7-mm. machine guns. I turned the 20-mm. cannon switch to the 'off' position, and closed in.

"For some strange reason, even after I had poured about five or six hundred rounds of ammunition directly into the Grumman, the airplane did not fall, but kept on flying. I thought this very odd—it had never happened before—and closed the distance between the two airplanes until I could almost reach out and touch the Grumman. To my surprise, the Grumman's rudder and tail were ripped to shreds, looking like an old torn piece of rag.

"With his plane in such condition, no wonder the enemy pilot was unable to continue fighting! Even as I studied the condition of the Grumman's tail, my Zero pulled ahead of the enemy fighter. I slid open the canopy and turned to look back at the enemy pilot. He was a big man, with an oval face and a fair complexion. We stared at each other for countless seconds; I would never forget the strange feeling when our eyes met.

"Keeping alert for any sudden moves by the Grumman, I waved my right hand in a gesture of 'come on if you dare!' The enemy was behind me now, and in position to attack my plane. He had an excellent opportunity to shoot me down. Perhaps, however, the pilot was seriously wounded. Changing his hand holding the control stick from the right to his left hand, he acted as though he were praying, 'Save me!' with his right.

"After closely observing the strange movements of the enemy pilot, I cut my throttle and fell to the rear of the Grumman. The time had come to destroy the enemy fighter. Switching the cannon position to 'on,' I closed in again and pushed the cannon trigger.

"I could see the shells exploding all over the Grumman, which went to pieces in the air. The enemy fighter plunged earthward. Far below I saw a parachute open, but lost sight of the pilot as he drifted over Lunga toward land.

"Later, as I recalled the details of the dogfight, I thought I had done a pitiless thing by destroying the Grumman. But at the time, seeing the enemy pilot administering a severe beating to my own boys, I was so excited that all I could think of was to deliver the fatal blow to the enemy. If the pilot is dead, I wish I could tell his family how well he fought. . . .

"As soon as the fight had ended, I realized my altitude was much too low for safety. As quickly as possible, I rounded up the pilots in my section. As we closed in toward each other, I took the muffler from my face to identify myself. They appeared overjoyed to discover I was unharmed.

"No sooner had we climbed in formation above the cloud layer at 15,000 feet than tracer bullets sprayed about us. The bullets were coming from our rear left. One of the enemy slugs smashed into the cockpit and bored a hole the size of my fist through the window just behind my head. That was close!

"Apparently a two-seat Douglas SBD dive bomber had followed us as we were climbing. Hiding in the clouds, he swung up to attack as soon as we had broken above the cloud layer. We climbed rapidly and swung around to attack the SBD from the rear and high above. After the first burst the dive bomber began to fall out of control.

"We reorganized our formation and continued on toward the main battle area. About six miles ahead of us, over what appeared to be Tulagi, I sighted a formation of eight enemy planes. My exceedingly good eyesight had always proven of great help before, enabling me to spot and make out details of enemy aircraft long before they could identify us.

"'Enemy planes!' I warned my pilots. I could tell they were enemy aircraft by the formation they held: two formations of four planes each, maintaining an altitude of about eighteen thousand feet.

"If the enemy formation had been aware of us, they would have immediately turned and pressed home an attack, taking advantage of their higher altitude. But it appeared that they had not sighted our fighters approaching them from below to their rear. 'If they are to fight,' I thought, 'they must spread out their present formation. No—they are narrowing the space between planes! They do not even know we are closing in—this is a chance to hit them hard!

"'If I can shoot down two planes from each formation in a single attack by surprising them from their rear and below, I shall be able to take care of half of them by myself. And my boys will take care of the rest.'

"I pushed the throttle lever as far forward as it would go, building up maximum speed. It didn't matter if the other Zeros fell behind. Speed is of paramount importance in a battle, and I could not afford to let the opportunity be lost.

"There was good reason to follow this procedure. On three separate occasions I had made surprise attacks on enemy formations, striking from a position below and to the rear of the enemy, and succeeded in shooting down at least two planes in each attack. The first time this happened was over Soerabaja, when I shot down two Dutch planes, while the second and third were over Port Moresby. On both of these last two occasions, my opponents were Bell P-39s. I would try the same attack today.

"The distance between my plane and the enemy formation narrowed steadily . . . 1,700 feet, 1,300 feet, 1,000 feet. As soon as I had approached within 1,000 feet, I made out the details of the enemy planes. I had run into a trap!

"Up to this moment I had believed the enemy planes to be fighters. But no! They were TBF torpedo bombers. No wonder they had narrowed the space between their planes before they *had* sighted our fighters and closed up for protection.

"I cursed myself for my own stupidity. I was only 300 feet away from the enemy planes. I could see clearly the turrets on each Grumman TBF—from each glass enclosure a single heavy 12.7-mm. machine gun—sixteen in all—were directed at my single plane!

"There was no way to escape. If I turned suddenly I would expose the underside of the Zero to the concerted fire of all sixteen heavy guns. I could only continue to attack. My plane rushed toward the enemy bombers—270 feet—200 feet—160 feet.

"I could go no closer. I jabbed down savagely on the firing button. My 20-mm. cannon and the enemy heavy machine guns fired almost simultaneously, bridging the narrow gap between our planes with smoking, streaking tracers.

"*Crash!* A terrible noise beyond all description. The whole world exploded, and the Zero rocked and shook like a toy. I didn't know what had happened. Was it a head-on crash? I couldn't tell.

"I felt as though I had been smashed on the head with a club. The sky flared up in red and I lost consciousness. I discovered later that two enemy planes and my own fighter began to fall simultaneously. Perhaps two thirds of the front windshield of the Zero had been smashed and blown off by the enemy machinegun bullets.

"My plane must have dropped like a stone. Within a few moments, the cold air streaming in through the shattered windshield restored me to consciousness. The first thing that came to my mind was the face of my beloved mother.

"'What's the matter with you? Shame on you, fainting from such a little wound!' She seemed to be scolding me.

"From a height of 18,000 feet I had dropped to about 7,000 feet. The plane was still falling out of control when suddenly I thought of a suicide bombing.

"'If I must die,' I thought, 'I will take an American warship with me. They are far preferable to a transport. I saw them only a few minutes ago; I can remember them well. The short and fat ships are transports, the long, slender vessels are cruisers. If I hit a cruiser, it will be all to my credit as a pilot.'

"Even as I thought about diving into an American warship I was scanning the ocean. I couldn't see any ships! I couldn't see *anything!* What was wrong? Only then did I realize that my face had been slashed and cut by numerous shell fragments, and that I was blind.

"The Zero continued its plunge toward the ocean. Because of the increased wind pressure howling through the shattered cockpit, due to the Zero picking up speed as it dove, I was hazy and was unable to judge the engine's condition or even gain a good idea of my flight position.

"Strangely, I felt no pain.

"Unconsciously, from force of habit, I pulled back on the control stick. Apparently the plane pulled out of its uncontrolled dive and regained a horizontal position; the wind pressure through the cockpit eased somewhat.

"I tried to move the engine throttle lever. My left hand was totally numb; I could not even flex the fingers. When I attempted to press on the rudder pedals to correct the Zero's awkward flight, I discovered that my left leg also was numb.

"In desperation I released the control stick and rubbed both eyes with my right hand. After rubbing as hard as possible for a few moments, I began to make out the left wing tip. I could see—though barely—with my left eye! Although I continued rubbing my right eye, it was useless. I could not regain my vision and the eye remained blind.

"I saw through a brilliant red film, as though the entire world and everything in it were blazing fiercely. I jabbed my left hand and left leg with my right hand, but felt nothing. They were both completely paralyzed. 'What happened?' I kept asking myself, over and over.

"Suddenly I felt in my head a terrible, agonizing pain, which left me weak and breathless. I reached up and uneasily probed about my head with my right hand; it came away sticky with blood.

"It was at this moment, when I was still gasping from the pain in my head, that I caught sight of something black racing below my left wing. With my left eye, I could barely make out what appeared to be large black objects swishing past the wing.

"I wondered what they could be when abruptly, above the roar of the engine, I heard machine guns chattering. Several bullets cut through the wings and the Zero trembled slightly from the impact. I was flying directly over the enemy troop convoy!

"I thought, 'So now my life is finally coming to an end.' I had given up all hope for surviving this flight. Since I had recovered, even if only slightly, my ability to remain conscious and fly the airplane, I could at any time make a suicide attack against an enemy ship. There was little use in prolonging a useless struggle. Once I had accepted the inevitability of death, I calmed down and took closer stock of the airplane's condition. Then I thought:

"'Didn't I shoot down several enemy airplanes today? I have probably brought my total up to sixty. I have sent those many airplanes to the same doom I am about to meet. Now it is my turn. I have always expected this to happen. On this very day I made the biggest—and the last—mistake of my life, when I mistook the enemy TBF bombers for single-seat fighters. Anyway, I have finally met the American Navy planes which I have long been looking for. There is nothing I have to regret.'

"It was at this moment that I began to weigh the possibilities of life or death.

" 'I've got it,' I thought. 'If I can, I'll engage an enemy plane and let it win over me. I will go out as a pilot should—in air battle. It still won't be too late to crash into an enemy ship after that.'

"Expecting an attack by an enemy fighter, many of which should be in the air to protect the troop convoy, I flew about in wide circles.

"The minutes went by slowly. Nothing happened. 'Will they come, after all? Will I suddenly hear the sounds of machine guns firing as enemy fighters dive against my Zero?' I waited, flying about aimlessly, but nothing happened. It seemed I was all alone in the sky.

"I looked at the sea below, and noticed my plane was headed toward Tulagi. As my head cleared further and I could see better from my left eye, I reached across my body with my right hand and pushed the throttle forward. The engine picked up and the Zero forged ahead.

" 'If this keeps up,' I said to myself, 'I might gain altitude. And if luck stays with me, I might even reach Shortland, or Buka, if not Rabaul itself.'

"Although I had accepted death as inevitable, I was still human and I wished to delay that death as long as possible. If the airplane could still fly, and I could stay conscious, then I had a good chance. But first the bleeding must be stopped. I took off my gloves and began to examine my wounds.

"As the wound on my head seemed to be the most serious and was still bleeding, I inserted the index and middle fingers of my right hand into my head through the gash in my flying cap. They penetrated deeply, and the wound felt sticky and rough. Obviously the wound was very deep, shattering the bones of the skull. Unbelievably, my head was clear and I was beginning to see even better than before.

"As I probed the wounds, I recalled a story about Ryuma Sakamoto, a courageous samurai, who remained alive even after an assassin had inflicted a terrible head injury. Well, if my luck held out, I'd make Shortland. I'd try to reach there if at all possible.

" 'Something must still be in my head,' I thought. It felt unusually heavy and the bleeding continued unchecked. (A medical examination later disclosed two 12.7-mm. machinegun bullets lodged in my brain, with many small fragments imbedded in my skull.) Blood, hot and sticky, ran down along my neck and was halted by the muffler around my neck and the collar of my flying suit. It clogged into an uncomfortable, sticky mess.

"Parts of my face and head which were exposed to the wind seemed to have been slashed and scarred like a corrugated board. The wind blowing in through the smashed windshield had dried the blood, caking it on my face.

"I was still in serious trouble. I could not make out the details of the compass because of my blind right eye, and could see only hazily through the left.

"In order to reach Shortland, I would have to retrace the general course we flew toward Guadalcanal this morning. But I could not determine the right direction. It was impossible to make out compass details.

"Fortunately, during our flight to Guadalcanal this morning I tried to prepare for an emergency in the event my compass went out of order, and I was separated from the other fighters. I decided that the only method for determining proper direction would be to take readings of the sun's position.

"I spit repeatedly on my right hand, rubbing my eyes again and again. But it was to no avail; I could not even find the sun! Throughout the growing hopelessness of my situation, the only consolation was the amazing fact that the airplane, somehow, managed to keep on flying, despite the great damage it had suffered. By all reasoning, the fighter should have crashed long ago.

"Unable to do anything at the moment to ascertain the proper direction to take to reach Shortland, I tried again to stop the head bleeding. I always carried triangular bandages with me in my Zero, for just such an emergency as this. I took the bandage out and tried to apply it to my wounded head in an attempt to stop the blood. The strong wind in the cockpit made the first two attempts unsuccessful. It was extremely difficult to place the bandage around my head, since I must simultaneously bandage myself and fly the airplane, and my left hand was useless.

"Before I knew it, the bandages were gone, and I was no better off than when I had started. I unwrapped the muffler from about my neck. Tucking one end under my right foot, and holding the other with my right hand, I cut the muffler into four pieces with a knife clenched tightly between my teeth. Three of these 'muffler bandages,' made with great effort, were snatched by the wind and I was left with only one piece.

"I forced myself to be calm. I had been too impatient, and had fumbled badly with the bandages and the muffler strips. To reduce the wind pressure as much as possible, I lowered the seat as far as it would go.

"Then I set the engine controls and the control stick in a position where the airplane would fly by itself, and started to apply the last piece of bandage to my head.

"Holding one end of the muffler strip in my teeth to prevent it from being blown away, with my right hand I pushed it inch by inch into the gap between my head and the flying cap. Holding my breath, I tightened the flying-cap strap as much as possible. The bleeding stopped.

"I felt as if my struggle with the bandages had lasted for at least half an hour. Just when I felt I could relax, I was faced with my worst enemy: overwhelming drowsiness. I felt like drifting off to sleep, into a warmth without pain or trouble. I could hardly fight off the overpowering desire to sleep.

"When, finally, I managed to keep my one good eye open and look about me, I discovered to my astonishment that the Zero was upside down. Quickly I pushed the stick over and corrected the flight attitude. I knew that if I did not remain fully alert from now on I would plunge to my death. I slammed my fist against my head; the consequent pain kept me alert for a while.

"In a few minutes the excruciating pain in my head increased to an almost unbearable intensity. I felt like screaming. My face felt as though a hot flame were being played across it. I was being burned alive. Even so, waves of exhaustion beat against me and I began drifting off to sleep again. The Zero wobbled in the air as my hand began to go limp. Even the terrible agony of my wounds could not keep me awake. I was forced to strike my head again with my right fist.

"Somehow I kept the Zero in the air, flying straight and level. I was forced repeatedly to hammer my fist against my head to stay alert. Even through my agony, the drowsiness washed in waves over me; each time I fought it off by striking my head with my fist.

"I was fighting desperately to keep alert. I knew I could not keep flying like this much longer. I thought suddenly of my lunch; there was still some left in the cockpit. About thirty minutes before the bomber and fighter formations had arrived at Guadalcanal, I had eaten half of the *maki-zushi*, rolled cakes of rice which I carried on long missions. Half of the food was still there, and it might be enough to keep me awake.

"With my bloody hands, I crammed the rice cakes into my mouth, forcing myself to eat. I managed to chew and swallow three pieces, but when I began to eat the fourth, I suddenly became sick and threw up everything I had swallowed. My stomach would not accept any food.

"Again, I drifted off toward sleep, and had to pound at my head to remain conscious.

"If I kept succumbing to the successive attacks of drowsiness, I knew that sooner or later I *would* fall asleep, and that would be the end. I would never reach Shortland or Buka. I decided it would be better to return to Guadalcanal and to dive into an enemy ship, rather than drift about the ocean until either I fainted completely or my fuel was exhausted.

"When I banked and turned the Zero back toward the battle area, my head miraculously cleared. My senses were sharp, and I was wide awake. Again my thoughts turned to my chances of returning to a Japanese airfield. I swung the plane about again and headed it in a direction I thought would take me home. In a short while I was sleepy again.

"By now I was moving almost from habit. For the third time I turned the plane about and headed for the battle area at Guadalcanal, determined once more to carry out my suicide attack. It was a succession of moments of clearheadedness and overwhelming drowsiness. I repeated the turns toward Guadalcanal, away from the battle area, and back again, and once more directed my plane toward my home base.

"I was caught in a dilemma between the overpowering instinct of self-preservation and the strong desire to finish this maddening flight with a glorious and honorable death. Somehow, each emotion would win out over the other every few minutes and I would subconsciously turn the Zero about.

"I went totally blind again. A shadow of islands which I had in sight disappeared abruptly from my view, and then the instrument panel faded before my left eye. I was in the worst possible situation. I could not determine where I was nor in which direction. Guadalcanal or my home base lay. I tried to rub my eyes with spit in the attempt to see again, but when I spat on my hands nothing came out from my mouth. It had become so dry not even a trace of saliva was left.

"Everything was going wrong at once. I was lost and totally blind, half-paralyzed, and with a shot-up airplane. Then the Zero began to buck and pitch, shuddering as it lost stability. I hung desperately to the control stick, trying to keep the plane level by feel alone.

Suddenly I could see again! Lines of white streaked at tremendous speed before me. The Zero was almost into the water! The white lines were the crests of waves whipping by just below the plane's wings.

"In another minute I made out an island ahead of the plane. 'God saved me!' I cried. But when I neared the 'island' it turned out to be a black squall cloud, hanging low over the water. I was fooled in this manner several times. I flew aimlessly about for nearly two hours.

"Finally, with my head clearing steadily, I was able to read the needle and large letters of the compass with my left eye. My chances of returning to a Japanese air base were better than at any time since i had been hit.

"Allowing for a wandering flight on my part, I judged my position to be roughly north-northeast of the Solomon Islands.

"With the sleeve of my flying suit, I did the best to wipe my blood from the smeared map, and spread it out on my knees. I marked an 'X' on the map where I estimated my position to be. Then I turned ninety degrees to the west, hoping to cross the Solomon Islands, which stretched almost due north and south.

"Forty minutes later I sighted a horseshoe-shaped reef. It was one of the Green Islands, which, because of its peculiar shape, had drawn my attention on the flight this morning.

"If I kept going like this, I would be all right soon. I had been in a hopeless situation for some time, but it appeared I was now well on my way to making it to a Japanese air base. Nothing is more discouraging to a pilot than to become lost, notably when fuel is running short.

"The danger of direction was thus met, but almost immediately I was beset with another almost fatal incident. I had barely turned the Zero on its new course when the engine died, and the fighter began to drop toward the ocean. The fuel in the main tanks had run out, with only some forty gallons left in the reserve tank.

"To economize on fuel, I had been running the engine on such a lean mixture that it did not start up again when I switched to another tank. I released the control stick and moved the throttle lever back and forth with my right hand, switching as rapidly as I could between these movements to manipulate the fuel pump.

"The Zero was almost into the water when the engine caught. I had been frantically operating the throttle lever, working the fuel pump, and trying to stretch my glide—all with a paralyzed left arm and left leg, and a blinded right eye.

"I was soaked with cold perspiration.

"Before long I sighted New England Island. Rabaul was not far away, and my hopes for reaching my own base rose high. I began to climb slowly, trying to gain altitude so I could take the shortest route by crossing the island.

"Climbing required much fuel. Despite the drain on my rapidly dwindling fuel reserves, I had to try to gain some altitude. Abruptly my hopes were dashed. A black squall cloud appeared directly before me when I had climbed to 5,000 feet. My only alternative was to detour along the coast of the island. I did not dare chance flying through the squall.

"I changed course to a southwest heading. Below me there appeared several white streamers on the water; they appeared to be from Japanese warships heading south at high speed.

" 'If I land in the water alongside the ships,' I thought, 'I can be rescued. But that might mean diverting the ships from an important mission. I cannot do that.' I held my course for Rabaul.

"The minutes fled by as the engine droned. Even though I was very tired, I was no longer beset by the attacks of drowsiness which had nearly caused my death before. After a while—I don't know how long it was—I searched the island below my right wing. I noticed a large crater in the ground . . . it was the crater by the airstrip!

" 'It' Rabaul!'

"I could hardly believe what I saw. It all seemed like a dream. Later, I found that I had been in the air for eight and a half hours that day.

"Landing the Zero would be extremely difficult, since my left leg was numb and my rudder control would be very poor. I had little hope of making a safe landing, since the Zero had been so badly shattered by enemy fire that it was a miracle the plane had remained aloft. In this case, the standing rule was to land on the sea. Even if the plane sank, the pilot could be rescued by the crash boats which would be waiting.

"I prepared myself for the crash landing, gently easing the throttle lever back. Gradually the plane lost altitude as I turned into the wind. Even as I dropped toward the water I changed my mind.

"I was sure my hours were numbered. 'Even if I make a successful water landing and am rescued,' I thought, 'I will not live very long. I am ashamed that I have considered causing so much trouble to my friends, who will rescue from the water a man who will be of no further use. Although it is more dangerous, I shall land directly on the field and save all the trouble a water landing will create.'

"I pulled up from my slow descent and circled the field, studying the strip for the best way to come in. After making one unsuccessful pass at the strip, I pulled up and decided to see if the landing gear would lower. I had little hope that it would work, since the plane had been so badly shot up. But the green light in the cockpit lit up, indicating that the two landing legs had lowered properly. I was even more amazed when the landing flaps slid below the wings. 'It's not hopeless, after all,' I thought.

"Prospects for a safe landing appeared to be good, once the undercarriage and the flaps had lowered. I circled the runway at one end of the strip and began my letdown. Since I could not tell what might happen upon landing—the undercarriage might collapse, for example—I cut the ignition switch to reduce the chance of fire or explosion. Usually I could cut off the ignition switch with my right hand with ease, but it was impossible to do so now. I managed to hit the switch with my right leg, after squirming about as much as my paralyzed left leg and arm would permit.

"Judging my altitude and my rate of descent by the top of a coconut grove which I could dimly make out, I drifted toward the runway. I controlled the plane in a daze, until I thought I felt the wheels strike the ground.

"Since the ignition switch was already off, the propellor stopped whirling immediately after the plane touched the earth. I could feel the ship slow down as it rolled along the strip.

"The indescribable feeling that I was at last back on the ground safely filled my whole body and mind. It is a supreme moment that belongs only to a pilot, and cannot be explained to anyone else.

" 'I've come home!' The thought surged joyously through my mind. Perhaps because of the sudden release of tension, I felt again the waves of drowsiness washing over me. This time there was no fighting back; I drifted into a dim world of red haze. I remember almost nothing of what happened after that.

"Before I lost consciousness completely, I felt hands striking my shoulder and voices calling my name. They were shouting, 'Sakai! Sakai! Never say die!'

"Several men clambered onto the wing of the battered Zero. They were Commander Kozono, the air officer, Lieutenant Commander Nakajima, my group commander, and Lieutenant Sasai, my squadron leader. The three men unfastened my parachute and safety belt, lifted me from the cockpit, and carried me gently to the ground.

"I was told later that my face was bloody and swollen so terribly that I appeared as a strange being from another world, so that even my own pilots feared me and stood aloof."

* * *

The story of Saburo Sakai is a tale almost beyond belief. Not only in the Japanese Navy, but also among the other navies of the world, this episode stands out above other great tales of courage and heroism. We do not believe that the performance of Saburo Sakai and his single-seat, single-engine Zero fighter, has been equaled in the entire war. This is in no way a deprecation of other truly heroic air war episodes, with which the writers are familiar. Sakai flew his small fighter airplane for nearly nine hours, including combat time in which he downed four enemy aircraft to run his total kills to sixty, and covered a distance of 560 nautical miles during his bitter struggle to return to his home base.

The deeds established by Saburo Sakai and the unit to which he belonged testify most vividly to Sakai's unusual skill and to that of his battlemates. It was a skill achieved only through constant combat experience, and ably supported by the high quality of the Zero fighter airplane.

Sakai remained in a hospital, undergoing medical treatment, for a year after this battle. He recovered from all wounds except that inflicted to his right eye, the sight of which he never regained. In June of 1944, when American forces launched a massive assault against the Marianas, Sakai was dispatched to Iwo Jima from the Yokosuka Naval Air group, to which he had been assigned after his hospital discharge. Despite blindness in one eye, he returned to air combat and succeeded in shooting down two American navy fighters over Iwo Jima. He later shot down two other American warplanes to bring his total to sixty-four planes destroyed.

Sakai flew with a seventeen-plane *"Kamikaze"* mission for an attack on the American Navy's Task Force 58. Thirteen planes were destroyed by defending enemy fighters before reaching their goal. The four remaining aircraft, including Sakai's, returned to Iwo Jima, where American bombers destroyed them on the ground.

A courier plane was rushed to Iwo Jima to pick up Sakai and sixteen other stranded pilots. All pilots were returned to Japan; thereafter, Sakai fought against the enemy B-29s which were carrying out mass raids against Japan's cities.

In March of 1945 Sakai (now an ensign) and a fellow pilot were commended by Admiral Soemu Toyoda, Commander in Chief of the Combined Fleet, for their exemplary record in destroying enemy planes. In August of 1945 he was promoted to the rank of Lieutenant (J.G.). Sakai ended World War II as the leading surviving ace of all our pilots.

On August 7, 1942, the same day Sakai experienced his terrible ordeal, our naval air forces reported the destruction of fifty-eight enemy aircraft in combat; on this date the United States Navy announced that it had lost twenty-one planes in battle.

The desperate air struggle which exploded with the initial attack of August 7 were the start of a series of long, wearisome battles in which Japanese air strength was inexorably sapped. The constant air war between American and Japanese air forces gradually, as though with some power of the Devil himself, sucked our naval air forces, and ultimately our army and naval surface strength, into a bottomless swamp wherein waited only defeat.

CHAPTER 17

Succession of Air Battles After Guadalcanal

ONE OF THE MOST formidable enemies confronting the Japanese Navy in the drawn-out struggle for Guadalcanal Island was its own negligence. The Navy had not considered the many possible threats which might result from a battle in which Guadalcanal and its environs were the stakes, and neglected to construct air bases on the islands which stretched for 560 nautical miles from Rabaul to Guadalcanal. Before the months-long fighting ended in defeat, this scarcity of base facilities proved to be a threat equally as serious as the American air attacks.

Our air crews of the smaller bombers were forced to the limit of their endurance, and too frequently these bombers dispatched from Rabaul failed to return because they ran out of fuel. Such incredible missions as that performed by Saburo Sakai, notably in the matter of flight endurance, came to be regarded as the rule and not the exception.

Bomber crews soon wearied of the strain of missions

from which their return was mathematically doubtful and often, in the cases of their flying mates, impossible. We could not maintain the pressure indefinitely, even with experienced and excellent air crews which were thrown into the fierce struggle for the vital Guadalcanal Island.

Medium bombers and Zero fighters based at Rabaul had sufficient range to attack American forces in the lower Solomons, and still return. Our Type 99 dive bombers, however, were dispatched in missions on which their crews despaired of survival. Simply stated, the airplanes could not carry sufficient fuel to make the round-trip flight from Rabaul to Guadalcanal and return. Within two days of the American invasion, we lost eighteen Type 99 bombers, but only a few planes fell to the enemy's guns. Their fuel ran out as they struggled to reach Rabaul, and all bombers crashed.

It was a terribly depressing situation. At the outset of the invasion, our Zero fighters were superior in almost every respect to the American planes which they opposed, yet their combat effectiveness was steadily being sapped by the strain which the pilots suffered from too many hours spent in the cramped confines of the planes' cockpits. This disintegration of our effectiveness in air attack was enough to drive the combat commanders to the verge of insanity; they had spent years in developing their air units to peak efficiency, only now to have them shackled by strategic blindness.

Had Japan possessed even one fifth of the American capacity for constructing air bases, the Guadalcanal air campaign might have ended differently. Had we possessed such air bases, we could have brought several times as much power to bear upon the American forces. One of Japan's greatest blunders in the Pacific War certainly lay in its failure to devote proper study to such matters as logistical and engineering support of our combat air forces.

Air combat units superior to the enemy's were shackled by a denial of adequate ground facilities. Such deprivation operated as effectively in the enemy's favor as actual destructive bombing of our personnel and planes.

Shortly after the Guadalcanal invasion we received urgent requests for Zero fighter planes of improved performance, with emphasis on increased maneuverability and extended flight range. American air opposition was constantly increasing in strength, and the enemy's fighter planes were rapidly improving in quality.

The wingspan of the new-type fighter (Zero) was restored to its original length, which served to improve the maneuverability. This increased wingspan likewise permitted the installation of additional fuel cells in the outer wing, appreciably extending flight range.

The initial phase of the land, sea, and air struggle ended within three days of the invasion. Despite our predominant strength in warships, we not only failed to prevent the enemy from successfully assaulting the island but also lost the ability to sustain a heavy air attack against the invaders. In those first three days we tallied forty-two of our planes destroyed and missing in combat, in addition to numerous aircraft lost in crash landings and many more heavily damaged in air fighting.

Despite the superior quality of our fighters, the combat efficiency of the Japanese naval air forces almost immediately fell to less than half that of normal. Those planes capable of making the round-trip missions from Rabaul to attack the American forces were rapidly being depleted, and the remaining aircraft types had become "one-way-mission" planes which meant an ever more rapid deterioration in our strength.

It was not until August 21, when the Army's Ichiki Detachment launched its first offensive to recapture former

Japanese airstrips, that our naval air forces in this theater were able to resume attacks in strength against the enemy. We received badly needed reinforcements of both carrier and land-based warplanes, and prepared to launch a sustained aerial assault against the American forces.

But the gods of war decreed otherwise. Although the Buka airbase on the northern tip of Bougainville Island was made available to our fighters and bombers by August 27, poor weather seriously handicapped our aerial operations. On numerous occasions, Zero fighters took off in dangerous weather and, after reaching Guadalcanal Island, were forced by even worse weather conditions to return to their bases without contacting the enemy.

During the twenty-three days from August 21 to September 12, just prior to the launching of the Army's first general offensive with the Kawaguchi Detachment on Guadalcanal, our ground forces received air support on only ten days. The terrible weather conditions encountered en route broke up four major bombing attacks. During the remainder of the time, the weather was so bad that the planes could not even get off the ground.

The troops on the front could only curse and fume at the solid sheets of rain and blanketing fog, while our bombers sank deep in mud at the air bases. For the twenty-three-day period during which heavy air support was needed, Zero fighters flew the meager total of 237 sorties, and our land-based medium attack bombers made only 312 sorties.

Under such conditions we could not prevent the enemy fighters and bombers from attacking our supply lines; our communications were savagely bombed and machine-gunned. This aerial interdiction proved fatal; we were unable to transport the minimum quantities of ammunition and foodstuffs required by the Army forces on Guadalcanal. The Army's first general offensive against the invading enemy ended in failure.

During the Guadalcanal campaign, the numerical superiority of the enemy warplanes was not so great that it could not have been more than equalized by the superior performance of our Zero fighters. As the battle got under way, the American fighter planes opposing us did not match the agility of the Zero in combat; nevertheless, the enemy air forces enjoyed a tremendous advantage through their ability rapidly to construct and constantly to supply new air bases.

As of September 24, following a month of bitter fighting in the theater, our actual naval air strength was as follows:

Fighters	Zero 21	Zero 32	Number Pilots
Tainan Air Corps	9	0	39
6th Air Corps	12	13	30
3rd Air Corps	20	0	27
Kanoya Air Corps	9	0	9
2nd Air Corps	0	16	14
TOTAL	50	29	119

Land-Based Medium Attack Bombers	On Hand	Operational	Available Crew Units
Kisarazu Air Corps	21	15	23
Misawa Air Corps	15	12	23
Takao Air Corps	20	19	20
Kanoya Air Corps	23	16	18
TOTAL	79	62	84

The normal complement of aircraft consisted of at least 232 Zero fighters and 180 land-based medium attack bombers, the latter group made up equally of Type 96 and Type 1 bombers. Our fighter strength, therefore, was only

34 per cent of the minimum desired, and medium attack bomber strength, only 44 percent of that deemed necessary effectively to combat the enemy.

The Guadalcanal situation demanded action and the Army planned for another general offensive to commence in late October. Repeated attacks were mounted against enemy forces on the island; 480 sorties were flown by Zero fighters, and 307 sorties by medium attack bombers during the period of September 28 to October 25. The attacks were pressed with determination, but our air forces failed to strike a decisive blow against the enemy.

On the night of October 13, naval support was brought up in the form of our battleships *Kongo* and *Haruna*. The two heavy warships steamed offshore near an enemy airfield and shelled enemy aircraft and installations with great success. Despite this, our Army's second general offensive, which began the night of October 24, was crushed by the savage fighting of the enemy defenders.

Two days later our carrier forces inflicted telling damage on the enemy in the Battle of Santa Cruz. Despite the losses which the enemy sustained, his position remained strong, and recapture of the dreadful Guadalcanal Island appeared more difficult than ever.

Our air forces in the Rabaul area were steadily reinforced with new fighters and bombers from Japan, but many of the aircraft we threw into the battle were lost, and therefore represented only a wasted effort. By October 28, after a month-long struggle with an enemy which fought fiercely, the six air corps in the theater could muster a total of only thirty Zero fighters and sixty-six land-based medium attack bombers. Our airmen fought desperately, but were unable to stem the tidal wave of enemy power.

From the beginning of the operation to recapture Guadalcanal, launched by the Ichiki Detachment on

August 21, until the termination of the Army's unsuccessful second general offensive, air battle casualties for both sides were as follows (seaplane combat not reported):

Three hundred and forty enemy aircraft were destroyed, and sixty-nine aircraft probably destroyed, for a total of 409. Our naval air forces had lost seventy-eight Zero fighters, forty-two land-based medium attack bombers, and fifty-four other types, all either destroyed or missing.

Before the third general offensive designed to throw the American forces off Guadalcanal was launched, the air war had taken a downward course from which there seemed to be little hope of salvation. We were unable to supply the landbased naval air forces in the theater with sufficient aircraft to maintain more than an average strength of 160 planes in combat at any one time. Although we resorted to desperate measures to build up an overwhelming air strength, they were of slight avail.

There is little question that, had our air combat forces received adequate support through construction of new air bases and the proper maintenance of existing facilities, we could have destroyed many more enemy planes and ships, and might have influenced the ground fighting in our favor. However, the situation deteriorated steadily as Japanese construction crews seemingly delayed endlessly their efforts to build new air bases. As late as September 6, 1942, the Navy had managed to construct only *one* new air base, and that was a single installation at Buin, on the south end of Bougainville Island, which lies between Rabaul and Guadalcanal.

The Army's third general offensive intended to retake Guadalcanal suffered the same fate as the two previous attempts. Six months of bitter fighting, during which we had expended many hundreds of planes, many warships, the lives of thousands of men, and staggering amounts of materiel, went for naught. On February 7, 1943, the last troops abandoned Guadalcanal.

For our land and surface forces, the period immediately following the evacuation of Guadalcanal came to be a temporary lull in the war; the absence of major action afforded the opportunity for regrouping and strengthening. There was, however, no respite for the naval air arm, which launched large-scale air attacks.

The first of a number of heavy air assaults against the enemy was the so-called *"I-go"* operation which was carried out from early to mid-April. The strategic air campaign was under the direct command of Admiral Isoroku Yamamoto, Commander in Chief of the Combined Fleet.

The land-based air force under the command of Vice-Admiral Jinichi Kusaka constituted 190 planes; 160 carrier planes under the command of Vice-Admiral Jisaburo Ozawa were likewise thrown into the operation. While the 350 aircraft participating in the *I-go* campaign represented considerably more strength than had been hurled against the enemy at Guadalcanal, the total number of aircraft was less than that of the Nagumo Force which had smashed Pearl Harbor.

Air attacks in strength were directed against Guadalcanal and southeast New Guinea, striking in particular at Port Moresby, Oro Bay, and Milne Bay. Four heavy raids appeared to have achieved the desired results in destruction of enemy aircraft and ground facilities, but disaster struck even as the new aerial offensive gained in momentum.

En route to an inspection trip on the front, flying in a bomber escorted by nine fighters, on April 18 Admiral Yamamoto was ambushed over the southwestern tip of Bougainville Island by Lockheed P-38 fighters of the

American Thirteenth Air Force and was killed in the devastating attack. His loss was a severe blow to the Japanese forces.

By now it was obvious to all our military leaders that the outcome of any conflict, whether waged on the sea, on land, or in the air, depended upon the ability of our fighters to establish control of the air. Accordingly, requests for air support made by sea and land commanders invariably were for fighter planes which could guard the sea and land forces against enemy destruction from the air.

The concept of important air battles may be simplified by imagining the clashing of great air fleets, the core of which is constituted of fighter planes. The fighter planes opposing the enemy should be superior in performance and range. Every effort should also be made to insure numerical superiority, for the difference even of a single fighter can decide the outcome of a major conflict.

By the time the *I-go* operation had been launched, it was obvious that the dour prewar predictions concerning a struggle with the United States and Great Britain were to be realized. The insistence of numerous Japanese military and industrial leaders that "a war against the United States and Great Britain might well become a prolonged battle with little prospect of victory for a nation of such limited resources as Japan" was now assuming ominous reality. In the Guadalcanal campaign, the inability of our Navy to replace the Zero fighters lost in combat with the enemy became clear, and this crack in our air-power wall spread ever wider as the war progressed. Replacement of Zero fighters on every front was becoming more and more difficult, and never achieved the numbers requested by combat leaders. Japan lacked other fighters in sufficient number to replace the Zero, and our air strength was steadily whittled down, even as enemy power gained monstrous proportions.

(The average monthly output of Zero fighters, from April of 1942 through June of 1943, totaled 221 aircraft, even with the combined production facilities of Mitsubishi and Nakajima.)

A severe handicap of the Guadalcanal campaign was the inability of the Army properly to integrate its air strength into combined operations with naval air units. The Navy should have received support at least to the extent that half of all missions were carried out by Army air power. Unfortunately, this ratio was never attained, partly due to the fact that the majority of operations were conducted over a vast expanse of ocean.

Consequently, the Navy's Zero fighters, which were designed for carrier use and originally assigned to fleet divisions, were forced to fight in inferior numbers against all types of fighters and bombers which were divided into categories consisting of carrier- and land-based craft. Float-type reconnaissance planes and Zero observation sea planes were forced to undertake what were virtually suicide missions. Superhuman efforts were demanded of our pilots because of the insufficient number of Zero fighters. The qualitative superiority of our Navy planes could no longer compensate for the lack of numbers.

In June of 1943 the Allied Powers resumed their offensives from both the Solomon Islands and New Guinea fronts. The Navy poured hundreds of Zero fighters and Type 1 land-based attack bombers into this decisive theater in an attempt to destroy the effectiveness of the enemy's air power, but the battle of land-based air forces resulted only in imposing an increasing burden upon our Navy.

Our position worsened steadily as American air strength inexorably gained the coveted position for which it struggled so relentlessly. How many of our "farsighted" planners and military leaders then arose openly to regret that the air arms of our Navy and Army were not welded into a single coordinated force resembling that of the Americans!

This desire for coordinated air control was no mere wish to ease our command structure; the inability of Japanese forces effectively to utilize air power lost us the Gilbert Islands. This bastion fell to enemy hands in late November of 1943, and for precisely the same reason—lack of naval air strength—we lost the key points of the Marshall Islands in February of 1944. This loss seriously threatened our combat potential in the entire Pacific.

The effectiveness of the enemy's incessant air blows raised a losing battle to the status of a tragedy. To prevent an almost complete loss of our forces in the Rabaul area, Admiral Mineichi Koga, the new Commander of the Combined Fleet, reluctantly ordered all naval air units to abandon Rabaul, the only major air base in the Southwest Pacific opposing the advancing enemy. On February 20, 1944, our unit (Masatake Okumiya's) evacuated the island as the last air unit of the withdrawal, leaving behind only our ground forces.

These successive withdrawals from our airbases could be regarded as nothing less than major disasters. Every base which was abandoned meant another enemy advance toward the heart of Japan, and another key point from which the enemy could dispatch his far-ranging bombers. Each air base lost involved not only ground installations taken over by the Americans, but a never-to-be-regained loss in our ability further to resist the enemy. Furthermore, those ordering the hasty withdrawals from advanced air bases often overlooked and abandoned the numerous maintenance crews. Men whose skills represented the experience of many years were deserted, despite desperate rescue operations undertaken by plane and submarine, in remote jungle facilities. Thus, we lost forever their ability to contribute to subsequent air operations; this loss became increasingly evident as the enemy's pressure mounted.

The absence of these invaluable mechanics and maintenance crews greatly affected our operations. Maintenance suffered disastrously, and mechanics rushed through hasty training programs proved woefully inadequate for their tasks. Our already enormous difficulties were increased by the fact that mechanics with little experience were forced to work on aircraft which had been rushed through expanded production lines. On too many occasions pilots and aircrew members fell prey to enemy guns because vital plane parts failed in the crucial moments of combat.

We were faced with a vicious circle of attrition for which there appeared to be no solution. The shortage of new fighter planes meant that we must often send our best pilots into combat with worn and damaged planes. Their chances of survival against an enemy whose strength was growing daily were thereby greatly lessened.

As enemy attacks and our own deficiencies placed a steady drain on our fighting strength, the Americans were free to strike and fight at their discretion. Although the Navy still possessed the two monster battleships *Yamoto* and *Musashi*, each of nearly seventy-four thousand tons' gross weight and each mounting nine eighteen-inch guns, we were forced carefully to husband our strength for only the most critical battles.

The hunters had become the hunted.

CHAPTER 18

The Guadalcanal Campaign: Evaluation of American Warplanes

THE FIRST FORMIDABLE OPPONENT which the Zero fighter encountered was the four-engined Boeing B-17 Flying Fortress. Before the war, thirty-five of the heavy bombers were reported deployed on Luzon Island, but the majority of these planes were destroyed on the ground before the war was yet a full day old. Those few B-17s which managed to take to the air were attacked by Zero fighters in such number that they were overwhelmed and shot down before our overeager pilots could study their characteristics.

During the period between these initial attacks and the successful completion of the Dutch East Indies campaign in March of 1942, the B-17s increasingly interrupted our operations with unexpected bombing raids. Their great radius of at least 750 nautical miles enabled them to fly from bases far beyond the reach of our Type 96 and Type 1 land-based bombers, upon which the Navy had placed such high hopes.

Thanks to the excellent protection afforded by their bristling 12.7-mm. machine guns, self-sealing fuel tanks, great load capacity, and far-reaching range, the B-17s continued to harass our forces in courageous and tenacious attacks. Our commanders believed the B-17 to be the enemy's only hope in the almost helpless plight in which he found himself in the early part of the war.

Immediately after our occupation of Rabaul in late January of 1942, B-17s based at Port Moresby launched a series of persistent day and night attacks which rained bombs on our installations. Zero fighters of the Tainan Air Corps, a veteran fighter unit which had fought constantly against enemy planes since the outbreak of war, swarmed up to intercept and destroy the big bombers.

It was not long before the Zero fighter pilots realized that they were confronted with an enemy plane well capable of defending itself, and one which could survive tremendous damage from the guns and cannon of the Zeros. On numerous occasions the Boeings flew undaunted on their bombing and reconnaissance missions despite the attacks of Zero fighters which swarmed about them and which the enemy's heavy machine guns too often destroyed.

Flying Fortresses on reconnaissance discovered the Japanese invasion convoy bound for Port Moresby in May of 1942; this led directly to the savagely fought Coral Sea Battle. Without the B-17's tremendous range, many of our operations would have been successfully executed without encountering enemy interference.

The Midway Sea Battle of June, 1942, was also due to far-reaching B-17s, which scoured the ocean surface in search of our invasion fleet and radioed the position of our ships to powerful American bombing forces. In the Guadalcanal campaign, the movement of our forces was constantly exposed to the prying eyes of B-17 crewmen. We came to learn that it was almost impossible to conceal our activities within seven hundred nautical miles of any base which might harbor Flying Fortresses, and within eight hundred nautical miles of bases from which consolidated-Vultee B-24 Liberator bombers might take off. The B-17s and B-24s seemed almost to ignore the intercepting Zeros as they flew into any area of their choice.

Sun, the great Chinese strategist, once wisely said: "Those who know the enemy as well as they know themselves never suffer defeat." This historical statement was never proved truer than by the probing missions of the B-17 and B-24 bombers, which endowed the Americans with a tremendous advantage in the far-flung Pacific War.

For years the Japanese Navy had followed a strategic concept laid down by tradition: that a small Japanese force could achieve victory over superior enemy strength only so long as we were informed of the enemy's strength and movement, while ours remained hidden. With the B-17s and B-24s thundering constantly over our ships, airfields, and staging areas, the situation was reversed. We were in the position of the traditional enemy and handicapped by the same limitations we had always regarded as the opponent's weakness.

Placed in the uncomfortable position of having our every movement fully known to the enemy, we were compelled to discard plans long prepared and resort to the application of mass strength and force in battle. The strength of quantity could well outweigh the value of quality in a modern war in which new pawns could be hurled into the theater of decision as rapidly and as long as the accumulated reserves would permit, especially in sea and air conflicts where the machine, not man, played such a decisive role. Mechanical strength in overwhelming quantity also had a direct bearing on the fighting ability of ground troops, whose fate in the Pacific War depended solely upon marine transportation and supply.

By September of 1942 the reconnaissance-mission-flying B-17s and B-24s had become a grave problem, and the Japanese Navy tried every possible means of destroying the troublesome raiders. With the Guadalcanal campaign in full swing, our fighter pilots became desperate, but failed to achieve any notable advance in increasing the number of destroyed American bombers. Only overwhelming numbers of Zero fighters could destroy the enemy marauders, and there was little hope that we might acquire fighter planes with heavier fire power than that of the Zero.

Although the B-24 lacked the protection of the B-17 in total number of defending guns and other characteristics, the two airplanes were unique in their ability to defeat enemy fighter attacks. Neither Britain, Germany, nor Japan produced bombers capable of protecting themselves as well as the Fortresses and Liberators.

We believed that the heavy American bombers, with their great defensive power and amazing aggressiveness in battle, stemming from a great national strength and a national policy which at all times proved itself to be aggressive, were fundamentally responsible for the defeat of Germany and Japan.

Before we could unearth a satisfactory solution to the problems presented by the Flying Fortresses and Liberators, we faced another dilemma with equally severe consequences; this was posed by the Army's twin-engined Lockheed P-38 Lightning fighter planes.

Although the American Curtiss P-40 Tomahawk and Bell P-39 Airacobra fighters featured high diving speeds, and the Navy's Grumman F4F Wildcat exhibited good maneuverability, their general performance failed to measure up to that of the Zero. Like these fighters, the P-38s first used in combat against the Zeros appeared to lack any distinctive features other than speed at great altitude and a very high diving speed.

The strange Lightnings made their combat debut in the Solomon Islands during the fall of 1942. Soon they were appearing in ever-increasing numbers, often challenging our Zero fighters. To the great delight of our pilots the P-38 pilots would attempt to dogfight with the Zeros, which managed to shoot down many of the enemy planes.

It was obvious, from contrast with later combat, that the Americans had not as yet learned the most favorable characteristics of the big, heavy P-38, and that the airplane was at first more misused in combat than properly flown.

Before long, however, the painful lesson of burning P-38s changed the situation. The Americans soon adopted new tactics which made the most of the P-38's superior performance at high altitude. Once the enemy pilots became aware of the Zero's poor high-altitude performance and its inability to dive at great speed, we were faced with an enemy of terrifying effectiveness.

It was no longer possible for the Zero fighters successfully to engage the P-38s, except under the most unusual conditions, which, unhappily, seldom presented themselves. The P-38s would patrol at extreme height, above the altitude at which the Zeros could fly. Their great speed at high altitude enabled them to maneuver into the most advantageous positions; then the big fighters would plunge from the sky to smash into the hapless Zero fighters.

The peculiar sound of the P-38's twin engines became both familiar and bitterly hated by the Japanese all across the South Pacific. Our ground crews, especially those servicing the Zero fighters, could only shake their fists in futile gestures as the P-38s with their high-pitched roar flew dauntlessly over Buin on Bougainville Island, Rabaul, and other South Pacific bases.

Pilots too were often heard cursing the speedy P-38s, which flaunted their flashing performance. The P-38 pilot was in a most enviable position; he could choose to fight when and where he desired, and on his own terms. Under such conditions, the Lightning became one of the most deadly of all enemy planes.

If the P-38s appeared to challenge our fighters, the Zeros were forced to wait until the P-38s attacked under conditions most favorable to themselves. A Japanese victory was possible only when the enemy fighters made a positive bid to engage in a dogfight. Since the P-38s could choose the exact place and moment of combat, however, such opportunities were exceedingly rare.

There is in this lesson of P-38 *vs.* Zero the fundamental difference between air battle and those conflicts which occur on the land or sea surface. The only possible means of commencing major air combat at a desired moment is through the possession of aircraft superior to those available to the enemy. To enhance the possibility of success in air conflict, the maximum possible number of aircraft should be committed to battle.

Since the Japanese naval air arm had made long and assiduous preparations toward achieving qualitative and numerical superiority long before the outbreak of war, it was possible to satisfy these two prerequisites in the early fighting. Before long, however, the enemy was rapidly whittling down the quantitative superiority and, one year after the war had begun, the qualitative superiority was hanging by a thread and was fast disappearing.

With our victorious sweep in the Pacific marred only by

the single minor incident of Wake Island, our naval air forces began to suffer even more than usual the difficulties of an air war which began to favor the enemy.

The first single-engine American fighter seriously to challenge the Zero was the Chance-Vought F4U Corsair. At first this fighter was reported to our naval intelligence as a carrier-borne plane which had failed in its carrier-qualification tests because of poor deck-landing characteristics. The main American counteroffensives which were launched from Guadalcanal, however, favored the use of the new fighter because of the availability of land bases.

In a short period of time the excellent qualities of the Corsair became only too evident, and the enemy rapidly increased the Corsair fighter strength in the Solomons campaign; the strongest increase was noted about February of 1943, when we withdrew from Guadalcanal Island.

Faster than the Zero in level flight and capable of infinitely greater diving speeds, the Corsairs soon proved to be a great nuisance to our fighters. So long as the number of Corsairs in any particular dogfighting engagement was not too great, the Zero fighters managed to cope with the enemy planes. As the total number of Corsairs increased, however, the outnumbered Zeros ran into serious trouble, and the Japanese fighter commands were soon faced with serious losses inflicted by the speedy American Navy fighters. The Corsair was the first single-engine fighter which clearly surpassed the Zero in performance.

During the Gilberts campaign in September of 1943, the enemy's new Grumman F6F Hellcat fighter made its debut. The carrier-borne fighter plane was to become one of the Zero's most formidable opponents.

Our first reports on the new Grumman fighter stated that its design had been affected by a careful American examination of a Zero fighter captured in the Aleutians in the spring of 1942. To some extent this appeared to be so, since the philosophy of weight-saving was carried throughout the Hellcat's structure to an extent without parallel in other American aircraft of that time.

There is no doubt that the new Hellcat was superior in every respect to the Zero except in the factors of maneuver-ability and range. It carried heavier armament, could outclimb and outdive the Zero, could fly at higher altitudes, and was well protected with self-sealing fuel tanks and armor plate. Like the Wildcat and Corsair, the new Grumman was armed with six 12.7-mm. machine guns, but it carried a much greater load of ammunition than the other fighters.

Of the many American fighter planes we encountered in the Pacific, the Hellcat was the only aircraft which could acquit itself with distinction in a fighter-*vs.*-fighter dog-fight. The Americans claimed that with the Hellcat the United States Navy had recovered for the first time since the war's beginning the ability to engage the Japanese *Zeke* (Zero) in close-in fighting. The favorite American maneuver was to assign a pair of fighters to attack a Zero fighter in a steep dive during which high speed was attained; once the Zero was within range of the enemy guns, the Hellcats would open fire, roar past, and make a sharp turn to withdraw.

Of the many American fighters the Hellcat was the only plane the design of which was undertaken after the attack on Pearl Harbor, and then placed in mass production for Pacific use. More than ten thousand F6F fighters were built before production ceased at the end of 1945.

Like the Corsair, the Hellcat was equipped with a Pratt & Whitney 2,000-horsepower, air-cooled, "Double Wasp" radial engine. The more powerful the engine in a fighter plane, the better its performance will be. This is especially true of fighters in which climbing ability is stressed. With increased engine power a fighter plane may also increase its armament, be fitted with self-sealing fuel tanks, armor plate, and other equipment, and not unduly sacrifice performance.

Japanese engineers had too long delayed their efforts toward producing practicable, powerful aircraft engines, and a wide gap existed between the superior products of the United States and the engines we could produce. Despite our strenuous efforts, we could not hope to match the superb products of American technology. In 1944, Mitsubishi rushed mass production of its 2,000-horsepower-class Ha-42 engine, but the engine's weight prohibited its successful use on fighter planes.

Lieutenant Commander Mitsugu Kofukuda, Flight Commander of the 6th Air Corps assigned to the Buin air base, participated in the Guadalcanal battle during the seven months following the American invasion. Commander Kofukuda later edited copious notes he had kept through the campaign; these afford unusual insight into air activities and combat of that period:

"Throughout the Guadalcanal campaign, a variety of American Army and Navy aircraft participated in combat against Japanese forces. The majority of fighter planes encountered during the invasion were Navy Grumman F4F Wildcats and Army Curtiss P-40 Tomahawks, but the F4F fighters increased greatly in number after the battle had begun. Bell P-39 Airacobras were observed in fair numbers when the campaign began, but these were gradually replaced with the big Lockheed P-38 Lightning fighters. Chance-Vought F4U Corsairs participated in the Guadalcanal fighting only toward the end of the campaign.

"The stubby Grumman Wildcats featured performance characteristics generally similar to those of our Zero fighters, but the enemy plane proved inferior in almost every respect to the Zero. Because of the general similarity, however, dogfights between the Wildcats and Zeros were not uncommon. In these combats the Japanese pilots possessed a decided advantage, since the Zero could outmaneuver its opponent and was able to outclimb, and could fly faster than, the Grummans.

"The initial and one-sided victories which the Zero fighters scored in the early phase of the war endowed the plane with 'mysterious' characteristics—mysterious only to the American pilots, of course. The Zero's flashing maneuverability and speed, which had resulted in the destruction of hundreds of enemy planes, seemed to convince the American pilots that the Zero could not be defeated in a close-in battle in which the opponents were of equal number.

"In fact, our pilots reported that, when an enemy fighter-plane force sighted a Zero formation of equal strength, it usually would refuse to join combat and would flee. This observation was made chiefly in the Solomons area, although, of course, such enemy timidity was not always to be relied upon. On many occasions, courageous enemy pilots would not only dive in to attack our formations when they were of equal strength, but would not hesitate to assault our fighter and bomber formations even when heavily outnumbered.

"However, there was no denying the fact that our pilots enjoyed absolute confidence in their ability always to emerge victorious from an air battle in which enemy and friendly forces were of equal number. Such confidence was not limited to the pilots; it was shared by the air force headquarters staffs.

"When our Zero pilots were forced into an engagement in which their strength was about half that of the enemy, the usual outcome was a wild melee which usually resulted in equal damage to both opponents.

"As the maneuverability of the Army P-38 and P-40 fighter was markedly inferior to that of the Zero, the enemy pilots soon learned to avoid dogfights, in which they were at a decided disadvantage. While the P-40 possessed approximately the same maximum speed as the Zero, it lacked the rate of climb of our fighter and could not hope to match the Zero in close combat.

"The P-40 pilots therefore took advantage of their superior diving speed, and almost always resorted to 'shoot and retreat' tactics. Thus, the P-40s usually refused combat unless they possessed the advantage of altitude, which enabled them to dive into the Zero formations with blazing guns and race away at a diving speed beyond that possible for the Zero.

"Soon after their introduction to combat, the big, heavy P-38 fighters learned to take advantage of their excellent high altitude speed and performance and of their superior diving speed. They adopted the tactics of diving from high altitude, slashing into the Zero formations with their heavy machine guns and cannon, and zooming upwards in a climb no Zero could hope to match. Taking every advantage of their superior high-altitude performance and high speed, they were rarely caught in a position in which they could be forced to engage in close-in fighting. It appeared to be a rule of the P-38 pilots not to fight with a Zero fighter at less than 300 miles per hour, at which point the Zero suffered from sluggish aileron action.

"On some occasions P-38 formations would descend from their usual great altitude in high-speed formation dives; the initial attacking wave scattered the Zeros. Other formations would follow from their vantage points to rip through the disorganized Zero fighter, inflicting unexpectedly heavy losses.

"Single-engined bombers encountered in the Guadalcanal campaign were the Navy's two-seat Douglas SBD Dauntless dive bombers and the three-seat Grumman TBF Avenger torpedo bombers. Twin-engined bombers included the Army's North American B-25 Mitchells and Martin B-26 Marauders. The Zeros sometimes caught Navy Consolidated-Vultee PBY Catalina flying boats. Although this is no reflection on their respective combat capabilities as bombers, none of these aircraft proved difficult opponents for the Zero fighter.

"The four-engined B-17 and B-24 bombers were, generally speaking, the most difficult enemy aircraft for the Zeros to shoot down. Because of their excellent self-sealing fuel tanks, they were extremely difficult to set afire with the Zero's 20-mm. cannon shells. Our fighter pilots soon learned that the B-17s and B-24s could rarely be destroyed unless the pilots or vital parts of the aircraft were hit and rendered useless.

"The fierce resistance with which the heavy American bombers opposed our fighters, unlike that of our own land-based medium attack bombers which too often fell easy prey to enemy fighters, was a most serious problem. In my opinion, which is shared by many Japanese combat officers, the ability of the B-17 and B-24 to defend themselves and carry out their intended missions despite enemy fighter opposition was the deciding factor in the final outcome of the war.

"A considerable number of these bombers fell prey to our Zero fighters, but their destruction was accomplished only after persistent and merciless attacks, usually at high cost to our own fighters. A survey of our air-combat operations against these bombers indicates clearly that they were rarely destroyed by the conventional attack of only a few fighters.

"As the war progressed, the ability of these bombers to

defend themselves became almost unbelievable; their defensive fire power, speed, operational ceiling, and ability to absorb the punishment of our fighters constantly astonished Japanese pilots.

"By the time the Boeing B-29 Superfortress appeared on the combat front, we had achieved great strides in increasing the fire power of our fighters and interceptors. However, even these steps came too late, for the B-29 represented a remarkable advance over the tough B-17, and we were unable to keep pace with American engineering developments.

"Another factor soon entered into the capacity of the enemy's heavy bombers to flout our air defenses. When the B-29s finally appeared in large numbers over the Japanese homeland, the quality of our fighter pilots had deteriorated disastrously. New pilots were unable effectively to press home their attacks on the enemy bombers, which soon began to run rampant over our cities.

"Had Japan developed such bombers as the B-17, I believe the war would have taken a different course. We did not have a single warplane comparable to these aircraft, and Japanese forces paid a heavy price for this lack. As was demonstrated by the qualities of the Zero fighter and the Type 1 land-based medium attack bomber, our aeronautical engineering standards had been raised to a high level. No one can deny, however, that our engineers and airmen, when comparing our bombers to those of the enemy, felt keenly the difference—the great difference—in the national strength of America and Japan.

"In all fairness to our aeronautical industry, there was a marked difference in the strategic concepts evolved by Japan and the United States, with a wide gap between the two nations' emphasis on the self-protection of large aircraft. But it is equally true that this difference stemmed from the Americans' scientific ability to keep their aircraft flying despite enemy damage. Developing this characteristic to its ultimate in World War II, they were able to send their unescorted bombers on missions deep within Japanese territory, secure in the knowledge that, despite our best efforts, they stood an excellent chance of returning to their home bases."

Authors' note: Japan had suffered serious losses in combat with the Type 1 land-based medium attack bomber (the G4M1), which was wryly nicknamed the Type 1 Lighter by its crews because of its highly inflammable qualities. When the bomber was revised into the G4M2 modification, the company designers and Navy engineers concentrated their efforts toward increasing the plane's flight range, and completely neglected any attempt to improve the bomber's ability to survive enemy fire power.

It is no exaggeration to say that this action constituted one of our navy's greatest technical blunders in the war, a mistake which was comparable to our strategic errors in the disastrous Midway and Guadalcanal operations in that the continued high loss of the Type 1 bombers to enemy guns seriously affected the final outcome of the war.

Commander Kofukuda's report continues:

Tactics of Enemy Aircraft: "During the Guadalcanal campaign, the enemy held to a policy of not committing his air forces to battle before attaining a local superiority of strength; these tactics appeared to hold true whether land, sea, or air forces were involved.

"In the air battles between opposing fighter plane formations, the enemy invariably refused to join in combat unless he enjoyed numerical superiority; when confronted with a superior number of Zero fighters, he refused to engage, lest he sustain unnecessary losses.

"As a result, our fighter pilots were forced to take great

risks when committed to battle, while the enemy based his fighter tactics upon conditions most favorable to his success. This peculiar situation resulted from the fact that, when the enemy chose to fight, he invariably did so when we were outnumbered. The enemy pilots left our men little opportunity to evade combat; for when they *did* engage the Zeros, the outnumbered Japanese pilots were forced to fight desperately to survive against the numerous American fighter planes.

"Another marked difference in the tactics of both opponents was to be found in the aerial weapons with which their respective fighter planes were armed. The United States mounted the heavy 12.7-mm. machine gun with a high rate of fire in almost all their warplanes, while the Zero carried two light machine guns plus two 20-mm. cannon. The wing cannon had a relatively low firing rate, but were designed to destroy an enemy aircraft with one or more hits. This weapon was indispensable to the Zero, which had been designed from the outset to contend with both enemy fighters and bombers."

Base Construction Capacity: "A world of difference existed between the ability of the Japanese and Americans to construct air bases in the combat theaters. Basically, we relied upon primitive manpower to clear jungles and pound out airstrips for our planes, while the Americans literally descended in a mass mechanical invasion on jungle, coral, and rock to carve out their air-base facilities. This difference in method undeniably and seriously affected the air operations of both belligerents, much to the benefit of the Americans.

"The construction of adequate air-base installations facilitated rapid and large-scale movement of the enemy's air forces, thus contributing directly to a great increase in his combat strength in any theater of action. Moreover, the vast and numerous bases gave the enemy the capacity to maintain large groups of interceptors in the air, and deny Japanese bombers the opportunity to destroy enemy planes on the ground.

"It was obvious that the ability of American engineers to establish air bases wherever and whenever they chose, while Japan struggled against the limitations of primitive methods and a lack of material and engineering construction skill, must affect the final outcome of the war to no minor degree in favor of the United States.

"One of the major points which has too often been overlooked in an evaluation of fighting power, but which determined to a large extent the efficiency of air units, was that of hygienic installations. Japanese engineers paid scant attention to this problem, dismissing the pressing matter of mosquito protection by simply rigging mosquito nets in personnel quarters. Sanitary facilities were basically crude and ineffective; certainly they contributed nothing to the morale of ground and air crews.

"The Americans, by contrast, swept clean vast areas surrounding their ground installations with advanced mechanical aids. Through exhaustive disinfecting operations, they banished flies and mosquitos from their air bases and paid similar attention to every phase of sanitation and disease.

"Some may consider this a prosaic matter, but it was vital to the men forced to live on desert islands and in the midst of jungles swarming with disease and insect life. The inevitable outcome of such neglect was a tremendous difference in the health of the American and Japanese personnel who were assigned to these forward air facilities."

* * *

In such matters as the support of our combat weapons, the Japanese Army and Navy proved to be woefully neglectful. It was a classic blunder, for which we paid dearly. Disease and insect plagues can hinder air operations as effectively as enemy attack.

The Navy, of course, made some attempts to organize mosquito-prevention and disease-prevention units, but only on a small and insignificant scale.

Even the efforts to expedite the construction of forward air bases with mechanical devices achieved little success. It was impossible to accumulate in only a few months the knowledge and experience which the Americans had gathered over many years.

To our distress, it became evident that our military and government leaders *had never really understood the meaning of total war.* Japan lacked the knowledge and the means with which to integrate its national resources into the most effective war machine. While these officials often spoke of total war, today it is clear that their knowledge of such matters was sorely limited and that their enthusiasm was confined largely to vocal efforts.

CHAPTER 19

"Operation A"—I-go Sakusen

OUR DEFEAT AT GUADALCANAL was due primarily to the great military strength and the tenacious attacks of the enemy on land, at sea, and in the air, but causes of that defeat were to be found also directly within the Combined Fleet.

The primary failure on our part lay in the utter lack of a fixed policy for the construction of island air bases. Even in the Philippines and the Dutch East Indies, when our forces swept aside enemy resistance in the opening attacks of the war, we established a policy of constructing air bases so that no more than three hundred nautical miles would separate these installations. Even when our planes were required to fly over open water, our air-base distances did not exceed three hundred and eighty nautical miles, as between Kendari and Koepang.

At Guadalcanal, however, the Navy bungled its planning for logistics support, and no explanation can possibly excuse the failure to provide air bases in the approximately six-hundred-nautical-mile stretch between Rabaul and Guadalcanal. This was perhaps the most serious error committed by our Navy in the southwest Pacific, and stemmed directly from the unjustified optimism created by our initial victories. This over-confidence, in retrospect an attitude which is seen to have engendered fatal consequences, prevented our commanding officers from evaluating soberly the inevitable enemy counterattack. It is also true that this episode illustrates the Japanese Navy's true nature, for we repeatedly failed to investigate our future needs for mutual assistance between military bases, the transportation and logistics requirements of our forces, and the anticipated distances between our air installations and those of the enemy.

Our second fault lay in the fact that we never studied properly the problems of air-base construction, maintenance, and supply. Neither did we appreciate accurately the limitations of air operations which could be conducted from any land installation. Despite our overwhelming initial successes, we literally ignored the priceless advantages afforded us in respect to the time in which we had to enlarge existing bases, to construct new facilities, and to determine to the last pound the supply requirements for our bases. Thus, while we could have prepared a bastion of air-power networks from which our planes could have assaulted effectively the Guadalcanal invaders, we did nothing toward this end. This failure on our part in great measure caused the loss of Guadalcanal.

It was a bizarre situation, for in such matters as aircraft performance, pilot skill, and efficient use of manpower we clearly exceeded the enemy's best efforts. Our overconfidence, however, cost us the results of years of painstaking labor and allowed the enemy to begin his long trek back into the Pacific which resulted eventually in our total defeat. This inability to coordinate the military and economic strength at our disposal was not restricted to the Navy air force only; it existed to a much severer degree within the ranks of the Army and, indeed, might accurately be described as characteristic of the entire nation.

The blame rested directly upon the shoulders of the Naval General Staff of Tokyo and with the staff officers of the Combined Fleet. They, too, allowed overconfidence to dim their appraisal of the Pacific situation and, since they were directly responsible for the war's conduct, the guilt is primarily theirs. This lack of competence undermined much of the brilliant work performed by Admiral Isoroku Yamamoto, who suddenly found his formerly advancing forces facing an enemy fighting savagely for an obscure island in the southwest Pacific.

All the admiral's meticulous plans, which had proven so effective in this battle area, foundered suddenly in the face of our own deficiencies. Certainly the interval between the time of our occupation of the Solomons and the enemy's return should have allowed us to hurl a wall of fire and steel at the invading forces; instead, our planes disappeared in the open sea from lack of fuel, our pilots became exhausted from over-extended missions, we encountered severe difficulties in replacement of men, materiel, and aircraft, and we watched helplessly as enemy strength inexorably increased.

The most bitter pill of all for Admiral Yamamoto to swallow was that, despite our obvious lack of preparation, we still had immediately available in the Guadalcanal area sufficient strength to mount a strong counterattack which could have wrecked the American invasion fleet and caused terrible casualties among the still comparatively weak landing forces. There was every reason to believe, from the available Japanese strength in the area, that we would make this counterattack. Not only did we have effective air power, but our Combined Fleet could at once muster at least twice the surface strength of the enemy fleet.

Instead, while the enemy committed to the defense of his initial, precarious beachhead all available aircraft, the new battleships *South Dakota* and *Washington*, and all available warships, units of our Combined Fleet remained uselessly at anchor at Rabaul and Truk. At the precise moment when the enemy's plans hung desperately on coordination of his efforts, and when our fleet was in a most favorable position to disrupt the invasion and destroy the enemy ships, we failed to act. This lack of decision later cost us dearly, for the advantages once presented in the early stages of the Guadalcanal fighting disappeared rapidly, and our own fleet suffered repeated defeats.

Many of our own strategists have compared the defeat at Guadalcanal with the havoc suffered at Midway; truly our same weaknesses responsible for the great American naval victory in the former battle appear to have been repeated.

The successful enemy invasion of Guadalcanal and subsequent enemy campaigns led many of our people to believe that Japan lost the war simply because the Navy overestimated the ability of our Army to defend the islands in the Pacific. They felt that this succession of Japanese Army defeats at the hands of the rampaging American amphibious forces was directly responsible for the Navy's own losses.

This is foolish reasoning, and with little basis in fact. We who evaluated realistically the capabilities of our own Army knew only too well that our ground forces never were prepared adequately for Pacific combat. For years our Army trained to fight a war with Russia which it regarded as inevitable. This same Army group of leaders woefully lacked a true understanding of the United States; they were not aware of the nature and strength of the American people, nor did they appreciate the overwhelming military strength American industry could bring to bear against any enemy.

I do not believe that our own Naval general staff was so ill-informed, or so unintelligent as to misjudge the Army's strength in times of emergency. It was a poorly held secret among the military hierarchy that our Army was never truly capable of extensive island operations. To us, the Army was a cripple, and at best its effectiveness would always be limited.

Ever since the beginning of the Second Stage Operation, prefaced by the disaster at Midway, Admiral Yamamoto faced a situation which became increasingly desperate. One might say frankly that, despite his most intensive future efforts the admiral was doomed to know only defeat for the remainder of the war. With the enemy finally in firm possession of Guadalcanal Island, we were now defending ourselves against future enemy attacks. The Pacific War had run through its first full cycle, and the enemy was on the move. Studying carefully our defense positions across the Pacific, Admiral Yamamoto discovered that our chain of island defenses and fleet units was riddled with weak points through which the enemy could strike. It was vital that these gaps be plugged, that we establish as close to an impregnable defense line as was possible. Yamamoto's greatest need was for time; it was necessary to hold back the mounting enemy blows until we had secured our defenses.

Abruptly the admiral's attention was drawn to the increasing tempo of enemy air attacks in the eastern part of New Guinea and the Solomons. The effectiveness of enemy air strength was brought to the admiral with the news of a crushing defeat which, if similar events were permitted to occur in the future, promised terrifying disasters for Japan.

On the afternoon of March 2, 1943, a large Japanese convoy was sighted by patrolling B-24 bombers north of Cape Gloucester, bound for Lae in an effort to reinforce our troops in the Lae-Salamaua area. The convoy consisted of eight destroyers (*Shikinami, Yukikaze, Asagumo, Uranami, Arashio, Asashio, Shirayuki,* and *Tokitsukaze*), a special service vessel (*Nojima*), and eight transports (the 3,800-ton *Shinano-Maru,* 6,870-ton *Teiyo-Maru,* 6,500-ton *Oigawa-Maru,* 5,500-ton *Kyokusei-Maru,* 3,750-ton *Taimei-Maru,* 2,746-ton *Aiyo-Maru,* 700-ton *Kenbu-Maru,* and 543-ton *Kokoku-Maru*). Aboard the convoy, in addition to the crews of the vessels, were five thousand ground troops assigned to the 51st Division. The *Kenbu-Maru* particularly was sorely needed at Lae, since she carried aircraft, fuel, spare parts, and other vital supplies.

When first sighted the convoy lay protected beneath a solid weather front, broken only occasionally. The B-24 sighting, however, had been dispatched immediately to nearby enemy air combat units. By daybreak of March 3 the Americans, aided by Australian units, hurled a savage attack against the convoy. One hundred and thirty-seven planes of the 5th Air Force and the R.A.A.F. battered our ships. Everything from fighters to heavy bombers, including B-17s, B-24s, A-20s, B-25s, P-38s, and Beaufighters swarmed at the helpless convoy. Other enemy fighters meanwhile attacked our airfields to draw off Zero fighters based at Lae and Salamaua.

Bombs crashed with deadly accuracy into one ship after the other, and the enemy planes raked the vessels with machine guns and cannon to add to the carnage.

Despite frantic defensive action by Zero fighters, we could do almost nothing to stem the vicious attack. By early afternoon closing weather afforded the convoy a respite as low clouds forced the enemy planes to withdraw. They left behind them a bizarre sea littered with bodies and wreckage.

During the night of March 3–4 enemy seaplanes tracked the convoy—what was left of it—and dropped bombs intermittently without effect. The breaking dawn confirmed the fears of survivors; the planes came screaming in again, skipping bombs across the water, and strafing with uncanny accuracy. By now the convoy lay some sixty miles east of Salamaua. But the weather no longer favored the ships, and the enemy fighters and bombers ran a shuttle from New Guinea bases to Huon Gulf to maintain the attack. Steadily the convoy dwindled as the ships went down.

During the night enemy torpedo boats raced through the convoy and sent a torpedo crashing into a cargo vessel which had been lying dead in the water. The ship went down at once. On March 5, as enemy fighters raked the wreckage and survivors in strafing attacks, a bomber brought the disaster to a finale by sinking the only destroyer still in the area.

Every transport, as well as the *Nojima* and four destroyers, was sent to the bottom. Only four destroyers, the *Shikinami, Yukikaze, Asagumo,* and *Uranami*, were able to reach friendly harbor. Desperately needed supplies littered the Bismarck Sea, and some three thousand corpses floated in the oily, bloody waters. The enemy planes shot ten Zeros out of the sky, and badly damaged five others. Despite the fact that destroyers and submarines bent every effort to rescue survivors, we saved only 2,734 men.

The enemy lost but three P-38s, one B-17, one B-25, and one Beaufighter.

Our losses for this single battle were fantastic. Not during the entire savage fighting at Guadalcanal did we suffer a single comparable blow. It became imperative that we block the continued enemy air activities before these attacks became commonplace. We knew we could no longer run cargo ships or even fast destroyer transports to any front on the north coast of New Guinea, east of Wewak. Our supply operation to northeastern New Guinea became a scrabbler's run of barges, small craft, and submarines.

Admiral Yamamoto personally assumed command of his air forces in the theater, establishing advanced command headquarters at Rabaul. He intended specifically to direct all air activities to destroy enemy air power in the area. This was "Operation A" (*I-go Sakusen*). Yamamoto established 21st Air Flotilla Headquarters at Kavieng on the northern end of New Ireland under Rear Admiral Toshinosuke Ichimaru, and sent the 26th Air Flotilla to Buin on southern Bougainville under Rear Admiral Kanae Kozaka. The air groups of the 1st Carrier Division under Vice-Admiral Jisaburo Ozawa moved into Rabaul. Also placed at Rabaul was the main body of the 21st Air Flotilla under Rear Admiral Ichimaru. The air groups of the 2nd Carrier Division under Vice-Admiral Kakuji Kakuda remained in Rabaul only when not in action; when attacking Guadalcanal, the division advanced its headquarters to our base on Ballale Island, near Buin.

Admiral Yamamoto had immediately available a total air strength of 350 planes, including 190 under Vice-Admiral Kusaka's command, and 160 carrier-based planes under Vice-Admiral Ozawa's command. The latter officer had replaced Vice-Admiral Nagumo.

Despite the scale of Yamamoto's intended operation, his force of 350 airplanes was numerically smaller than that of the Nagumo Force employed in the Pearl Harbor attack, or even the Tsukahara Force used in the Philippines and Malaya area operations. Yamamoto's air fleet could carry a slightly greater weight of bombs, since he would employ twin-engined attack bombers.

Nevertheless, the total air power assembled by the admiral presented an alarming picture. His forces constituted the main strength of Japan's first-line air power after only eighteen months of war, during which time our Navy afforded aircraft construction its first priority. In other words, the Navy Air Force had not expanded. Indeed, we now had less combat airplanes than we did at the war's outset. This fact alone demonstrated dramatically the adverse conditions under which our Navy planes combated the enemy, for in this same time interval the Americans (as well as the English and the Australians) hurled ever-increasing numbers of fighters and bombers at us.

Further difficulties arose in our pilot-replacement program. Guadalcanal had cut sharply into the ranks of qualified pilots and our Navy air force suffered increasingly from difficulties resulting from pilots with insufficient training. Before the outset of Yamamoto's Operation A, I (Okumiya) was air staff officer to Admiral Kakuda, and was required to train many lieutenants directly out of pilots' school. These men had behind them barely thirty days of carrier training, and our veteran air leaders hesitated to send the fledglings into combat against the aggressive and experienced American pilots. Not only did we fear for the safety of these new pilots in combat, but many had great difficulty merely in properly flying their fighters and bombers. More than once this lack of experience cost us our invaluable warplanes, as the unqualified pilots skidded, crashed, and burned on takeoff. Admiral Yamamoto hoped that his personal presence in the Rabaul area would spur his instructors to bring these student pilots to a point where they could fly against the enemy with some chance of survival.

On April 7, 1943, the attack began in full force. Our planes in heavy strength raided a concentration of enemy vessels anchored at Guadalcanal; on the 11th we attacked enemy shipping at Oro Bay and Harvey Bay on the east coast of New Guinea; on the 12th our planes raided the Port Moresby airfield; and on the 14th we attacked the Milne Bay airfield on southeast New Guinea as well as enemy ships within the harbor.

Pilots' reports of the four heavy raids indicated that we had inflicted severe damage on the enemy, and intelligence officers reported to Admiral Yamamoto that we sank one cruiser, two destroyers, and twenty-five cargo and transport ships; shot down in air combat 134 planes, and wrecked others in ground attacks which severely damaged four enemy air bases. (Again our pilots overestimated the efficiency of their attacks, for postwar investigations revealed that the Americans, while hit hard, suffered far less damage than we were led to believe.) Our losses included at least forty-nine planes shot down and missing, in addition to those which were damaged.

Convinced by his pilots' reports that his original goal of wreaking great havoc among the American airfields and reducing the effectiveness of enemy air power had been accomplished, Yamamoto declared Operation A as concluded successfully, and ordered his land-based air forces to resume their original attack missions. He sent the carrier-based planes back to Truk, where they rejoined their original groups.

I had participated actively in the entire operation, and remember clearly the final conference on the campaign. Our officers expressed great concern over the severe bomber losses we had experienced at the hands of the enemy fighter pilots, for only four missions had cost us fifty planes. No other action could have demonstrated so effectively the fact that the Americans were now matching and exceeding the performance of our own aircraft. The meeting concluded in a pessimistic air; we could anticipate only expanding enemy air strength and an ever-increasing drain of our own air power.

The demands of Operation A disorganized the 1st Carrier Division's air groups, which was ordered to return to Japan for reorganization, new aircraft, and extended training. To compensate for the loss of the 1st Carrier Division's planes, Admiral Kakuda regretfully split into two units his own 2nd Carrier Force, assigning half his strength to Truk and the remainder to the Marshall Islands.

CHAPTER 20

Admiral Yamamoto Dies in Action

A S COMMANDER IN CHIEF of the Combined Fleet, Admiral Isoroku Yamamoto held the unreserved respect and admiration of every man who served under him. Neither the debacle at Midway nor the shock of the Guadalcanal defeat marred the confidence of his men in the admiral. This was not merely the result of military conduct, but Yamamoto was afforded a personal loyalty which bordered on the fanatic. No other officer ever approached the immense popularity of this single man who, when confronted with the unexpected disasters in the Pacific, personally accepted the responsibility for failure, and at no time tolerated accusation of his subordinates.

Yamamoto was every inch the perfect military figure, and conducted himself on all occasions with military reserve and aplomb. Even at Rabaul and Truk, he suffered the intense heat of the tropical sun impeccably attired in the pure white Navy officer uniform. This figure of the Commander in Chief, oblivious to heat, tropical humidity, and insects, never failed to impress every officer and enlisted man. Yamamoto was not merely an admiral, he was the personification of the Navy.

The admiral's Operation A was to be launched with a heavy air blow against the enemy on April 7. On the afternoon of the sixth, Vice-Admiral Kakuda planned to leave Vunakanau for our air base at Ballale, a small island south of Buin. The admiral would fly in a Type 1 Betty bomber, which would lead a fighter-plane group to join the "X Raid," the first step of the operation.

The weather on the sixth was very bad. Constant heavy rains covered the airfield with volcanic ash, and there seemed little prospect for brighter skies. The ground crews worked ceaselessly to maintain our airplanes in readiness, despite the airfield's condition. The roads leading from the field to Rabaul became muddy quagmires, and travel by automobile was a risky affair. Despite the weather and the risk of becoming caught in the mud, Admiral Yamamoto drove to the field personally to see Admiral Kakuda off. The seventeen-mile trip to the field from Rabaul was a jolting, mud-splattered journey, yet Yamamoto appeared no more uncomfortable than if he were in his Tokyo headquarters.

The Commander in Chief spoke briefly to the assembled pilots and crew members, wishing them good fortune in the forthcoming battles. To the Japanese pilots, this was a great moment. They were fortified by Yamamoto's good wishes and no obstacle seemed too great to be overcome. I was in Admiral Kakuda's bomber, the first airplane to leave the mud of the Rabaul field. Behind us the fighters jockeyed for takeoff position, rocking the landing wheels to clear them from the sucking mire. One by one the fighters struggled along the strip and lifted into the murky skies. I looked back at the dwindling field, where the white uniforms of Admiral Yamamoto and Vice Admiral Ugaki stood

out distinctly against the drab ground. It was an incongru-
ous scene, for Yamamoto looked little different in these
forsaken surroundings than when I had last seen him as we
left Hiroshima Bay.

We assembled our fighters and, with formations complete, set a course south of Rabaul. A massive cloud front
filled the entire sky before us, and the black, boiling squall
blocked our course. In our bomber we had little to fear
from the weather, but forty-five single-seat fighter planes
clung grimly to our tail, knowing that to lose our guiding
plane in the storm ahead meant almost certain death.
Despite our anxiety to reach the main battle force at Ballale, the storm's severity forced a disappointed Admiral
Kakuda to return to Rabaul. We had searched in vain for
twenty minutes for a break in the clouds. Our battle plan
called for the planes to arrive at Ballale at sunset, so that
American reconnaissance planes photographing the area
would not see the new force of forty-five fighters. By the
time we returned to Vunakanau one hour later, dusk had
settled.

We sent the fighter planes in to land first. Forty-three
Zeros made their precarious landings in the mud without
damage, but two planes sank into the treacherous surface
and damaged their propellers and undercarriage. Finally, in
the dark, our own bomber landed. I was astonished to see
Admiral Yamamoto waiting for our plane; informed of our
radio message that we were returning to base, he remained
to see Admiral Kakuda.

The initial mass attack against the enemy could not be
postponed after the sixth, for our forces had long prepared
for the raids, and were in the most advantageous position
to strike. Our forty-five fighter planes were desperately
needed to escort the bombers against the expected heavy
opposition; while it was imperative that we get to Ballale,

further flight tonight was impossible. After our plane landed, I proceeded at once along the muddy, darkened road from the field to Admiral Ozawa's headquarters to receive new orders. We conferred at length on the attack requirements and not until many hours later did I leave the admiral's headquarters with an order that our planes were to leave Ballale early in the morning of the seventh. We would fly directly to our rendezvous and participate in the air blows. Even as I returned to the field I met a car dispatched for me by an anxious and worried Admiral Kakuda.

The sudden change in plans involved hasty last-minute briefings of the pilots, for we were to leave from the Vunakanau airfield and join the attack directly. Our flight time would be increased, and the pilots were unfamiliar with the areas over which they would pass. Our pilots were, however, confident that they would completely fulfill Admiral Yamamoto's expectations for the success of the attack. We carried out "Raid X" as scheduled.

Following the completion of Operation A, which Admiral Yamamoto was led to believe had caused great damage to the enemy, the admiral prepared to make a personal survey of our forward bases. He conferred with the commanders and officers of the various air corps, stressing that the future of the war could not permit complacency. The admiral stated further that many great sea battles were yet to be fought, and that victory or defeat in those same battles, and consequently the outcome of the war, would depend largely upon our conduct in air battles. Every man who attended these special meetings could not help but be impressed by the admiral's sincerity, nor could our staff officers ignore the consequences of failure so dramatically brought to their attention.

At 0600 hours on the morning of April 18, Admiral

Yamamoto left Rabaul on a flight to Ballale in southern Bougainville, to inspect personally our air base which lay so close to enemy forces. Almost simultaneously with Yamamoto's departure, I flew from Rabaul with Admiral Kakuda for our return flight to Truk. When we returned to his flagship, the aircraft carrier *Hiyo*, his staff communications officer ashen-faced, personally delivered a confidential telegram to Admiral Kakuda.

Kakuda was a veteran combat naval air officer, known for his iron self-discipline under any circumstances. I was astonished to see the admiral's face grow pale as he read the message. He uttered something unintelligible, and for some time afterward could not or would not speak to anyone.

Admiral Isoroku Yamamoto was dead.

The incidents leading up to the attack by American fighter planes against Admiral Yamamoto's plane, and the death of Japan's greatest naval leader, are recorded in detail in the diary of Vice-Admiral Matome Ugaki, Chief of Staff of the Combined Fleet, who was with the admiral at the time of his death. The following passages in quotation marks are from Ugaki's diary:

"Admiral Yamamoto wished to fly from Rabaul to Buin, via Ballale, to inspect front-line Navy forces, and to pay a personal call on General Hyakutake, commander of the 17th Army. The admiral planned to return on the nineteenth to our base at Truk."

(The flight was planned with Admiral Yamamoto's usual meticulous care. Personally aware of even the smallest difficulties of the Navy and Army forces in the Solomons, particularly those troops under General Hyakutake which had been hard pressed by savagely fighting enemy troops and ever-increasing air attacks, Yamamoto hoped by this frontline visit to better his own understanding of future problems. Aware that enemy intelligence would literally go to any lengths to discover his presence in the area, the admiral discarded his white uniform and for the first time donned the Navy khaki garb.)

"At 0600 hours Admiral Yamamoto left the Rabaul airfield in the lead aircraft, a Type 1 Betty bomber, which carried, in addition to Yamamoto, Commander Ishizaki, his secretary, Surgeon Rear Admiral Takata, and Commander Toibana, his air staff officer. In the second aircraft with me were Paymaster Rear Admiral Kitamura, Commander Imanaka, of the communications staff, Commander Muroi, air staff officer, and Lieutenant Unno, our meteorology officer.

"As soon as I entered the second bomber, both aircraft began their takeoff runs down the field. The lead bomber took to the air first. As our planes passed above the volcano at the bay's end we slid into formation and took a southeast course. Clouds were intermittent and, with excellent visibility, flying conditions were good.

"I could see our escort fighters weaving in their protective pattern; three fighters flew off to our left, three remained high above and behind us, and three others, making nine in all, cruised to the right. Our bombers flew a tight formation, their wings almost touching, and my plane remained slightly behind and to the left of the lead ship. We flew at approximately five thousand feet. We could clearly see the admiral in the pilot's seat of the other bomber, and the passengers moving within the airplane.

"We reached the west side of Bougainville Island, flying at twenty-two hundred feet directly over the jungle. A crew member handed me a note reading: *'Our time of arrival at Ballale is 0745 hours.'* I remember looking at my wristwatch, and noting that the time was exactly 0730. In fifteen minutes we would arrive at our first stop.

"Without warning the motors roared and the bomber plunged toward the jungle, close behind the lead airplane, leveling off at less than two hundred feet. Nobody knew what had happened, and we scanned the sky anxiously for the enemy fighter planes we felt certain were diving to the attack. The crew chief, a flight warrant officer, answered our queries from his position in the narrow aisle: 'It looks as if we made a mistake, sir. We shouldn't have dived.' He certainly was right, for our pilots should never have left our original altitude.

"Our fighter planes had sighted a group of at least twenty-four enemy planes approaching from the south. They began to dive toward the bombers to warn them of the approaching enemy planes. Simultaneously, however, our bomber pilots also sighted the enemy force and, without orders, raced for low altitude. Not until we had leveled off did our crewmen take their battle positions. Screaming wind and noise assailed our ears as the men unlimbered the machine guns.

"Even as we pulled out of the dive and returned to horizontal flight above the jungle, our escort fighters turned into the attacking enemy planes, now identifiable as the big Lockheed P-38s. The numerically superior enemy force broke through the Zeros and plunged after our two bombers. My own plane swung sharply into a ninety-degree turn. I watched the crew chief lean forward and tap the pilot on the shoulder, warning him that the enemy fighters were fast closing in.

"Our plane separated from the lead bomber. For a few moments I lost sight of Yamamoto's plane and finally located the Betty far to the right. I was horrified to see the airplane flying slowly just above the jungle, headed to the south, with bright orange flames rapidly enveloping the wings and fuselage. About four miles away from us, the bomber trailed thick, black smoke, dropping lower and lower.

"Sudden fear for the admiral's life gripped me. I tried to call to Commander Muroi, standing immediately behind me, but could not speak. I grasped him by the shoulder and pulled him to the window, pointing to the admiral's burning plane. I caught a last glimpse myself, an eternal farewell to this beloved officer, before our plane again swung sharply over in a steep turn. Tracers flashed by our wings, and the pilot desperately maneuvered to evade the pursuing fighter plane. I waited impatiently for the airplane to return to horizontal position, so that I could observe the admiral's bomber. Although I hoped for the best, I knew only too well what the fate of the airplane would be. As our own plane snapped out of its turn I scanned the jungle. Yamamoto's plane was no longer in sight. Black smoke boiled from the dense jungle into the air.

"Alas! It was hopeless now!

"Even as I stared at the funeral pyre of the crashed bomber, our own plane straightened out from its frantic maneuvering and at full speed raced toward Moila Point. Shortly we were over the open sea. We noticed the concentration of dogfighting planes in the area where Admiral Yamamoto's bomber had plunged into the jungle; other fighters were separating from the group and turning after us now. I stared helplessly as a silver H-shaped P-38 half-rolled in a screaming zoom, then turned steeply, and closed rapidly toward our plane. Our gunners were firing desperately at the big enemy fighter, but to little avail.

"The bomber's 7.7-mm. machine guns could not reach the approaching P-38. Taking advantage of his superior speed, the enemy pilot closed in rapidly and, still beyond the range of our defensive machine guns, opened fire. I watched the P-38's nose seem to burst into twinkling flame, and suddenly the bomber shook from the impact of the enemy's machine-gun bullets and cannon shells. The P-38 pilot was an excellent gunner, for first his fusilade of bullets and shells crashed into the right side of the airplane, then into the left. The drumming sounds vibrated through the airplane, which rocked from the impact of the enemy fire. We knew we were now completely helpless, and waited for our end to come. The P-38 hung grimly to our tail, pouring in his deadly fire.

"One by one our answering machine guns fell silent. Abruptly the crew chief, who had been shouting orders to his men, fell from our view. Several of the crew were already dead, as the bullets screamed though the airplane. Commander Muroi sprawled over the chair and table in the fuselage compartment, his hands thrown out before him, his head rolling lifelessly back and forth as the plane shuddered.

"Another canon shell suddenly tore open the right wing. The chief pilot, directly in front of me, pushed the control column forward. Our only chance of survival was to make a crash landing in the sea. I did not realize it at the time, but a Zero pilot above us in a futile attack against the grimly pursuing P-38, reported heavy smoke pouring from our bomber. Almost into the water, the pilot pulled back on the controls to bring the airplane out of its dive, but he could no longer control the aircraft. Enemy bullets had shattered the cables. Desperately the pilot killed our power, but again it was too late. At full speed the bomber smashed into the water; the left wing crumpled and the Betty rolled sharply over to the left.

"Prepared for an emergency landing, I do not recall being injured in the crash. Apparently the shock of the plane's meeting the water at such high speed numbed my senses, for when I was hurled into the aisle from my seat my body was bruised and cut.

"The impact of the crash momentarily stunned me, and everything turned black. I felt the crushing force of salt water pouring into the fuselage and almost immediately we were below the surface. I was completely helpless. Convinced this was my end, I said a requiem to myself. Naturally it was difficult to remember coherently everything which happened in those incredible moments, but I vaguely recall that I felt as if life had come to its end; I could not bring myself to move and could only lie perfectly still. I do not believe I was actually knocked unconscious. I did not swallow any sea water. Everything was hazy, and I could not tell how much time passed before . . ."

(Several lines of the diary are omitted here.)

"The following day search planes discovered the wreckage of the lead bomber in which Admiral Yamamoto had flown to his death. The reconnaissance pilots found no sign of life and reported that fire had entirely consumed the wreckage. On the day of the attack a native reported to an Army road-construction crew that a Japanese plane had crashed in the jungle along Bougainville's west coast. Army headquarters dispatched a rescue force, which reached the wreckage on April 19. They picked up the corpses and began their return. It was this same group that our Navy rescue force encountered.

"The Army group had found Admiral Yamamoto's body, still in his pilot's seat, hurled clear of the airplane. A sword was held tightly in his hand. His body had not yet decomposed and even in death dignity did not leave the great naval officer. To us, Isoroku Yamamoto virtually was a god.

"Our doctors later examined his body aboard a submarine chaser, and found bullet holes through the lower part of the skull, as well as in the shoulder. Presumably the admiral died instantly aboard the airplane. In addition only the chief medical officer, his body partially burned, could be identified, as the remainder of the group were burned beyond recognition.

"As to the wreckage of my own airplane, divers went to sixty-seven feet below the water's surface, but found only the wheels, engines, propellers, machine guns, and one officer's sword. The following day (April 20) the bodies of the two crewmen were washed up on the shore.

"Of all the personnel aboard both bombers, only rear Admiral Kitamura, the pilot of my bomber, and I survived. More than twenty men and officers perished. Although death is an everyday occurrence in war, I feel that I am to be blamed for this incident.

"I was informed at a later date that the enemy, which had in the past made only single-plane reconnaissance missions, had, only one or two days before April 18, increased his reconnaissance to fighter-plane groups. This information from our field forces did not reach Vice-Admiral Kusaka's headquarters until twenty-four hours after the incident. Had we been informed immediately of the sudden appearance of the enemy fighter formations, we could have averted the terrible loss of Admiral Yamamoto. But we were too late."

In the same area where so many of his own men had shed their blood for Japan, Admiral Isoroku Yamamoto came to the end of his brilliant career. Not only did we suffer an irreplaceable loss in his death, but Japan lost also Commanders Toibana and Muroi, considered the two "brains" of the Navy's air staff. The injured Admirals Ugaki and Kitamura, and their pilot, were rescued by our ships which sped to the scene of the water crash.

The itinerary of Admiral Yamamoto and his staff was, of course, a closely guarded secret. Behind the chain of events leading to the successful enemy attack, however, lay the direct cause for the incident. Partially as a courtesy message, the commander of the Shortland seaplane base southwest of Buin had notified his forces, in naval code, that the admiral would personally inspect their area. This same message was intercepted and decoded by American Navy headquarters at Pearl Harbor. The Navy immediately informed Army Air Forces headquarters at Henderson Field, Guadalcanal. Late in the afternoon of April 17 the Henderson Field message center delivered to Major John W. Mitchell, P-38 commander at Guadalcanal, a cablegram from Frank Knox, Secretary of the Navy, with the complete information on Admiral Yamamoto's scheduled inspection tour. The message also noted that Yamamoto was most punctilious, and could be counted upon to follow his schedule rigidly. Included in the message was a list of other officers accompanying the admiral, as well as the fact that the staff would fly in two new-type Mitsubishi bombers escorted by six Zero fighters.

The only planes capable of performing the interception mission were the Henderson Field P-38s, which had the speed, range, and destructive fire power for the attack. The big fighters would have to fly at least four hundred and thirty-five miles from Guadalcanal before they could intercept west of Kahili. Contrary to Vice-Admiral Ugaki's report of "at least twenty-four enemy planes," Mitchell had available only eighteen P-38 fighters. He planned to use six fighters as the attack force against the bombers, which he estimated would fly below ten thousand feet, while the remaining twelve airplanes at twenty thousand feet would try to draw off the Zero escort. Interception was planned when Yamamoto's plane was only thirty-five miles from its destination. Two planes aborted the mission at the start; Mitchell then assigned four of his sixteen P-38s to make the attack against the bombers.

Lieutenant Thomas G. Lanphier was the pilot who shot

down Yamamoto's plane and also shot down a defending Zero fighter in his attack. Lanphier reported that he put a long burst into the right engine, then the right wing, and, still beyond the range of the bomber's defending tail cannon, watched the wing break into flame and tear off the airplane. Caught by two pursuing Zeros, Lanphier went into a steep climb and lost the Zeros.

Lieutenant Rex Barber, attacking with Lanphier, raced through three intercepting Zero fighters and shot down the second bomber. Lieutenant Besby F. Holmes shot down two Zeros, making our losses for the day three fighters and two bombers. Our pilots shot down Lieutenant Ray Hine's P-38; and, we verified later, most of the fifteen P-38s which returned to Guadalcanal were badly shot up.

Some time later when I (Okumiya) was at Buin during a new attack against the enemy, I visited Admiral Yamamoto's tomb. This was a small, inscribed stone placed over the site where the body was cremated, near the Buin headquarters.

Full credit must be given to the fine activities of the American intelligence services which broke the Japanese code and kept secret the fact that the Americans were fully acquainted with our naval activities. It was this advance knowledge which did so much to defeat our fleet at Midway and which destroyed the admiral's plane. These unheroic and behind-the-scenes moves not only frustrated the Midway Operation and took the life of our most able officer but contributed directly to our eventual defeat.

Ironically, Admiral Yamamoto prophesied his own fate immediately after the Midway conflict. Similarly, our position in the war degenerated specifically as the admiral had predicted even before December 8, 1941.

To me, who had in the past served with this great man, my return to Truk, when we were informed of his death, was a particularly sorrowing moment. From the bridge of the aircraft carrier *Hiyo*, with grief-stricken Vice-Admiral Kakuda, I watched Admiral Yamamoto's flag being lowered from the mast of the world's greatest battleship, the *Yamato*. I thought to myself at the time:

"Those who so strongly insisted upon war with the United States and England may still be dreaming of success, although victory slips further and further from our grasp. Perhaps, however, we who are carrying the fight to the enemy, as we are ordered to do, may still survive this conflict. It is impossible for me, or any other man, to express in words the mixed emotions which must have been experienced by the admiral who so long ago realized the dark future of our country should we be forced by those in power to launch this war. Despite his apprehensions, as the Commander in Chief, Yamamoto was obliged to serve his country to the best of his ability. This he did, but with his command went the feeling of guilt that he had failed in his efforts to convince his government and its ruling heirarchy that war could bring only disaster.

"Whatever history will decide, the admiral now can rest peacefully in his grave. At least his death came in a plane of the Naval Air Force for which he was directly responsible. His unflagging efforts had given his country the most powerful naval air arm in the world.

"And who can forget the personality of this man, typified by his first action in 1924 as the executive officer of the Kasumigaura Air Corps, when he embarrassed the entire corps by insisting that he fly with the poorest pilot of all!"

CHAPTER 21

Battle of Santa Cruz

THE ONLY DECISIVE VICTORY achieved by the Japanese Navy after the disastrous Battle of Midway was scored in the engagement of air-sea forces off Santa Cruz, east of the Guadalcanal area. After Midway and the fleet reorganization, our surface forces operated with the aircraft carrier as a nucleus. Admiral Yamamoto divided our major naval strength into two units, each with three aircraft carriers. These were the Vanguard Force of Vice-Admiral Nobutake Kondo, Commander of the Second Fleet, with three carriers, two battleships, five heavy cruisers, one light cruiser, and twelve destroyers; and the Carrier Task Force under Vice-Admiral Chuichi Nagumo, Commander of the Third Fleet, with three carriers, two battleships, four heavy cruisers, one light cruiser, and sixteen destroyers.

Both fleet units operated in the seas east of the Solomon Islands. Kondo's force coordinated its activities with Army groups on Guadalcanal Island, while Nagumo's ships patrolled east of Kondo's fleet to ward off possible enemy carrier attacks.

By October 23, 1942 intelligence reported an ominous buildup of enemy carrier strength. Meanwhile, we had suffered our own losses, including the sinking of the aircraft carrier *Ryujo*, which went to the bottom on August 23 in the Second Solomons Sea Battle, and the aircraft carrier *Hiyo*, which limped home with battered engines. Kondo's force was left with only a single carrier, the *Junyo*, under Rear Admiral Kakuji Kakuda, Commander of the 2nd Carrier Division. I (Okumiya) was then air staff officer to Kukuda.

After October 16 we could find no trace of the enemy carriers in the area; they had apparently disappeared. A week later we encountered a sudden increase in enemy reconnaissance-plane activities; the two facts appeared to be linked together. The Americans often withdrew their combat fleet units from an operational theater, taking advantage of the tremendous range of their land-based reconnaissance planes, which kept the warships fully advised of our activities. We sought vainly for some indication of the whereabouts of the enemy ships. On October 24 we picked up an American radio broadcast which stated that "a major sea and air battle is expected in the near future in the Solomon Islands area."

Something was in the wind. October 27 was Navy Day for the enemy, and perhaps the carrier-task-force commanders would choose this day for a surprise assault. I was familiar with the American "love of adventure" on such dates, and expected the worst to happen. Our military forces were even then committed to the second all-out attack designed to throw the enemy troops off Guadalcanal, and the Americans might take advantage of the situation to force a decisive sea battle at a time when our land forces desperately needed all our support.

On the morning of October 25 enemy flying boats surveyed the Nagumo Force which, despite strong fighter patrols, could do little to keep the long-range planes from making detailed observations of our fleet strength and maneuvers. Apparently a major enemy effort could be expected. Vice Admiral Kondo turned his ships to the south and by late October 25 prepared his planes for air strikes against enemy forces on Guadalcanal. One hundred nautical miles to the east of Kondo, Nagumo's force also worked its way southward as a buffer against the anticipated enemy carrier attacks.

Nagumo had learned a bitter lesson at Midway, and he used to advantage the tactics which that defeat revealed to him. Sixty to eighty nautical miles ahead of his flagship, *Shokaku*, steamed the battleships *Hiei* and *Kirishima*, the heavy cruiser *Chikuma*, and seven destroyers; the heavy cruiser *Tone* and the destroyer *Teruzuki* cut the Pacific waters two hundred nautical miles east of the *Shokaku* to protect his flank.

Approximately at 0050 hours on October 26 a large aircraft, presumably a flying boat, appeared over the carriers of the Nagumo Force and dropped a salvo of bombs which exploded alongside the *Zuikaku*, the fleet's second largest carrier. The bombs missed the vessel so narrowly that the entire bridge became enveloped in the smoke of the detonation; fortunately, there were no casualties.

Captain Toshitane Takata, senior staff officer of the Nagumo Force, then on the *Shokaku*'s bridge, reported the attack to Admiral Nagumo and Chief of Staff Rear Admiral Ryunosuke Kusaka. Nagumo felt he was being drawn into a trap, and dispatched to the fleet the following orders:

"Emergency turn, together, 180 degrees to starboard." This was followed by: *"All ships, execute turn, speed 24 knots."*

The assembled ships of the Nagumo Force, shrouded in the darkness of the early morning, executed the sudden reversal of course. Where the fleet had attempted to approach the enemy under cover of night and attack in full strength under the shroud of darkness, it was now in hasty retreat to the north. The turn was ordered approximately two hundred and fifty nautical miles northeast of the Gaudalcanal airfield.

In the early morning of October 26 I was the staff officer on duty at the *Junyo*'s bridge, and was the first officer to learn of the bombing and Nagumo's sudden withdrawal. I transmitted the information at once to Rear Admiral Kakuda and the Chief of Staff Captain Mineo Yamaoka. Shortly afterward Admiral Kondo's flagship, the heavy cruiser *Atago*, dispatched new fleet orders. The entire Kondo Force turned and headed northward at high speed, following the action of the Nagumo Force. It was exactly 0200 hours when the ships turned.

For the last ten days we had been without any information as to the movements of the enemy aircraft carriers. We had little knowledge of any American fleet movements, beyond a single report that two battleships and four cruisers had been sighted approximately three hundred nautical miles south of Guadalcanal. The attack earlier during the night, however, indicated strongly that American carriers were within striking range of their planes. Admiral Nagumo launched sixteen reconnaissance seaplanes and eight Type 97 Kate bombers from the advance and main fleet units to search to the east and south of our ships. The planes took off before dawn.

As Takata had forecast, enemy carriers were found in the immediate area. A *Shokaku* reconnaissance plane searching southeast of the carrier reported at 0450 hours:

"Have sighted one enemy aircraft carrier and fifteen other vessels. Enemy fleet is bearing to northwest."

The long-sought carrier (or carriers) was two hundred and fifty nautical miles southeast of the *Shokaku*, or one hundred and forty nautical miles, fifteen degrees, from Nudeni Island. The other reconnaissance planes in the area flew to the reported area and continued to track the progress of the enemy ships.

The 1st Carrier Division Attacks

The three carriers of the 1st Carrier Division had been in readiness for the fighting; the planes were hastily fueled and rushed to the decks for takeoff locations. Admiral Nagumo ordered immediate air strikes. At 5:15 A.M. the first attack force left the *Shokaku*; forty-five minutes later the second group thundered off the ship. Nagumo ordered the latter formations launched ahead of their scheduled departure; even as the first unit prepared for takeoff, the *Shokaku*'s radar picked up what appeared to be enemy planes approaching our force. Since the *Zuikaku* lacked radar, the great carrier depended upon the radar reports from the *Shokaku*. Aboard the former carrier the armorers worked feverishly to load torpedoes.

The first attack group, under Lieutenant Commander Mamoru Seki of the *Shokaku*, consisted of twenty-two Val dive bombers; Lieutenant Jiichiro Imajuku took off from the *Zuikaku* with eighteen Kate torpedo bombers. Protecting the slow and vulnerable torpedo planes were twenty-seven Zero fighters led by Lieutenant Commander Hideki Shingo of the *Shokaku*.

The second attack group was made up of twelve Kates under Lieutenant Commander Shigeharu Murata of the *Shokaku*, and twenty Vals under Lieutenant Sadamu Takahashi of the *Zuikaku*; the same ship provided a fighter escort of sixteen Zeros led by Lieutenant Kenjiro Nohtomi.

The relative numerical weakness of the attacking groups was due directly to the losses sustained in the air battles in the Solomons area; the fleet had not yet received its replacements.

Approximately at 5:00 A.M., even as the first attack group prepared for takeoff, two enemy reconnaissance planes appeared suddenly from low clouds and dropped several small bombs on the *Zuiho* of the 1st Carrier Division. Captain Sueo Obayashi reported that a single bomb struck the rear of the flight deck, tearing a hole in the deck and curling the plates. He could not land any planes, but was able to launch his aircraft.

Forty minutes after the first group was airborne, enemy planes attacked the 1st Carrier Division. The bombers appeared suddenly over the *Shokaku* after emerging from scattered clouds and went into glide bombing attacks. The enemy formations appeared to consist of fifteen to sixteen planes; five or six medium-size bombs scored direct hits on the carrier. The explosions tore great holes in the carrier deck and touched off fierce fires below decks. Excellent and rapid work by the crew extinguished the flames; fortunately the attack came after the *Shokaku* had launched her planes. Damage was confined to relatively small areas, but the ship could not launch or receive planes, and her communications were literally paralyzed. A single enemy plane attacked the *Zuikaku*, but a patrolling Zero fighter destroyed the bomber before it neared the ship. Far to the east of the *Shokaku*, the *Zuikaku* sought cover beneath scattered clouds and escaped further attacks.

With his flagship crippled, Nagumo ordered Kakuda to take command of the *Zuikaku* and to continue the battle. The *Shokaku* left for northern waters and repairs.

Prior to the raid on the 1st Carrier Division, Rear Admiral Hiroki Abe's advance force came under enemy attack. The force reported that an estimated forty dive bombers and ten torpedo bombers were attacking the battleships *Hiei* and *Kirishima*, and the heavy cruisers *Tone*, *Chikuma*, and *Suzuya*. Ten dive bombers concentrated on the *Tone*, thirty dive bombers swarmed over the *Chikuma*, and the *Suzuya* received the assault of the ten torpedo planes. The warships put up a withering antiaircraft barrage and by excellent evasive maneuvers avoided what might have been a disastrous blow. The ships received some damage, which was regarded as minor. Only the *Chikuma*, which bore the brunt of the attack, sustained heavy casualties to its officers and men, including Captain Keizo Komura. The bombers scored two direct hits on the bridge and a direct hit in the torpedo tubes, but the cruiser was able to continue action.

On their way to raid the enemy carrier, Lieutenant Commander Seki's first attack group from the 1st Carrier Division passed a force of about twenty enemy dive bombers headed for the *Shokaku*. Our escort-fighter commander failed to recognize the planes as enemy aircraft and took no action. Ten minutes later Seki's force encountered eight enemy dive bombers protected by six fighters. The escort fighters from the *Zuiho*, led by Lieutenant Hidaka, ripped into the enemy formations and scattered the planes with heavy losses to the Americans. The wild scramble drained the fighters' fuel and ammunition, and the planes turned back, leaving Seki's force virtually unprotected. The interception enabled the *Zuiho* to escape bombing, but Seki's planes began their attack with only a few Zeros flying escort.

At 6:55 A.M. the bombers arrived over the enemy fleet. On the bridge of the *Junyo*, I heard the radio conversations of our pilots.

First: *"Enemy aircraft carrier in sight."* Then, a report that the American carrier was still some two hundred and fifty nautical miles distant from the *Shokaku*. Shortly afterward: *"Enemy's course is 300 degrees, speed 24 knots."* A short wait, and: *"All planes go in!"*

At 7:10 A.M. Imajuku's torpedo bombers began their low-level assaults. The group sent back frequent radio reports, with the important message that "... one *Saratoga*-class carrier is on fire." Subsequent investigation revealed that the enemy fleet was made up of one heavy cruiser, one light cruiser, four destroyers, and the carrier *Hornet*, the latter surrounded by the lighter ships. Our pilots reported they hit the *Hornet* with five 550-pound bombs and two torpedoes, which crippled the great ship.

I had special interest in this attack. Although I was delighted at the greatest success scored by our carrier planes since the Midway defeat, Seki was my old and good friend, and Imajuku a former student; I feared for the lives of both men. My apprehensions were well founded, for their radio reports of their attacks were the last words they ever spoke. Their planes went down before the *Hornet*'s defenses.

We suffered additional severe losses. Lieutenant Shohei Yamada, the *Shokaku's* 2nd Squadron Leader and the hero of many air battles after Pearl Harbor, was shot down. We received the full story from Lieutenant Kazuo Yakushiji, 3rd Squadron Leader and the senior officer surviving the attack.

"Lieutenant Commander Seki's plane seemed to have taken several direct hits soon after he gave the order to attack. His craft was directly in front of mine as I went into my dive. I noticed the bomber enter the dive and suddenly begin to roll over on its back. Flame shot out of the bomber and, still inverted, it continued diving toward the enemy ship."

Lieutenant Commander Murata of the second attack group of the 1st Carrier Division was another former classmate. He specialized in torpedo-attack procedure at the Yokosuka Air Corps and had become one of the world's foremost authorities on the subject. With his extensive background, exceptional flying skill, and outstanding leadership, he became the commander of the torpedo units at Pearl Harbor and actually launched the first torpedo of the war. After the opening battle he served with the Nagumo Force. He was wounded at Midway while aboard the *Akagi* but had recovered and now flew as the *Shokaku*'s group leader and the over-all commander of the Nagumo Force torpedo planes.

Murata was one of Japan's outstanding naval officers. We had the opportunity at Truk to discuss the forthcoming battle in which we were now engaged. "I am grateful, Masatake, for all the work you have done with us in the past," he told me at Truk. "This time especially we are depending on you." He smiled, "The operations command does not always understand the finer points of air attack. Remember the Second Sea Battle of the Solomons? Even those ships on which Mamo (Lieutenant Commander Mamoru Seki) scored direct hits and which were set afire managed to escape. This time I hope the staff will be wise enough to use as many torpedoes as possible. Perhaps then we will be able to avenge our losses at Midway."

Murata's second attack group reached the enemy warships at approximately 8:25 A.M., and attacked a fleet unit which included one aircraft carrier. Murata encountered the new force about twenty miles southeast of the carrier which already had been heavily damaged. We received reports from his group that three 550-pound bombs and at least two torpedoes struck a *Yorktown*-class carrier, and that a battleship was hit with two torpedoes and a cruiser with one torpedo.

We heard Murata give the familiar *"All planes go in!"* command. That was our last contact with him.

Lieutenant Sadomu Takahashi of the *Zuikaku* suddenly discovered an enemy fighter on the tail of his dive bomber. Frantic maneuvers saved him from being shot down but his plane was so seriously damaged that the rudder jammed and the bomber flew in wide circles. After six hours of frustrating circling flight, Takahashi's fuel was nearly exhausted and he decided to abandon the airplane. By a stroke of luck he sighted one of our tankers and dropped the plane into the water near the ship, which rescued Takahashi and his crew. Lieutenant Yutaka Ishimaru, another former student of mine, was shot up by enemy fighters as he was returning to his carrier. Seriously wounded, he ditched his plane near a destroyer which picked him up. A few minutes later he died.

The Second Carrier Division Pursues the Enemy

The Kakuda Force listened anxiously to the battle reports of the 1st Carrier Division. The news of the damaging strikes against the first carrier cheered our men, who were anxious to join the assault. Shortly after 10:00 A.M., Lieutenant Masao Yamaguchi led eighteen dive bombers escorted by twelve fighter planes under Lieutenant Yoshio Shiga from the *Junyo*. Soon afterward the second attack group of nine torpedo bombers and five fighters led by Lieutenant Yoshiaki Irikiin took off. One of the fighter plane leaders, Lieutenant Shigematsu, was forced to return to the carrier because of mechanical difficulties. There was talk among the other pilots of the unusual "mechanical trouble"; Shigematsu waited impatiently on deck for engine repair and took off alone to rejoin his planes. A courageous fighter at Midway who survived the loss of the *Hiryu*, Shigematsu realized the vital role even one experienced pilot could play in a large-scale air battle.

A little past the noon hour the first attack force sighted a burning enemy aircraft carrier and several other warships, but failed to sight the second carrier which had been reported in the area. The attack-force leader notified Kakuda that he was going to attack a battleship in the enemy fleet; as his planes formed for the dive-bombing attacks, Kakuda received a message from one of his reconnaissance planes which had sighted an undamaged enemy carrier. Kakuda ordered his planes to attack the carrier; Lieutenant Commander Okada, communications staff officer, transmitted the new order to Lieutenant Yamaguchi.

The minutes dragged by and finally the radio crackled with the familiar combat commands. We heard Yamaguchi's voice:

"Enemy aircraft carrier in sight. . . . All planes go in!"

Aboard the *Junyo*'s bridge one of the officers grinned and shouted with joy. We now had a chance to destroy two of the largest American carriers. Everything depended upon Yamaguchi's men. Rear Admiral Kakuda smiled at the news of the attack and turned to Okada and me: "Our men have become quite proficient. The ship functions as a team. Perhaps we shall compensate for Midway."

As Lieutenant Irikiin led the torpedo planes of the second attack group to the scene of action he learned that the formations preceeding his planes had attacked the undamaged carrier. Irikiin anticipated that the carrier would either be crippled or sinking before he arrived; his expectations were justified, for when he arrived at 1:15 P.M. the ship was aflame. The lieutenant's planes dove in to attack. Three torpedoes blew open the carrier's hull for the final strike against the ship.

The battle appeared to be entirely in our favor.

Once her planes were launched, the *Junyo* continued toward the enemy ships under full steam with only three destroyers as escorts. Kakuda ordered this bold maneuver because he wished to shorten the distance between the carrier and the planes returning from the attack. Kakuda was an aggressive fighter; the lessened distance between his carrier and the enemy fleet would permit, if it should prove necessary, additional bombings to be made.

In the early afternoon our lookouts sighted in the eastern sky several small planes rapidly approaching the *Junyo*. The planes skimmed just over the waves, so low that our radar failed to pick them up. We could not identify the aircraft and alerted the ship for the air attack. Finally we identified the first plane as a friendly; the pilot rocked the airplane, raising and lowering his wingtips to identify himself; he was a stray who had lost his own carrier.

Shortly afterward the *Junyo*'s planes began to return. Lookouts sighted the planes straggling toward the carrier; only six Zeros flew formation. The remainder flew in from all directions. We searched the sky with apprehension. There were only a few planes in the air in comparison to the number launched several hours before. We could see only five or six dive bombers. The planes lurched and staggered onto the deck, every single fighter and bomber bullet-holed. Some planes were literally flying sieves. As the pilots climbed wearily from their cramped cockpits they told of unbelievable opposition, of skies choked with antiaircraft shell bursts and tracers.

Amidst the confusion of the returning planes Kakuda turned to me. "Air Staff, go to the hangar deck and see how many of our remaining planes can be sent out immediately for further attacks." The admiral had only one thought in mind: he wanted that carrier!

Flight Officer Yoshio Sakinaga was occupied with the landing planes and could not leave his post. I ran down the three long ladders to the hangar deck where the mechanics attended to the battered airplanes. Of all the planes aboard the *Junyo*, including the strays from the 1st Carrier Division, only six dive bombers and nine fighter planes were in condition to fly.

Kakuda ordered a third attack to be launched as soon as the planes were armed and fueled. The carrier's captain, Okada, sent the orders throughout the ship. "Prepare nine fighters and six dive bombers for attack. Planes will take off immediately after servicing."

Lieutenant Commander Sakinaga assembled his pilots for the mission, and assigned Lieutenant Shiga, the *Junyo*'s flight group leader, to lead the new flight. Lieutenant Ayao Shirane of the *Zuikaku*, who had made a forced landing on our ship, also received orders to fly with the group.

Shirane was a veteran warrior who had fought in China and who had led the Nagumo Force's fighter planes into Pearl Harbor. He was an outstanding fighter pilot who came from a distinguished Japanese family. Skilled, well-educated, and of unusual build, he commanded the respect of his fellow fliers. The eight fighter pilots who would fly again for the third time today were more than pleased to have Shirane with them.

The dive-bomber unit had lost its leaders, Lieutenants Yamaguchi and Naohiko Miura. The surviving senior pilot was Lieutenant (J.G.) Shunko Kato, a young officer with an unusually childlike face. Because of his weight his fellow pilots jokingly called him *Ton-chan*, or Fat Pig. Kato was the youngest reconnaissance officer assigned to the *Junyo*; his baby face and cheerful disposition made him one of the most popular men aboard the ship.

When the third attack was ordered, however, Kato was anything but cheerful. Today was his first experience in battle against an enemy carrier force, and Kato had literally gone through hell. Enemy fighter-plane attacks and the incredible antiaircraft defenses had taken a heavy toll of Kato's friends; his own plane had been hit many times and he had narrowly escaped death on several occasions on his first missions. When he reported the details of the dive-bomber attack to Captain Tametsugu Okada, Kato was so shaken that at times he could not speak coherently. Young and lacking experience in circumstances where his friends died all around him, he had suffered a nasty shock.

Less than a half hour after he completed his report, the admiral issued the new attack orders. I found Kato in the aircrew waiting room on the flight deck, and told him he was to fly again. To our astonishment, Kato rose from his seat and asked, "Again? Am I to fly *again* today?" He could not believe after the terrible losses we had suffered that he would be ordered to return to the carnage he had gratefully left. It was difficult for me to explain to someone like Kato why he *had* to fly again; I remained on the ship.

Lieutenant Shiga jumped to his feet and shouted across the room. "Ton-chan; this is war! There can be no rest in our fight against the enemy . . . we cannot afford to give them a chance when their ships are crippled. Otherwise we will face those same ships again. We have no choice . . . we go!" A veteran of China, Shiga fought at Pearl Harbor and in the Aleutians and since that time had served with me in the Kakuda Force. Ever since the Aleutians attack he had been the *Junyo*'s fighter-unit leader. Even now he was preparing to take off with the few remaining planes.

Kato stood silently and then stated simply: "I will go." He was not a coward; he had been unnerved by his shattering introduction to actual combat and, in a weak moment, he needed the harsh but sincere assistance of his senior officer. I silently thanked the Fates which allowed me, on this ship at least, the company of experienced and capable officers. We had avoided what could have been a serious blow to the morale of the ship. Kato would be all right.

Before takeoff, the young pilot addressed his dive-bomber crews. "We are about to leave for our third attack mission of the day. Our mission is to destroy the enemy's aircraft carriers. Follow me when I attack. Take your planes as low as possible to assure hits. That is all. Man your planes."

All through the preparations for the third attack Admiral Kakuda did not utter a single word. His subordinates carried out their tasks quickly and efficiently. The *Junyo* was a good ship. Kakuda ordered full steam ahead in the direction of the enemy. That was his only message to his men. So long as the ship continued on this course, every airplane capable of taking off from the deck would be launched to attack the enemy forces. If it were necessary, Kakuda would not hesitate to sail his ship directly into the enemy fleet and ram the largest enemy carrier he could find. Kakuda was a hard but a courageous taskmaster.

The third attack force took off to deliver the *coup de grâce*.

By late afternoon several hours had gone by without any attacks against the Nagumo Force. We estimated that by this time the *Zuikaku*'s third attack force should have completed its missions and, were this true, Kato's small force would be the only air-attack strength remaining of both the American and Japanese battle fleets. It was a ludicrous situation, for Kato controlled greater power than any of the dreadnaughts, cruisers, and other warships on the vast ocean surface below him. I regretted that I could not be in his place; I would have given anything to be flying that lead dive bomber. But I never flew at the controls of a plane again after my last crash; I was no longer strong enough to handle the plane. I could not help but feel uncomfortable, for *I* remained on the ship while Kato and his men followed my orders.

Every man on the *Junyo* had his heart with Kato. Everyone waited, anxious and quiet, for the first reports to come in. The first metallic words over the radio startled us.

"Enemy aircraft carrier is now in sight." Then silence, and the familiar, cheering words: *"All planes go in!"* How many times this day had we heard the last command before combat; now, only six dive bombers of the former great air fleet were left to execute the order.

On the bridge of the *Junyo* we sweated out the next reports. The minutes dragged by. Officers and crewmen paced back and forth silently. I stayed close to the speaking tube which led to the radio room, waiting for the first news.

Suddenly the tube roared into life *"Succeeded in bombing. The attack is successful!"* The commander called to the communications room: "Is Kato still flying?" Then silence, and the cheerful single word to us as he put down the phone: "Good!"

An hour later we sighted the first returning plane. The sky was darkening quickly and the blinking red and green lights in the wings of the bomber grew brighter as the plane glided in for its landing. A flushed and triumphant Kato climbed down from his bullet-riddled bomber.

The day's operations were complete. Our men had

fought continually and had suffered severe losses in their attacks against the enemy carriers. I summarized the day's events in my personal memo book:

"The efficient radio communications between the carriers and airborne planes allowed the first attack force to locate a new enemy aircraft carrier. In the vicinity of the carrier broken clouds were thickening at seven thousand feet. Lieutenant Shiga discovered the enemy ship through the clouds but soon lost sight of the vessel because of the rapidly forming cloud masses. Lieutenant Yamaguchi dove toward the sea in an attempt to find the enemy warship but soon became lost in the swirling banks. Finally breaking into the clear, he discovered an enemy battleship directly beneath him and released his bombs. He scored several direct hits and the other pilots in the formation attacked cruisers which were nearby. Consequently only a part of the original force which finally found the carrier was available to attack the ship. Fighters which later flew over the combat scene reported the carrier in flames.

"We judged that the second torpedo-plane unit had succeeded in breaking through a fierce antiaircraft defense and intercepting fighter planes to score at least four or five torpedo strikes against the burning warship. The attack was extremely costly, for only two of the planes of our torpedo force returned to their ship. As the third attack failed to arouse enemy fighter opposition, we confirmed our estimated direct hits against the ship.

"These reports were brought in by the fighter pilots who flew escort high above the dive and torpedo bombers. The battle proved so intense and enemy opposition so severe that the bomber crews were unable to assess the results of their attacks."

With the operation completed, the *Junyo* was still

steaming at full speed toward the enemy fleet. We had many reports which claimed that both American carriers had gone to the bottom; however, most of these reports were assumptions and could not be confirmed. We must be ready to carry out additional attacks on the following day. All through the night the weary mechanics and aircrew personnel labored to prepare their battered airplanes for flight.

Last Moments of the Hornet

Admiral Yamamoto was kept fully informed of the battle's progress during his stay at Truk. With the battle clearly in our favor, he ordered the entire fleet to pursue the remaining enemy ships and to take every means of destroying the major combat vessels of the enemy force. This was sweet revenge, for the plight of the enemy fleet fleeing after losing its aircraft-carrier strength was exactly what we had experienced—only on a larger scale—at Midway. We could not afford to lose for a moment the advantage we had fought for so desperately.

All through the night, as our warships plunged at top speed through the Pacific, we could hear enemy flying boats searching for our fleet. The pursuit became increasingly difficult to maintain. The destroyers escorting the *Junyo* and the *Zuikaku* sent out urgent appeals for fuel oil. Their plight was so desperate that they risked enemy attack by sending out direct radio signals. Other vessels began to lag behind and the fleet's formation began to stretch out. Many of our captains hesitated to race at full speed toward an enemy fleet which we suspected might harbor yet another aircraft carrier; they did not want to expose their vessels to heavy unexpected air assault. We had moved recklessly at Midway in almost this same situation and paid the price for our folly. We could not be sure that a third carrier was not waiting to attack, for our second attack group had encountered enemy fighters after previous planes had poured their bombs and torpedoes into the carriers under attack on the twenty-sixth.

Because of this overcautious maneuvering and the reluctance of many commanders we failed to catch the fleeing enemy warships, although we continued the chase until the morning of the following day. At midnight of the twenty-sixth advance warships were maintaining full speed when they suddenly encountered several enemy destroyers preparing to sink the crippled *Hornet.* We were under instructions from Combined Fleet headquarters to capture, if possible, the *Hornet,* which we knew to be seriously disabled. Our fleet units, however, did not close; at least we confirmed that the *Hornet*'s demise was but a matter of a few minutes.

From the *Junyo*'s bridge I saw a red glow lighting the horizon far to the east of our carrier; this I presumed to be the blazing hulk of the sinking American carrier. I wondered at the time how the war might have been changed had our Navy been fortunate enough to have more combat officers like Read Admiral Kakuda.

The other enemy carrier which had been attacked by our planes was the *Enterprise.* The badly damaged ship managed to make good its escape from our pursuing fleet and, as we had been warned, we could not afford to allow even a single enemy warship to survive. By the middle of November the *Enterprise* had been repaired.

The big carrier returned to battle with a vengeance which was stunning. On November 12 her planes alone delivered the final blow to the battleship *Hiei,* which had been damaged off Guadalcanal, and sent the dreadnaught to the bottom. Two days later the planes caught and mercilessly bombed the heavy cruiser *Kinugasa*, which also went down. Also on the fourteenth, and continuing through the following day, the planes from the *Enterprise* shattered a valuable transport convoy attempting to fight its way to Guadalcanal with supplies and reinforcements for our beleaguered troops. The *Enterprise* clearly played the dominant role in halting decisively our Army's third all-out offensive of Guadalcanal.

On the morning of October 27 Kakuda brought the *Junyo* into fleet formation with the *Zuikaku*. The all-night repair work of the two carriers gave Kakuda a combined striking force of forty-four fighters, eighteen dive bombers, and twenty-two torpedo planes. The reconnaissance planes which had been launched from the two carriers before dawn failed, however, to discover any enemy ships or planes. The fuel situation had become desperate, with the escorting destroyers ready to fall out of formation. The fleet then received an order from Vice-Admiral Nagumo to assemble and return to base.

Nagumo had left the scene of action when the *Shokaku* received crippling damage, and had ordered Kakuda to command the subsequent air battles. Once he discovered, however, that he could not direct the over-all operation from the disabled carrier, Nagumo ordered the big ship to return for repairs to Truk; he transferred to a large destroyer which became his flagship for the general operation. Since our reconnaissance planes could not locate the enemy fleet by the morning of the twenty-seventh, Nagumo ordered his scattered vessels to reassemble. Shortly after noon of the same day the warships regrouped their formations and refueled at sea. Nagumo once again transferred his flag, this time to the *Zuikaku*.

The carrier's commander, Captain Tameteru Nomoto, had run his vessel and commanded the air battles for three consecutive days, without sleep, remaining at all times on the bridge of his ship. Nagumo personally offered his thanks to Nomoto for the latter's superhuman efforts. This was the first time in the Navy that a warship commander personally directed the actions of carrier-based planes without his staff, no small feat in itself.

Vice-Admiral Nagumo ordered a special conference held aboard the *Zuikaku* as the ship returned to Truk to discuss in detail the sea and air battle of the twenty-sixth. I attended the conference as the Kakuda Force's representative. When I boarded the *Zuikaku* I went directly to pay my respects to Nagumo; he was on the bridge, his face wan and drawn, and in deep thought. It was hard to ascertain the admiral's thoughts, but obviously he had thrown off the apathetic feeling which had weighed upon him after the Midway defeat.

Pleased that we had discharged in full Admiral Yamamoto's trust, Chief of Staff Kusaka warmly praised the accomplishments of the Kakuda Force. Kusaka was in a genial mood and, indeed, the entire staff attending the conference rejoiced in the newly won victory. For me, the price we had paid was bitter; Lieutenant Commanders Seki and Murata, old and good friends, were gone forever.

Even as the conference compared notes, we did not know accurately the losses our own ships and planes had sustained; some of our men had landed on other carriers, several reconnaissance planes had set down on our Solomons bases, and the crews of a number of planes which had ditched had been picked up by surface vessels. The data submitted to the conference enabled us to arrive at these tentative conclusions:

Enemy Losses:

Planes shot down	80 (55 by our planes)
Ships sunk or	
seriously damaged	3 aircraft carriers
	1 battleship
	2 cruisers
	1 destroyer
Ships damaged	3–4 cruisers
	3 destroyers

Japanese Losses:

Planes lost	69 (crashed into enemy or shot down)
	23 (forced landings at sea)
Ships sunk	*None*
Ships damaged	2 aircraft carriers (*Shokaku* and *Zuiho*)
	1 cruiser (*Chikuma*)

We based the estimates for the enemy carrier losses on the confirmation of the *Hornet*'s sinking and, the following morning, on the fact that our reconnaissance planes could not find any enemy carriers; the planes, however, did sight a large slick in the immediate vicinity where an enemy carrier had been reported as fiercely burning. We were forced to rely upon such information because we had lost two of our three dive-bomber leaders, all three leaders of the torpedo planes, and many other important officers.

Up to the time of this battle, both the Americans and the Japanese had lagged badly in shipboard defenses against aerial attacks; commencing with this conflict, however, antiaircraft defense rapidly improved in quality and quantity. This sudden increase in the defense available to the enemy ships was felt to account for the exorbitant losses sustained by our planes. Because we had lost so many of our experienced men, the conference had no choice but to accept the reports of young officers who were prone to allow the excitement of battle to color their observations. We could not follow any other course but to base our future plans on what these young officers reported to us.

Much later we discovered that our estimates were far from accurate. The *Hornet* eventually went to the bottom, sunk by the destroyers *Mustin, Anderson,* and our four destroyers; the destroyer *Porter* also was sunk. These two ships, however, were the only vessels which did go down. The second carrier to be attacked (there were only two, not three, carriers) was the *Enterprise.* Contrary to our pilot reports, the ship did not receive any torpedo hits, and its damage was confined to three direct bomb hits which, fortunately, inflicted serious damage to the vessel. The reports of the torpedo hits are understandable; superb maneuvering by the *Enterprise*'s captain permitted him to escape our torpedoes which slipped within a hair's breadth of the ship. Our planes also damaged the battleship *South Dakota* (which bristled with new defensive armament) and the destroyers *Smith* and the *San Juan.* We lost approximately one hundred and forty men in combat, most of them irreplaceable veterans; American personnel losses of air crews amounted to about one hundred men.

Despite the gross overevaluations, we had inflicted telling blows upon the American warships. The sea battle henceforth was officially titled the Sea Battle in the South Pacific, and Imperial General Headquarters made much of the victory.

Since the outbreak of the war, the United States had made constant anti-Japanese propaganda radio broadcasts. When I was aboard the *Ryujo* off the Aleutians I heard William Winter's broadcast which ridiculed the Nagumo

Force as *Ahodori*, or the foolish bird. Winter crowed long and loud (presumably with justification), since Nagumo's ships had been overwhelmingly defeated at Midway. This morning, at exactly 6:00 A.M. on October 26, I laughed aloud at Winter's words when he admitted that never in its history had the American Navy had so little cause to "celebrate" its Navy Day.

The battle was over, and, although we had suffered grievously in losing many of our best pilots, the enemy fleet had been soundly trounced. The victory was to be short; this was our only decisive conquest since Midway, and it was to be the last.

CHAPTER 22

Our Situation Becomes Critical: Air Battles in the Solomons and Rabaul Areas

B Y MID-1943 WE could no longer ignore the visible deterioration of the Pacific War situation. We still maintained powerful army forces, and our Navy posed a dangerous threat with its surface fleet. Despite this land-sea power, however, enemy attacks rapidly depleted our available planes, and it was obvious to all that without mastery of the air Japan could no longer hope successfully to conclude the war.

Our loss of air control centered directly about the situation with reference to the Zero fighter. Early in the war and, in fact, until the later stages of the Guadalcanal battle, the Zero clearly demonstrated its superior performance over enemy fighter planes. The Americans, however, bent every effort to augment and replace their inferior fighters with new planes of outstanding performance, and soon the Zero met increasing numbers of remarkably fast and powerful enemy fighters. In the interim we were forced to retain the Zero as our frontline fighter; the Navy did not have a suitable successor to the Zero, nor did the Army have an airplane which could favorably contest the American planes.

As the war continued, the dwindling number of Zeros were forced to fight under the most difficult circumstances against such planes as the Army Air Force's P-38, which was faster, could outclimb and outdive the Zero, and featured high-altitude performance, all coupled with heavy firepower, self-sealing fuel tanks, and armor plating. Soon there appeared the Navy's F4U fighter, the first enemy single-engined airplane clearly to outperform the Zero, notably in maximum speed and in diving speed. The second direct cause of our loss of air control was the numerical superiority of the American fighters in the south Pacific, then the main war theater.

The rapid diminution of our air strength is evident in a running summary of the Pacific War in the year following Admiral Yamamoto's death, when Admiral Mineichi Koga became Commander in Chief of the Combined Fleet. Koga's first planned large operation was stopped in its tracks. In May of 1943 an American force invaded Attu Island in the Aleutians Chain; if successful, the invasion would cut the defense chain we had established across the Pacific. Koga planned a massive aerial counterattack to drive the enemy back to the mid-Aleutians, and for this campaign concentrated the major strength of the fleet in Tokyo Bay. The enemy's rapid moves, however, caught Admiral Koga off balance and, before he could make his bid for the counterattack, the Americans controlled Attu.

One month later the Americans began a powerful assault against Rabaul, rolling northward through the Solomon Islands from Guadalcanal. By November the enemy secured his forces on the southern half of Bougainville Island, threatening our positions in the entire area. Another massive enemy thrust crushed our defenses in the Gilbert Islands, and this, too, became an American bastion. Seemingly in coordination with this move, the American and Australian forces in the New Guinea area intensified their air, ground, and sea attacks. The furious tempo of air and ground fighting visibly reduced our available fighting forces and weapons. By late 1943 the enemy assaulted our positions on the Merkus Peninsula in the western end of New Britain, the very island on which lay our Rabaul airfield.

We could now appreciate at first hand the incredible power of the American military machine, for despite furious and courageous defensive fighting and counterattacks the enemy ground his way northward. By the close of 1943 we were in a precarious position. Our Zeros no longer showed themselves over enemy territory, for every venture against enemy positions met awaiting swarms of high-performance American fighters. Indeed, our pilots were hard pressed even to maintain air control directly over Rabaul. Both quantity and quality played a direct part in this constant reduction in our air strength, for the American Navy now threw into combat its deadly Grumman F6F Hellcat fighter plane. Appearing for the first time in November of 1943, the Hellcats increased rapidly in number. Not only were they superior to the Zero, but out pilots faced literally hordes of the new enemy planes.

In late January of 1944 the enemy took the Marshall Islands and, several weeks later, stormed ashore on the Green Islands, some one hundred and thirty nautical miles east-southeast of Rabaul. Even as the troops hurled our own forces back into the jungles and mountains of these islands, the American engineers performed miracles of air-base construction and again established new fields from which to increase air attacks. The Americans demonstrated

their mushrooming power on February 17 with an irresistible carrier raid against Truk Island, our Navy's largest
and most powerful naval base in the inner southern Pacific.
Disdainful of even the fierce opposition they confronted,
the carrier planes wreaked chaos throughout our installations. Six days later, flushed with victory, a carrier task
force hurled hundreds of planes against our Mariana Island
air bases and again sowed a path of terrible destructions.

By this time we tottered on the brink of total defeat in
the southern Pacific. Enemy Army Air Force planes slashed
by day and night at our installations, and unbelievably
powerful carrier task forces roamed the Pacific, striking
where and when they desired. By February 20 our position
at Rabaul was no longer tenable, and our naval air force
units abandoned the island. This evacuation drew down
the curtain on two years of the greatest air battles of the
Pacific War, which began with our occupation of Rabaul in
January of 1942.

The remainder of this section describes in detail how
many of the air battles were fought in the Solomons and
Rabaul theater, for the most part taken from my (Okumiya's) personal experiences in the area. These episodes
reveal the transition of power from the Zero fighter to the
enemy, representing, as it were, the yielding of strength on
our part to the enemy across the entire Pacific.

Simultaneously with the American invasion of Attu
Island, in May of 1943, enemy counterattacks and island
invasions in the Solomons increased steadily in tempo. On
June 30 a vast assembly of ships poured men and supplies
ashore on Rendova Island. This latest invasion directly periled Rabaul, and Admiral Koga ordered all the air groups of
the 2nd Carrier Division, then at Truk, immediately to
transfer south to our base at Rabaul, and to Buin in southern Bougainville. Rear Admiral Munetaka Sakamaki

assumed command of the assembled air groups; at the time I was the air staff officer to Admiral Sakamaki.

In the central Solomons and east New Guinea our forces waged furious battles, retreating steadily before the aggressive enemy attacks. The jungle ground became red with blood of our troops who, despite every effort, could not stem the relentless enemy drives. The Navy Air Force centered at the Buin air base made every effort to destroy the enemy air units then based at Guadalcanal, and to provide air cover for our land forces and surface vessels in the area. To maintain an air blanket over our forces was in itself a major undertaking, for American planes in round-the-clock attacks hammered at troops and ships.

Consequently, the air battles centered about our Buin air base developed into violent day and night raids by both forces. The campaign was deadly, for the stakes included the entire southern Pacific and perhaps the war's outcome. Both the United States and Japan concentrated their main air strength in the theater.

Buin, a wretched air base, was not comparable in air-field facilities to the enemy's magnificent engineering achievements. Our pilots had only one runway, 4,000 feet long and 800 feet in width, running at a right angle to the coast. Extending from each side of the airstrip were numerous small roads leading into the jungle, where we concealed the majority of our planes from aerial observation. Each night we moved every plane from the field into the jungle revetments and, during the day, did the same except for those ships which were on call. This dispersion kept our losses from enemy bombing and strafing to a minimum.

Our air-force headquarters and sleeping quarters were located on the beach, approximately a mile and a half west of the field. Our "quarters" were simply barracks or, more accurately, tents scattered haphazardly over the ground.

We raised the floors about six feet above the soil for protection against the severe heat and moisture.

I remained at Buin approximately three months, from July 2 to September 28, 1943. During this time I kept detailed notes of our harassed life at this jungle air outpost:

"The daily activity at the air base begins at least three hours before sunrise. In the steaming humidity, surrounded by insects, the mess crews begin the task of preparing meals for the day. Most of the maintenance crews also arise at this time to prepare the planes for the day's missions. The work of our mechanics is most strenuous, for they must bring all the aircraft which are to fly that day from their jungle revetments onto the field. One by one the planes move from the jungle cover, a band of men tugging and pushing the heavy aircraft over the soft ground. Everything must be done by hand; there is not a single tractor on the field! Two hours later, with sixty minutes yet to go before the sun shows over the horizon, the entire field awakens, and all men take their posts. The pilots and the air-crew members carry their flying gear to the assembly point, which is the flight personnel pool near the runway. Here they eat their breakfast while they await their orders of the day.

"Even as the pilots receive their briefings, reconnaissance planes bound for routine search missions in the Guadalcanal area thunder along the runway and disappear into the brightening sky. By now every Zero fighter in flying condition is ready for an immediate takeoff, to defend the base against attacking enemy planes. The Zeros are fueled and armed, placed along the runway so that the pilots have only to fly straight ahead to take off. The 'standby' fighter pilots wait near the personnel shack, listening to the radio reports from our reconnaissance planes and from the distant ground-watching stations on the islands close to the enemy's airfields.

"Now the loudspeaker blares its warning. The outermost watching stations have sighted enemy planes wheeling into formation over their bases and heading for our area. The fighter commander checks the reports of each station, estimating the enemy planes' time of arrival. He waits until the last possible moment before ordering the Zeros into the air. The fighters rock and bounce slightly as they roll along the runway; then faster, the motors thundering, dust streaming behind the planes. Then they are in the air, dwindling to small black specks, and finally disappearing as they claw for altitude. They will wait high above the field, so that they can dive out of the sun against the enemy formations. Superior altitude in launching an attack can decide the outcome of the air battle.

"The base is quiet now. The only sounds are the metallic crackle of the loudspeaker, the hammering of mechanics, and the voices of men. Suddenly the lookout on our tower stiffens behind his binoculars; his voice carries to the ground. We see him pointing to the south. Yes . . . there they are! Enemy planes, fast approaching the air base. The siren screams its warning and the men on the field dash for cover, never too soon, as the enemy bombers close on the field with great speed.

"No one really stays down in the ditches and culverts. Hundreds of men stare at the sky, seeing the bombers and searching for the Zeros which should even now be diving against the enemy planes. Here they come, racing from their greater height to break up the bomber formations. But even before they reach the slower, heavier planes the escorting enemy fighters scream upward to intercept the Zeros. No matter how determined the Zero attacks, the bombers maintain their formations. Even as the Zeros and American fighter planes scatter over the sky in swirling dogfights we can hear the rapidly increasing shriek of the falling bombs. The earth shakes and heaves; great blossoms of fire, steel, smoke, and dirt erupt from the airfield as salvos of bombs 'walk across' the revetments and the runway. Sharp sound cracks against the eardrums, and the concussion is painful. Our own machine gunners fire in rage at the droning bombers above, even as the explosions come faster and faster. There is the rumble of bomber engines, the rising and falling whine of the fighters, the stutter of machine guns, and the slower 'chuk-chuk' of aerial cannon. The sky is filled with dust and flame and smoke. Planes on the field are burning fiercely, and wreckage is scattered across the runway, which by now is cratered with great holes.

"Through the smoke we can see the hurtling fighter planes, diving and climbing in mortal combat. Our men curse or only stare silently as we watch Zeros suddenly flare up in scarlet and orange flame, and then plunge from the sky like bizarre shooting stars, leaving behind them a long trail of angry flame and black, oily smoke. Parachutes can be sighted drifting earthward, clearly silhouetted against the deep blue sky.

"Then, abruptly, the raid is over. The crashing, earth-heaving thunder of the bombs is gone. As soon as the last bomb has expended its fury, the ground crews clamber from their air-raid shelters and with shovels in their hands race for the runway. They work frantically, sweat pouring from their bodies, ignoring the ever-present mosquitoes and flies, shoveling dirt back into the craters, rushing to patch up the field so that the damaged Zero fighters can land.

"The men jump aside as the crippled fighters, metal skin torn and holed by enemy bullets, stagger toward the runway. Most of them land safely, but every so often a badly damaged fighter spins under a collapsed landing gear or flips over on its back. As soon as it has stopped rolling, each arriving plane is surrounded by the maintenance crews. They push the fighters off the runway one by one, and immediately refuel the tanks and load fresh machine-gun bullets and cannon shells. The pilots, weary from another early morning encounter, assemble at the command post where the intelligence officers record their reports of the fight. As soon as the conference is ended, the pilots return to the assembly pool.

"These daily attacks are a familiar story. Even now our attack bomber group is waiting for takeoff. Finally the reconnaissance planes report the most favorable targets, and the bombers trundle down the runway and soar into the air. The Zeros will be flying close escort. The American fighters are becoming tougher every day.

"The long day passes. The gathering dusk is a welcome sight, for it means some rest and, at least, respite from heavy raids. Neither we nor the enemy has the proper equipment to permit large-scale night attacks. Once the sun has set the air crews, back from their missions, walk wearily to their respective sleeping quarters.

"Not, however, the maintenance crews. Their full day of work is no assurance of relaxation and sleep. The planes which have fought today are riddled with bullet holes, shrapnel, and gaping cannon tears in the wings and fuselage. Motors grind noisily and must be brought to smooth operation. Sheet-metal work must be done. Machine guns which have jammed must be cleared, brakes tightened or replaced, radio sets repaired, new sheets of clear plastic put in the bullet-riddled nose sections.

"The maintenance crews are exhausted, but they drag their weary bodies about the field, heaving and tugging to move the planes back into the jungle. They pray for tractors such as the Americans have in abundance, but they know their dream of such 'luxuries' will not be fulfilled. Three hours after the sun has gone down, the mechanics and technicians emerged red-eyed and haggard from the jungle to take their supper. It is blue-black twilight now, and the men eat, too tired to talk to one another, groping for their food in the darkness imposed by air-raid blackout orders. Hot, sweaty, dirty, and tired, they eat their food and walk to their sleeping quarters. They are too weary to read, or write letters, or even to talk very much to each other. Sleep is their only concern and they fall heavily to their mats.

"It is dark now, and the field is quiet. Maybe, if we are lucky, it will be a restful evening. Before long we know differently. Even as the siren screams, we hear the distant sound of approaching bombers. Anti-aircraft guns cough raucously at the black shapes far above, and dazzling searchlight beams stab through the sky, swinging in circles to search for the raiders. A series of tremendous explosions smashes at the eardrums. Again the earth heaves and shakes, and dust and smoke shower over the entire field. Perhaps there is only one airplane up there, circling the field, dropping a bomb every now and then, but he keeps us awake for hours, and before he leaves another nocturnal raider takes his place.

"Eventually the ear-splitting shock waves and the thunder leave. Again the field is quiet. This does little good! The mechanics and other ground crewmen curse the day, still black, as they begin another exhausting period of work.

"And this is but one day, typical of the seemingly endless succession of day and night periods, filled only with work, exhaustion, the ceaseless enemy attacks, and the ever-increasing number of pilots and air crewmen who do not return."

When the 2nd Carrier Division, commanded by Rear Admiral Sakamaki, to which I was attached as air staff officer, arrived at Buin, we found the 26th Air Flotilla already on the field. The two headquarters groups coordinated their activities and I was assigned responsibility for night raids. All pretense at a normal workday vanished, and I would be called on to work at any hour of the day or night. Since I had to "work with the moon," which rises at different times each night, I found regular sleep impossible. Here my long training stood me in good stead, for soon I could snatch sleep at any time, whether it was light or dark, and for any interval. I could sleep as well for twenty minutes as I could for three hours. Without this ability to relax under any conditions I would have broken down physically and, perhaps, mentally.

Usually I arose about one and a half hours before the time scheduled for departure of our planes. Without washing or breakfast, I groped through the blackout to the radio station. Here I checked the positions of enemy surface vessels, land-based air units, and the expected weather. With an hour to go before takeoff, I would then drive to the field's command post. Unless special conditions warranted their absence, our commander, the senior staff officer, and the command staff would remain directly on the base. Each time I arrived at the command post I would hear the mechanics warming up the engines of the planes scheduled to fly. I could see the blue-white flashes of flame spitting from the exhaust pipes, the only light visible on the entire base.

Thirty minutes before takeoff Captain Sakae Yamamoto, the 582nd Air Corps commander, briefed his air crews under a dim electric bulb at the command post. Although I often advised the captain, I never gave orders directly to the pilots and crew members. That was not my job, for I remained in the background, studying carefully the facial expressions and the actions of our flying personnel. My responsibility was to ascertain their morale and physical condition.

Finally Yamamoto gave the order to take off. One by one the planes rumbled down the field and lifted into the darkness. All work was carried out through signals, a simple flash of light between the command post and the take-off line. The runaway itself was shrouded black; at the extreme end one could barely make out two dimly glowing lights, shielded from above, marking the end of the runway to the pilots.

With the last plane gone we snatched some rest on cots at the command post, waiting on call in the event that any of the planes were forced to turn back. The C.P. rose like a fire watchtower to a height of sixty-seven feet, and its top matched the height of the surrounding jungle trees. Atop the tower was the lookout station; the actual command headquarters rested within the tower, about eleven feet off the ground. Our working space was little bigger than a wrestling ring. During an enemy attack the C.P. was filled with men and became a center of utter confusion. There was little room, even if everyone were to remain still, to use mosquito netting. We could protect ourselves from the vicious insects only by covering our bodies with a rain-coat. In the muggy atmosphere we perspired profusely. The lower parts of our bodies were protected by long, heavy trousers and pilot's boots, which we did not take off even when sleeping.

The hours always passed by slowly. Our lookout finally identified the returning bombers, which showed a coded light signal. The landing procedure was seldom uneventful, for often courageous American pilots would trail our bombers back to the base, flashing the light signal similar to that used by bombers. We had to be absolutely alert at all times, for the favorite American trick was to scream down upon the field in a surprise attack. Once, we brought the first bomber in for a successful landing, then signaled the second plane to make its approach. The airplane drifted toward the ground in a normal landing run; suddenly, we heard the sound of motors being pushed to full throttle and the "Japanese" bomber came into view as an enemy night intruder, machine guns spitting tracers into the command post and over the field. Fortunately, in this attack I escaped injury, but we lost several maintenance crewmen and suffered damage to some airplanes. The American pilots were the most adventurous fliers I have ever encountered; apparently they would stop at nothing.

As our planes landed and were pushed into their jungle revetments, I interviewed the pilots and aircrews. With the data from every man condensed into an intelligence report, I radioed all units concerned the information obtained on the night raids. Before I realized it the darkness was fading before the first signs of dawn. Another day!

When there was no moonlight to guide our planes on night raids, we modified the attacks so that the planes would be able to strike at dawn or dusk. If we attacked at dusk, the planes could leave during daylight and attack their objectives under conditions of good visibility, but they also ran the risk of enemy fighter interception. The dawn attacks required split-second timing, for if the planes were forced by weather to postpone their takeoff, usually they could not arrive over the target until the sun was up, reducing the favorable element of surprise. Therefore we now used also the airstrip on Kolombangara Island, which lay close to Munda, where our troops were engaged in bitter fighting with the enemy. Not only did this new arrangement raise the morale of the marines at the base, isolated along the front lines, but the ground crews at Kolombangara now had some work to perform for the first time in many weeks.

In mid-August four Kates led by Lieutenant (J.G.) Taka-hashi arrived secretly at the Kolombangara airstrip, sliding into the field just at dusk. Even though the airstrip person-nel knew the planes were on their way, a runway pitted with holes from repeated air attacks greeted pilots. They were apprehensive about landing, for each Kate carried a 1,760-pound bomb for the next day's attack. After circling the field slowly and noting the location of the craters, the four Kates finally made precarious but safe landings.

The pilots and crew members could scarcely believe their eyes when they descended from their planes. The maintenance crews which greeted them stared from blood-shot eyes; they were bearded and unkempt, and their short pants were filthy. Malnutrition had pulled back the skin on their faces and bodies. They ran tender hands over the planes they had not seen for so many months, and could not help crying with joy after their long isolation.

The bomber crews bedded down for the evening which, as always, brought with it hordes of mosquitoes and other insects. The mosquito nets which the mechanics respect-fully offered them were rags, utterly useless, and the pilots and crew members tossed and turned the entire night, besieged by insect swarms.

To Lieutenant Takahashi's astonishment, the air-base personnel slept soundly through the night. Despite their lack of netting, and the consequent exposure to the mos-quitoes, they awoke refreshed and eager to service the Kates. Takahashi's group took off early in the morning and successfully bombed the enemy objectives. Returning to Buin, which we had long despaired of as probably the "worst air base" in the Pacific, Takahashi vowed never to complain again. He described to his fellow pilots in detail the terrible conditions at Kolombangara, compared to which Buin was an "engineering paradise."

The absence of ground fighting near the Buin air base allowed us one pleasure: the luxury of bathing. This was, in fact, the only pleasant aspect of life at the jungle airstrip, and even to enjoy this we had to squeeze in our bathing time within the space of about thirty minutes after the daily battles. Eventually the Americans intensified their attacks and raided Buin at any time of the day or night. Frantic movements to extricate oneself from a tub because of flaming tracers soon made us forgo even this last moment of relaxation!

I must give credit where it is rightfully due. The American pilots who raided Buin were some of the bravest fliers I have ever seen. They flew at treetop level, racing at great speed over the field, their machine guns spraying lead and tracers into every possible target.

The loss of merely the pleasure of bathing may appear as a trivial matter to the reader. However, we lived under the most primitive conditions, without decent food, yearning for rest, beseiged day and night by American bombers and fighters, waging a battle which could have but one outcome, watching our friends leaving on missions never to return, suffering from jungle diseases, annoyed day and night by insects; with this in mind, then, perhaps this fervor at least to be clean can better be understood. Finally our dreams of pure luxury centered about an uninterrupted bath and an evening's sound slumber beneath several layers of mosquito netting, with bright lights all about us instead of dreary blackout.

At this time the only serious land battles being fought in the Pacific area raged in our area and along the east coast of New Guinea. Large-scale air battles were fought mainly between the American planes from Guadalcanal and our Buin-based forces. We were the one force which held back the mounting enemy pressure and, were we to fail, the Americans would burst northward from Guadalcanal. As the director of the air battles in the area, I prepared the communiques for release by the Imperial General Staff (*Daihonei*) in Japan. One such communique, as an example, read:

"NEWS FLASH ON AIR BATTLES BY THE BUIN AREA AIR FORCE

"BUIN: AN AIR GROUP OF TWELVE TYPE 99 CARRIER-BASED DIVE BOMBERS AND FORTY-EIGHT ZERO FIGHTERS, LED BY LIEUTENANT JG TACHIBANA, LEFT THIS BASE AT 0600 HOURS TODAY TO SEARCH FOR A LARGE ENEMY CONVOY. ONE OF OUR RECONNAISSANCE PLANES ON THE NIGHT OF THE FOURTEENTH SIGHTED THE ENEMY FLEET MOVING NORTH IN THE SEA SOUTH OF RENDOVA ISLAND. OUR AERIAL FORMATIONS SIGHTED AN ENEMY LANDING FORCE OFF THE EAST COAST OF VELLA LAVELLA, BELIEVED TO BE THE ENEMY CONVOY PREVIOUSLY SIGHTED AT SEA. LIEUTENANT TACHIBANA LED THE DIVE BOMBERS AND THE FIGHTERS IN AN ATTACK AGAINST THE ENEMY FORCE, DESPITE INTERCEPTION WITH APPROXIMATELY FIFTY ENEMY PLANES.

"OUR BOMBERS SANK TWO LARGE AND ONE SMALL TRANSPORT SHIPS, DAMAGED TWO LARGE AND TWO SMALL TRANSPORT SHIPS. WE SHOT DOWN SEVEN ENEMY PLANES AND DAMAGED FIVE. OUR LOSSES INCLUDED FIVE TYPE 99 DIVE BOMBERS AND THREE ZERO FIGHTERS. LIEUTENANT TACHIBANA GAVE HIS LIFE IN THE ATTACK.

"OUR FORCE WILL RETURN TO VELLA LAVELLA AGAIN TODAY TO PRESS BOMBING ATTACKS AGAINST THE ENEMY LANDING SHIPS."

The government released this news flash to the public immediately after the enemy established a beachhead on August 15 at Vella Lavella. We mounted three attacks against the invasion force, placing over the target area a total of 141 Zero fighters, 36 Val bombers, 23 Betty twin-engined bombers, and 20 seaplanes.

On the evening of the day when I sent the news report to Imperial General Headquarters, we listened to the radio broadcast to our people. The program opened with a recording of the "Navy March," after which the announcer repeated my news flash verbatim. When I heard that more than half the program time was allotted to my report I first realized to what extent I could control the feelings of our people at home.

On September 1 the Navy ordered the Commander of 26th Air Flotilla to return with his staff to Japan, and directed Admiral Sakamaki and his staff to assume the combat responsibilities of the departing flotilla. As the division air staff officer, I assumed the air-operations duties which had been conducted by the flotilla's air officer. We now were the only remaining high echelon headquarters unit in close proximity to the enemy, for which I comprised the entire air staff! What the situation actually indicated was that our planes were the only force left to face the main body of American air strength in the area. Our conduct would reflect accurately the national air strength of my country.

From this moment on I no longer recognized night or day. Often I worked right through stretches of forty-eight hours or more, laboring to dispatch my airplanes where they could most effectively attack the enemy and, equally time-consuming, trying to be elsewhere when the American raiders assaulted Buin. My position was anything but unique, for Rear Admiral Sakamaki, Captain Yamamoto, and their immediate staffs were suffering the same tribulations.

On September 14 enemy planes bombed Buin three times, placing over the air base at least two hundred and twenty planes. The rain crashing bombs turned the field temporarily into complete chaos. Every available Zero fighter took to the skies to intercept, and many of these planes and their pilots failed to return. The September 14 attacks were the largest fought since my arrival. So severe was the damage to the field, and so great was the number of planes either damaged or wrecked by the enemy bombs, that every single officer and enlisted man worked more than twelve hours without rest or food. We knew only too well that unless we quickly became operational again we would be at the full mercy of the enemy bombers. By nightfall we had cleared away most of the debris, and the base was returning to "normal" operations.

Despite the damage suffered that day, we dispatched our night bombers on their harassing raids. Our pilots were determined to repay the enemy, at least in part, for his damaging attack. On this particular mission I was unable personally to dispatch the planes, since I still had to prepare the daily report to Tokyo. As usual, I hurried to the field after midnight. The planes were already due, but for some reason Captain Yamamoto and his flight officer failed to appear at the command post. Most probably they had been exhausted by the bombing and were sound asleep.

Soon the bombers began to return, assembling over the field. The ground crews did not know what to do; although the bombers waited for the landing signal lights; only Captain Yamamoto and his flight officer had the authority to order these on. I fidgeted uneasily, for it is intolerable to keep pilots who have just completed a long and grueling night mission circling in the dark. Further, the situation was ready-made for an effective sneak attack by an enemy intruder. And the entire base now was wide awake, waiting with uncertainty for the planes to land. One can never be *sure* that the planes above are friendly.

It was beyond my authority, but as the air staff officer I ordered the ground crews immediately to switch on the landing lights to bring the bombers in. One by one the black raiders slipped onto the airstrip, and the signal lights winked out. At that moment Yamamoto and his flight officer came running into the command post. At once I apologized, for to overextend one's authority is a serious matter. Rather than taking offense, the captain was grateful for my intervention. His action was typical. To every one of us the welfare of the aircrews was our primary consideration. Our purpose was to ease as much as possible the burden of the men who carried the fight to the enemy. This required the unhesitating cooperation of all concerned; to do less was to shirk one's responsibility.

The aircrews best of all personified Japan's people in the battlefield, for they came from every walk of life. Some of them carried the names of well-known families; some noncommissioned officers were simple laborers. Some were the only sons of their parents. While we maintained strict military discipline on the ground, with proper observance for rank, class, and age, those differences no longer existed when a crew's plane lifted its wheels from the ground.

The enemy cared little about the groups which constituted our air crews, and there existed no discrimination on the part of the pilot who caught our planes in his sights! Our air crews were closely knit teams, for it mattered not one whit whether an enlisted man or an officer manned the machine guns or cannon. The effect was exactly the same. Unfortunately this feeling of solidarity of our air crews was unique in the Japanese military organization.

The continual air battles against the savagely fighting Americans exacted a heavy and steady toll of our men. The constant fighter-plane interceptions and bombing missions meant that hardly a day passed without men dying or receiving serious wounds. The pilots and air crews did not honestly expect to survive their Buin duty tour, for the steady loss of men meant that no one could predict the time of his own passing. I could not understand the attitude of our Navy command, which treated its men with unnecessary harshness and apparent disregard. Of the one hundred and fifty air-crew members who had arrived one month ago with me at Buin, at least fifty were dead. Before the month passed we were certain that more than one half of the remaining men also would be lost. Even in the costly Guadalcanal beachhead operation we did not lose more than a third of our personnel. Here at Buin we suffered most heavily in the loss of our lieutenant J.G. personnel, who formed the nucleus of the fighter pilots. Thirteen of these men had arrived in the south Pacific eighteen months ago; only one was still alive.

I was not entirely aware of the attitude of these men, either of those who had died, or the ones who remained. Perhaps many of the men accepted their fate willingly, with the realization that in sacrificing their lives for their country they went beyond merely the act of dying. I do not know the answer, but I found it gratifying to see that those who remained to fight and almost certainly to die exhibited no signs of psychological disturbance.

For our ground forces it was a different matter. It was not difficult for our troops to whip themselves into emotional frenzies, for there existed no greater honor than to die in defense of their homeland. Perhaps some of our troops obtained their courage from the long-cherished desire to die, as they knew eventually they must, before their comrades with the fearless *Banzai!* cry upon their lips.

This world of human emotions did not seem to touch our flying personnel. Their courage and solidarity as a team under fire arose from something more profound and lasting. Certainly they realized that if war conditions did not change drastically, their demise was but a matter of time. Just when that time would come was, of course, the question. They had to continue fighting, ignoring the ever-present specter of flaming death, simply because there was a task to be done.

It was important to our men to be remembered for the brave manner in which they met death against the enemy. Our airmen who for so long fought a steadily losing battle often were denied in their last minutes of life the knowledge that their passing would be related at home. On the majority of occasions the end came without witness by a man's flying mates. Those men who failed to return simply were listed as "died in action" or "failed to return." Despite the lack of what was to them a matter of great consequence, our pilots and airmen fought courageously.

The philosopher would state that "it is the basic principle of the theory of evolution to be unmindful of one's own destruction for the sake of propogating the species." This is all very well in the classroom, but the philosopher often is conspicuously absent from the battlefield. What is it which allowed our men to act as they did? I cannot answer, and never really will know, but I feel that I saw something wonderful, deep, and pure in their eyes, a reflection, perhaps, of the serene peace they knew in their souls. If I am compelled to identify this motivation, I can reply only with the inadequate phrase of "love of their country." Could this be classed merely as patriotism? It is difficult to answer.

Through my association with these men I learned that there are those who fight merely for the sake of fighting, who seek out mortal combat with the enemy, who wish to stake their lives against that of the enemy pilots. They did not do this from patriotic motives, but merely because they *wanted* to fight. This is no longer explained by logic. Had the real conditions of the battleground, with its overwhelming lack of decent facilities for our men, been shown to the people back home, there would have been a terrible outcry against our leaders. The decision for war itself would have been questioned seriously, and, perhaps because of this, the war might have ended sooner.

And yet, our airmen did not care to shoulder the task of such public enlightenment. *Our men were not so lacking in scientific knowledge as to believe in happiness after death.* They had enjoyed in their present life what they considered to be the greatest spiritual moments a human being can attain.

The matter so disturbed me that on occasion I secretly left my barracks and visited the sleeping quarters of my men. I would contemplate, with little success, the drive behind these courageous airmen. Officers higher than the rank of lieutenant (Japanese Navy division officers) were afforded the luxury of sleeping in twos and threes in one room, but the lieutenant J.G. personnel crowded eight together, usually in an old, dirty tent superficially protected by mosquito netting. Our noncommissioned officers also suffered quarters in dilapidated tents, crowded in together. Worst of all, however, were the terrible conditions under which our maintenance crews lived. Their quarters were comparable to the worst jungle slums, and the men slept like sardines in a can, so tightly jammed together that it was impossible for a man to roll over on the damp floors. Tropical rains poured water over their bodies, making sleep impossible. Their mosquito netting amounted to pitiful shreds of cloth, of virtually no use. With poor food, lack of toilet facilities, and jammed quarters, theirs was indeed a miserable lot. We could do nothing to alleviate the terrible conditions, for the few ships which broke through the enemy screen of submarines, warships, and bombers carried only the most essential items.

I feared for the health of the aircrew personnel. Even the slightest illness could wreck the smooth teamwork necessary in air combat. The effects of malnutrition especially denied us certain combat advantages. In any aerial engagement the opponent who first discovers his enemy gains an immediate advantage. Our pilots and crew members, suffering from malnutrition, also underwent a corresponding loss in vision. We had a most forceful demonstration of this handicap. Lieutenant Commander Mochifumi Nango, a distinguished ace in the Sino-Japanese Incident, persisted in flying despite marked malnutrition. He was a superb flyer. We were convinced, however, that he did not even see the enemy fighter into which his Claude rammed with terrifying impact.

Buin was in the tropical zone, but lacked the customary native dwellings and, indeed, could only boast cocoa. Neither fruit nor vegetables grew in the forsaken strip of jungle land. At Rabaul and Buka (an island north of Buin) there grew some fresh fruit, but in such niggardly quantities that they could not meet even a fraction of our needs. Every so often I dispatched a transport plane to Kavieng, at the northern tip of New Ireland, with orders to bring back bananas, papayas, and vegetables. The flight required a round trip of more than eight hundred nautical miles and the use of valuable fuel, but I felt it imperative that our airmen receive at least this minimum quantity of fresh food. Rear Admiral Sakamaki would not take the food, but ordered it distributed only among the pilots and air-crew members.

Occasionally high-ranking officers from our Tokyo headquarters and from Combined Fleet Headquarters at Truk would visit Buin to confer with me about the air war in the Buin theater. I know that what they learned from me would influence to no small extent the future conduct of our naval air arm, and I was always cautious to answer carefully their every question. One particular interrogation proceeded as follows:

"We understand that since the 2nd Carrier Division transferred to Buin, air operations in the theater have suddenly increased. According to our intelligence reports, our raids are causing the enemy great difficulty. Has the present commander employed tactics differing greatly from those of the former commanding officer?"

Actually we had not modified our tactics to any unusual extent. The truth of the matter was simply that most of the air staff which preceded us at Buin had suffered severe emotional disturbances. Not only were they exhausted mentally and physically from their grueling work under enemy fire, but the lack of proper housing and food and the murderous climate hastened their collapse. Under such conditions they could not possibly have employed their aircraft effectively against the enemy. I replied:

"There has been little change, if any at all. I believe the increased efficiency of our men stems from the fact that our commander receives the unquestioned trust and support of his subordinates. As you realize, the present air battles are fought chiefly by our younger officers, and by men below the rank of lieutenant. Frankly, I myself want quite badly to make a reconnaisance flight over Guadalcanal, for personal observation would aid my duties; however, as you are aware, my old wounds do not permit me to make a high-altitude flight. I could only be a burden to a reconnaisance plane and, as much as I would like once again to fly, I have refrained from doing so."

"However, Commander Okumiya, as the staff officer in charge of air operations, haven't you specific ideas you have followed, or would like to see put into practice?"

The question was difficult to answer, but finally I said:

"My idea of an air staff officer may differ from the conception you hold. To me his duties should parallel, if you will pardon my analogy, the task of a sports trainer. The air staff officer should outline his plan of attack, but similarly should bend every effort to ease the work of his airmen. Let us face facts: the air staff officer has no place in actual combat; his every effort should be made to formulate the most effective plan of attack and to provide his men with the greatest chance of survival. I am simply carrying out my duties with this attitude in mind."

"Will you elaborate a bit further, Commander?"

"Perhaps the best example is found in the manner in which we ordinarily attend to our personnel. Usually everybody takes great care to insure that the needs of officers are met, but these same people are surprisingly negligent of the cares of the greater majority of our flying personnel, the noncommissioned officers. To me this is foolish, for the best officer is useless in combat unless he has the support of a well coordinated and able crew. Therefore I have given every possible minute to devising means to raise the morale of our noncommissioned officers. I have taken special pains to provide these airmen with the food and medicine necessary for their health. Our mechanics bend every effort to maintain our planes in flying condition; few things are as effective in destroying morale as a lack of aircraft against an enemy who daily grows stronger."

"I see!. . . . Is there anything that, as the air staff officer, you would specifically like to see done?"

"Many things! But of all which I feel should be done, I particularly want to send some of my men back to Japan while they still are in good health. It is unimportant if we return to the homeland only one or two of our airmen who are not yet ill, or wounded. More than two months have passed since I arrived in Buin; in all this time, although many more men have since come as replacements, not a single healthy man has left the base. This same situation applies to our maintenance crews, who live under the most primitive conditions. Why? If our personnel could believe only that they had a chance, even the slimmest chance, of returning to Japan *before* they were seriously wounded, or become seriously ill, our morale would soar. The prospect of returning home under conditions other than, so to speak, being carried out on a stretcher would provide a tremendous incentive for work.

"Another question. Why in the name of heaven does Headquarters delay so long in according our combat men the honors they deserve? The most unbelievable acts of courage and bravery before the enemy have gone without notice from Tokyo. From the looks of things, Japan is no more impressed with the man who singlehandedly defeats a hundred enemy planes than with the administrative clerk who is never fired upon! Look at the methods of our enemies. Henderson Field on Guadalcanal, the largest enemy base in the area, is named after their Major Lofton Henderson, a Marine torpedo-bomber pilot who died at Midway. I am impressed with the wisdom of the American method of raising the morale of their fighting men.

"In contrast, our Navy does absolutely nothing to recognize its heroes. The outstanding men of the Pearl Harbor Attack, and the Sea Battle of Malaya, to this day have not received a single individual honor or citation. These men are now dying one after the other in battle, and their numbers decrease every day. The situation at times becomes ridiculous. Recently Vice-Admiral Jinichi Kusaka, Commander in Chief of the Southeast Area Fleet, was forced to take *some* steps to recognize one of our pilots. The admiral awarded an honor sword to Flight Petty Officer Okabe, who in one day shot down seven enemy planes. Okabe himself was happy to receive this citation, but little is left for his memory, since he died in action several days later. Our aircrew members do not complain or even discuss this lack of recognition or honors for their deeds; because of this silence especially I plead that you may convince Headquarters to give these men the attention they so rightfully deserve."

(It is astonishing, and perhaps shameful, to realize that throughout all World War II *not a single living member of the Japanese armed forces ever received any form of government honor, award, or citation*, despite the actions of many men above and beyond their duty to their country.)

In late September of 1943 I was reassigned as the air staff officer of the 2nd Carrier Division, and soon afterward I returned to Japan. By mid-October the enemy air raids against the 26th Air Flotilla at Buin had become intolerable. With its base constantly subjected to enemy bombs and strafing attacks, with living facilities reduced to the lowest possible level, and with a mounting loss of supply ships, the Navy pulled out, moving its air strength directly to Rabaul. From October of 1943 to January of 1944 our planes engaged the enemy air units in some of the most bitter air fights of the war. Increased numbers of enemy land-and carrier-based fighters and bombers attacked our positions; these were met by planes of the 25th and 26th Air Flotillas, and the air groups of the 1st Carrier Division. The Navy could not continue to bear indefinitely the ever-increasing enemy air strength, and our position deteriorated rapidly.

The Last Rabaul Air Force

During the summer and early fall of 1943 the reorganized 2nd Carrier Division, under Rear Admiral Takaji Jojima, was forced by a shortage of aviation fuel to recognize and train its air groups in the Singapore area. With its training barely completed, the division received orders from Admiral Koga to transfer to Truk, and arrived at the Pacific bastion by December. By the close of 1943 the Marshall Islands and Rabaul were periled by the advancing enemy, whose planes daily filled the skies over our bases. Truk itself was threatened by the approaching bulk of enemy air strength. For the third time, Admiral Koga dispatched the 2nd Carrier Division's air groups to bolster Rabaul's tottering defenses.

Preceding the main body of planes, on January 20, 1944, I flew to Rabaul to set up my working quarters. In charge of Rabaul's air defense was the 26th Air Flotilla, the air group I had worked with at Buin. After paying my respects to Vice-Admiral Jinichi Kusaka, commander of the new aerial defense operation, I hurried to the flotilla's headquarters to visit my old friends. I was anxious to see the men with whom I had shared the bombings and deprivation at Buin.

I was pleased to see that, instead of the ramshackle quarters of Buin, the 26th staff now worked in a splendid native house, with a high tropical floor. A section was apportioned off as sleeping quarters, and the building was well furnished. With facilities such as these, obviously the commander and his staff would be able to direct their operations with the greatest efficiency. I did not even wait for my car to stop, but climbed out when it still was moving and ran up the stairs leading to the operations room.

The moment I passed through the door I realized something was wrong. Outwardly the staff personnel were the same. Nevertheless they had changed. Six months ago they were cheerful and hard workers, despite the rigors of life at Buin. Now, they were quick-tempered and harsh, their faces grimly set. The fighting spirit which enabled us to ignore the worst of Buin was gone. The men lacked confidence; they appeared dull and apathetic. No longer were they the familiar well-functioning team.

It was difficult to determine the reason for this startling change. Perhaps it was the never-ending pressure of enemy attacks, or the realization that American troops battered their way closer to Rabaul every day. It was possible that finally they had despaired entirely of victory, and were only waiting for the end to come. Their expressions and actions indicated clearly that they wished to abandon Rabaul at the earliest possible moment.

Yet, despite the American boast that by Christmas their forces would be in Rabaul, the 26th Air Flotilla had somehow managed to hold back the Americans from sweeping over Bougainville Island. Although this was only a defensive action, any respite from the giant war machine's pounding its way north in the Pacific could have come only from a great fighting effort. Even the success of this delaying operation failed to buoy the spirits of the headquarters staff.

Before long, I could understand the prevalent apathy. I

learned that even the Buin attacks could not compare to the devastating enemy assaults against Rabaul. The Americans hurled hundreds of planes in incessant day and night attacks at our crucial base. Sleep became impossible as high-flying bombers and night intruders dropped bombs during the evening. The men were completely exhausted.

In the air war raging around Bougainville and Rabaul, the bomber crews were required first to be competent engineers before they could become effective in combat. In the aircraft types employed by our air flotilla, composed of single-seat fighters, two-seat dive bombers, and three-seat level and torpedo bombers, the highest levels of teamwork were necessary to survive the strong enemy air opposition. This demanded, of course, considerable training and coordination of effort on the part of the crew members. We found that replacements who lacked the intimate knowledge which allowed them to fit smoothly into a bomber's established routine became not an asset but a liability. Past combat experience was insufficient to replace the teamwork built up through months of working together. The steady attrition of our personnel in combat denied our men the teamwork they considered so essential, and we were forced constantly to draw upon our administrative staffs for aerial gunners, radiomen, bombardiers, and other crew replacements.

Our air staffs lost invaluable subordinates rapidly, and our commanders cursed the necessity for breaking up their headquarters teams which had been developed over so many months. Before long the strain of sending out men every day to their deaths began to tell even on the top headquarters staff officers. It is one thing to know that you have a mission to perform, but it is another to stay behind, at a desk, when the pride of Japanese manhood dies because *you* have committed them to battle. Many of our top commanders would talk to no one for long periods of time; they could not help but reproach themselves for remaining alive at the expense of our young fliers.

And yet, absolutely nothing could be done to alleviate the situation. American air pressure increased steadily; even a momentary lapse in our air defense efforts might lose us Rabaul and our nearby fields. The endless days and nights became a nightmare. The young faces became only briefly familiar, then vanished forever in the bottomless abyss created by American guns. Eventually some of our higher staff officers came to resemble living corpses, bereft of spiritual and physical strength. The Navy would replace as quickly as it could the necessary flight personnel, but failed at any time during the war to consider the needs of its commanding officers. This was an error of tragic consequence, for no leader can properly commit his forces to battle when he does not have full command of his own mental and physical powers. Neither did the Navy ever consider the problems of our base maintenance personnel, who for months worked like slaves. From twelve to twenty hours a day, seven days a week, these men toiled uncomplainingly. They lived under terrible conditions, rarely with proper food or medical treatment. Their sacrifices received not even the slightest recognition from the government.

The Naval General Staff failed also in its evaluation of our front-line fighting men, choosing to believe that *all* of our combat veterans were heroes. Clearly this was a supposition without the slightest basis in reality! Courage is something which fluctuates widely; it is determined by a thousand large and small factors—the place and time of battle, the men with whom one serves, the caliber of enemy opposition, and so on. For the average pilot and air-crew member, the required mental outlook and physical stamina necessary for effective combat cannot last longer than a month under heavy enemy pressure. Some men, of course, do not lose any of their physical and mental stamina even when facing savage enemy air blows over a period of two months; these men, however, are the exception and not the rule. Should the demands of combat require that a unit be kept directly in combat for more than a month at a time, the flight personnel should be provided with rest periods at regular intervals. It is immaterial whether this rest period is no longer than a single day; even a "short break" has an excellent effect upon the men. Again our Navy failed to consider such aspects of the war, and many men who finally went down before enemy guns did so only because their physical and mental exhaustion had sapped their ability as pilots.

For these and other reasons, I found on my arrival at Rabaul an astonishing conviction that the war could not possibly be won, that all that we were doing at Rabaul was postponing the inevitable. Our executive personnel at Rabaul were not deluded by promises of future successes; they were experts in military aviation affairs and had personally undergone many combat engagements. As the months went by they watched the qualitative superiority of the Zero fighter fade before the increased performance of new American fighter planes which, by now, not only outfought but also outnumbered the Zeros. There existed a growing feeling of helplessness before this rising tide of American might. Our men felt keenly the great difference between American industrial and military strength and the limited resources of their own country. Despite these convictions, they could only continue to send our pilots and air crews into combat and to their deaths. Who could blame them, then, for the mental regression into spiritual apathy and defeatism?

I found in my discussions with the 26th Air Flotilla flight personnel that they held the same impressions of futile combat, that further fighting could only postpone eventual defeat. The most astonishing reaction to the 2nd Carrier Division's arrival at Rabaul was that the knowledge that the flotilla could return to Truk did not engender relief. Instead, many of the flotilla's men could see only reproach in their replacement. They felt that they were being removed from the front line because their performance was unsatisfactory, that the Navy expected the 2nd Carrier Division to accomplish what they had failed to do. An attitude of this nature is dangerous, for it can lead in a short time to the spiritual disintegration of even the strongest army.

As I took over my new duties as the Rabaul air staff officer, I reflected that to date I had been extremely fortunate. Although I had gone through many battles, I was never forced to remain under severe mental strain for undue lengths of time. Either the campaign developed in our favor, or transfer to other duties relieved me of any excessive worry. Because of this past experience, I arrived at Rabaul in excellent physical and mental health.

My own convictions as to the proper use of our air power differed from the Navy's plan of operation at Rabaul. I was not entirely in favor of throwing our remaining carrier-based air strength, which had been trained specifically for decisive sea battles, into another one of the seemingly endless campaigns fought against enemy land-based air power. This was the twelfth specific occasion in which the Navy pitted our carrier aviation against enemy land-based warplanes, and it was the sixth such campaign for my own air group. Personally I believed this use of carrier aviation to be wasteful; it could not produce any positive results for Japan. However, these thoughts constituted my own personal convictions, not those of the Navy. Despite my own viewpoint, I could not justify allowing personalities to intrude upon my official status. My position as an officer demanded only absolute adherence to the policies of my Navy, and I would not do otherwise than to support to the fullest our efforts against the enemy.

I knew that the defeatist attitude prevailing at Rabaul could only cause dissension among my own staff. I had to take every step to prevent the lethargy affecting the 26th Air Flotilla's staff from being transmitted to my own group. Until I arrived at Rabaul, we permitted the replacement staffs to work together with the groups being relieved; the overlapping duties permitted rapid familiarization with the procedures of the base. In this case, however, I preferred not to allow this contact to occur, and as soon as my unit arrived at Rabaul I relieved the 26th Air Flotilla, permitting them to return at once to Truk.

On January 25 the 2nd Carrier Division's planes arrived at Rabaul. Rear Admiral Takaji Jojima assumed active command of his forces. The admiral did not have long to wait before he tried the mettle of his pilots, for the very next day a powerful enemy force of approximately two hundred fighters and bombers attacked the Rabaul airfield. Admiral Jojima threw into the interception every available Zero fighter, totaling ninety-two airplanes. The Americans exacted a heavy toll. For many of the fighter pilots, this was their first taste of combat, and they faced experienced enemy pilots who flew excellent airplanes. Ten Zeros were shot out of the sky. The exorbitant loses did not permit us merely to record the dead pilots as having "crash dived."

Combat experience teaches that it is always impossible to predict the outcome of battles, no matter how extensive the planning and preparation. Unknown factors can disrupt even the most perfectly arranged operation, and it is beyond the ken of any man to predict accurately what shall comprise these factors. Despite their realization of the uncertainty which accompanies any combat operation, Admiral Jojima, and indeed the entire flight personnel of the division, had absolute faith in my ability to extricate our air groups from our precarious position. My past combat record indicated that certainly I was most likely to wrest victory from an enemy which now not only possessed excellent and plentiful airplanes but which exercised unusually aggressive tactics. I admit willingly that my position as the Rabaul air staff officer caused me no end of personal anguish; there could be but one outcome to the war of attrition, and that would be in the favor of the Americans.

The days passed in a blur. Every day we sent the Zeros up on frantic interception flights. The young and inexperienced student pilots had become battle-hardened veterans, their faces showing the sudden realization of death all about them. Not for a moment did the Americans ease their relentless pressure. Day and night the bombers came to pound Rabaul, to smash at the airfield and shipping in the harbor, while the fighters screamed low on daring strafing passes, shooting up anything they considered worth-while target. So intense were the enemy attacks that we literally were unable to find time to attack their bases. Our losses mounted steadily, and the list of dead and missing pilots grew visibly. Throughout this enemy effort we exacted a heavy toll of bombers and fighters, but even our most successful interceptions failed to affect adversely the air offensive of the Americans. They threw in more and more replacements, and the ratio of enemy planes to ours widened steadily. Under such conditions the air division could not last much longer.

It was obvious that so long as we continued the battle

in its present fashion, the Americans would grind us under. A change was called for, and I recommended to Admiral Jojima what was to our air force a startling change in tactics. Lieutenant Commander Saburo Shindo, the division's fighter-group commander and the former flight officer who had won a special letter of commendation for the outstanding initial victory of the Zero fighter in China on September 13, 1940, assembled his pilots and passed on the new orders:

"In the future you will no longer be required to engage enemy planes whenever they are encountered. You will attack or defend yourselves only when the battle circumstances appear particularly favorable to you."

What sad words these were! How do our pilots determine what are "particularly favorable" circumstances? In the flashing, ever-changing situations of air combat it is literally impossible to determine when you are in the better position to engage the enemy. The words come easily; the actions, with difficulty. It is a different matter with surface vessels; there, at least, the responsibility for engaging, or avoiding, combat rests upon a senior naval officer. I was fully aware of the fact that my air crews could not properly judge all the varying factors of air war which would permit them wisely to "attack or withdraw," but I could not arrive at a better solution. Even the issuing of the new orders had a depressing effect, for to our men such words were clearly an official admission of our inferiority to the rampaging Americans.

To counter the effects of the new order, I reinstituted small night offensive raids with single-engine Kates. At no time did I believe that the night attacks would affect noticeably the enemy's northward drive, but the feeling of returning to the offensive would improve morale. The Kates attacked enemy transports in the Dampier Strait between New Britain Island and New Guinea. At times we sent Val dive bombers into the Tripoiru air base (just north of Buin), where they remained overnight and early the following morning bombed enemy transports at Mono Island in the Treasury Islands south of Bougainville. Less often we sent out the twin-engined Bettys to hit enemy land installations. We could not muster more than twenty planes to use in these raids and the results, of course, were negligible.

Ignoring our feeble bombing attempts, the enemy launched his newest invasion and put several thousand troops ashore on the Green Islands, north of Bougainville and one hundred and thirty miles from Rabaul. Danger to our Rabaul positions mounted rapidly with the accompanying increase in enemy air offensive operations. Our air losses became appalling. No longer did anyone at Rabaul harbor any doubts as to the monumental gap between the national strength of Japan and the United States.

Every enemy raid was on a large scale. The bombers thundered over regularly, disdainfully flying in large formations in which weak defensive gaps were readily apparent. Had we taken advantage of these formation faults, we could have exacted a heavy toll of the enemy bombers. However, the enemy's confidence was well founded! In the face of such large formations our numerically inferior Zeros were utterly helpless. Had the Zero fighter been superior in performance to the enemy planes, we might have been able to deal the enemy a heavy blow. But no longer could the Zero flaunt its performance, for the former terror of the Pacific now ran a poor second to the Grumman F6F Hellcat, and could not hope to engage the Corsairs and Lightnings unless the enemy fighter pilots so desired. With basically the same fighter airplane we had used at the war's beginning, we could not hope to do much against an enemy who pursued technological progress so prodigiously.

There are other factors in aerial combat even more important than the quality of the individual opposing aircraft, and perhaps the most vital of these is having experienced pilots and air crews. After every mission the Americans sent out flying boats to areas in which their planes had fought, searching for and rescuing air crews which had been shot down and stood a good chance of surviving aboard life rafts. Every lumbering flying boat, normally an easy catch for our fighter planes, went out on its search mission with nine to twelve escort fighters. Although their duties were extremely hazardous, the crews of these flying boats performed their missions gallantly, and there arose few occasions during the war when groups of men so consistently exposed themselves to multiple dangers. Our pilots could not fail to be impressed with these daring search missions and, despite the fact that enemy pilots manned the flying boats, our men regarded them as unusually courageous.

On the other hand, although the Japanese high command realized (perhaps in theory only) the value of saving human lives, and believed that every human life should be held as irreplaceable, they would not emulate the American rescue policy. Our naval commanders were so afraid of the possible sacrifices which might be the consequences of attempting to rescue our crews which were shot down that often we abandoned on the open sea those men whom we could obviously have saved. The naval command's attitude toward the situation was that they could not tolerate the *possible* loss of a large flying boat merely to effect the *certain* rescue of one air crew.

I pondered this situation more than once. For this apathy toward rescuing downed pilots was not merely the attitude of the high command ... our own combat men, the flying mates of the same men who were shot down and adrift at sea, would not, even under orders, take any unnecessary chances to save their lives. Lest this attitude be misconstrued as indicating that our men lacked compassion for their friends, it should be added that they would not expect otherwise should they be the ones to be shot down. Any man who was shot down and managed to survive by inflating his liferaft realized that his chance for continued survival lay entirely within his own hands. Our pilots accepted their abandonment stoically. At any rate, the entire Japanese Navy failed to evince any great interest in rescue operations of this nature.

There were exceptions, of course, and during my final stay at Rabaul the seaplane group commander proved to be one of these. He and his men often flew dangerous missions to save the lives of those air-crew members downed at sea. Their seaplanes were small and few in number; despite their most intensive efforts, they could do little.

These were some of the "behind-the-scenes" factors at Rabaul. Our situation worsened steadily, and finally reached the point where we were deluged by a storm of enemy bombs and bullets. Clearly we could not remain much longer at Rabaul. Incredibly, all during my stay I did not once become ill. Every last member of Rear Admiral Jojima's staff, including the admiral, suffered either from dengue fever or malaria, or both. Perhaps the reasons why I escaped sickness was that, although I had had land duty longer than any member of the headquarters staff, and I was obliged to remain outdoors longer than usual, I always exercised the greatest care in selecting food and water. Further, I ignored the oppressive heat and wore nothing but long trousers and boots. These were not as comfortable, I admit, as the cooler short trousers, but they were preferable to fever and illness.

On February 29, 1944, after having lost the majority of its men and most of its planes in a single harrowing month of incessant battle, the 2nd Carrier Division gave up the fight for Rabaul. The embittered division abandoned this vital air base and withdrew to Turk.

CHAPTER 23

The End Is in Sight: Defense of the Mariana Islands

WITH RABAUL ABANDONED to the enemy, the Navy realized that soon it would be forced to commit its planes and ships to another vital defense operation. American aircraft-carrier task forces roamed the entire Pacific Ocean in unbelievable strength, hammering with rapid blows at even our strongest island bastions. By the end of May of 1944 it appeared probable that the Marianas were next on the list for an all-out assault. When the Americans finally struck, it was with overwhelming quantitative and qualitative power. So severly beaten were our sea, air, and land forces that the Battle of the Mariana Islands drove Prime Minister Hideki Tojo from office. Further, the loss in ships and planes so crippled the Navy that it was never able again to engage the enemy in what could be described as a "well-organized operation."

By late 1943 the Navy high command realized that the Pacific War was rapidly approaching its climax. America's devastating carrier task force assaults, especially against the Gilbert and Marshall island groups, proved beyond any doubt that the enemy regarded our surface fleet strength with increasing disdain. Tokyo realized further that the Marianas attack was but a matter of time; we would be called on to defend this crucial island with our maximum strength and many of our officers feared that the anticipated American assault would be the war's last decisive battle. The United States possessed far greater air and naval strength and increased its advantage by employing fighter planes considerably superior to the aging Zero.

There was good reason to believe that the Marianas conflict might give the enemy the final advantage necessary to defeat Japan. Should American marines and troops successfully occupy the islands, then the Japanese homeland itself would fall within the effective bombing range of the Army Air Force's new B-29 bomber, which could well cripple our production. We had never seen the B-29, but Navy intelligence believed it had completely reliable information on the airplane, obtained from a former B-29 test pilot who had been shot down in the Solomon Islands in the summer of 1943. The information later proved to be accurate.

Another danger arising from American occupation of the Marianas was that the enemy could employ the islands as a home base for their aircraft carriers, which could then strike directly at New Guinea, the Philippine Islands, and even the Japanese mainland. A successful American move in this direction would gravely imperil our position in the Pacific. Even should our Army remain intact in the Philippines and on Formosa and Okinawa, the enemy carrier task forces, longrange land-based bombers, and submarines could cut the vital communications lines between our factories and our sources of raw materials in the Pacific. Not only would our industry suffer, but the loss of these supply lines would create serious food shortages among our people.

With these factors to consider, the Navy prepared to hurl against the expected enemy attack every available airplane and warship. The Marianas' defense was to be a maximum effort; we would greet the Americans with an impenetrable wall of fire and steel. To make certain that our planes would be flown by veterans as well as novices, the Navy drew instructors from its training air corps and assigned them to the front. Every serviceable plane and ship moved into the area of decision.

Even before the two great opponents were committed to battle, however, our defense preparations suffered what proved later to be a damaging blow. The Navy knew almost for a certainty that the showdown would come soon, but could not convince the Army of the urgent need for immediate action. General Hideki Tojo, then Minister of the Army as well as Prime Minister, stated emphatically that there existed no need for such feverish and "hysterical" defenses, since the Americans would not attack in strength. So believing, he refused to commit a single Army plane to the Mariana Islands. We could do nothing to disabuse him of his mistaken confidence.

On June 11, 1944, the enemy carrier task forces began their bombardment of the Marianas. At the time the Japanese Combined Fleet defense lines consisted of the following:

1. Admiral Soemu Toyoda, Commander in Chief of the Combined Fleet, directed the over-all operations from his headquarters aboard his flagship *Oyodo*, in Hiroshima Bay.

2. Vice-Admiral Kakuji Kakuda, Commander of the First Air Fleet (land-based aircrafts), controlled approximately one thousand warplanes. Operating from headquar-

ters on Tinian Island, he assigned his planes to the Marianas, Carolines, Iwo Jima, and Truk.

3. Vice-Admiral Jisaburo Ozawa, Commander of the First Task Fleet and the Third Fleet, was assigned a carrier task force made up of the largest number of aircraft carriers gathered together since the Hawaiian Operation. His force waited the oncoming battle at Tawitawi anchorage in the southwest area of the Sulu Sea, west of the Philippine Islands. Under Ozawa's command was a fleet of seventy-three vessels, including nine aircraft carriers, and the 74,000-ton battleships *Yamato* and *Musashi*, each with nine eighteen-inch guns. Admiral Ozawa's orders were to coordinate his movements with the Kakuda land-based air fleets; to conserve his limited fuel supply Ozawa elected to remain as long as possible at Tawitawi before engaging the enemy.

4. In addition to these forces, Vice-Admiral Chuichi Nagumo, Commander in Chief of the Central Pacific Fleet and the commander of the Pearl Harbor attack, controlled the Marines and other naval units which were to defend the Marianas against enemy amphibious operations.

On June 13 the enemy confirmed our worst fears, and began the initial aerial bombardment against the Marianas. Fighters and bombers in great number attacked ground positions of the islands, pursued all shipping in the area, and began to exact a heavy toll of our defending planes. Admiral Toyoda ordered the Ozawa Force to move against the enemy fleet at once; unfortunately, Ozawa had to refuel his ships and could not arrive west of the beleaguered islands prior to June 18.

During the week necessary for Ozawa's carriers to reach the Marianas, the Kakuda land-based air force waged a desperate defense against the swarms of enemy carrier-based fighters and bombers. It was a losing battle from the start, and Kakuda's available planes decreased alarmingly in strength, forfeiting control of the local air to the Americans. Their planes pounded Kakuda's positions mercilessly, destroying vital installations and causing heavy casualties to his men. Kakuda's pilots lacked the training necessary to offer strong resistance to the aggressive American pilots, and the defending Zeros fought hopeless battles against the marauding Hellcat fighters which outperformed and outnumbered our own planes. Our dive bombers and torpedo bombers launched several raids against the enemy carriers, but never stood a chance against the determined defense of the Hellcat fighters and the unbelievable accuracy and volume of the ship's antiaircraft guns. By the time Ozawa arrived at the scene of battle, Kakuda's defenses had been shattered. Most of his planes were gone, he lacked experienced pilots, and the Marianas installations were reduced to a shambles.

The Americans could not have planned their operation better. Events occurred almost as if we were cooperating with the attack, for, by the time the Ozawa Force drew within bomber range of the American carriers, Kakuda's land-based planes no longer existed as an operational air fleet. He had been so soundly defeated that Ozawa was forced to fight alone, without the support from Kakuda for which he had originally hoped. Of the two major opposing air groups the Americans were called on to face, they first virtually annihilated the land-based units, then turned, with almost their original strength intact, to deal with Ozawa.

Our intelligence reported that the Americans were attacking the Marianas in four separate carrier groups, with a total of twelve aircraft carriers. Against these Ozawa had nine such ships in three groups, with the three largest carriers, the *Taiho, Shokaku,* and *Zuikaku*; two medium carriers, the *Junyo* and *Hiyo*; and the four smaller ships, the *Ryuho, Chiyoda, Chitose,* and *Zuiho*.

The 1st Carrier Division, under the direct command of Vice-Admiral Ozawa, consisted of the *Taiho, Shokaku,* and the *Suikaku* and the *Zuikaku*. Aboard these three large vessels were the 601st Air Corps with eighty-one Zeros, nine Type 2 Judy reconnaissance planes, eighty-one Judy dive bombers (*Suisei*), and fifty-four Jill attack bombers (*Tenzan*). Each carrier accommodated approximately a third of the total striking force. Under Rear Admiral Takaji Jojima's command was the 2nd Carrier Division with the *Junyo, Hiyo,* and the *Ryuho*. Aboard the three carriers were the 652nd Air Corps' eighty-one Zeros, twenty-seven Val dive bombers, nine Type 2 Judy dive bombers, and twenty-seven Jill attack bombers. The third group was Rear Admiral Sueo Obayashi's 3rd Carrier Division with the *Chiyoda, Chitose,* and the *Zuiho*, which carried the 653rd Air Corps' sixty-three Zeros, six Jills, and twelve Kates.

The nine aircraft carriers accommodated a total of four hundred and fifty planes, or more than fifty planes over the maximum number available to the Nagumo Force which attacked Pearl Harbor. Furthermore, Ozawa had a greater advantage in that he controlled nine aircraft carriers, not six. If he were to lose one or more of these carriers, he could minimize his aircraft losses by landing the planes from a sunken vessel aboard its sister ships.

The nine carriers concentrated at Tawitawi were regarded by many of our naval officers as assurance of victory in the Marianas battle. We had never assembled in one striking force so much carrier aviation, and our pilots were convinced that they would shatter the attacking American fleet. It appears, however, that these people who enjoyed such premature success thought only in terms of the total available aircraft carriers and their planes, failing to give due consideration to the human factor. Vital to every battle is the indefinable element we term aggressiveness, or spirit, or *esprit de corps*; whatever it is, the Americans had it. Our forces lacked the close coordination and unity of the American groups, and so were at a disadvantage. Those officers who boasted—prior to the battle, of course—of the terrible havoc our fleet would wreak among the Americans were due to suffer terrible disappointments.

On June 19 the great carrier-vs.-carrier air battles began, west of the Mariana Islands. Ozawa threw every available airplane against the American carriers in an all-out attempt to destroy the American ships. The effort failed to produce any results whatsoever, and, while Ozawa suffered considerable losses to his fighters and bombers, the American ships sailed on undaunted. Rear Admiral Raymond A. Spruance, informed that our carriers were several hundred miles from his own vessels, wisely decided to postpone his bomber attacks against our fleet. Instead, he ordered every Hellcat fighter plane into the air to meet our attacking bombers. As a result of this fierce resistance from enemy planes which easily outflew our own aircraft, only a few bombers managed to break through the American fighter screen to the carriers. Here they met a veritable cyclone of antiaircraft fire. The results of the attack were negligible. Ozawa, on the other hand, lost the majority of his planes in the battle and simultaneously lost what future advantage he had hoped for in the way of making mass air attacks against the enemy.

Ozawa's powerful aircraft force did not suffer the expected enemy aerial attack and, even as his men began to relax with the realization that the American planes were not approaching, disaster struck. Aboard his flagship, *Taiho*, Ozawa received word from his radio room that a submarine attack was under way. The next moment, at 0800, the *Taiho* literally blew up under his feet; the enemy submarine *Albacore* had loosed six torpedoes, most of which struck the *Taiho*, but Japan's newest and strongest 35,000-ton carrier neither listed nor slackened her speed. Despite the comparatively minor damage of the torpedo strikes, gasoline vapor from a broken large tank and pipelines gradually seeped out to fill the entire interior of the big carrier. Ozawa was obliged to transfer by destroyer to the cruiser *Haguro*. Ninety minutes after the *Albacore* fired her torpedoes *Taiho* was wracked by a tremendous explosion. The tremendous detonations shattered all control aboard the vessel and at 1640 hours she went down.

Ready to board his new flagship, Ozawa suffered another blow. At 1120 hours another enemy submarine had attacked, and four of the six torpedoes fired (by the *Cavalla*) had shattered the *Shokaku*. The great carrier blew apart several hours later and sank.

Ill fortune did not stop here. On the following day, June 20, Ozawa changed his flagship to the *Zuikaku* and prepared to launch a maximum-effort bombing and torpedo attack against the American fleet. Even as the planes were being fueled and armed, enemy dive bombers, torpedo bombers, and fighter planes in great number raided our carriers. The American attack was savage and well executed; split asunder by bombs and torpedoes, the *Hiyo* went down, along with two tankers loaded with critically needed fuel. The *Zuikaku, Junyo, Ryuho*, and *Chiyoda* all suffered heavy damage, as did the battleship *Haruna* and another tanker. Reeling from the devastating blow, Ozawa's carriers launched a punitive night attack with ten torpedo bombers. None of our planes could hit the enemy carriers.

The combination of sea and air losses shattered the effectiveness of Ozawa's task force as a fighting unit. It was impossible for him to even attempt a comeback against the formidable American fleet which stormed, almost without a scratch, against his fleeing ships.

The Americans called their smashing air victory the "Marianas Turkey Shoot," and with good reason. With the battle concluded, Ozawa had only forty-seven airplanes in fighting shape; twenty-five Zeros, six torpedo bombers, two dive bombers, and twelve miscellaneous aircraft. The enemy losses were trifling in comparison, for they lost but twenty-six aircraft in combat.

Thus ended the Marianas Sea Battle, which our Navy had entered with the greatest carrier and air strength in its history. The great battle concluded with the Navy suffering its worst defeat, the consequences of which exceeded even our losses at Midway.

We examined the various phases of the action in an attempt to determine what had denied Admiral Ozawa the victory which, on paper at least, his great carrier and air strength should have afforded. As air staff officer to Rear Admiral Jojima, 2nd Carrier Division, I (Okumiya) had available the data from which I drew the following conclusions.

First, our aircrews lacked the training necessary to coordinate their attacks in combat. For two years prior to the Marianas battle I had been the 2nd Carrier Division's air staff officer, and at no time did I feel our air group leaders possessed the minimum capabilities required for combat leadership. The preceding two years had witnessed a marked lowering of the requirements necessary for air-group leadership, and it soon became obvious that we were entrusting vital combat command to men who were greatly in need of further operational training.

When I was first assigned to the air staff of the 4th Carrier Division, just prior to the Midway-Aleutian Operation, the Nagumo Force's over-all air-group leader was Commander Mitsuo Fuchida, who had led the air attack against Pearl Harbor. Fuchida had graduated from the fifty-second (1924) class of Etajima Naval Academy. In the Battle of Santa Cruz in October 1942, Lieutenant Commander Mamoru Seki was Nagumo's over-all air-group leader; like myself, Seki entered Etajima in 1927 as a member of the fifty-eighth (1930) graduating class. However, the air-group leaders who participated in the Marianas Battle included Lieutenant Commander Jyotaro Iwami of the Jojima Force from the sixty-second (1934) graduating class, and Lieutenant Commander Akira Tarui of the Ozawa Force, and Lieutenant Commander Masayuki Yamagami of the Obayashi Force from the sixty-forty (1936) graduating class.

In other words, in only the two-odd short years since I was appointed to the carrier division's air staff, the average age of the senior air-group leaders had dropped by at least ten years. Unfortunately, too, the skill of the air crews which flew in the Marianas conflict had deteriorated in direct proportion to the average reduced age of their commanding officers.

One example especially illustrates the marked loss of combat flying skill. When my carrier force (the 2nd Carrier Division) joined the Santa Cruz battle, our dive-bomber pilots had established and maintained an enviable rate of accuracy in their attack. In a bombing operation by nine planes against the target ship *Settsu*, an old battleship 160 meters in length and 20 meters in width, which could maintain an evasive pattern speed of sixteen knots on the open sea, the nine planes frequently scored nine hits. Just prior to the Marianas fight, however, the same nine-plane formation diving against the *Settsu* rarely scored more than *one* hit. We could not expect our aircrews, only recently assigned to aircraft carriers, to achieve high flying skill and bombing accuracy in only a few weeks. And it was these men, sorely in need of months of training, who flew against the powerful, well-defended American fleet. Within two and a half years after the war's start, our training standards and air-crew proficiency had deteriorated to a point where the men stood little chance of survival against the enemy. The marked loss in minimum qualifications underscored dramatically the fact that our personnel preparations for this war never had been adequate.

Second, there were few officers in the Ozawa Force with experience in carrier-vs.-carrier warfare, and this lack of familiarity with this type of conflict was clearly evident. Vice-Admiral Ozawa, his chief of staff, his entire senior, operations, and air staffs had never participated in a battle against enemy aircraft carriers. Moreover, with the exception of only two air staff officers, Vice Admiral Ozawa and his supporting staffs knew little about the problems of air groups. They had only the barest knowledge of aviation problems. Even Rear Admirals Jojima and Obayashi, who both had participated in combat as the captains of aircraft carriers, knew little about the intrinsic problems of general aircraft operation. With myself as the sole exception, the immediate staffs of Jojima and Obayashi all lacked carrier battle experience. As the Marianas conflict was to be waged against an American task force under command of Rear Admiral Raymond A. Spruance, the talented leader at Midway, I could not help but feel, prior to battle, that we suffered from a severe handicap in leadership.

Third, Ozawa lacked a sufficient number of high-performance aircraft, so necessary against the effective American defenses. We still employed as our first-line carrier-based fighter plane the aging Zero; there did not exist in the Navy another plane with performance superior to that of the fighter which had fought in China in 1940. The six aircraft carriers under command of Jojima and Obayashi were slow and hampered by short carrier decks. It proved difficult, under ordinary conditions, to launch from these carriers the new *Suisei* (Judy) dive bombers brought into service after the Battle of Midway. The nine Judy's aboard the *Junyo* could not even be used for training purposes for the month while the fleet was anchored at Tawitawi; the carrier was too slow in the limited training area to launch its planes. Even the new *Tenzan* (Jill) attack bombers were difficult to use efficiently when aboard the small aircraft carriers.

Faced with these operational difficulties, and also searching for increased escort fighter coverage, the Navy experimented with the Zero fighters as dive bombers, carrying a 550-pound bomb. Nine modified Zero fighter-bombers went aboard each carrier of the Jojima Force, and each of Obayashi's three carriers received twelve Zero fighter-bombers. A total of sixty-three modified Zero fighters were placed aboard Ozawa's six carriers, and these planes were broken up into two special attack groups.

Led by the *Tenzan* attack bombers, which provided navigational direction, the two Zero fighter-bomber groups left their ships on June 19 to attack the enemy task force. Our hopes for the new planes' victory were fruitless. Our Zero pilots, covering nearly three hundred and fifty nautical miles to the enemy fleet, arrived in exhausted condition, unable to fly with their usual skill. Nearing the American carriers, they ran into an effective defensive screen of Hellcat fighters and suffered severe losses. This final effort dropped the curtain on our Navy's complete defeat at the Mariana Islands.

It was evident, however, that although the Zero fighter-bomber required assistance in long-range navigation, it achieved better results against enemy carriers than did any of our dive bombers. This sudden increase in bombing accuracy was the greatest single cause of the sudden rise of the famous *Kamikaze* suicide squads which participated in the hopeless sea battle off Leyte Island in the Philippines, four months later.

Thus the Zero fighter plane which once had been the undisputed master of fighter-plane combat in the western Pacific and the Indian Oceans, seemed destined to play a further leading role in the Pacific air war. Not, however, any longer as the champion of air combat, but as the main character in the mounting tragedies which prophesied only the total defeat of Japan.

If the war leaders of our nation had at that time realized the true condition of our naval air force, they would certainly have made a serious effort to conclude the war as rapidly as possible. Had such negotiations been undertaken, the *Kamikaze* suicide attacks would never have occurred, and much loss of life, both Japanese and American, could have been averted. In this sense, especially, our failure to defend successfully the Marianas played a significant role in the history of the Pacific War.

CHAPTER 24

The Kamikaze Suicide Attacks

DURING THE GREAT AIR battles of the Pacific War, many pilots while directly over enemy war ships or land installations were caught in situations in which either they were seriously wounded or their aircraft became disabled. Under such conditions, not a few pilots chose, while it was still possible to maneuver their airplanes, to meet their end in a final suicide dive against the enemy objective. These occasions, not at all rare in air assaults, were not "suicide attacks" in the true sense of the word, since the pilot stood almost no chance of survival. There were instances, of course, when certain individuals elected to sacrifice their lives in order to accomplish their missions, but these were isolated cases.

The *Kamikaze* attack, however, was an entirely different matter. In this operation the pilot, or the entire crew, of an attacking aircraft, eliminated even the remotest opportunity for survival once committed to the final dive against the enemy. Death was the companion of the *Kamikaze* pilot, as it was of the *Kaiten*, the human torpedoes employed in the war's latter stages.

There has been, and there will continue to be, much criticism of the Japanese Navy for adopting for the first time anywhere the deliberate mass suicide method of attacking the enemy. The *Kamikaze* operations have evoked much dissension among our own people, for such tactics cannot help but to be accompanied by incomparable mental anguish and sacrifice on the part of all concerned. I neither condemn nor condone the decisions which led to, and maintained, the *Kamikaze* flights, but present here the developments leading up to, and following, the decision finally to launch the suicide attack.

The Zero fighter, long the Navy's mainstay against enemy air operations, again played a leading part in our military activities through its position as the most widely used *Kamikaze* aircraft. There were good reasons to employ the Zero fighter for this role, all of which were necessitated by combat inadequacies. Despite the severe losses sustained by the Navy in the Marianas Sea Battle (often described by the Americans as the Battle of the Philippine Sea), in which three large aircraft carriers went to the bottom, despite the fact that we no longer had available the air crews to man the remaining six carriers, and despite the fact that we could no longer reorganize a balanced fleet with our remaining vessels, Tokyo still elected to continue the war. After the Marianas debacle, the Zero still remained as the mainstay of the Navy's air fleets, outnumbering by a considerable margin any other type of plane. If the *Kamikaze* attacks were to be instituted, then the Zero, by virtue of its available numbers and also because its performance made it the most likely airplane to break through the defending screen of Hellcat fighters, was the logical choice for the *Kamikaze* groups.

The human element, of course, contributed much to the final decision. Members of the Navy and the Army had been raised in an environment startlingly different from that of our enemies. The time-honored custom and sentiment of the Japanese people would not recognize existence as a prisoner of war; capture by the enemy was to be feared even more than death, for such capture was always accompanied by disgrace to one's family and homeland. Rather than to surrender to the enemy and spend a life of shame, our men naturally considered, once they had been confronted with repeated and chaotic defeats, means of achieving an honorable and a glorious death.

It was but a matter of time before the American fleet, incredibly powerful and now clearly the master of the Pacific, launched the final all-out assault against the Philippine Islands. Our defending officers in the Philippines were faced with a problem apparently without solution. With a Navy air force comparable in strength to only one large American aircraft carrier, it was impossible to hurl back the colossal attack which the enemy clearly would soon begin. If we could not entertain the possibility of surrender, and if accepted means of defense obviously would be impossible, the Philippines' Navy air commanders could not help but turn to tactics which until then had never been employed.

Under these circumstances, then, the Japanese Navy Air Force planned and finally executed the *Kamikaze* suicide attack.

With all the air bases in the Mariana and Caroline islands and along the northern coast of New Guinea in the hands of the enemy by early September of 1944, the rich prize of recapturing the Philippines tantalized the Americans. Before they could dispatch even their formidable fleets, with the thin-hulled and vulnerable transport ships, to the shores of the islands, they must first destroy or render inoperative the air bases from which our fighters and bombers could strike out at any invasion force. We could expect, then, first an attack by carrier task forces, which would be followed by a mass troop assault. The Navy air force received the responsibility for defending the Philippines, and upon our success or failure rested control of the great island group. With these assumptions as the basis for action, the First Air Fleet, with land-based aircraft, established its headquarters at Davao, and began the reorganization of its units with those planes permanently assigned to the Philippines, as well as the surviving aircraft from the Mariana Islands.

Our groups worked with feverish haste, but the mounting power of the Americans allowed them to strike with greater speed and effectiveness than we had anticipated. On September 9, 1944, their task force closed in on the Philippines and blasted Davao for its first air raid of the war. The following day, with many of our ground installations already in wreckage, the carrier-based planes returned again to bomb and strafe the airfield.

As the Davao attack raged, the Zero fighters then undergoing training at Clark Field on Luzon Island were hastily fueled and armed, and ordered to transfer immediately to our base at Cebu Island in the central Philippines. The fighters arrived too late to participate in Davao's defense, for the Americans had completed their attack and withdrawn to the open sea. Or so we thought. Two days later the carrier task force steamed under full speed for Cebu and launched an all-out aerial effort against our planes. Something happened to snarl our communications and for some unknown reason Cebu Field failed to receive the proper notification of the attacking planes which our outposts had sighted on their way. The communications mix-up was fatal, for the arriving American pilots came upon a scene which not even they had hoped for. About one hundred Zero fighters sat on the Cebu runways, ripe and helpless for an air attack. The Americans did not forfeit the rare opportunity; when the nightmare of screaming dive bombers and strafing fighters was over more than fifty Zero fighters either were charred wreckage or had been blown to pieces. It was a loss of great magnitude; in a single stroke the enemy had destroyed nearly two thirds of our entire serviceable fighter-plane force in the Philippines, and had left in damaged condition many other Zeros.

By late August of 1944 I had returned to Japan as the air staff officer attached to the Naval General Staff of the Imperial Headquarters. As the American carrier force raided Cebu, I was flying under orders from Davao to the Cebu air base; my transport plane arrived on the scene almost simultaneously with the first wave of enemy fighters and bombers. Our pilot swung clear of the field lest we be caught by the Hellcats, which would quickly have shot us out of the sky. We were able to see, before the transport fled the area, the dive bombers plunging from the sky, and the fighter planes as they screamed back and forth over the field, their wing guns spitting tracers into the parked Zeros. Within minutes Cebu became utter confusion. The American pilots were remarkably accurate, and the flames and black smoke boiling from the burning Zeros reminded me of a crematorium . . . ours.

That evening I returned to Manila and conferred with the pilots whose Zeros had been gunned and bombed into wreckage. The pilots were enraged at their helplessness, and talked heatedly of revenge against the Americans at any cost. It was obvious that there would soon be radical changes in our battle tactics.

In an attempt to overcome the effects of the devastating Cebu airfield attack, the Zeros were transferred from Cebu to Clark Field and Manila. Under the highest priority Tokyo dispatched aircraft replacements, spares, fuel, and other material to rebuild the shattered fighter-plane force. Even as the groups reformed, the American carrier planes struck again; on September 21 and 22 enemy fighters and dive bombers strafed and bombed the fields, once again breaking up the Zero groups. Another attempt to establish a powerful fighter defense in the Philippines had failed.

Even as the American carrier planes swept over the Philippines, other large formations pounded our air bases on Okinawa on October 10 for the first raid against that island. From the twelfth to the fourteenth the irresistible American carrier-based planes thundered against Formosan air bases; on the fifteenth they returned to Luzon Island to sweep our airfields into burning, tangled wreckage.

Again the carrier attacks frustrated our attempts to reestablish a defensive fighter-plane force. Not only did we fail in every attempt to reinforce our fighter groups in the Philippines, but we could not even maintain our minimum strength. Every additional day meant a further drain on the planes which would be called on to defend the Philippines when the American troops first stormed ashore; exactly when and where, however, was a matter yet to be determined. On October 17 enemy troops invaded and secured their position on Suluan Island, east of Leyte. The situation in the Philippines was no longer merely serious; it had become critical.

Admiral Soemu Toyota, Commander in Chief of the Combined Fleet (Admiral Mineichi Koga was lost at sea in a Kawanishi flying boat on March 31) judged that the Americans were making their all-out bid for the Philippine Islands and, acting on plans long before prepared, started in motion his powerful defensive fleet. On the seventeenth he ordered every warship in the entire Philippines area to proceed under full steam for the southeastern area of the island waters, there to assemble in battle formation. Simultaneously, he issued orders to his other fleet units, which included the Second Fleet under Vice-Admiral Takeo Kurita, then in Singapore waters and consisting of the two 74,000-ton battleships *Yamato* and *Musashi*, five additional battleships, nine heavy cruisers, two light cruisers, and twenty-three destroyers; Vice-Admiral Kiyohide Shima's Fifth Fleet of two heavy cruisers, one light cruiser, and seven destroyers then in the Formosa area; and Vice-Admiral Jisaburo Ozawa's Third Fleet of four aircraft carriers, two battleships, three light cruisers, and eight destroyers, then in Hiroshima Bay. It was an imposing force, with seven battleships (two of them the world's most powerful), eleven heavy cruisers, six light cruisers, thirty-eight destroyers, and four aircraft carriers. On the same day there arrived at Manila Headquarters the new naval commander of the First Air Fleet, Vice-Admiral Takijiro Onishi.

Onishi was a capable veteran pilot who had assisted the late Admiral Isoroku Yamamoto over a period of many years. Onishi was personally responsible, along with Yamamoto, for the build-up of our naval air arm. As a rear admiral he commanded the first air flotillas with Zero fighters in the Sino-Japanese Incident. Assisted by Commander Minoru Genda, he drew up the original plans for the Pearl Harbor attack and, when the war began, as the Chief of Staff to Vice-Admiral Nishizo Tsukahara, Commander in Chief of the Navy Land-Based Air Force, he distinguished himself in the extensive aerial operations which extended from the Philippines to the Dutch East Indies. Now he returned to the battlefield where once he had led the attack, only this time his opponents thundered toward the Philippines with the greatest massed carrier air power in history. Ironically, the planes which he would order into combat were chiefly the familiar Zero fighters with which he had fought some four years before.

Vice-Admiral Onishi's hands were literally tied even before he made his first official move. Not only were his fighter planes primarily the all-too-familiar Zero, but he could not scrape together from every field in the Philippines more than thirty serviceable fighters. By patching up every remaining Type 1 Betty bomber on the islands, he managed to increase his defensive force of operational aircraft to the pitiful total of only sixty planes. Onishi realized the futility of his task: that not even by the wildest stretch of the imagination could be hope, through orthodox methods of attack, to inflict heavy damage upon or to destroy the American carriers so well guarded by the Hellcat fighter planes. Without fighter-plane escort, Onishi mused, even the mighty battleships *Yamato* and *Musashi*, despite their eighteen-inch guns and slabs of armor plating, would be destroyed by American carrier bombers long before they would have the opportunity even to *see* the enemy fleet, let alone engage it in combat.

Since orthodox methods of attack could no longer be pursued to carry out his mission, Onishi turned to the possibility of *Kamikaze* attacks—suicide dive bombing with Zero fighters carrying 550-pound bombs. The airplane most likely to break through the defending cordon of Hellcats, and the most accurate of all our dive bombers, the Zero was the only logical choice for the suicide missions.

However, the admiral could not simply order his subordinates to commit suicide in mass numbers, not even in the Japanese Navy where surrender could not be tolerated. Suicide attack on a mass, calculated scale was unknown to war, and Onishi knew that he would have to make the request to his pilots personally. On the evening of October 19 the admiral arrived at Clark Field on Luzon Island, the major Zero fighter base in the Philippines, to confer with the executive officers of the Zero Fighter Corps. At the meeting he made his formal request for the *Kamikaze* attacks.

Even to the pilots who had fought against overwhelming odds, the request was not received without a certain shock. The precarious position of the Japanese fleet and air groups in the Philippines was, however, well understood by every man. They fully knew how slight were the chances of staving off the anticipated American assaults. All the pilots unanimously agreed to the admiral's request. Onishi designated the Zero groups which would engage in the suicide operations as the *Kamikaze Tokubetsu Kogekitai (Kamikaze* Special Attack Squad), after the *Kamikaze* (Divine Typhoon) which Japanese history records as having twice wrecked Kublai Khan's powerful Mongolian invasion force attacking Kyushu in the thirteenth century.

While Onishi prepared his suicide squads, the Philippines resounded with the thunder of new battles. Kurita, Shima, and Ozawa rushed to the islands to attack the vulnerable American transports which even then poured men, tanks, guns, and supplies ashore on Leyte. On the twenty-fourth the great showdown began. American carrier planes sighted the long-sought battleship fleet of Vice-Admiral Kurita steaming at full speed for the waters east of Leyte Island. The enemy dive bombers, torpedo bombers, and fighters screamed in to attack in unending waves. Every ship put up a withering antiaircraft barrage, but even this shower of steel and fire did little to divert the attacking planes. Helldivers hurled their bombs at great speed into the battleships, and the lumbering Avengers, protected by Hellcat fighters all the way, slid their torpedoes into the water and sent them true to their mark. Before long the giant *Musashi* was a shattered hulk which, according to Captain Kenkichi Kato, the ship's executive officer, had received at least thirty bombs and twenty-six torpedoes. Her crew attempted to beach her on Sibuyan Island, but the battleship capsized and sank, taking more than twelve hundred men with her. Heavy bombs smashed into the deck of the *Yamato*; despite the surface damage, the ship's fighting power was unimpaired. The heavy cruiser *Myoko* staggered with a torpedo hit in her side and was put out of action. The battleships *Haruna* and *Kongo* were damaged, as were several other ships.

This was exactly what Onishi had forecast; without air superiority, even the two greatest warships ever built were helpless before the enemy carrier dive and torpedo bombers. By this time Onishi's Zero pilots were beginning to regard the suicide attacks which they were planning as the only possible course to take. Conventional attack would produce nothing but a higher total for the American fighters and antiaircraft guns; nothing could be done against the granite-like defenses of the carrier task forces. On October 12 and 23, two *Kamikaze* Zeros with 550-pound bombs left their air bases on their first missions, but failed to find enemy carriers and returned.

Battered by the carrier plane attacks, Kurita withdrew his fleet from San Bernardino Strait, where he lay at the mercy of the enemy planes. In seven hours the Americans made more than two hundred and fifty sorties against his ships. Kurita felt that if he were to continue to attempt to force his way through the strait, he would merely offer the enemy planes an unexcelled opportunity to wipe out the remainder of his fleet. Later the same day, Kurita came about in the Sibuyan Sea and withdrew to the west; he would attempt to force a decisive last battle with the enemy ships on the twenty-fifth. Kurita did not retreat for long; the tough little admiral, stung by his defeat, soon turned and headed back toward San Bernardino Strait. As the darkness of the night faded, Kurita's group of four battleships and other warships, groping their way through the strait without benefit of air search, blundered into an American group of six escort carriers, three destroyers, and four destroyer escorts. The light enemy force should not have had the slightest chance of survival, but they fought with amazing courage. Against Kurita's heavy guns, they lost the *Gambier Bay*; when Kurita withdrew, the *Hoel, Johnston*, and *Samuel B. Roberts* were either sunk or on the way down, and the *Fanshaw Bay, Kalinin Bay, Dennis*, and *Heermann* had suffered crippling damage.

The battle—involving all three Japanese fleet units—was at its climax. On the morning of October 25, the *Kamikaze* Zeros led by Lieutenant Yukio Seki left on their first missions. One Zero plunged into the carrier *Santee*, exploding just forward of the deck elevator. Two others dove at the *Sangamon* and the *Petrof Bay*; our reports stated the ships were hit, but we learned later that defending antiaircraft fire caused the diving fighters to hit the water close by the ships. (A few minutes later, although Onishi was not aware of it at the time, one of our submarines put a torpedo into the damaged *Santee*.) The fourth Zero crashed into the carrier *Suwannee*, exploding in the ship's hangar and causing heavy casualties, and severe damage. Before noon six other Zeros went into their final dives. The Zero plunging into the carrier *St. Lo* sent its bomb through the flight deck, which set off violent explosions. Another Zero crashed into the *Kitkun Bay*. Three Zeros attacked the *Kalinin Bay*; two of them exploded on the flight deck.

Less than thirty minutes later the *St. Lo* broke in two and sank. The escorting Zero fighters confirmed these hits. Onishi felt he was fully justified in the *Kamikaze* attacks, as illustrated in the case of the carrier *St. Lo*; this ship had escaped the eighteen-inch guns of the *Yamato*, and, like other Ameri-can carriers, its planes had fought off our weak air attacks. A single *Kamikaze* destroyed the vessel.

This second battle of the Philippines demonstrated clearly that future attacks against the American warships, notably the carriers, would have to be performed by the *Kamikaze* planes, if Japan was to have even the slimmest opportunity for salvaging an effective defense of her homeland. Our Navy had suffered disastrously in the far-flung sea-air battle, and we had lost the battleships *Musashi*, *Yamashiro*, and *Fuso*; the large carrier *Zuikaku*; the light carriers *Chitose*, *Chiyoda*, and *Zuiho*; the six heavy cruisers *Atago*, *Maya*, *Chokai*, *Suzuya*, *Chikuma*, and *Mogami*; the four light carriers *Abukuma*, *Kinu*, *Tama*, and *Noshiro*; and the eleven destroyers *Wakaba*, *Yamagumo*, *Michishio*, *Shiranuhi*, *Uranami*, *Akitsuki*, *Asagumo*, *Hatsutsuki*, *Nowake*, *Hayashimo*, and *Fujinami*.

In contrast, the American ships sunk were the light carrier *Princeton*, the escort carriers *Gambier Bay* and *St. Lo*, the destroyers *Johnston* and *Hoel*, and the destroyer escort *Samuel B. Roberts*.

Encouraged by the potentials of the *Kamikaze* attacks, Onishi hastily recruited his new suicide forces and modified the airplanes to be used. As his new units became available, they were thrown into the mounting battle against American warships and transports. As anticipated, we achieved results far beyond those possible through the orthodox method of attack. Not only the Zeros were used for the *Kamikaze* dives; as there arrived in the Philippines

Val and Judy dive bombers and Frances twin-engined bombers, these were added to the roster of the suicide attack groups. Stimulated by Onishi's success in the *Kamikaze* operations, Army air force units in the Philippines studied our planes and methods of operation. Soon the Navy groups were joined by the Army pilots and air crews in the increasing suicide bombings. Despite the high ratio of strikes against the American fleet forces, we could not prevent the enemy from invading the various islands. The initial carrier strikes against our airfields had accomplished their purpose; we did not have enough airplanes in the Philippines, even when employed for *Kamikaze* attacks, to thwart the American operations.

One of our most successful *Kamikaze* attacks occurred on November 25, 1944. Twenty-seven fighters and bombers were converging on an enemy carrier task force; a group of six Zeros and two Judys led by Lieutenant Kimiyoshi Takatake, on their way to join the other planes for the attack, sighted another carrier fleet. Escorted by six Zero fighters, the *Kamikaze* planes raced in to attack the enemy ships. The large aircraft carrier *Essex* was only lightly damaged, but our planes caused heavy damage to two sister carriers, as well as the small carrier *Independence*. Two of the six escorting fighters were shot down; the returning four provided confirmation of the attacks.

On January 25, 1945, our planes made the last *Kamikaze* attack in the Philippines. American troops fought savagely for, and won, a beachhead on Lingayen Bay in Luzon Island; during the landing operation we mounted the final *Kamikaze* assault with every available airplane. Even this last maximum effort, while increasing the list of damaged and sunk enemy ships, could not prevent the Americans from effecting their invasion operations where and when they chose.

The table immediately below lists the types and number of planes used for the *Kamikaze* attacks:

Aggregate of aircraft which left on *Kamikaze* missions:	Zeros	331
	Others	116
	Total	447
Number of aircraft which completed their suicide attacks:	Zeros	158
	Others	43
	Total	201
Number of aircraft unable to complete suicide attacks because of weather, antiaircraft, enemy fighter interception, etc.:	Zeros	51
	Others	16
	Total	67
Number of aircraft which returned to base:	Zeros	122
	Others	57
	Total	179

As these figures indicate, the Zeros were used most often for *Kamikaze* attacks in the Philippines area; of the aggregate aircraft which left their bases, 74 per cent were Zeros; 79 per cent of all planes actually executing the suicide dives were Zeros. We maintained, separate of the *Kamikaze* groups, a minimum number of fighters which both guided and escorted the suicide planes to their targets and, of course, confirmed the results of these attacks. We employed an aggregate of 249 planes for this purpose, of which 238 were Zeros.

In January, 1945, after the bulk of the First Air Fleet transferred from the Philippines to Formosa, four *Kamikaze* attacks were made; two each on January 15 and 21.

Aggregate of aircraft which left on *Kamikaze*
    missions:

Zeros	19
Others	<u>8</u>
Total	27

Number of aircraft which completed their suicide
    attacks:

Zeros	4
Others	<u>3</u>
Total	7

Number of aircraft unable to complete suicide
attacks because of weather, antiaircraft, enemy
fighter interception, etc.:

Zeros	4
Others	3
Total	<u>6</u>

Number of aircraft which returned to base:

Zeros	11
Others	<u>3</u>
Total	14

Between October 25, 1944, when the *Kamikaze* pilots made their first successful attack, and January 25, 1945, we estimated that our suicide pilots inflicted from light to severe damage to at least fifty American vessels of all types. These included six large aircraft carriers, four of which were identified as the *Intrepid, Franklin, Essex,* and *Lexington*; the two small aircraft carriers *Belleau Wood* and *Independence*; and the escort carrier *St. Lo*. It was impossible at the time, of course, to determine specifically the names of those carriers our planes had struck, such as the *Santee, Suwannee,* etc., until corroboration could be received through American reports. Confirmation by our escorting Zero fighters was at best a questionable affair, because of the speed of the attacks, the fierce fighter and antiaircraft defenses, and the short period of time over the target area.

On January 21, 1945, the Formosa air base reported that one of its *Kamikaze* planes had scored a direct strike on the large American aircraft carrier *Ticonderoga*, setting the vessel afire, and that later another suicide plane dove into the burning ship, the explosion of the impact spreading the flames and causing heavy damage.

Although the first *Kamikaze* attacks occurred with the Zero fighter plane in October of 1944, the Navy had considered this "last chance" means of assault several months prior to the first suicide bombing. In the several months preceding the actual inception of *Kamikaze* attacks, the Navy studied various proposals for such raids from several sources within the organization. The first recommendation, in fact, for employing the *Oka* (Cherry Blossom) suicide plane was obtained from an Ensign Mitsuo Ota. In late 1943 and early 1944 Ota participated in the desperate battles waged by our land- and carrier-based air groups against the Americans, notably the hard-hitting, fast-moving enemy task forces. Later, caught in the overwhelming defeats in the Mariana and Caroline islands, defeats again inflicted by enemy carriers, Ota had an excellent opportunity to study at close hand the deficiencies of our attack methods. Clearly the only means of salvaging a war in which the enemy ravaged our most powerful bases with relative impunity was to destroy his weakest link—his carriers.

Ota proposed to his superiors that, since conventional level, dive, and torpedo bombing accomplished little against the American task forces other than an alarming loss of our planes, we achieve the accuracy required to destroy enemy warships through piloted bombs. The young ensign's proposal met little opposition, and was pushed through official channels for high-level consideration. Those officers consulted on the new plan had little choice but to concur with the decision for suicide bombing; in a Navy which would not sanction defeat, and whose planes rarely could break through the defending screens of Hellcat fighters, suicide bombing provided the sole means of inflicting heavy damage upon, or sinking, the enemy capital ships.

In August of 1944 the Naval Air Research and Development Center instituted an emergency development program of special piloted glide bombs, which bore the first character of *Ota*, and which henceforth came to be known as the *Marudai* project. From late October to November we held accelerated flight tests of the new glide bombs. Tokyo established a new air corps charged with the mission of operating the *Marudai* weapons, and by the close of November pilot training was well on its way. Captain Motoharu Okamura, one of Japan's most famous senior fighter pilots, became the corps commander; Okamura selected as his first fliers experienced fighter and dive-bomber pilots. Actually these pilots were selected prior to the first *Kamikaze* attacks in the Philippines. The selection was unnecessary, beyond the critical choices made by Okamura; volunteers poured in by the thousands for the new operation, despite the "special nature" of their future missions.

The new unit was designated *Jinrai Butai* (Corps of Divine Thunder). Even as they trained in their new, small piloted bombs, Japan received the news of the first *Kamikaze* attacks with Zero fighters in the Philippine theater. Frankly, the *Jinrai Butai* pilots were disappointed in that they had not led the first of the *Kamikaze* bombings.

Where the suicide-bombing Zero planes were limited by the 550-pound bombs they carried with respect to the damage they could inflict upon the enemy vessels, the *Marudai* glide bombs would carry a 2,640-pound warhead, powerful enough to sink even a large warship with one suicide plane. The first service glide bomb was designated the *Oka Model II*. The first production *Oka* (Cherry Blossom) bombs were to be assigned first to the Philippines, then Formosa, and last to Okinawa.

The Americans never realized that they had struck a telling blow against our initial operations with the glide bombs. In late November of 1944 the giant 68,000-ton aircraft carrier *Shinano* left Yokosuka on its maiden voyage. Aboard the converted *Yamato*-type battleship were fifty of the new *Oka* bombs. On November 29 the *Shinano* went to the bottom off Shio Point, south of Osaka, several hours after the enemy submarine *Archerfish* had put six torpedoes into the world's greatest carrier. All fifty glide bombs were lost with the ship. Later in the war we shipped a number of *Oka* bombs to Formosa and Okinawa. During the savage fight for Iwo Jima island in February of 1945, we made several combat experiments with the Oka bombs, but failed to find an opportunity then in which we could determine the new weapons' effect.

On March 21, 1945, the *Okas* were first used in actual combat. American carriers had stormed off Japan's western shore, sending fighters and bombers out to attack our factories and cities with machine guns, cannon, rockets, and bombs. The task forces literally dared the Navy to do its worst. On the eighteenth, with the enemy fleets beginning their withdrawals, Vice-Admiral Matome Ugaki, Commander in Chief of the land-based Fifth Air Fleet and commander of all Navy airforce units in the Kyushu area, ordered Captain Okamura to attack the American carriers with his *Oka* bombs.

Lieutenant Commander Goro Nonaka led sixteen Type 1 Betty bombers, each carrying an *Oka Model II*, and two regularly armed Betty bombers from the Kanoya air base on Kyushu in search of the enemy carrier fleet. Thirty Zero fighters escorted the bomber formation; originally fifty-five fighters had been scheduled for the escort mission, but the preceding day's battles resulted in the loss or damage of many fighters. Okamura's staff felt that the thirty Zeros could not provide sufficient protection to allow the bombers to break through the defending Hellcats, but Admiral Ugaki ordered the attack to be pressed despite any opposition. Lieutenant Commander Nonaka led his planes over the open sea with little hope for his own personal survival. Three hundred miles southeast of Kyushu and only fifty nautical miles from the enemy carriers, it appeared as if he would actually have the opportunity to strike a hard blow at the fleet. Suddenly at least fifty Hellcat fighters screamed down to attack; the thirty defending Zeros fought a furious but futile battle. Shortly afterward every one of the eighteen bombers plunged into the ocean, as well as fifteen Zeros. The Hellcat "screen" still was too tough to break through.

The only other occasions during which *Oka* glide bombs were used against the Americans took place during the defense of Okinawa. A total of seventy-four *Oka* bombs left their bases; fifty-six *Okas* either were released from their mother planes, or were shot down while still attached to the carrying plane. Of this number we received confirmation of an *Oka* hit on April 16, and pilots reported many other successful suicide dives into enemy ships. However, in many cases our observation planes failed to elude the pursuing Hellcat fighters, and confirmation was at least quite questionable. Not until the war's end did we receive definite reports that the majority of the *Okas* had in fact caused appreciable damage to the American warships and that, as was to be expected, the appearance of the piloted suicide bombs had a telling effect upon enemy morale.

The Americans had their own identification for the *Oka*

bombs, giving the suicide planes the code name of *Baka* (stupid). Our officers regretted that they did not have the opportunity to employ the *Okas* on the scale originally planned; they felt that several hundred of these suicide gliders with their powerful warheads could have raised havoc with the American fleets.

During the last year of the war the Navy pressed development of *Oka* variations for suicide attacks. These included the jet engine propelled *Oka Model 22*; the turbojet-propelled *Oka Model 33* and *43*; the turbojet-engined *Kikka* (Mandarine Orange Blossom); the pulse-jet *Baika* (Plum Blossom); and the *Shinryu* (Divine Dragon) glider, which utilized solid rockets for takeoff. Developing their own model from Navy types, the Army launched a program to build the all-steel *Tsurugi* (Sword), in which any type of reciprocating engine could be mounted; the Navy version of this plane was the *Toka* (Wisteria Blossom). However, even as the first test flights of the *Kikka*, *Shinryu*, and the *Tsurugi* began, the war ended.

Even as the Navy and the Army labored to perfect and to place in production the small, speedy, piloted bombs, the scene of *Kamikaze* operations with existing fighters and bombers shifted from the Philippines to the waters near Japan. In the defense of Iwo Jima Island in February of 1945 our pilots made several suicide attacks against the enemy carriers, with one strike confirmed.

After March of 1945 more than half of our pilots resorted to *Kamikaze* attacks. American and British vessels in the waters off western Japan and Okinawa were subjected to repeated raids by the Third, Fifth, and Tenth Air Fleets in Kyushu, and the First Air Fleet in Formosa. We employed a variety of aircraft types for the suicide bombings; these were, in order of the number used, the *Zero*, *Suisei* (Judy), *Ginga* (Frances), Val, *Shiragiku* (a navigation and crew trainer), Kate, Betty, Nell, *Tenzan* (Jill), Type 96 carrier-based dive bomber, and various types of reconnaissance seaplanes.

An aggregate of 597 Zeros left their bases in Japan to raid the enemy ships; 330 of these planes actually made suicide dives. An aggregate of 865 planes of all other types took off on missions, and 516 of these bombed the enemy fleet. Thus, 846 planes out of an aggregate of 1,462 which left on missions actually completed the bombings. From the Formosa bases, an aggregate of 239 Zeros and 118 other-type planes flew against the enemy; thirty-four Zeros and forty-four other types completed their suicide dives. The majority of the *Kamikaze* missions flew from Japan simply because the Zero fighters, operating from Formosa, lacked the range necessary to search for and attack their targets.

Among the enemy warships damaged in these *Kamikaze* operations were the carriers *Wasp, Franklin, Hancock, Intrepid, Bunker Hill*, and *Enterprise*. During the same period of time, our planes damaged only a few enemy vessels through attacks other than suicide dives. Despite the frantic attempts to break up the American fleets, the enemy continued to invade the islands along our shrinking defense lines, and sent his carriers to smash any objective within the range of his airplanes, which, of course, meant the very heart of Japan. Even the desperate suicide measures could not halt the colossal war machine advancing against our country.

During these last-ditch defense measures, the Zero fighter again played the dominant role. A total of 2,363 Navy planes, including the *Okas*, took off on *Kamikaze* flights; 1,189 were Zero fighters. Of the 1,189 planes which actually completed their suicide missions, 530 were Zeros.

The *Kamikaze* suicide attacks took the lives of approximately 2,530 Navy pilots and air-crew members, and at least an equal number of Army pilots and air crew perished. On August 15, 1945, the day of our surrender, Vice-Admiral Matome Ugaki, who had commanded the suicide bombings from Kyushu, flew the last *Kamikaze* mission of the war and followed his men by diving against an enemy warship off Okinawa. Also in the war's closing hour, Vice-Admiral Takijiro Onishi, Vice-Chief of the Naval General Staff and the originator of the *Kamikaze* operations, chose death by *hara-kiri* rather than surrender.

Thus ended the *Kamikazes*.

CHAPTER 25

Air Raids and Earthquakes

BY SEPTEMBER OF 1939 the Zero fighter was a proven combat airplane, and its pilots had demonstrated their superiority over the best of the enemy's fighters in China. The one-sided combat box scores attested dramatically to that fact. During this same month the Navy prepared for its great mass-production program, and discussed with Nakajima Airplane Corporation its role as the producer of the Mitsubishi-designed Zero fighter. Late in September, representatives from the Navy and the two companies drew up the final manufacturing agreements, and Mitsubishi's director of design transferred to Nakajima the blueprints necessary to initiate the new production program. The two companies agreed further to exchange all data required for future fabrication techniques and modifications. The conference ended with the understanding that Nakajima would bear the greatest portion of Zero production, and that Mitsubishi would engage in design alteration, as well as in production in parallel, with the proviso that Nakajima be kept fully informed of all changes. Eventually Nakajima produced more than half (6,500 out of slightly more than 10,400 planes) of all Zero combat models built, including the Rufe seaplanes modified from the fighter. In June of 1944 the Navy ordered the Hitachi Corporation to prepare the industrial facilities needed to manufacture Zero fighters; the Hitachi program failed eventually to produce any fighters because of materials shortages and air raids.

Despite the tremendous production effort, the Zero fighter failed to meet the Navy's fighter-plane requirements. This failure extended beyond the superiority later achieved by American fighters; the more than ten thousand fighters produced could not meet even the numerical demands of the Navy. Behind this failure lay the obvious reasons of a shortage in engineers, lack of sufficient skilled workers, lack of materials, and so on, but apart from these, other factors hampered our production activities.

Jiro Horikoshi fills in the rest of the picture:

"Soon after its introduction to combat we cut back the production of the *Raiden* interceptor plane; despite our plans that this fighter should replace the Zero, it suffered from poor pilot visibility and lacked the fight endurance necessary for Pacific operations. We invested our greatest hopes in the *Reppu* carrier-based fighter, the performance of which might well return to Japan its lost air superiority in carrier-*vs.*-carrier combat. The *Reppu*, true to my predictions of several years back, disappointed the Navy with poor performance caused by difficulties and power loss associated with the production-type *Homare* engine. Even frantic efforts to mass produce the *Shiden-Mod* interceptor were fruitless as an endless stream of 'last-minute' design changes and disorderly arranged blueprints drove the final production line crazy. As the confusion and bickering mounted to a crescendo, the Allies continued to increase their superiority in the air. The Navy had little choice but to depend upon the Zero as its major front-line airplane until the war's end.

"Throughout the war Mitsubishi was responsible for the improvements and modifications to the Zero fighter, many of which were based upon front-line reports from our pilots. So frequently did the Navy forward these '*Rush*' orders for modifications that it became impossible to maintain a steady production flow. Mitsubishi suffered especially from the Navy's inability to crystallize its decisions regarding the Zero and *Raiden* fighters. We would receive orders to boost the output of the Zeros, with the *Raiden* taking second priority. A month later the Navy would reverse its order, and engineers would try frantically to unravel their new setups. Three months later, perhaps, a new change in policy would come through ... it became an incredible see-saw game between the two fighters.

"Nakajima did not suffer from such frequent changes and, freed of the time-consuming necessity for changing assembly lines, maintained an average monthly production rate of over two hundred planes from the fall of 1943 to the spring of 1945; their peak was 270 planes in March of 1944. The average monthly production during the same period for Mitsubishi, however, was barely over one hundred planes, with a peak of 155, reached in October of 1944. Mitsubishi suffered not only from the policy tantrums of the Navy but, early in December of 1944, with the war nearing the critical stage, reeled from the shock of a severe earthquake (Tokai district earthquake) which rocked the city of Nagoya and its southeastern suburbs.

"The earthquake was only the beginning of a series of incredible misfortunes to befall the aircraft industry. The Nagoya Aircraft Works of the Mitsubishi company, a giant airframe production center, was built over a weak ground foundation of reclaimed land east of Nagoya Harbor. The quake so severely jolted the factory that gaping cracks and strains developed in the concrete floors. Every assembly jig was thrown out of line, and several of the important shop buildings on separate ground collapsed. Thus in a single blow the production of both Mitsubishi's and Aichi's giant planes ground to a halt. Both companies made frantic efforts to readjust the assembly jigs, working day and night to complete the job so that production could resume.

"Even as the plants returned slowly to normal operations, on December 13, 1944, B-29 bombers from Mariana Island bases ripped the Mitsubishi Engine Works at Daikocho, Nagoya, and, five days later, hurled their high-explosive and incendiary bombs at the Aircraft Works at Ohe-machi, Nagoya.

"Up to the time of this heavy raid the military authorities could not reach a final decision on the matter of plant dispersal. Torn between the vital need for more and more airplanes and the knowledge that the American bombings would increase in severity and effectiveness, they hedged continually on the matter. After the attacks against the Mitsubishi plants, however, the government ordered immediate plant dispersal and Mitsubishi put into practice its long-standing plans. Its first move was to transfer the major part of its Engineering Division to the school buildings in Nagoya. The company separated its Airframe Production Division into three separate units, one Navy and two Army, and dispersed these to widely scattered areas; Navy facilities went to Suzuka, Ohmi, Nagoya, Nankai, Hokurika, and to Gakunan. Army installations were set up in Nagoya and its southeastern suburbs, and in Ohfu, Nagoya, Ueda, Gifu, Daimon, Toyama, and Kanazawa. These dispersed factory units remained within the central part of Honshu island. The company rented spinning and textile factory buildings to house its scattered machinery. Finally the Engineering Division, separated from the production units, transferred to a silk-manufacturing building and to schools on Matsumoto in Nagano Prefecture. The hasty move concentrated Zero fighter production in the Suzuka and Ohmi districts. Following these initial activities, factory dispersals coincided with the mass evacuation of city residents to rural areas. This latter move found little favor with the people; they felt it was certain to bring the B-29's after them, even in the remote country districts.

"Even as the Mitsubishi company began its complicated dispersal program, the B-29s returned. Again and again they showered bombs on Nagoya, with the result that traffic and communications became hopelessly entangled in a snarl of raging fires, blocked streets, and destroyed telephone lines. The well-laid dispersal plans went up in smoke with the flaming buildings. We found it impossible to maintain adequate communications among our scattered workshops. Production control vanished, and the manufacturing schedules became worthless scraps of paper. From March of 1945, Nagoya reeled beneath an unbelievable cascade of high explosives and incendiaries from the B-29 fleets. So effective was this aerial interdiction that, despite every effort, the Mitsubishi company managed to produce during the entire month of July the ridiculously small total of fifteen fighter airplanes.

"Nagoya and Tokyo became the two most frequently bombed cities in Japan. The Americans chose their targets wisely, for the two cities were the most critical centers of the entire nation. Nagoya was Japan's aircraft manufacturing center; one great factory at Daiko-cho alone produced 40 per cent of all our aircraft engines, and the sprawling plant at Ohe-machi assembled 25 per cent of our aircraft.

Tokyo, of course, was our military and political center. The incessant raids rapidly disorganized internal functions, and government activities nearly reached a standstill.

"The Nakajima Company spread its airframe factories through the northern section of the Kanto Province and, fortunately, escaped the brunt of the earlier enemy bombing attacks. Despite the dispersal program, which ruins manufacturing schedules, Nakajima produced 138 Zero fighters in June of 1945. All did not go well, however, with the great Nakajima firm. The company dispersed the critical engine plants which produced the Zero's *Sakae* power plant to the Tokyo suburbs. The move failed to hide the factories from the B-29s, and the resulting torrent of bombs so severely shattered machinery and assembly lines that engine production dropped well behind the airframe program.

"In September of 1943 the sprawling airframe factory at Mizushima in Okayama Prefecture, in western Honshu, was separated from the Nagoya Aircraft Works; the former single combine now was broken into two separate manufacturing centers. In January of 1944 Mitsubishi again divided another large plant, this time the Kumamoto Aircraft Works in Kyushu's Kumamoto Prefecture. The former factory produced the Type 1 land-based attack bomber (Betty) for the Navy, and the latter turned out the *Ki*-67 bomber (Peggy) for the Army. Mitsubishi divorced the activities of the two factories from its primary concern, which increased Zero fighter production. In February and March of 1945 the two plants dispersed throughout nearby suburban areas; they failed, however, to escape the B-29s, and by July their production lines were almost still.

"The fate of these vital factories, despite their high target priority to the enemy, was not at all different from that of other production centers. By May of 1945 munitions plants and the most important civilian goods factories were reduced to shattered remnants of once-efficient industries.

"Many a factory which went through the time-consuming steps of dispersing its most important machine and assembly lines now found itself no better off than before dispersal. The B-29s relentlessly and literally tracked down every move; no sooner had the new factory sections settled down in their new locations than the bombs showered down. The plant managers searched frantically for new sites, and sought refuge in factory buildings surrounded by steep mountains, or placed their vital machines within emergency caves drilled into the sides of hills. Eventually the dispersal plan proved to be a complete failure. At the time when we most desperately needed production, our industrial personnel scrabbled in the hills for new machine sites. Devastation in Japan mounted daily, as the B-29s were joined in the daily assaults against the homeland by long-distance land-based fighters and swarms of carrier-based fighters and bombers.

"This loss of fighter-plane production directly weakened our defensive tactics against the enemy fighters and bombers. This was especially applicable in the battle against the great fleets of four-engined B-29s. During the earliest Superfortress attacks our fighters inflicted heavy damage against the enemy planes; by May we were so short of fighter airplanes that the B-29s, constantly increasing in number, roamed the skies almost at will. As a result of both the enemy air attacks and our own chaotic plant dispersal, our aircraft production dropped alarmingly, as indicated in the following tables:"

MONTHLY AIRCRAFT PRODUCTION
(All Companies)

1944	Navy Planes	Army Planes
August	1,249 (367)	1,228
September	1,005 (244)	1,320
October	1,167 (339)	1,146
November	1,260 (360)	1,297
December	958 (268)	1,096
1945		
January	992 (251)	951
February	812 (167)	450
March	990 (247)	965
April	1,001 (267)	815
May	713 (285)	894
June	628 (208)	784
July	480 (153)	523

(The figures in parenthesis indicate the number of Zero fighters produced.)

MONTHLY AIRCRAFT ENGINE PRODUCTION
(Mitsubishi Only)

1944	For Navy Planes	For Army Planes
August	961	861
September	818	980
October	780	790
November	626	713
December	279	437
1945		
January	182	269
February	386	211

1945	For Navy Planes	For Army Planes
March	244	263
April	170	158
May	207	57
June	157	199
July	111	234

The peak of monthly airframe production for the Army was reached in July of 1944 with 1,331 aircraft completed, and for the Navy in November of 1944 with a total of 1,260 airplanes. Mitsubishi's aircraft engine production peak for the Army was reached in September of 1944 with 980 engines. One month previously the company hit its Navy aircraft engine top with 961 units. These figures do not include those airframes produced by the Hitachi Aircraft Company (which manufactured a small percentage of Navy aircraft, or those of the Manchurian Airplane Manufacturing Company, which produced from 10 to 15 per cent of all Army airframes).

The severe production losses sustained in late 1944 and in 1945 greatly hindered our defense against the approaching enemy and our interception of the enemy fighters and bombers which ranged over Japan. The greatest causes for this sudden production failure were, of course, the severe damage inflicted by the B-29s and the effects of the Tokai district earthquake. By no means, however, were these the only two causes, for many other factors indirectly affected aircraft production, even before the first B-29 raids against the homeland. Perhaps the greatest cause other than the B-29 attacks and the Tokai earthquake was the difficulty in obtaining certain types of critical materials, notably aviation gasoline. Once the enemy submarines, mine-laying planes, patrol bombers, carrier task forces, and surface warships had effectively sealed off the sea routes to the southern area of resources on which we depended, the end was in sight. This "resource isolation" of Japan both directly and indirectly contributed to our losing air superiority over the vital arterial route to the south. Eventually enemy pressure through direct bombing and air attack became so severe that our air forces found themselves helpless against the activities of the American submarines and carrier-based planes, as well as against the B-29s.

This paralysis of the sea routes upon which Japan depended for its very existence brought about the virtual isolation of the country. The air-raid damage and the frantic reshuffling of supplies available directly within Japan threw our internal transportation facilities into chaos. The hindrance of transportation and the loss of raw materials reduced aircraft-factory assembly lines to a meaningless crawl. Further, those aircraft which we did manage to produce under these difficulties were less effective than usual, for the inferior materials employed in their manufacture reduced flight performance and increased the time spent in maintenance and overhaul. Vital equipment failed all too often, and our pilots cursed the planes which consistently failed them just as they attacked the great enemy air fleets.

Before we could realize the confusion into which our aircraft production had descended, our industry had disintegrated to an extent where recovery seemed impossible. Not only were our raw materials cut off from the factories, but we struggled under the heartbreaking hardships of earthquakes, severe bombings, factory dispersal, and, later, of incompetent workers dragged off the streets through resort to the conscription laws. Even as the industry became lost in this sea of hopeless chaos the military services demanded modifications in a steady stream. We could hardly produce even the basic model; to say nothing of altering partially completed planes.

The trail of grief did not end here. As the limited number of airplanes came off the disorganized production lines, many of them remained on the ground, while the others were flown only on short and usually meaningless flights. There was a total lack of gasoline with which to fly these machines except on the briefest flights; even those airplanes flown on test hops were liable to encounter enemy fighters and bombers which daily defied our weak air resistance and flew where they pleased. After the fall of the Mariana Islands to the enemy, the entire aircraft industry labored under the shadow of inevitable defeat. By May of 1945, several months before the capitulation of Japan, we despaired of ever increasing our production. Personal effort was now meaningless, for the factories were on the verge of collapse for lack of parts and materials. The atomic bombings of Hiroshima and Nagasaki contributed absolutely nothing to this industrial disintegration; it was complete long before August 5 and 9, 1945.

To their credit, the Navy's officers never ceased their attempts to obtain through qualitative gains what we no longer could hope to accomplish with our outnumbered planes. In the final months of the war our engineers feverishly pushed the development of jet propulsion, rocket-powered guided missiles, rocket-powered interceptors, and similar projects. Japan started late in this work, and American engineers later considered our progress, in the face of a tardy beginning and ceaseless destruction of our planes, as "amazing." The need for haste naturally resulted in the appearance of inherent technical defects in the new equipment. Given sufficient time, these defects would have been eliminated and the new jet and rocket aircraft and missiles might have been developed successfully. The time, of course, was not to be had.

When the occupation forces came ashore on Japanese

soil, the enemy's technical intelligence officers soon visited our research and development centers. They paid special attention to the Yokosuka Naval Air Research and Development Center, where we had conducted the bulk of our aeronautical engineering activities. The scene which greeted the American technicians was not one of which we were proud, for our leading research installation was by then a confused collection of thin-walled wooden and stucco buildings. Lack of repairs had allowed the green and brown camouflage paint to peel from the riddled aircraft hangars. Those airplanes still on the field were in terrible condition, desperately in need of maintenance. Many of the planes were scarred with bullet and cannon-shell holes from the strafing of the American fighters. Equipment lay haphazardly on the ground, left by the disheartened engineers and crewmen.

The surface picture did not tell the entire story, for much of our research work went on within the security of the Yokosuka limestone hills. In these subterranean chambers we had set up aircraft hangars, machine shops, assembly lines, storage facilities, and living quarters. The underground installations were actually complete experimental aircraft factories.

Here, too, the misery and dissolution of a hopeless battle were evident, for the once-efficient and neat workshops had given way to filth and uncertain routine. Our work had become disorganized and, as defeat became ever more inevitable, even haphazard. The loss of supplies, machine tools, and vitally needed materials meant that our technicians must obtain their "precision parts" through the use of hand benches and tools, and by painstakingly hammering out the thousands of small items of equipment which go into the modern airplane.

This was the engineering and technical status of the air

force which only four years before had dominated more than seven thousand miles of Pacific and Indian oceans.

Technical and Administrative Factors Which Hampered Production

1. The urgent needs of the combat air corps forced the Army and Navy to place in production several types of experimental aircraft which lacked the required test flights and design modifications. Airplanes were rushed from the experimental hangars to the production line, with the result that the planes were dispatched to the front lines before we could determine the missions which they could most effectively perform. Our engineers lacked the time necessary to prepare maintenance manuals and texts; thus the front-line mechanics, plagued with primitive working conditions, were forced to service airplanes about which they understood little. The confusion of the maintenance crews inevitably caused equipment malfunction and breakage on a prohibitive scale. Typical of these planes were the *Raiden, Shiden, Shiden-kai, Ginga, Tojo,* and the Type 4 fighter.

2. Shortages in raw materials and aviation fuel contributed primarily to the final collapse of the aircraft industry. The items most in demand were aluminum and the alloy steels. The allocation of aluminum for aircraft production decreased from a 1942 figure of 6.5 tons per airplane to 5.3 tons in 1943 and, in 1944, to only 3.8 tons. By late 1944 the industry was slowing down because of the scarcity of alloy steels. The use of substitute materials for vital engine parts further slowed production, as our workers were forced to pay more attention to heat treatment, forging, and final assembly. We suffered a sudden increase in the failure of crankshafts, gears, and other critical

engine parts. The inadequacies of the Material Mobilization Plan made it impossible to alleviate the situation.

Our natural crude oil resources, compared to our national requirements, are barely worth mention. Consequently an extended war in which our sea routes were cut—as happened in 1944 and early 1945—could only mean critical fuel shortages. By July of 1944 we found ourselves severely handicapped by a lack of aviation fuel. Pilot training was cut drastically, and commanding officers on the front were ordered to send their planes out on only the most essential missions. Engineers were forced to reduce the bench-test time for new engines and consequently ordered those same engines into production even when they were plagued with operating difficulties. The best example was the *Homare* (*Ha*-45) power plant used in several Navy and one Army combat plane. Despite their aerodynamic configurations and high power, constant engine trouble and long hours of maintenance consistently grounded the airplanes.

3. Throughout the war the aircraft industry labored under the unrealistic demand that it manufacture an excessive number of production *types*; that it slow production in order to build numerous prototypes, and that it effect far too many modifications to aircraft already on the assembly lines. These military requirements severely overburdened the small group of competent engineers available to the industry; the endless attrition of engineering manpower eventually resulted in great confusion between the drafting rooms and the production line. The fundamental sources of the trouble were the Army and Navy; the two organizations lacked a fundamental understanding of the actual nature of engineering, and were given to making unreasonable demands. The engineers further aggravated the situation by failing to take a determined stand against these

constant orders from military headquarters; had they done so, many of their problems could have been obviated.

4. Japan's generally low industrial capacity always proved detrimental to our attempts to realize mass production of precision equipment. Engine production, for example, never equaled the output of airframes, causing a surplus of the latter. Frankly, Japan did not meet the European technical standards of such basic industries as those which processed raw materials and produced the machined tools necessary for the aircraft factories. Another great fault was that our plant managers never mastered the techniques of controlling the sprawling aircraft plants. Naturally, the inefficiency which inevitably arose indirectly cost us many airframe and engine units.

Management inadequacies were highlighted when war broke out and the government called for a substantial increase in production. Not only did the major plants suffer from their own deficiencies, but they were forced to accept parts produced by subcontractors which were clearly of inferior quality. These subcontractors were small machine shops scattered throughout the cities and towns; there did not exist a single criterion of quality for the thousands of small shops. As a result, the major plants were forced to destroy a great deal of the material received.

5. The majority of our engineers were handicapped from the beginning of their design programs. Anxious to acquire the world's leading fighters and bombers, the military services issued performance specifications clearly beyond the capacity of our industry. Attempting to meet these unrealistic demands, engineers often overextended themselves and produced designs which, while admittedly modern, actually lay outside the realm of sound engineering. Impressed perhaps by the performance results of prototype aircraft, the government ordered new planes,

engines, and equipment into mass production. We paid for our rashness in time, material, and energy, for the production machines had to be sent to modification centers for extensive alterations. Production likewise suffered as the engineers repeatedly modified their products to eliminate many of the technical "bugs."

6. Our industry never filled its minimum requirements for qualified technicians and skilled factory workers. This unhappy situation resulted from the nation's general low industrial standard; furthermore, the aircraft factories could borrow from other industries only a handful of able technical personnel. In this respect, the military services seemed bent on increasing our difficulties for, except on rare occasions, they refused to consider individual cases in the conscription program, and we watched our experienced men drift away to war along with the unskilled laborers.

7. Japan paid heavily for her failure scientifically to plan the location of aircraft factories, and by 1942 our airframe, engine, instrument, and equipment factories had become concentrated in and around large cities. This failure to disperse enabled the enemy B-29s to perform their task of destruction with little difficulty in finding targets; the massed factories literally invited the rain of bombs. We paid heavily to prepare facilities in outlying areas when the government ordered plant dispersal; but not until we began to suffer heavy damage was the dispersal order given. We never managed to return our plants to normal operation after the air attacks commenced. An added crippling blow was the Tokai area earthquake in December of 1944. Not only were the great Mitsubishi and Aichi airframe plants paralyzed completely for at least a month, but they never overcame fully the effects of the devastating earthquake.

CHAPTER 26

Defense of the Mainland: The B-29 Appears

WHEN JAPANESE SHIPS AND planes swept over more than six thousand miles of the Pacific and Indian oceans to launch the Pacific War, the government had a specific plan of defense for the homeland. We would capture every enemy air-base outpost within bombing range of Japan to deny the Americans or the British the installations from which to mount air attacks; further, we would destroy the majority of enemy aircraft carriers so that their smaller planes would not be able to bomb our cities. It was chiefly for this reason that the Japanese Navy occupied Wake Island, Guam, and air bases in the Philippines and along the sea coast of China. Even the Pearl Harbor attack was planned, to a great extent, with the defense of the Japanese mainland in mind.

These early operations achieved their objectives, but only to a limited extent and for a limited period of time. We occupied every air base we had intended to, but the Pearl Harbor attack failed to catch any of the American carriers we wished to sink. And, on April 18, 1942, the first American planes flew over Tokyo in what was admittedly a raid essentially for morale-boosting and propaganda purposes. Eventually B-29 formations were to blacken our skies and reduce our cities to charred wreckage, but this still was far in the future.

The details of the air attacks upon Japan which culminated in the atomic bombings of Hiroshima and Nagasaki are known to every Japanese, and have been more than adequately described in the United States. There are certain aspects of this aerial strangulation, however, which have not previously been presented, and are here made available. Some material appearing in these pages cannot, of course, be entirely unknown to the student of the Pacific War, but the air war against the Japanese mainland cannot be overemphasized, for its effects were beyond the comprehension of both the Japanese and the enemy.

At the time of the Doolittle raid on Japan I (Okumiya) was an air staff member of the 11th Combined Air Flotilla with headquarters at the Kasumigaura Air Corps base approximately twenty-five miles northeast of Tokyo. I was able to witness part of the raid, watching a B-25 skimming low near our headquarters.

We knew that "something was up" in the Pacific. Since April 10 the wireless communications of the American Pacific fleet indicated that a carrier task force might approach the Japanese mainland. It seemed that sometime after April 14 the Americans would launch a carrier-plane attack against the main island of Honshu. Admiral Yamamoto ordered immediate countermeasures. He alerted all the patrol vessels in the Pacific Ocean within six hundred nautical miles of the mainland to make special daily patrols of the sea east of Japan and, at the same time, ordered all available Navy planes to assemble in the Tokyo area.

At 6:30 A.M. on April 18 Tokyo headquarters received a flash warning from our patrol boat No. 23, *Nitto-Maru*, which was on regular duty in the specified danger area. The boat's captain radioed that he had sighted three American aircraft carriers six hundred nautical miles east of Inubo Point; we never heard from the ship after the first report. Obviously the carrier escorts had destroyed the vessel. Several hours later, at 9:45 A.M., a Betty patrol bomber confirmed the existence of enemy planes in the area; it had sighted two enemy bombers between five and six hundred nautical miles east of Tokyo.

On the basis of the original patrol vessel report, the commander of the Yokosuka Naval Station and the Army commander of the Tokyo area issued an air-raid warning at 8:30 A.M. Their respective fighter planes were ordered to be in the air by twelve noon. By the noon hour three Type 96 (Claude) fighters from the Kasumigaura Air Corps circled at ten thousand feet, and two other fighters waited at the air base for take off orders. None of us at Kasumigaura expected the enemy air attack before the late afternoon at the earliest, since the American carriers had only single-engine bombers.

We could not know, of course, that Lieutenant Colonel James H. Doolittle's sixteen bombers aboard the *Hornet* would be fast, twin-engined North American B-25s, or that the attack had been planned so that the B-29s would leave the carriers four hundred miles from Japan. The patrol vessel sighting forced the Americans to launch their planes six hundred and twenty miles off the coast, which consequently meant they would arrive over their target several hours earlier than we expected. Actually, Doolittle's men left the *Hornet* ten hours ahead of schedule.

The enemy bombers flew toward Japan at a height of only fifteen to twenty feet. At approximately 1:00 P.M. we received word that American planes, flying very fast, low, and not in formation, were over the mainland. The enemy's tactics were superb. Their "on-the-deck" flight had completely fooled our air-defense system, and the three fighters circling ten thousand feet over the Flotilla base never even saw the B-25s. Since we were a primary training unit, we did not have available a single Zero fighter at any of the four bases around Kasumigaura. When the B-25s bombed Tokyo, not a single anti-aircraft gun fired at the bombers and not a single fighter plane went in pursuit. The sixteen B-25s scattered their hits and struck at north, central, and south Tokyo, Kanagawa, Yokohama, Yokosuka, Kobe, Osaka, and Nagoya.

When the sixteen B-25s attacked Honshu, the Navy had already completed its plans for the Midway Operation, but not without serious opposition from some high-level Navy quarters. The Doolittle attack served Yamamoto's needs in that the bombing thoroughly silenced the dissenting voices. Fortunately, the public was well aware that this type of sporadic air attack could not cause serious damage and was little disturbed. We understood, however, that the Americans had accomplished their primary purpose of boosting the morale of their own people—then apprehensive because of the attack on Pearl Harbor, and the loss of so many islands and ships in the Pacific—with this single raid.

The Doolittle raid spurred plans to strengthen Japan's homeland defense against future bombings. Ever since the start of the war homeland defense had been the Army's responsibility, with the Navy relegated strictly to cooperate with the Army at the latter's convenience. The April 18 attack brought forth a government order that henceforth both services would take every measure to create an effective air defense.

Passive defense measures were considerable, but little actually was done to increase the number of fighters and interceptors for mainland patrol against bombers which might not appear for long months or years. The disastrous plane losses incurred at Midway, the air battle at Guadalcanal, and the unexpected attrition of planes in the Solomons and Rabaul areas had steadily drained our available fighter strength. Neither the Army nor the Navy had anticipated such devastating defeats, and the requirements of the frontline forces dictated that every available fighter plane and anti-aircraft weapon originally assigned to homeland defense be shipped to the Pacific. In later months, with the war steadily approaching the home islands, the people called for increased defenses against impending enemy air attacks. We could do little to answer these pleas, for we desperately needed every plane along our shrinking defense lines.

In the summer of 1943 we obtained for the first time accurate information concerning the new Boeing B-29 bomber, the Superfortress, which reputedly had a radius of action far in excess of that of the Consolidated B-24 Liberator. On June 15, 1944, the B-29 appeared over the mainland for the first time. The Americans had opened the final battle for Japan.

Between the evening of June 15 and the following morning, the same day when the Americans launched the beachhead operation to take Saipan, more than forty-five B-29s flew over northern Kyushu from a staging base at Chengtu in China. (*Editor's note:* Sixty-eight planes took off on the mission, forty-seven arrived in the Kyushu area, and five were lost because of operational mishaps.) The planes attacked the steel center of Yawata, but the bombing was ineffective and only a small number of civilian structures suffered damage. Despite its lack of destructive results, however, the first Yawata attack had a grave psychological effect on the Japanese people. Where they regarded the Doolittle raid as a nuisance, the Yawata assault promised tremendous bombing raids in the future. All Japan discussed what might happen when the Americans increased the severity of their raids. The iron chain the enemy was closing on the homeland was becoming ever tighter.

On July 8 and on August 11 and 20, the B-29s flew from their China mainland bases to attack our southern cities. Every bombing followed a certain pattern from which we could determine in advance of the attack how many planes would make the raids, when the attack would come, and other details of the missions. Because of this advance information, our mainland air defenses were able to have their fighters in the air waiting for the bombers as they arrived for their bomb runs.

Our first information came two or three days before the attacks. American transport planes increased their shuttle flights between a British air base near Calcutta, India, and the B-29 fields in China, ferrying gasoline and other materials for the big planes. Our Navy radio listening stations in Tokyo caught the details of every coded communication which, we determined, were from the American planes reporting the exact times of their arrivals and departures. These radio communications were so clear that we could calculate the exact number of planes flying the China missions.

Two or three days later, a similar number of B-29s would arrive over Japan. We never failed in these bombing forecasts, which received corroboration from Army and

Navy units scattered widely in China. These reports were dispatched at once to Tokyo. Within ten minutes every antiaircraft battery and every fighter base was informed of the estimated time of arrival of the American bombers.

Despite the remarkable good fortune of anticipating the enemy attacks in detail, our defenses proved ineffective. The Superfortress made their first three attacks during the night. We had few Navy fighters available for interception, and they proved of little value against the large and powerful enemy planes. Even the Army found itself handicapped in night interception, and Army fighters attacked only a limited number of planes. On the evening of August 20 Navy fighters made our first effective interception. Approximately sixty B-29s attacked targets in Kyushu, Chugoku, and western Shikoku. Intercepting Navy fighters shot down one B-29 and damaged three others; Army fighters damaged several other bombers. These attacks were always extremely dangerous, for the B-29s carried the remarkable defensive armament of at least twelve heavy machine guns in power turrets.

One of our night fighters under Lieutenant Endo demonstrated the effectiveness of the twin-engined night fighter *Gekko* (Irving) during this attack. An experienced night-fighter team which had fought against B-17s and B-24s over the Solomons and Rabaul, Endo's crew shot down the B-29 we confirmed as destroyed. He brought his fighter plane directly beneath the tail of a B-29 over Sasebo and, flying almost with the bomber's speed, fired the 20-mm. cannon which was fixed in an oblique position behind the pilot's seat. The upward-firing cannon pored shells into the huge airplane, which burst into flames and fell from the sky. Several minutes later Endo slipped beneath another Superfortress and heavily damaged the airplane. Another *Gekko* fighter piloted by one of Endo's men repeated the maneuver and shot up a third B-29. Following the August 20 attack, the B-29s did not return to attack Japan proper until late October.

Five days before this last bombing raid I was appointed as the Air Staff Officer, Japan Homeland Defense, Navy Section, at Imperial General Headquarters. To my disappointment I discovered that we had only 192 planes of all types assigned exclusively for air defense. Of these, the majority of the day fighters were Zeros and the remainder, a small number of *Raidens* (Jacks) and *Shidens* (Georges). The night fighters were all *Gekkos*. These fighters were distributed to three areas; forty-eight day and twenty-four night fighters to Yokosuka; forty-eight day and twelve night fighters to Kure; and forty-eight day and twelve night fighters to Sasebo. The Army had available for homeland defense some two hundred planes of all types, and assigned one hundred and ten planes to Tokyo, sixty to north Kyushu, and thirty to Osaka. In addition to these planes there were available in Japan nearly four hundred additional Army and Navy fighter planes assigned to such special missions as escorting bombers for attacks against enemy ships. But they cooperated with the homeland defense force in special emergencies.

On August 16 two B-29s, which we believed were based at the new Saipan airfields, flew a reconnaissance mission over the Bonin Islands. On October 30 there no longer was any doubt as to the use of Saipan as the B-29 base; eight of the giant bombers attacked the naval base at Truk.

At 1:30 P.M. on November 1 the first B-29s appeared over Tokyo. Aircraft spotters were astonished suddenly to discover the two huge planes on a reconnaissance mission high over the city. They dropped no bombs and left shortly after their arrival, but their appearance was a great shock to the military personnel charged with the mainland defense. Until these planes were sighted directly over the city, we had no idea that the airplanes were over Japan. Our patrol planes and ships had failed to sight the bombers and, despite the excellent flying weather, our interceptors could not catch the enemy planes. Within the next two weeks additional B-29s flew over Nagoya on reconnaissance missions, again with impunity.

On November 24 Saipan-based B-29s raided Tokyo for the first time. For approximately three hours during the afternoon some seventy bombers attacked the Tokyo area, concentrating their missiles on the Musashino Works of the Nakajima Airplane Company at Kichijoji, a vital engine factory. The bombings killed and injured 260 people, and destroyed at least a hundred civilian homes. Those losses were immaterial; what mattered was that the B-29s had wrought tremendous destruction in the critical factory, causing a loss of more than 50 per cent of normal production.

Five days later the B-29s bombed Tokyo proper for the first time, setting great fires in the Kanda and Nihonbashi areas in the heart of the city. Some twenty-five hundred homes were destroyed; one hundred people died and some fifteen thousand were made homeless. By now every Japanese citizen realized that the American air attacks would cause devastation and misery on a scale they had never anticipated. The future was ominous. The first raids also made it evident that the B-29s would strike not at military establishments, but at strategic industrial plants and civilian homes. For the first time our people knew the meaning of fear from air attack.

The B-29s ranged across half of Asia, attacking factories and other targets in Manchuria, Korea, Formosa, and other areas. On October 25 the bombers from China returned to the Kyushu area, and a total of at least one hundred and fifty B-29s smashed most of the Navy's Twenty-first Air Arsenal at Omura, twenty-five miles south of Sasebo. Seventy fighters, including Zeros, *Raidens*, and *Gekkos*, made intercepts, and our pilots reported they had either shot down or damaged at least nineteen planes. The losses and damage sustained by the enemy were meaningless compared to the effect of their bombs.

The B-29s had proven deadly opponents to our fighter planes in air combat, and the light losses sustained by these airplanes, as well as the terrible damage to our factories, prompted our pilots to discuss *Kamikaze* attacks against the huge airplanes. On November 21 Lieutenant Mikihiko Sakamoto dove his fighter into a B-29 over Sasebo, giving up his life to destroy the enemy bomber. The aerial death struggles continued steadily until early January of 1945, with the B-29s constantly increasing the severity of their attacks. We learned finally that the Americans had abandoned their China mainland bases to concentrate their attacks from Marianas installations.

On December 13 the Marianas-based Superfortress for the first time attacked the great Nagoya Aero Engine Works, and five days later smashed the Nagoya Aircraft Works. From late 1944 until early February of the following year they repeatedly attacked the aircraft factories in the Nagoya area in daylight raids and, on night missions, bombed the civilian areas in Tokyo, Yokohama, Osaka, and Kobe. The B-29s made the limited attacks against aircraft plants in the Kwanto and Kobe area. Our aircraft plants were smashed wreckage, for the high explosive and incendiary bombs had shattered machinery, broken steel supports, burned out vast factory sections, and killed hundreds of workers. Mitsubishi's Nagoya aircraft and engine factories, Kawasaki's Akashi engine plant west of Kobe, and

Nakajima's Ohta aircraft factory forty-five miles northwest of Tokyo all sustained great damage. Each of these factories were vital centers of airframe and engine production for both the Army and the Navy, and the B-29 attacks caused a drastic reduction in their production.

To bolster our air defense, the Navy assigned about one hundred serviceable planes of all types, including *Raidens*, Zeros, *Shidens, Gekkos*, and *Gingas* (remodeled night fighters), to Atsugi air base. To my disappointment there were only fifteen Zeros at the Meiji air base twenty miles southeast of Nagoya, and thirty Zeros at the Naruo air base to defend the Osaka and Kobe areas. The Army, on the other hand, stationed in the Tokyo area for both day and night air defense some two hundred fighters, including *Hayabusas, Shokis, Hiens, Hayates, Toryus*, and remodeled Dinahs. There were in the Nagoya area eighty fighters, and fifty planes to defend Osaka and Kobe.

During the early stages of the B-29 attacks our fighters generally proved ineffective against the fast, high-flying, and powerfully armed B-29s. Enemy losses were remarkably low, and the B-29s exacted a stiff toll from our fighters. By the time the B-29s were concentrating their attacks against the aircraft plants we had greatly improved our air-defense system. Three battle incidents reflect the increased effectiveness of our pilots.

On December 3, 1944, our fighters intercepted an estimated eighty B-29s raiding Tokyo, and pilots reported that they had shot down thirteen planes and probably destroyed another seven. These losses included three B-29s which were destroyed by Army fighters which rammed the bombers. Two pilots succeeded in bailing out before the collisions.

On the afternoon of December 27 antiaircraft guns and

fighters were reported to have destroyed nine out of an estimated fifty bombers, probably destroyed five others, and damaged twenty-seven.

On the afternoon of January 27, 1945, fighters and antiaircraft reputedly accounted for twenty-two out of seventy-five B-29s which raided the Ginza and Hibiya areas in the heart of Tokyo. The majority of Army and Navy officers ridiculed the reports of twenty-two B-29s destroyed on this date as being impossible. However, on the twenty-ninth we received a wireless report from Zurich, Switzerland, which stated that during the raid in question the B-29s encountered unexpectedly heavy fighter opposition, and that thirty planes failed to return to their home bases. One plane staggered into its airfield after flying more than sixteen hundred miles on two engines. The losses actually incurred, then, appeared to exceed our reports of twenty-two planes destroyed.

(Postwar investigation revealed that we, as well as Zurich, had greatly overestimated the effects of the fighter planes during this attack. The B-29s bombing Japan were from the Army Air Force's 73rd Wing, and their pilots reported that they had met "fighter opposition of unparalled intensity." The American crews reported that our pilot's "pressed their attacks right down the formations' stream of fire, dove into formations to attempt rammings, and sprayed fire at random." The American losses for January 27 amounted to five bombers destroyed over the target, two bombers ditched on the way home, and thirty-three planes badly shot up.)

The majority of B-29 attacks had been daylight raids, which gave our fighters the best opportunities to intercept the enemy planes. Lieutenant Teramura, the squadron leader of the 302nd Navy Air Corps (at Atsugi) describes the intercept mission on February 2, 1945, over Tokyo:

"At 28,000 feet I found a nine-plane formation of B-29s. I flew parallel to the bombers in an attempt to get in front of them and, finally, pulled ahead of the enemy planes, which kept up a constant fire at my fighter. I could see only a few tracers which drifted slowly toward me in parabola, and felt little danger.

"About three thousand feet ahead of the B-29s I turned sharply and picked up speed in a shallow dive, dropping below the bombers and then pulling up for the attack. I opened fire against the first B-29 in the formation, attacking from the lower front side of the airplane. As the two planes closed rapidly I did not have the opportunity to maintain a long burst. The nose turrets of three B-29s surrounded my fighter with tracers. I opened fire and watched the tracer shells of my four cannon coverage on the bomber ahead of me. When I was extremely close to the giant bomber I kicked right rudder and pushed the control stick forward and to the right, dropping away from the B-29 in a diving turn. My shells had hit, for one of the B-29 engines was burning fiercely.

" *'I got it!'* I shouted to myself. One of my pilots, Harukawa, followed my plane and executed the same attack. Taking advantage of our diving speed, we turned and climbed to attack the bombers from below and behind. One of the B-29s dropped out of the formation, trailing a thick plume of white smoke from under the outer left engine. Jettisoning its bombs, the airplane took a southeast course, toward the Pacific Ocean, steadily losing altitude in an attempt to escape our attack. I continued firing but soon exhausted my cannon-shell supply. Our *Raiden* fighters, however, were equipped with a single 20-mm. cannon mounted to the left and behind the pilot's seat, fixed to fire upward at a thirty-degree angle. Diving to attack from the right and behind the bomber, I closed the distance between our planes. By this time Harukawa had expended his ammunition and was returning to base.

"The enemy gunners kept up a steady defensive fire. I continued to pursue the bomber until I reached the ocean; by then my fuel was almost gone. When finally I turned to head for home, the B-29 was still trailing heavy smoke and descending almost to sea level. I doubted whether it could return to its base.

"I made an emergency landing at Kohnoike Naval Air base, where the mechanics discovered that enemy bullets had damaged my plane's engine and oil cooler."

As was so effectively demonstrated before the war's end, even our most strenuous air defense efforts failed to keep the ever-growing fleets of B-29s from carrying out their missions to destroy our industries and our cities. We reached the height of our air defense measures on the night of May 25–26 in 1945, during the American's "Mission 183" against Tokyo's urban area. Of the 498 planes dispatched for the attack, 464 bombed their primary target over Tokyo. Our fighters and antiaircraft racked up their greatest single mission total of the air defense period, destroying twenty-six of the sixty-five-ton airplanes. One hundred bombers, 21.3 per cent of the attack force, were shot up by antiaircraft and fighters. We paid an even heavier price, for the B-29s burned out nearly nineteen square miles of the city.

By the close of 1944 the Americans actually had committed only a minor portion of their B-29 strength against Japan. In 1944 no more than one hundred B-29s ever bombed their targets on a single operation; in early August of 1945, however, the enemy sent more than eight hundred of the great raiders on a single night's operation over the mainland. This was not the entire picture, of course. In November of 1944 the B-29s carried an average bomb load of 2.6 tons per airplane; in July of 1945 this figure had increased to 7.4 tons. Our best interception and destruction ratio, assisted by antiaircraft fire, occurred during the month of January, 1945, when the enemy lost 5.7 per cent of his attack force. By July of the same year the Americans enjoyed an unprecedented safety factor for bombing missions, losing only 0.4 per cent of the raiding planes. Greatly responsible for the lowered loss ratio, of course, was the new ability of the B-29s to bomb at any time of the day or night and in almost any weather. In July of 1945, the record month of B-29 attacks, the Americans dropped more than 75 per cent of all their bombs by radar.

On the night of March 9–10, 1945, Major General Curtis Le May instituted a new and devastating method of B-29 attack. In every previous attack, night or day, we had never encountered the B-29s below twenty-four thousand feet, and we could expect to meet the airplanes at this height or above. On the night of March 9, Le May sent in more than three hundred unarmed, stripped-down B-29s to attack Tokyo from an average height of only seven thousand feet. Each of the planes carried from six to eight tons of new jelly-gasoline fire bombs, and swept low over the city in flights which caught our defenses by surprise. The Americans in this daring raid lost fourteen bombers, but they also carried out what was then the most destructive air attack in history, burning out more than sixteen and a half square miles of the city. The enemy pilots reported that Tokyo "caught fire like a forest of pine trees."

Thirty minutes after the attack began the fires were out of control, fanned by a high ground wind. It was impossible to combat the racing conflagration. As one of our newspapermen reported: "The fire clouds kept creeping higher, and the tower of the Diet Building stood out black against the red sky. The city was as bright as at sunrise; clouds of smoke, soot, even sparks driven by the storm, flew over it. That night we thought the whole of Tokyo had been reduced to ashes." Estimates of the dead and missing ranged from eighty to three hundred thousand; the final figures will never really be known because of the destruction of vast housing areas and the chaos which followed.

In all missions the great B-29s dropped 157,000 tons of bombs, of which nearly 100,000 tons of incendiaries were directed against sixty-six target cities, ranging in size from Tokyo to Tsuruga with a population of thirty-one thousand. The Americans burned out more than one hundred and seventy square miles in these incendiary attacks.

It is impossible to determine accurately all the bombing effects because of the terrible state of chaos to which Japan was reduced by August of 1945. More than 30 per cent of our total aircraft industry suffered heavy damage; these attacks, we estimate, denied us the production of more than seven thousand planes annually. We lost 70 per cent of our total output of airplane propellers, which alone was a devastating blow. By the war's end the bombers had caused a total shutdown, at least temporarily, of our high-grade lubricating-oil capacity. While we had a surplus of refining *capacity*, by August 14, 1945, the B-29s wrecked our eleven most modern refineries. We could hardly assess the over-all effect upon our industry merely by adding the total square footage of factory space destroyed. Many plants left standing were useless, denied as they were the materials and parts to work with, and suffering from a shortage of laborers who had fled to the hills in terror of future raids.

By the end of July some ninety cities had become literal ash-choked funeral pyres. Only four major cities in the country, Kyoto, Hiroshima, Nagasaki, and Sapporo remained undamaged, or had experienced only a few stray bombs. Our industry had been strangled, and even the relatively undamaged plants in Tohoku and Hokkaido stood quiet and unproductive. The machines lay idle because the plants no longer received working materials and, further, because they lacked the means to transport their products to Honshu. The blanketing swarms of carrier-based planes paralyzed our communications and all but halted sea transportation between Hokkaido and the mainland.

Once the Americans had attended to our larger cities, they went after the smaller industrial cities in an unbelievably methodical fashion. They concentrated their attacks on cities with less than one hundred thousand population as their primary targets. An example of these raids, the bomb tonnages of which indicate their terrible effects, follows:

Date	Target	Bomb Tonnage	B-29s
June 17	Omuda and small cities	3,195	457
June 19	Toyohashi; other cities	3,335	481
June 22	Kure, Wakayama; small cities	2,290	412
June 26	Osaka; small cities	3,058	468
June 28	Okayama-Sasebo and Moji	3,519	485
July 2	Kure, Kumamoto; small cities	3,709	532
July 4	Kochi; small cities	3,752	483
July 7	Chiba; small cities	4,227	568
July 10	Sendai; small cities	3,872	536
July 13	Utsunomiya; small cities	3,640	517
July 16	Numazu; small cities	3,678	471
July 20	Fukui; small cities	3,255	473
July 24	Osaka and Nagoya	3,445	570
July 28	Tsu; small cities	4,427	548

Date	Target	Bomb Tonnage	B-29s
August 2	Toyama, Tachikawa; small cities	6,600	855
August 6	Saga; small cities	4,122	573
August 7	Toyokawa arsenal	830	131
August 8	Yawata	1,296	245

Perhaps the over-all effect of the bombings against the homeland—an incredible story—is best summarized in the statement of a Tokyo newspaperman. When he was questioned as to B-29 crew reports of damage to Tokyo and other cities which had suffered the most intensive aerial bombardment in history, the reporter replied:

"Superfortress reports of damage . . . were not exaggerated: if anything, they constitute the most shocking understatement in the history of aerial warfare."

Japans's four most critical industrial centers were the areas of Tokyo-Yokohama; Osaka-Kobe, Nagoya, and Kita-Kyushu. What happened to these cities is representative of Japan's condition by the time our country surrendered. The five largest cities, not including Kita-Kyushu, received nearly half of all bombs dropped by the enemy Twentieth Air Force. So thoroughly gutted were the major sections of these cities, with a combined total of 103.22 square miles destroyed, that the Americans eliminated them as targets.

CHAPTER 27

Carrier Planes Raid the Homeland

THERE IS LITTLE DOUBT that the primary reason for the American invasion of tiny Iwo Island (Iwo Jima) was to reduce the loss of B-29s flying against Japan from the Mariana Islands. We knew that the great four-engined bombers were running into serious trouble on the return flights after attacking the mainland; dozens of crippled planes, unable to fly the sixteen-hundred miles from Japan to Saipan, were ditched in the open sea. We expected the Americans to make an all-out assault against Iwo Jima, for with the island in their possession the enemy could land his crippled planes on the eight-mile-long haven. (Admiral Ralph A. Ofstie: "The reason for the bloody seizure of Iwo Jima . . . was the pressing need to have an additional field for emergency landings. . . .") The enemy could also employ Iwo as a springboard for his long-range fighter planes which escorted the B-29s on their bombing missions.

It was only a matter of time, Tokyo reasoned, before the island would be attacked; further, the attack would undoubtedly involve a preliminary strike elsewhere to draw off our air power. As we had anticipated, the attack came. On February 16, 1945, three days before the invasion force assaulted Iwo Jima, American carrier-based planes opened a massive series of air blows against the mainland. A total of one thousand fighters and bombers swept over military air bases and civilian aircraft factories, chiefly in the Kanto (Tokyo) area. The enemy Task Force 58 assembled sixteen aircraft carriers, eight battleships, seventeen cruisers, seventy-five destroyers, and other vessels to support the carrier strikes. The following day an additional six hundred planes returned to batter our targets, dropping in the two-day period a total of five hundred and thirteen tons of bombs, in addition to the attacks with machine guns, cannon, and rockets.

Japanese Imperial Headquarters announced that our defending fighters and antiaircraft guns had destroyed at least two hundred and seventy-five enemy planes, while we lost only seventy-seven fighters. The American Navy's official combat reports stated otherwise, claiming that their planes had shot down 322 Japanese planes, strafed and damaged 171 on the ground, and had lost 49 to our defenses. There is a wide difference in these two reports, as seems to have been the case throughout the war. Certainly our claims appeared to be as widely exaggerated as were the Americans. We never did ascertain accurately all the losses, due to the chaotic condition of our communications and chain of command at the time. In my opinion, as a responsible officer of Japanese Naval Headquarters, the actual losses of both combatants appeared to have been approximately the losses each opposing force announced; i.e., Japanese loses probably amounted to seventy-five planes, and American losses to forty-nine planes.

One cannot, however, contest the fact that the attack of

the sixteenth was a complete surprise to our homeland defenses. Tokyo expected the carrier assault, but not directly against the heart of the homeland. Consequently, the Grumman F6F Hellcat fighters overwhelmed our Army and Navy fighter planes, both numerically and qualitatively. Our fighters fought a difficult defensive battle against overwhelming odds and against planes which brazenly swept low against every possible ground target.

There was one especially bright note which served to overcome the general oppression of an overwhelming enemy success. There was no doubt that the Americans had achieved their original objective and that our battered air force could do little to halt further mass carrier raids. The majority of our pilots were inexperienced and consequently were at a decided disadvantage against the Hellcat pilots.

However, Flight Warrant Officer Kinsuke Muto of the Yokosuka Navy Air Corps put up a brilliant singlehanded defense against tremendous odds. About noon of the first day the enemy planes attacked, fighter-plane pilots awaiting orders at Atsugi Navy Airbase sighted a single *Shiden-Mod.* fighter, fleeing southward over Yokohama and pursued by twelve Hellcat fighters. There could only be one outcome to the chase, and the pilots waited for the *Shiden* fighter to fall in flames.

However, the unexpected happened. As the Hellcats closed the distance between their groups and the *Shiden*, the Japanese fighter suddenly turned sharply and at full speed raced directly at the enemy planes. The Hellcats formation scattered before the unexpected maneuver and the thirteen fighters swung into a wild melee of twisting and turning airplanes. Taking advantage of the fact that, in a battle of twelve planes against one, the enemy force often "gets in its own way," Muto hung to the tail of a Hellcat, pouring cannon shells into the Grumman until it blew apart.

The remaining eleven Hellcat pilots frantically tried to "latch on" to the elusive *Shiden*, and their tracers could be seen filling the air about the agile Japanese fighter. Muto saw his opportunity, turned directly into one of the Grummans, and pressed the head-on attack. His cannon shells shattered the plane and the pilot bailed out. By now Muto played what was obviously his superior flying skill to the hilt; abandoning his defensive maneuvers, *he* became the attacker and in short order two more Grummans plunged from the sky. Four down! The remaining eight Hellcat fighters abruptly broke off the engagement and fled the area.

The incredible battle ended and a tired but jubilant Kinsuke Muto brought his fighter, riddled with enemy bullets, to a safe landing at Yokosuka air base. Pilots watching from Atsugi did not know the name of the pilot in the *Shiden* fighter, but after watching the Grummans being shot out of the sky, they quickly identified him as Muto.

This was only natural. Muto was famous as one of the leading Navy aces. He shot his first enemy plane out of the air at least eight years before this battle, as a fighter pilot flying in China in 1937. Muto was assigned to the Yokosuka Navy Air Corps as a combat test pilot, and on February 16 had taken one of the new *Shiden-Mod.* fighters up on a test flight against enemy fighters. He left his base and circled about the Tokyo area in a search for enemy planes. Failing to meet the expected American fighters, he turned to return to Yokosuka when he noticed the twelve Hellcats diving upon his fighter.

On February 17 the enemy carrier planes made two heavy attacks against the Tokyo area, one morning and one afternoon raid. The Americans flew almost unopposed against their objectives, and the majority of the fighters and bombers machine-gunned, rocketed, and bombed their targets with little opposition. Again, the only bright spot of the day was that relating to a single fighter pilot, this time Lieutenant (J.G.) Sadanori Akamatsu, the Navy's senior fighter pilot ace. Flying a Zero fighter from Atsugi, Akamatsu shot down two Hellcats over Tokyo Bay. When the enemy planes returned for their second attack, Akamatsu intercepted two Grummans directly over the Atsugi field and shot both planes out of the air for a one-day tally of four enemy fighters destroyed.

When flown by thoroughly experienced pilots like Muto and Akamatsu, the Zero could prove a formidable opponent even against the versatile Hellcat; however, the greater majority of our fighter pilots were green youngsters with little or no combat experience. In their hands the Zero was no match for the Grumman fighter. There existed no doubt in our minds that we had long since lost qualitative superiority to the Americans.

Our mainland air defense force, fully occupied with interception of the increasing B-29 attacks, lost all power to cope with the enemy carrier air raids. Our defending fighter force could be well described as completely helpless. This situation arose in great part from the fact that Japan lacked a single operational fighter plane which could match the Hellcat fighter, and stood little chance of seeing its prototype planes manufactured in sufficient quantity to improve our situation.

Without superior defending fighter planes our mainland air-defense force was virtually useless. We could throw our dwindling reserves against the B-29s and the carrier attacks, shoot down some planes, and still in no way diminish the severity of the enemy air blows. Whatever number of planes we could destroy would not cause the enemy to slacken his efforts to pound Japan into absolute submission. By the spring of 1945 the B-29 attacks reached catastrophic proportions, and the great bombers thundered over our cities in furious day and night assaults. We could do relatively little against these systematic and large-scale bombardments, for we had never built a satisfactory high-altitude fighter plane. The Americans caused unimaginable havoc, especially when bad weather grounded our planes. Our fighters sat impotent on their runways while the hundreds of B-29s roared overhead, using their radar bombsights to smash with uncanny accuracy at our factories and cities.

The price the Americans paid for Iwo Jima was high; forty-eight hundred dead, fifteen thousand eight hundred wounded, and four hundred missing. The tiny island, however, paid handsome dividends. From March 4, when the first crippled B-29 landed on the still-crude runway, to the war's end, a total of 2,251 Superfortresses made emergency landings. The crew members in these airplanes, most of which never could have returned to Saipan or Guam, amounted to 24,761 men. In the bitter defense of Iwo we lost 22,322 men killed.

When the Iwo conflict ended on March 13, our losses in patrol boats in the southern sea rose to alarming figures. Enemy planes scoured the ocean in search of our patrol vessels and made these small ships their special targets. Soon we could no longer count on the survival of a single patrol boat in the area and were forced to rely for warning of enemy attacks entirely upon the radar reports of our southern island outposts. Under these conditions we were wide open to attack at any time by powerful enemy carrier forces.

As we expected, the carrier planes returned. Between March 18 and 21 the enemy fighters and bombers swept almost at will over the mainland, pouring their shells, rockets, and bombs into every conceivable target. Not even the remotest areas of Japan were safe from the marauding planes.

At this time, the Navy's 343rd Air Corps, considered the most powerful fighter plane unit of the entire Army and Navy, was stationed at the Matsuyama air base in Shikoku. Equipped mostly with the newer *Shiden* fighters, the plane which had become the Navy's great hope for a carrier-based fighter, the 343rd was manned by outstanding Navy fighter pilots, all of whom had considerable combat experience. The commander was Captain Minoru Genda, an able and experienced leader who had made the preliminary draft for the Pearl Harbor attack and who had served as an air staff officer of Imperial General Headquarters for the preceding year.

On March 18 and 19 the enemy carrier planes raided the Kure Naval Base. They met completely unexpected opposition from Genda's pilots. Combining extensive air-combat experience with a fighter plane which featured a maximum speed exceeding 400 mph and effective armor plating, they caused heavy losses to those planes they encountered.

This constituted the only decisive victory of all the Japanese fighter-plane units against the American carrier-plane attacks. Tokyo announced that for the two days of fighting in the Kure area our land, sea, and air defenses destroyed 119 planes, and that the majority fell victim to the 343rd Air Corps. Again, we at Naval headquarters could not determine the actual number of enemy planes destroyed, but obviously Genda's men provided effective opposition.

Before the month was past the terrible and one-sided air conflict entered another and equally disastrous phase. Heavy bombing by carrier-based and Army planes shattered defense installations on Okinawa and, following several weeks of protracted aerial bombardment, enemy troops landed on the island. From the invasion day of March 25 until two months later, our defending fighters fought furiously against the carrier planes and the relentless B-29s. By now it was a familiar story; the enemy exacted a murderous toll from our available aircraft and air strength continued to dwindle.

On March 21 one of our reconnaissance planes photographed the first North American P-51 Mustang fighter on Iwo Jima. On April 7 the Iwo-based VII Fighter Command launched the first Mustang fighter attack against the mainland. One hundred and eight P-51s escorted B-29s on a daylight mission against Tokyo, and rapidly proved their superiority over our fighters by shooting down twenty-one defending planes. We destroyed two Mustangs.

The new P-51s flew only ten escort missions since, after their arrival on Iwo, the B-29s resorted mainly to attacks at night and in foul weather. (After the war we learned that weather proved to be the P-51s' greatest foe; on June 1, returning from an escort mission against Osaka, twenty-four of the Mustangs disappeared in a seething caldron of violent weather, and two other planes collided and crashed.) On April 16 the Mustangs began their first series of sweeps against our ground installations, and by the war's end we counted thirty-three such missions. These attacks denied us the use of many of our airfield facilities in the Tokyo-Nagoya-Osaka area (Okinawa-based P-51s shot up airfields in Kyushu and Shikoku). The dispersal procedures forced by the strafing fighters complicated even further our maintenance problems, which already had reached monumental proportions. With most of our airfields reduced to wreckage, the fighters turned their attention to railroads, powerhouses, factories, and coastal shipping.

By May the eventual loss of Okinawa was clearly foreseen. The relentless drive of the Americans, which had started with the Guadalcanal invasion, was now on the very doorstep of the homeland. There was little doubt in our minds that the next great invasion of the war would be the assault against Japan itself.

To prepare for this final calamitous blow, Imperial General Headquarters ordered our remaining fighter planes to ignore future enemy air attacks, except in emergencies which would be determined by Tokyo itself. We were under new orders now; to save as many planes as possible for the final defense against the enemy invasion fleet. We feared that were we to continue our aerial defense operations against the B-29s, the carrier raids, and the Mustang sweeps, our defending fighter force would be annihilated. We could not face the enemy fighters and bombers without sustaining critical losses.

By June, enemy medium and heavy bombers from Okinawa bases began to raid the Kyushu area. Coordinating their attacks with these blows against our southernmost island, the B-29s increased the bomb tonnages dropped on our cities by leaps and bounds. On August 2 alone, Tokyo received reports that more than eight hundred and fifty of the giant raiders were over the mainland.

July became a nightmare of carrier-plane attacks. On July 10 the enemy Task Force 38 steamed off Japan with fifteen aircraft carriers, nine battleships, nineteen cruisers, and sixty-two destroyers. Warships shelled shore installations and the planes roamed at will over the mainland. Eight days later a British force of four fleet carriers, one battleship, six cruisers, and eighteen destroyers joined the

Americans. With our pilots under orders not to engage in combat, the enemy planes reduced literally every target they flew against to wreckage, and the battleships and cruisers hurled waves of shells into industrial targets.

The finish was near. Japan lay completely helpless before the tremendous tidal wave of enemy fighters and bombers. Our fleet was through. Our pilots, choked with rage at their inability even to dent the wall of fire and steel hurled at us by the enemy, waited for the final day of reckoning when enemy troops would storm ashore.

Japan could not avoid total defeat, but the enemy would pay dearly for every foot of Japanese soil. So stated the government which, despite the knowledge that by midsummer of 1945 our nation was nearly prostrate, elected to conclude the war in a bath of blood by resisting the imminent invasion with every available man.

CHAPTER 28

The Atomic Bombings: Personal Observations of Masatake Okumiya

B Y AUGUST OF 1945 the Pacific Ocean and the waters surrounding the four main Japanese islands had become an "American lake." Enemy warships in powerful task forces roamed along our coast, safe from attack, hurling thousands of shells into anything which moved on the shore, or into any buildings or other structures they deemed worth-while targets. Enemy planes flew literally thousands of sorties over every square foot of the mainland. Western Japan fell under the control of enemy planes based on Okinawa. Eastern Japan reeled under the hammering strikes of the B-29s and P-51s from Saipan and Iwo Jima. The Americans ruled the sea and the air surrounding and over the entire country. We were denied freedom of movement even in the interior, for the searching planes shot up trains, small boats, cars, trucks, communications facilities—anything and everything.

The Army and Navy kept its planes on the ground, hidden beneath camouflage, in underground hangars, and scattered to dispersal areas as far as five miles from the air-fields. We hoarded this last air fleet of 5,130 combat planes, in addition to several thousand trainers, which we would hurl against the invasion fleet which even then was assembling for the attack against Kyushu. These consisted of twenty-five hundred Army planes, of which sixteen hundred were *Kamikazes*, and twenty-six hundred and thirty Navy planes, including fourteen hundred suicide fighters and bombers. When the attack came we could throw in every airplane in Japan which could fly and carry bombs, including the slow and flimsy trainers.

It was clear to everyone that Japan could not avoid overwhelming defeat. We knew that our all-out defense of the islands was little more than a delaying operation which could result only in hundreds of thousands of lives lost in the bitter fighting to come. Despite this realization, the government elected to fight to the last man. It is difficult, if not impossible, to explain in logical terms the mental state of Japan's leaders, who insisted upon resisting what certainly would be the greatest invasion force in history.

This determination did not last very long. On August 6, 1945, there arose a new factor. The impact of the atomic bombing, first to Hiroshima and then, on August 9, of Nagasaki, was not immediate, because it required time before the government could assay the tremendous machine of destruction which the enemy had hurled at Japan. Once, however, our military and government leaders gained a fuller appreciation of this fantastic weapon which could make even the horror of the incendiary raids seem as only minor irritations, they could not commit themselves to the insane folly of continuing the war.

The city of Hiroshima had escaped the fury of the B-29s, and yet it held certain installations which we knew might invite a rain of bombs upon the city. It contained the

2nd Army Group Headquarters, which commanded the ground defense of the southern half of Japan. Tens of thousands of troops had assembled at Hiroshima during the war, and the city had become a major storage point and communications center. Hiroshima lay on the wide and flat delta of the Ota River. The seven river channel outlets divided the city into six islands which jutted out into Hiroshima Bay. Except for a single hill in the center of the city about two hundred feet high, Hiroshima was almost entirely flat and just slightly above sea level. Only seven square miles of the city's total twenty-six-square-mile area was built up, and 75 per cent of the population crowded into this area.

Except for its center, which featured a number of reinforced-concrete structures, the city overflowed with a dense collection of small wooden houses and wooden workshops. Even the majority of industrial buildings were of wood.

A little after seven o'clock on the morning of August 6, our early warning radar network picked up several enemy planes approaching southern Japan. Military authorities gave the air-raid alert and many cities, including Hiroshima, ceased their radio broadcasts. By eight A.M. the Hiroshima aircraft spotters clearly identified the incoming planes as only three aircraft flying at a very high altitude, and the all-clear signal was given. Hiroshima's radio station broadcast the news of the three planes and informed the people that, should the planes appear over the city, it might be advisable to seek shelter.

Approximately at 0830 hours, Lieutenant (J.G.) Nakajima, the air-defense duty officer, notified me that an emergency telephone call had come in for me. At the time I was on duty in the second basement of the underground air-raid shelter which had been built inside the Navy

Department's compound at Kasumigazeki, Koji-machi, Tokyo. The three-story subterranean shelter was the brain center of naval operations and the communications center of Japan's naval air defense (the Navy Department headquarters building was destroyed by fire May 27). All reports from the radar stations, patrol vessels, and aircraft spotters regarding enemy plane movements from the Marianas or aircraft carriers centered here.

The telephone call was from the Air Defense Command headquarters at the Kure Naval Station. I heard Commander Hiroki's voice ". . . about fifteen minutes ago there was a terrible flash over Hiroshima. Immediately afterward a terrible mushroomlike cloud rose into the sky over the city. Many of the people here heard a heavy roar, something like distant thunder. I don't know what happened there, but from the flash and the cloud it must have been something big. I tried to reach Headquarters of the Second Army Group by phone, but there is no answer. This is all I know right now. . . . I'll send in the details just as quickly as I get them—"

Kure Naval Station is about twelve miles south of the center of Hiroshima City.

I interrupted. "Do you know if it was an air raid, or some other explosion on the ground?"

"I don't know what it was. Only a few B-29s were seen, that's all."

"What's the weather like?" I asked.

"Fine."

"All right. Call me as soon as you get more information."

The entire affair made me feel uneasy. There was no ordinary explanation for a "bright flash" and a "tremendous cloud." I felt as though something ominous had happened. I queried the members of the Naval General Staff, but without success. No one had any idea of what could have happened at Hiroshima. There was one other place, however, which might provide the answer, and I called Captain Yasui of the Naval Bureau of Aeronautics.

I related the details as given me by Commander Hiroki. Captain Yasui's reply was staggering. I remember clearly his words that "... it may be an atomic bomb, but I can't tell until I actually look at the city. ..."

Atomic bomb! It *was* possible! The words struck a familiar note in my mind. I remembered that long ago the Navy in secret conferences had discussed the possibility of nuclear weapons. The basic theory was no secret. Several years ago the Navy had requested Dr. Arakatsu of Kyoto University, where the brilliant Dr. Yukawa worked, to study the possibilities. The Army too was investigating the theory of an atomic weapon; Dr. Nishina of the Physical and Chemical Research Institute had studied the matter in detail. But this work was hardly more than scientific investigation.

Could the enemy actually have used such a fantastic weapon?

Meanwhile several phone calls had come in from the Army General Staff. The Army was concerned; they had been unable to raise Hiroshima, either by telephone or by radio. Hiroshima was a vital strategic center of Army operations ... they were anxious for a report.

Just before noon we heard again from Kure.

"At 0815 hours this morning, immediately after two B-29s passed with high speed over the city, there was a searing flash, like a fantastic flash of lightning. It was followed by a sudden, roaring sound. In the next instant houses collapsed all across the city. It is as though a great steel fist had suddenly descended on Hiroshima. Fires broke out everywhere. Everything is all confused. The raging flames and the streams of refugees have made it impossible to get in touch with any place closer than Kaidaichi (about five miles southeast of the city)."

These reports were unbelievable. Everything was so sudden. Regardless of what happened, it was imperative that I, in command of the navy's homeland air defense, must get to the scene. Headquarters ordered that I proceed with Captain Yasui to Hiroshima to investigate personally what had occurred. We could not take off the same day, despite our anxiety; enemy planes in successive raids roamed over Japan.

On the afternoon of the following day, August 7, we took off with difficulty from Tokyo. We wished to make a full investigation from the air but by the time we arrived over Hiroshima the sun had set. Even on the second day, however, we found an incredible scene confronting us. A ghastly and terrible light flared from the stricken city. The still-burning Hiroshima cast a deep-red, flickering glow which was reflected from the black smoke which billowed upward from the earth.

Shortly afterward, our transport glided in for a landing at the Iwakuni Naval Air Base. Early the next morning, we rushed to Hiroshima.

Nothing—neither films, magazines, books, eloquent speeches—nothing can possibly express to any other person except those actual witnesses at Hiroshima what had happened to the city, and what occurred after the bomb fell. It was an appalling spectacle beyond the power of words to describe. Cold printed or celluloid media cannot carry the sounds and smells and "feelings" of the shattered city.

Hiroshima's debacle is a familiar tale, but all the thousands of stories do not reproduce the shuddering and screaming cries of the victims who already were beyond all possible help; they do not show you the dust and ash swirling about the burned bodies which groveled and

writhed in indescribable agony; the twitching and spas-
modic jerking of fingers which were the only expressions
of agony; the seeking of water by *things* which only a
short while before had been human beings.

Words do not convey the overwhelming, choking, nau-
seating stench, not from the dead, but from the seared
living-dead. The unharmed, or only slightly injured, survivors, placed these burned, dying men and women on
planks and mats in long, impersonal rows like decaying
fish, so that when they died their bodies would not have to
be stacked by people attending to those still living. How
many times has the story been told, but with the limited
effects of words, of the young mother whom I watched in
the agony of dying, not a word passing through her blis-
tered lips, her stomach sheared open, her intestines
sprawled in the ash and dust, her living but unborn infant
caked in blood and dirt on the ground beside her?

This was the Hiroshima I saw. Even today the full story
remains obscure, for it is impossible to tell all of the many
things which the subconscious happily refuses to allow one
to remember. I have never yet seen a single report of the
white soldier, a prisoner of war we can identify only as
white, as the corpse was terribly seared, sprawled in the
wreckage of the city's main street, only three hundred feet
from ground zero. Here was one man's direct sacrifice to
the atom of his countrymen or, at least, of his Allies.

Where Hiroshima had existed now there was only a
dirty brown scar on the face of the land. The people did literally nothing, they could *do* nothing, to extract themselves from the incredible misery thrust upon them. Staff
officers from Tokyo who flew to Hiroshima with me, and
others who followed, joined in the first relief measures.

Sixteen hours after the bomb struck intelligence officers learned for the first time what really had ripped the

city apart. The radio carried the American announcement of the atomic bomb.

Three days later, at 7:50 A.M., Japanese time, the air-raid sirens sounded over the city of Nagasaki, which lies at the head of a long bay which forms the best natural harbor on Kyushu. The city spread across two valleys through which two rivers flowed. Separating the residential and industrial areas was a mountain spur which contributed to Nagasaki's irregular layout, and which confined the built-up portion of the city to less than four square miles of the city's limits of thirty-five square miles.

Nagasaki was one of the largest seaports in southern Japan and was vitally important to our military forces with its many and varied industries, including those producing weapons, ships, military equipment, and other materials. Along one narrow strip of the city the Mitsubishi Steel Works and Dockyards lay to the south, and to the north sprawled the Mitsubishi-Urakami Torpedo Works. Unlike the industrial portions of the city, the residential areas were the typical flimsy, tile-roofed wooden buildings, jammed into a dense concentration particularly susceptible to fire.

The air-raid warning was given at 7:50 A.M., but forty minutes later the all-clear signal brought the people from their shelters. When at 10:53 A.M. our spotters sighted two B-29s, high over the city, they assumed a reconnaissance mission was on, and did not sound any further alarms. However, on seeing the B-29s, several hundred people hurried to shelters. Only nine days before, some high explosive bombs had been dropped on the city, and several of them fell in the shipyards and dock areas. Others exploded at the Mitsubishi Steel Works and Ordnance Works, and six bombs smashed into the Nagasaki Medical College and Hospital, with three direct hits on the buildings. While the bombs caused little damage, they frightened the people, who were led to believe that heavy incendiary raids were in store for the city.

At 11:30 A.M. there occurred the blinding flash of an explosion such as had destroyed Hiroshima slightly less than seventy-five hours before. Another city joined the ever-growing list of Japanese centers destroyed and wrecked.

Even the worst diehards in the government could see little cause for continuing the folly of resisting an enemy which threatened to hurl a rain of these bombs against Japan.

On August 15, 1945, with a country literally beaten to its knees, the Emperor accepted the surrender terms. The war was over.

Soon after the surrender the Army announced that in Hiroshima 78,150 people had died, that 51,408 were injured or missing, that 48,000 buildings were totally destroyed, and that 22,178 other structures received light to severe damage. At least 176,987 people were made homeless. Listed casualties in Nagasaki included 23,753 dead and 43,020 injured.

These lists were at the best only informed estimates, and the steady numbers of persons succumbing to the aftereffects of the two attacks caused the total list of casualties constantly to rise. Many Japanese sources openly questioned the announced casualty figures and today the best-informed Japanese sources believe that at least two to three times as many people were killed and injured as was originally stated.

The immediate postwar casualty survey conducted by the Army, which since then has added many names to the dead and injured lists, was as follows:

Casualties	Dead	Injured	Missing
Incendiary and explosive attacks	198,961	271,617	8,064
Atomic bombings	109,328	78,488	15,971
Warship bombardment	1,739	1,497	29
Total	310,028	351,602	24,000

Japan faced the coming winter of 1945–46 in perilous condition. Almost all of our important cities—ninety-eight in all—were burned out. The official Army report on the bombings stated that seventy-two of these had few if any important military establishments, that the B-29s had gone after both industry and the civil populace. In the Tokyo-Yokohama area, 56 per cent of the buildings were gone; 52 per cent in the Nagoya area; and 57 per cent in the Kobe-Osaka area. The cities suffered varying degrees of loss of residential structures, Nishinomiya losing only 9.1 per cent, while Fukuyama lost 96 per cent, Kofu and Hama-matsu 72 per cent, and Hitachi, 71 per cent. The initial studies indicated that one million, four hundred and thirty thousand buildings were totally destroyed; later this figure rose to more than two million, directly affecting more than nine million people.

At the war's end, our communications and transportation lines were in a chaotic state. Ships which formerly plied between the main islands as well as those which had sailed to Korea and China remained hidden in harbors to escape the guns, bombs, and rockets of searching enemy planes. We had lost staggering numbers of these supply vessels and had all too few available at the time of surrender. Even had we been well supplied with ships, we could not have used them to great advantage, for the waters in and around bays, ports, and straits were thick with deadly enemy mines sown by B-29s. We suffered from a serious shortage of men for land transportation work and stevedores to load ships. Almost all these great cracks in the national economy were traceable to the loss of control of the air over the mainland.

On Kyushu, a fraction of the normal train schedules were kept during the day. Many trains which left on trips were shot to pieces by fighters and failed to arrive at their destinations. The constant aerial interference completely disrupted the ferry service between Aomori and Hakodate. Honshu's mainland communications and land transportation lines functioned, but in a wild state of confusion and disrepair, and these operated only because the bombers had not concentrated on our rail lines.

We were dangerously short of food supplies for our people. In July of 1945 the government reluctantly ordered a cut of 10 per cent in the staple food ration, which amounted to a ration of 312 grams per adult person per day of staple food, including substitutes. In the seasons between rice-crop harvesting, we feared a possible famine, for the islands were virtually cut off from outside food supply. The supply of non-staple food and seasoning was reduced by 20 per cent in meat, 30 per cent in fish, and 50 per cent in seasoning from the amounts available in 1941.

As against what was available to the Japanese people in 1937, they could obtain only 2 per cent of cotton goods, 1 per cent of woolen goods, 4 per cent of soap, and 8 per cent of paper.

These poverty-stricken conditions caused wild and runaway inflation and contributed much to lower the morale of the people and to destroy their will to continue the war.

Our industries, including those which had escaped the terrible blows of the B-29s, were virtually at a standstill, great ghosts of factories no longer with meaning or purpose. Our industrial production had plummeted with the steady and increasingly severe bombings. For the first fiscal quarter of 1945 (April to June), coal production was down 29 per cent, iron and other metals 65 per cent, chemical products 48 per cent, and liquid fuels 66 per cent, compared to the highest fiscal quarter of the war. The aircraft factories especially had been terribly damaged, with several of our larger plants as much as 96 per cent destroyed.

In Hiroshima and Nagasaki, our people had sunk to despair. Even by December of 1945 many thousands who had fled the cities after the bombings had not returned. Their paralysis was remarkable; they could not immediately throw off the full terror of the bombings. Their lot was merely representative, however, of the great devastated areas, where the people lived in primitive squalor, hungry and with few creature comforts, in want of medical attention and other necessities.

And what of our Navy, once one of the most powerful battle fleets afloat? When the war ended we possessed, able to cruise under their own power, only two aircraft carriers, one of which was damaged, three damaged cruisers, only a few of forty-one destroyers left in docks and harbors, and fifty-nine submarines. We still had a total of 829 vessels of all types, but only the handful of ships mentioned above were capable of sailing.

Still armed and equipped on the mainland were seventy powerful Army divisions, more than one million fighting men who formed the core of the defense forces which were to resist the invasion. The Pacific War, fought chiefly in the air and on the sea, came to a halt before these Japan-based troops fired even a single shot in the defense of the country.

CHAPTER 29

Jiro Horikoshi's Final War Diary

AS WE HAVE RELATED in this book, without the Zero fighter Japan could not possibly have effected her early war gains in the Pacific and Indian oceans and on the Asiatic mainland. Everything depended upon the Zero's ability to wrest the all-vital command of the air from the enemy in every theater of action. This the airplane did with amazing effectiveness during Japan's widespread initial operations.

Jiro Horikoshi, the engineer responsible for the Zero fighter and other Japanese front-line fighter planes, is seen thereby to be an exponent, so to speak, of Japan's position in the war. The following pages contain extracts from his personal diary which refer to the final nine months of the war. They provide an unusual look at inner Japan during these months of great crisis:

"*December 5, 1944*: I left Nagoya by train today for Yokosuka. I was scheduled to attend the Navy-industry conference on the new *Reppu* fighter plane, to be held on

December 6 at the Naval Air Research and Development Center. I would return to Nagoya after completing the necessary liaison work with the Navy on the new plane, traveling about the Tokyo and Yokosuka areas after the conference.

"On December 7, however, a heavy earthquake rocked the Tokai area (the southern coast of central Japan). The quake caused extensive damage and wrecked the long railroad bridge of the Tokaido Line on the Tenryu River. In a single stroke Japan's most vital rail transportation line was cut. My concern for the factories in the Tokai area rose when I learned that the earthquake had been so severe as temporarily to halt all manufacturing operations at the Mitsubishi Aircraft Works in Ohe-machi, Nagoya, where I worked with my design staff.

"My first impulse was to start out at once for Nagoya to do what I could in returning the factory to production. However, I was warned against making the trip by train, since the wrecked bridge meant that I would have to travel by foot in the cold of the winter night before I could reach another train. For months I had been exhausted from constant overwork, and I realized that the trip might cause me to become seriously ill. Nagoya granted me special permission to remain in Tokyo, and to carry on all the work necessary with the Navy on the *Reppu* until the next scheduled conference at Yokosuka on the fifteenth.

"Misfortune did not stop with the earthquake. On the afternoon of the thirteenth B-29s for the first time struck a devastating blow against Nagoya, concentrating on the Mitsubishi Engine Works factories in Daiko-cho, Nagoya. The sprawling buildings suffered extensive damage which caused a severe setback in production.

"*December 16, 1944*: The Tokaido Line still had not

repaired the bridge damaged by the earthquake. I had to return to Nagoya, and I was compelled to take a round-about mountain route to reach the city. I took a Shinetsu Line Train which left Uyeno Station in Tokyo on the seventeenth, and arrived at Nagoya via Nagano City late in the night of the seventeenth. I had been on the train for more than twenty hours; the regular Tokaido Line journey required only five and a half hours by express train between Tokyo and Nagoya.

"*December 18, 1944*: This afternoon B-29s returned for their second attack on Nagoya, attacking the Mitsubishi Airframe Works, to which I belonged. As soon as the air-raid warning screamed we ran to a vacant lot near the main factory buildings and dropped into 'trenches' and 'dugouts' prepared as shelter areas. Protected against bomb shrapnel and blast, we searched the sky for the bombers; we noticed several waves of B-29s, appearing white at a height I estimated to be thirty thousand feet. The great planes maintained a steady formation, releasing their bombs in salvos aimed to 'walk' across the factory buildings from the east to the west. This was my first experience under heavy air attack, and I remember vividly the screeching sound of the falling bombs and the unbelievable sound of the bomb explosions. My ears rang and I was deafened for hours afterward.

"*December 19*: The Mitsubishi plant manager has ordered an emergency dispersal program. We fear that the bombers will return in ever-greater numbers and, if the machines remain so exposed to the giant B-29s, we soon will lose all production. The men have begun the task of transporting machines to schools and factory buildings in the city and in the suburbs.

"*December 25*: The Engineering Department, to which I

am attached, has completed its evacuation from the main factory buildings. We are now located in several school buildings in eastern Nagoya.

"*From December 25, 1944, to April, 1945*: The long hours of exhaustion and overwork have exacted their toll. Suffering from pleurisy, I have been compelled to confine myself to bed, beginning on December 25. It is strange to remain bedridden, and to hear the sounds of the bombing attacks, which now come often, during both day and night. There is what is to me the now-familiar scream of the falling bombs, the thundering explosions in the city, and the roar of the great fires. From my house I have on many occasions watched the frightful flames devouring the homes and buildings, and the towering clouds of smoke which completely cover the sky over the city.

"During this period I maintained contact with my projects at Mitsubishi—the *Reppu* and other fighters. Many of my colleagues and assistants visited me frequently. I had noticed as far back as December that our employees' will to work had suffered badly; the reports from my men now indicated that this mental deterioration had progressed even further. Complicating the natural state of despondency because of the progress of the war were the increasing difficulties in their private lives, the lack of food, and problems of travel to and from work, and so on.

"It is now the middle of March. Apparently the B-29s have changed their bombing tactics. Where they formerly concentrated on the factories and military establishments, they are now attacking the populace through terrible fire attacks on their homes. With a sense of impending total doom, I received the reports of the terrible incendiary attack against downtown Tokyo, which lasted from the night of March 9 to early morning of the following day. The overwhelming incendiary saturation raid appears to be only the first of a new series of attacks. I have been told the heart of the city is gutted, and they have already counted more than eighty-three thousand dead and missing. Tens of thousands of people were injured and burned. (Here I have added a postscript. The loss of life in this great air attack exceeded even the atomic bombings of Hiroshima or Nagasaki. What happened to our cities is unbelievable.)

"It is now Nagoya's turn. From the night of March 11 until the early morning of the twelfth, B-29s hurled tens of thousands of incendiary bombs into the city. Great fires arose and swept unchecked through the flimsy wooden homes and other buildings. The people fortunately managed to escape a fate similar to the March 9 raid on Tokyo. The comparatively small city area of Nagoya enabled many of the populace to escape the advancing sheets of flame. The loss of life has been relatively small.

"It is obvious now that the B-29s will attack each of our cities in this fashion. (Postscript: More than half of all my relatives living in Tokyo had lost their homes by May.)

"*March 12, 1945*: Against their protests, I ordered my family, except for my wife, to leave Nagoya at once. Much of the city is already gutted and desolate, but the B-29s may return. My family, escorted by my brother-in-law and my housekeeper, left for my home village, which is located near the city of Takasaki in Gumma Prefecture, about sixty miles northwest of Tokyo.

"It was strange to be alone in this empty house while my wife is at Ozone Station in Nagoya seeing off the family. It was a time for thought, and I felt deep concern about the future life of my family and my people, about our jobs, the future of the company with which I had worked so long. When I thought of the inevitable course the war would follow, the certain defeat of my country and my people, I could not prevent the tears from coming. I must confess in these pages that the misery which is in store for Japan has caused me to cry; I was unable to stop the tears.

"When we awoke on the morning of December 8, 1941, we found ourselves—without any foreknowledge—to be embroiled in war. The realization was astonishing. Since then, the majority of us who had truly understood the awesome industrial strength of the United States never really believed that Japan would win this war. We were convinced that surely our government had in mind some diplomatic measures which would bring the conflict to a halt before the situation became catastrophic for Japan. But now, bereft of any strong government move to seek a diplomatic out, we are being driven to doom. Japan is being destroyed. I cannot do other but to blame the military hierarchy and the blind politicians in power for dragging Japan into this hellish cauldron of defeat.

"*April 8*: The cabinet has changed. The new lineup suggests strongly that a big change may appear soon in the government's diplomatic policies and its attitude toward the war.

"*April 15*: My health has improved remarkably, and there are times now when I can leave my bed. It is a wonderful feeling to know that I have cheated death and that soon I will be up and around again. For the first time in four months I was able to get a haircut, to take a long-desired bath, to walk around the familiar rooms of my own home. I had improved so much that I was able to walk by myself to an air-raid shelter when the B-29s came, instead of being helped as if I were a cripple.

"*May 15*: I was now well enough to return to travel by train. The No. 1 Works of the Mitsubishi Heavy Industries, Ltd., to which I was now assigned, was located at Matsumoto in Nagano Prefecture. I left Nagoya by train for the plant. For the first time I really saw the effects of the incendiary raids on Nagoya. The city is a wasteland, charred and unspeakably desolate. My former factory is a ghostly, steel-ribbed wreck, shattered by bombs and torn apart by the dispersal crews. It is hard to believe that all this is true.

"I knew that soon I would be well. Strangely, however, I had little desire to return to work. The impression of the shattered city and the wrecked factories will not leave me.

"*May 22*: Apparently my illness had weakened me much more than I believed. I was ordered to rest, and I left Matsumoto to join my family. For the next two months (until July 21, when this entry was completed), I remained with my family, including my aged mother, and rested as much as possible to regain my strength. Fortunately, the village is small and has not been bothered by air attacks.

"Even here, however, the air-raid warnings sound across the countryside. The enemy planes are everywhere, bombing and shooting and hurling their rockets against our buildings. When the heavy B-29s thundered overhead to attack Maebashi, Takasaki, and Ota in Gumma Prefecture, we could hear the distant explosions which sounded like deep rolls of thunder, even though we are quite far away.

"Every now and then I could see the American carrier-based fighters and bombers racing low over the countryside, searching for targets. Our planes can do little against the tremendous power of the enemy air fleets, which completely control the air over Japan.

"This has been the first time in eighteen years, since my college days, that I have spent more than one month continuously with my parents in their home. The hills and the rivers are the same as ever, but the fields are different. Most of the copses and groves where I played in my childhood are no longer playgrounds for youngsters, but have been tilled to produce food. The country is hungry. Our ships are not getting through with supplies.

"Our national situation is deteriorating swiftly. It feels as if certain elements are rotting the country from within. There has been a tremendous increase in the number of people who suffer directly from the bombings; inflation has spread like wildfire throughout the country, and the salaried class most of all suffers from it; cunning people propose new random policies and measures to the bewildered government offices and somehow get new jobs which provide them with both good income and position— while the honest people (the majority of our country) are driven to war or to a life of hardship and bitterness; many foxy merchants and industrial people flatter and beguile the military; they seek and they obtain big profits through unjust, dishonest business dealings; the government is at a loss to distinguish true from false; the clamor of the favored grows ever louder; many a government official is bent solely upon shirking his responsibility; high-ranking officials frequently change their positions; they move about constantly.

"The country seems as if it were rife with corruption. Rottenness in government is spreading. The whole nation has been exhausted. Japan is quickly losing the strength, it hardly has the will, to continue the war.

"I met many of my old school friends and had the opportunity to discuss the old days. Often I walked through the hills and along the river banks. Often I was reminded of a line from an ancient Chinese poem; *'Mountains and rivers remain unchanged in this war-ruined land.'* During my stay in the village I often was tempted to forget my duties and responsibilities in the war effort. The war situation had deteriorated to such an extent that even the people in the countryside desperately wanted peace. They often discussed the possibility of requesting the Soviet Union, the only powerful neutral country between the Allied Powers and Japan, to intercede in the war and end the conflict. Japan has made special efforts to maintain neutrality with the Russians, and we hoped that we could rely on her fairness and friendship in mediating with the Allies.

"*July 22*: I returned to the Mitsubishi No. 1 plant in Matsumoto City, where I was assigned a new engineering position. Matsumoto was one of the very few cities which had been spared the enemy air attacks; the others were Kyoto, Hiroshima, Nara, Nagasaki, Fukuyama, and Mito. The company had tried desperately to organize the new workshops and to establish effective liaison with the other divisions and workshops scattered about the country as a result of the dispersal program. The effort, however, had done little good, and affairs were in chaos. Management was inefficient, and we accomplished little because of the unending confusion. Our efforts appeared hopeless. Bombing damage had become so great throughout the entire country that everybody realized that the war could not possibly be won. It was senseless to continue fighting, but the very momentum of our combat activities appeared to carry us on.

"*August 7*: A report says that the enemy has used an apparently altogether new type of bomb yesterday. We learned that the bomb is incredibly more powerful than an ordinary weapon, and that yesterday morning it was dropped over the city of Hiroshima. There are very few details concerning the new bombing, but we have learned that the horrible effects of the bomb, the human suffering and loss of life, the destruction of buildings, are beyond all description. This is all we know so far.

"*August 10*: Yesterday, again Japan was struck with the

new bomb. This time the city of Nagasaki was the target. A still more shocking report came in to us, saying that, like a lightning bolt from a blue sky, Russia has declared war and has commenced the invasion of Manchuria and North Korea. We hear that mighty land armies and hordes of bombers already have struck.

"This means the final blow to a Japan which already is reeling from the unremitting American assault. The local authorities recommended, but with little official enthusiasm, that the residents of Matsumoto quickly evacuate the city which has, so far, escaped air attack. The majority of the company's employees now are busily occupied with dispersal of their private belongings, of hiding factory machines and equipment. Their daily shop work has been forgotten. They seem to have accepted defeat as only a matter of time.

"*August 15*: The radio has announced that the Emperor would broadcast a special and a very important message. I knew at once that this would be the rescript of a surrender. The transmission was poor, and I missed many passages of the talk. It was of little matter. Japan had been helpless against the enemy for months.

"The war is over. We were defeated after what amounts to literally a total exhaustion of our national power. This is the first defeat my country has ever experienced, and it is a strange feeling for the populace. Let us face the reality that the Japanese people do not have a social organization which lends itself to a cohesive national effort. We have never been highly trained to combine our intellectual abilities and to think and work in scientific or efficient terms. We have poor natural resources and the land is terribly overcrowded.

"Japan has too many vital problems which we cannot solve through our own resources and abilities or efforts.

My country will not be able to maintain a civilized and prosperous existence unless we can rely upon the generous aid and industrial and trade intercourse of the world. We require an open-door principle from the world for the good of our people and all nations. I have little doubt that the lack of such things was probably the greatest of the remote and the basic causes of this insane war. Things that our people see before them are economic difficulties and moral confusion. If Japan must grow, then we must face our responsibilities of the future in a fashion entirely different from that adopted by the government which led us into the abyss of war and utter defeat. And then we must endeavor to secure the fair and generous attitude of all this world.

"It is easy to recognize the struggle which lies ahead for Japan. I know what my country needs, but I have absolutely no ideas as to how my people should meet their needs in the future. Japan requires and *must* find those great and sincere statesmen who can and will lead us to a future of peace and guarantee a secure national existence."

COMPANY COMMANDER VIETNAM
BY JAMES ESTEP

ISBN 0-7434-5250-X

One of the most important works about personal frontline command in Vietnam. Vietnam has been called the "company commander's war"—these were the young officers who ran the war on a day-to-day basis, making life and death decisions in the jungles, rice paddies, and villages. Estep quickly learned what it meant to be a leader of men: to comfort an 18-year-old who had killed for the first time; to give confidence to an intimidated platoon leader; to revitalize the morale of a "hard-luck" company; to gain the trust of his crusty first sergeant and, most of all, to confront and conquer his own fears. *Company Commander Vietnam* is an honest and compelling story of American infantrymen caught up in a war that could not be won. But more than one man's story, it is a revealing look at "the way of war"—how young boys become fighters and leaders, what they give, what they gain—and lose—in the end.

ALSO AVAILABLE

ZERO
BY MASATAKE OKUMIYA and JIRO HORIKOSHI
with MARTIN CAIDIN

ISBN 0-7434-4491-4

The story of Japan's Air war in the Pacific during World War II, as seen by the enemy! From the co-author of *Samurai!* and *Thunderbolt!*, and the author of *The B-17* and *Fork-Tailed Devil*

With a Foreword by John Gresham, the bestselling co-author of Submarine.

This is the thrilling saga of war in the air in the Pacific Theater of Operations during World War II from Pearl Harbor to Nagasaki, as told by the men who created, led, and fought in the deadly Zero fighter plane. A classic in military aviation history.

OPERATION VULTURE
BY JOHN PRADOS

ISBN 0-7434-4490-6

For the first time ever, the complete, shocking true story of high-stakes diplomacy during the Eisenhower administration that brought the United States to the brink of atomic warfare intervention in Vietnam in 1954 during the height of the battle of Dien Bien Phu. *Operation Vulture* contains new information from recently declassified documents. It is a gripping behind-the-scenes story of how the U.S. came within a heartbeat of making the decision to drop atomic bombs on Vietnam during the Eisenhower administration.

THE LOST HISTORY OF GETTYSBURG
BY COLONEL JAMES K. P. SCOTT
WITH AN INTRODUCTION BY CRAIG L. SYMONDS

ISBN 0-7434-4489-2

A lost classic of the greatest battle in the Civil War,
written by a Civil War veteran.

No other military engagement on American soil has captured the attention and imagination of the American public as much as the Battle of Gettysburg. It was the deadliest
battle of the deadliest war in American history. Now an
extraordinary long-lost history of the opening rounds of
this great battle returns for a new generation. Scott's narrative is impressive in its ability to speak across the generations. It conveys a knowledge that can only be told by
one who fought with and against the participants on the
bloody battlefields of the Civil War. The result is a history
rich in detail and authority.

THE BATTLE FOR JERUSALEM
BY LT. GENERAL MORDECHAI GUR

ISBN 0-7434-4488-4

A stunning profile in courage of Israeli paratroopers in the crucial battle of the 1967 Mideast War, written by the field commander of the troops who captured the Temple Mount.

Lt. General Mordechai Gur, who played a major role in Israel's military operations since statehood, has vividly written an unforgettable account of the events surrounding the critical Battle for Jerusalem during the 1967 Mideast War. General Gur's fast-paced narrative brings alive all the tension, terror, uncertainty, hope and desperation of the conflict.

MARCH TO GLORY
BY ROBERT LECKIE

ISBN 0-7434-3493-5

The landmark history of the 1st U.S. Marine Division and their incredible fighting withdrawal from the Chosin Reservoir in Korea written by the bestselling author of *Helmet for My Pillow*

This is the incredible saga of the famed 1st Marine Division and its savage battle for survival in the frozen mountains of North Korea. Battling bitterly cold winds and temperatures that dropped to -25 degrees Fahrenheit, the Leathernecks blasted their way through roadblocks, ambushes, and wave after horrifying wave of Chinese Communist army attacks. Robert Leckie brings to life all aspects of the epic struggle and the men who wrote one of the greatest chapters in Marine Corps history with their frozen blood.

ALSO AVAILABLE

THE CIVIL WAR READER: 1862
BY THE EDITORS OF *CIVIL WAR TIMES ILLUSTRATED* AND *AMERICA'S CIVIL WAR MAGAZINE*
INTRODUCTION BY CRAIG L. SYMONDS

ISBN 0-7434-4466-3

A fresh and bold re-examination of the epic year that was the "spring of the Confederacy."

From blood-stained battlefields to smoke-filled antechambers of political power-brokers, 1862 was a year of tumultuous events in America. Flush from its victories of the previous year, the Confederacy stood poised and powerful—tantalizingly close to sundering the shackles of the Union and establishing itself as a new and independent nation-state on the North American continent.

With contributions by James M. McPherson, Stephen W. Sears, Tom Wicker, Geoffrey Perret, and many more.